The New Answers Book 3

Over 35 Questions on Creation/Evolution and the Bible

Ken Ham General Editor

First printing: February 2010
Tenth printing: January 2016

Master Books®, P.O. Box 726, Green Forest, AR 72638
Master Books® is a division of the New Leaf Publishing Group, Inc.

ISBN: 978-0-89051-579-2
ISBN: 978-1-61458-108-6 (ebook)
Library of Congress Number: 2008903202

Please consider requesting that a copy of this volume be purchased by your local library system.

Printed in the United States of America

Please visit our website for other great titles:
www.masterbooks.com

For information regarding author interviews,
please contact the publicity department at (870) 438-5288.

ACKNOWLEDGMENTS AND SPECIAL THANKS

Acknowledgments and special thanks for reviewing or editing chapters:

Steve Fazekas (theology, AiG), Frost Smith (biology, editor, AiG), Mike Matthews (editor, AiG), Gary Vaterlaus (science education, editor, AiG), Tim Chaffey (theology, Midwest Apologetics), Dr. John Whitcomb (theology, president of Whitcomb Ministries), Dr. Larry Vardiman (atmospheric science, chairman of the department of astro-geophysics at the Institute for Creation Research), Ken Ham (biology, president and CEO of Answers in Genesis), Donna O'Daniel (biology, AiG), Dr. Tim Clarey (geology), Christine Fidler (CEO of Image in the UK), Mark Looy (editor, AiG), Dr. Terry Mortenson (history of geology, AiG), John Upchurch (editor, AiG), Dr. Jason Lisle (astrophysics, AiG), Dr. John Morris (geological engineering, president of the Institute for Creation Research), Dr. Andrew Snelling (geology, director of research at AiG), Dr. David Menton (retired, cell biology, former associate professor of anatomy at Washington University School of Medicine, now AiG), Dr. Tommy Mitchell (internal medicine, AiG), Dr. Georgia Purdom (genetics, AiG), Roger Patterson (biology, editor, AiG), Bodie Hodge (engineering, materials, AiG), Dr. John Whitmore (geology, associate professor of geology, Cedarville University), Lori Jaworski (editor, AiG), Dr. Danny Faulkner (astronomy, physics, chair of the division of math, science, nursing & public health at the University of South Carolina, Lancaster), Stacia McKeever (biology, psychology, AiG), David Wright (student of engineering, AiG), and Dr. Elizabeth Mitchell (MD).

Special thanks to Dan Lietha for many of the illustrations used in this book, and to Laura Strobl, Dan Stelzer, and Jon Seest for much of the graphic design layout and illustrations, unless otherwise supplied.

We would also like to thank the authors for their contributions to the Answers Book Series and all the research and hard work they put into these chapters.

Contents

INTRODUCTION

Evolving Tactics

KEN HAM

Over the past 30 years of my personal, intimate experience in the biblical creation ministry, I have observed "evolving" (in the sense of "changing") tactics used by prominent secularists to respond to arguments from creationist scholars and researchers. Based on my experience, I would divide the interactions of biblical creationists and outspoken secularists into four basic eras.

The Debate Era of the 1970s

When I first became aware of the U.S. creation movement in the 1970s (while I was a teacher in Australia), I learned that Duane Gish (Ph.D. in biochemistry from the University of California, Berkeley) of the Institute for Creation Research was actively debating evolutionary scientists from various academic institutions.

At that time, creationist arguments against evolution consisted of arguments against so-called ape-men, and arguments that the Cambrian Explosion and lack of transitional forms illustrated that Darwinian evolution did not happen.

Evolutionists argued back with supposed counters to these arguments. For instance, they claimed that *Archaeopteryx* was a transitional form between reptiles and birds (since refuted), that the "mammal-like reptiles" were transitional forms, and so on. However, in the long run, such "evidences" were just interpreted differently by both sides according to their starting points — creation or evolution!

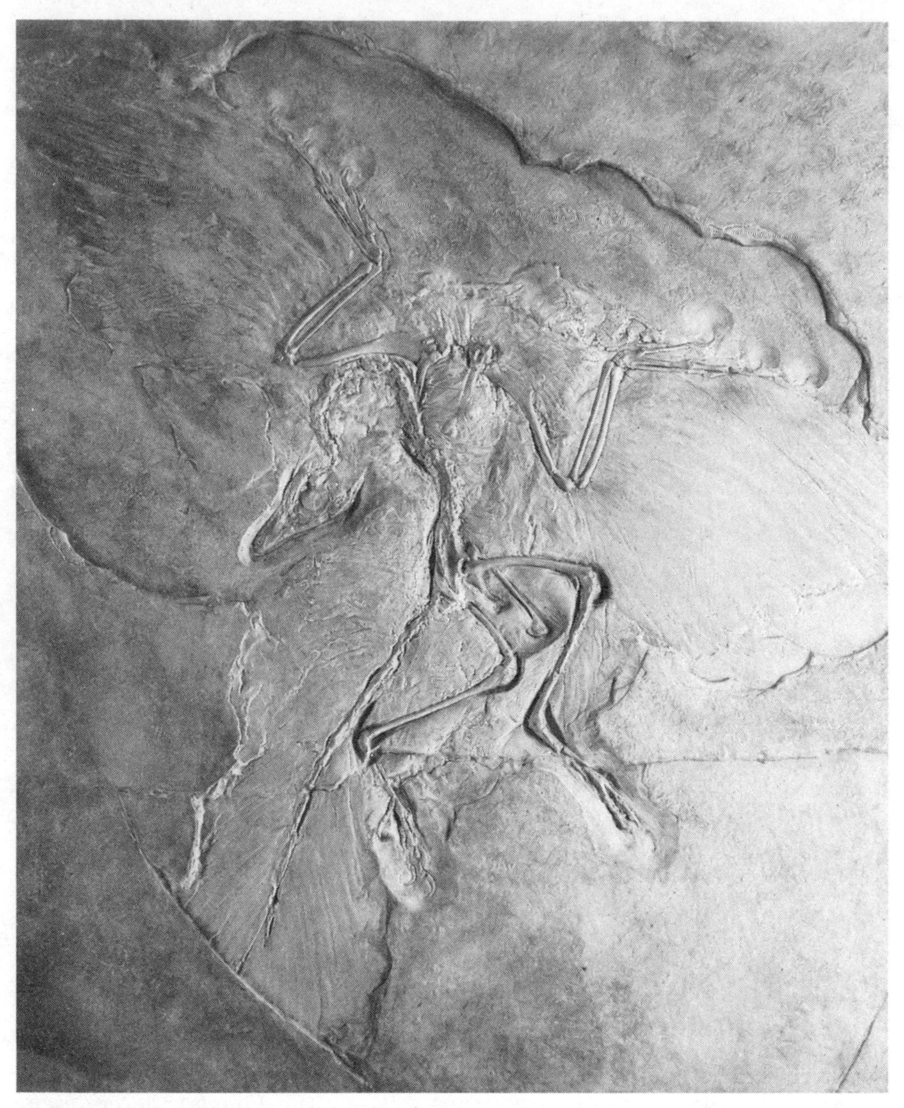

Evolutionists still use this fossil to support the transition of one kind of animal to another. Creationists interpret the same evidence in light of the Bible and come to different conclusions.

The Rise of Creationist Media in the Early 1980s

Although secular educational institutions and secular journals, by and large, taught evolution as fact, I noticed more deliberate attempts to increase public indoctrination about evolution and earth history occurring over millions of years. For this reason, I might also call this the *Intensified Evolutionary Indoctrination* era.

At the same time, evolutionists increasingly refused to debate creationists. In today's world (early 21st century), such debates are rare.

Nonetheless, the biblical creation movement began publishing more and more books, videos, and other materials; and the "creation versus evolution" issue rose to greater prominence in the culture and secular media. Secularist opposition to the creation movement intensified, with many articles in print. Although they included some ridicule, many articles tried to outline the supposed scientific reasons why creationists were wrong.

The Public School Controversies of the 1980s and 1990s

Frustrated by how evolutionary teaching had taken over much of the secular education system, and seeing that creation was basically outlawed from the classroom, many Christians tried (unsuccessfully) in the courts to force public school teachers to teach creation in their classes, or at least to allow critiques of evolution.

This era eventually sparked the rise of the non-Christian "intelligent design" movement[1] —which many Christians thought might be the answer to the education problem — but soon found it was not.

Secularists fought hard to falsely accuse creationists of being anti-science. They typically labeled belief in the Genesis account of history — or even the simple belief that God created — as just a "religious" view, while belief in Darwinian evolution was a "scientific" view.

The Name-Calling Era of the Early 21st Century

Some secularists have reverted to name-calling in a desperate attempt to discredit biblical creationists. In the early part of the 21st century, articles against the creation movement became more scathing, sarcastic, and mocking, with increasing name-calling. Rather than attempting to use logical arguments to dissuade people, evolutionists mocked not just the Genesis account of creation but also belief in any unnamed intelligence behind the universe.

No longer satisfied to argue that creationists could not be real scientists and that belief in creation is anti-scientific, secularists began accusing creationists

1. The intelligent design movement does not claim to be Christian. It is a movement (with both Christians and non-Christians) that is against naturalism, teaching that an unnamed intelligence is behind the universe.

of being anti-technology. I began to see the argument appear that people who believe in creation are inconsistent if they use modern technology, such as computers and airplanes, which are products of man's scientific ingenuity.

Increased name-calling against creationists, in an attempt to defame their integrity, began to appear, not just in newspaper articles but in various evolutionist books and reputable science magazines. Biblical creationists were equated with terrorists, as secular writers used words like *fundamentalists* to describe both Christians and terrorists. All of this name-calling by unscrupulous secularists is part of a deliberate attempt to smear Christians and use fear tactics to brainwash people into a false understanding of what Christians believe.

This era also saw the rise of the "New Atheists," who began overtly attacking Christianity and preaching atheism around the world. This radical atheist movement is spearheaded by Dr. Richard Dawkins of Oxford University, summed up in a quote from his best-selling book *The God Delusion*, in which he vehemently attacks the Christian God:

> The God of the Old Testament is arguably the most unpleasant character in all fiction: jealous and proud of it; a petty, unjust, unforgiving control-freak; a vindictive, bloodthirsty ethnic cleanser; a misogynistic, homophobic, racist, infanticidal, genocidal, filicidal, pestilential, megalomaniacal, sadomasochistic, capriciously malevolent bully. Those of us schooled from infancy in his ways can become desensitized to their horror.[2]

In June of 2008, Paul Myers, associate professor of biology at the University of Minnesota–Morris, decided to oppose me on his blog by beginning a name-calling exercise.

> Millions of people, including some of the most knowledgeable biologists in the world, think just about every day that you are . . . [and then he launched into a long list of names, from airhead to birdbrain, blockhead, bonehead, and bozo to sap, scam artist, sham, simpleton, a snake oil salesman, wacko] and much, much worse. You're a clueless schmuck who knows nothing about science and has arrogantly built a big fat fake museum to promote medieval [expletive] — you should not be surprised to learn that you are held in very low esteem by the community of scholars and scientists, and by the even larger community of lay people who have

2. Richard Dawkins, *The God Delusion* (Boston, MA: Houghton Mifflin Co., 2006), p. 31.

made the effort to learn more about science than you have (admittedly, though, you have set the bar very, very low on that, and there are 5 year old children who have a better grasp of the principles of science as well as more mastery of details of evolution than you do).[3]

More troublesome is the accusation, which I now observe from different sources, that creationists and Christians are "child abusers." Such an emotionally charged term is really meant to marginalize Christians in the culture. If the secular elite had total control of the culture, they could prosecute this in the courts.

Richard Dawkins agrees that this term is appropriate for Christians who teach about the doctrine of hell: "I am persuaded that the phrase 'child abuse' is no exaggeration when used to describe what teachers and priests are doing to children whom they encourage to believe in something like the punishment of unshriven mortal sins in an eternal hell."[4]

3. Posted on blog of P.Z. Myers on 6/21/2008.
4. Dawkins, *The God Delusion*, p. 318.

In chapter 16 of the best-selling book *God Is Not Great*, entitled "Is Religion Child Abuse?" another New Atheist, Christopher Hitchens, answers the chapter title in the affirmative, claiming that all related customs, such as circumcision, are child abuse. He even equates teaching children about religion to indoctrination and child abuse.

When the Creation Museum opened near the Cincinnati International Airport on Memorial Day weekend 2007, secular scientists and an atheist group demonstrated outside the museum with signs simply mocking my name, such as "Behold, the curse of Ham," rather than using logical scientific arguments to argue their case.

Resorting to such name-calling not only shows that this issue strikes at deep spiritual problems, but that those who can't prove their position by logic or science are driven by emotion. We can expect such name-calling to increase as secularists become more frustrated in not being able to refute the powerful truth that the Creator is clearly seen (see Romans 1:18–20) and "in the beginning God created the heavens and the earth" (Genesis 1:1).

We need to remember what God said in Proverbs 21:24: "A proud and haughty man — 'Scoffer' is his name; he acts with arrogant pride." In contrast, God expects His people to take the higher ground, to earn a reputation for kind and gentle words, as we speak "the truth in love" (Ephesians 4:15). The theme verse of my life and Answers in Genesis includes every Christian's duty to give answers "with meekness":

> But sanctify the Lord God in your hearts, and always be ready to give a defense to everyone who asks you a reason for the hope that is in you, with meekness and fear (1 Peter 3:15).

1

Where Was the Garden of Eden Located?

KEN HAM

Most Bible commentaries state that the site of the Garden of Eden was in the Middle East, situated somewhere near where the Tigris and Euphrates Rivers are today. This is based on the description given in Genesis 2:8–14:

> The LORD God planted a garden eastward in Eden. . . . Now a river went out of Eden to water the garden, and from there it parted and became four riverheads. The name of the first is Pishon. . . . The name of the second river is Gihon. . . . The name of the third river is Hiddekel [Tigris]. . . . The fourth river is the Euphrates.

Even the great theologian John Calvin struggled over the exact location of the Garden of Eden. In his commentary on Genesis he states:

> Moses says that one river flowed to water the garden, which afterwards would divide itself into four heads. It is sufficiently agreed among all, that two of these heads are the Euphrates and the Tigris; for no one disputes that . . . (Hiddekel) is the Tigris. But there is a great controversy respecting the other two. Many think, that Pison and Gihon are the Ganges and the Nile; the error, however, of these men is abundantly refuted by the distance of the positions of these rivers. Persons are not wanting who fly across even to the Danube; as if indeed the habitation of one man stretched itself from the most remote part of Asia to the extremity of Europe. But since many other

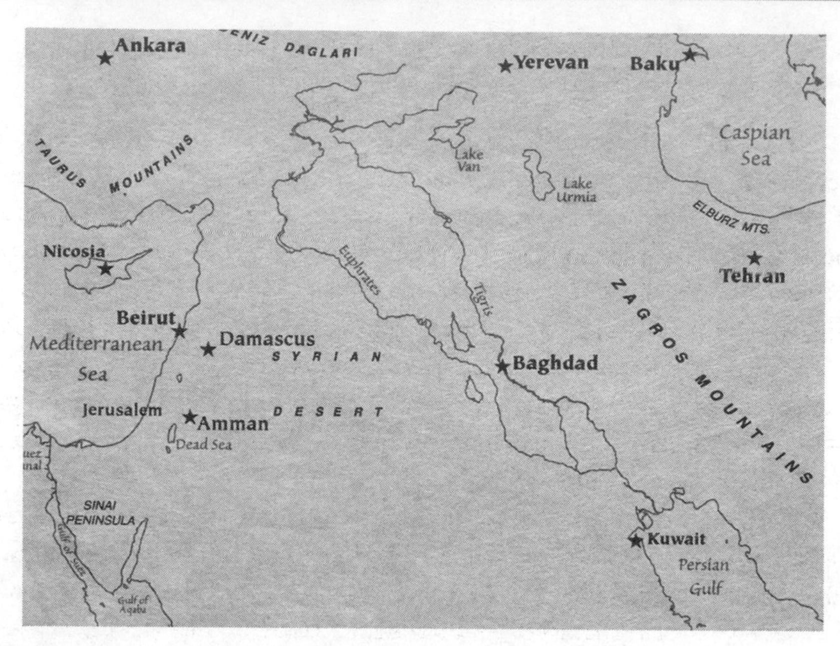

Many wrongly conclude that the Garden of Eden was somewhere in the Middle East based on the names of the rivers in Genesis 2.

> celebrated rivers flow by the region of which we are speaking, there is greater probability in the opinion of those who believe that two of these rivers are pointed out, although their names are now obsolete. Be this as it may, the difficulty is not yet solved. For Moses divides the one river which flowed by the garden into four heads. Yet it appears, that the fountains of the Euphrates and the Tigris were far distant from each other.[1]

Calvin recognized that the description given in Genesis 2 concerning the location of the Garden of Eden does not fit with what is observed regarding the present Tigris and Euphrates Rivers. God's Word makes it clear that the Garden of Eden was located where there were four rivers coming from one head. No matter how one tries to fit this location in the Middle East today, it just can't be done.

Interestingly, Calvin goes on to say:

1. John Calvin, *Commentary on Genesis*, Volume 1, online at: www.ccel.org/ccel/calvin/calcom01.viii.i.html.

> From this difficulty, some would free themselves by saying that the surface of the globe may have been changed by the deluge. . . .[2]

This is a major consideration that needs to be taken into account. The worldwide, catastrophic Flood of Noah's day would have destroyed the surface of the earth. If most of the sedimentary strata over the earth's surface (many thousands of feet thick in places) is the result of this global catastrophe as creationists believe, then we would have no idea where the Garden of Eden was originally located — the earth's surface totally changed as a result of the Flood.

Not only this, but underneath the region where the present Tigris and Euphrates Rivers are located there exists hundreds of feet of sedimentary strata — a significant amount of which is fossiliferous. Such fossil-bearing strata had to be laid down at the time of the Flood.

Therefore, no one can logically suggest that the area where the present Tigris and Euphrates Rivers are today is the location of the Garden of Eden, for this area is sitting on Flood strata containing billions of dead things (fossils). The perfect Garden of Eden can't be sitting on billions of dead things before sin entered the world!

This being the case, the question then is why are there rivers named Tigris and Euphrates in the Middle East today?

In my native country of Australia, one will recognize many names that are also used in England (e.g., Newcastle). The reason is that when the settlers came out from England to Australia, they used names they were familiar with in England to name new places/towns in Australia.

Another example is the names given to many rivers in the United States. There is the Thames River in Connecticut, the Severn River in Maryland, and the Trent River in North Carolina — all named for prominent rivers in the UK.

In a similar way, when Noah and his family came out of the ark after it landed in the area we today call the Middle East (the region of the Mountains of Ararat), it would not have been surprising for them to use names they were familiar with from the pre-Flood world (e.g., Tigris and Euphrates), to name places and rivers, etc., in the world after the Flood.

Ultimately, we don't know where the Garden of Eden was located. To insist that the Garden was located in the area around the present Tigris and Euphrates Rivers is to deny the catastrophic effects of the global Flood of Noah's day, and to allow for death before sin.

---

2. Ibid.

2

What Did Noah's Ark Look Like?

TIM LOVETT (WITH BODIE HODGE)

Most of us have seen various depictions of Noah's ark — from the large, box-like vessel to the one in children's nurseries with the giraffes' heads sticking out the top. But what did the ark really look like? Can we really know for sure?

Depicting the Ark — A Sign of the Times?

Noah's ark has been a popular subject for artists throughout the centuries. However, it is not easy to adequately depict this vessel because the description in Genesis 6 is very brief. To paint a complete picture, the artist must assume some important details.

As the invention of Gutenberg's movable-type printing press in the 1400s made rapid and widespread distribution of the Holy Scriptures possible, Noah's ark quickly became the subject of lavish illustrations. Many designs were pictured, and some were more biblical than others. Often, artists distorted the biblical specifications to match the ships of the day. For instance, the picture shown in figure 1 has the hull of a caravel, which was similar to two of the small sailing vessels used by Christopher Columbus in 1492.

Unlike most other artists, Athanasius Kircher (a Jesuit scientist, 1602–1680) was committed to accurately depicting the massive ark specified in Genesis. He has been compared to Leonardo da Vinci for his inventiveness and his works' breadth and depth. This early "creation scientist" calculated the number

Figure 1. Artist's depiction of the construction of Noah's ark, from H. Schedel's *Nuremburg Chronicle* of 1493.

Figure 2. Athanasius Kircher (1600s) was careful to follow the Bible's instructions and used a rectilinear hull, based on the dimensions in Genesis 6:15, including three decks, a door in the side, and a window of one cubit.

of animals that could fit in the ark, allowing space for provisions and Noah's family. His realistic designs (figure 2) set the standard for generations of artists.

For the next two centuries, Bible artists stopped taking Noah's ark quite so seriously, and ignored the explicit biblical dimensions in their illustrations. These artists simply reflected the scholars of the day, who had rejected the Bible's history of the world. Few Christians living in 1960 had ever seen a biblically based rendering of Noah's ark. Cute bathtub shapes and smiling cartoonish animals illustrated the pervasive belief that Noah's ark was nothing more than a tool for character-building through fictionalized storytelling.

Then in 1961 Dr. John Whitcomb and Dr. Henry Morris published *The Genesis Flood*, which made sense of a global cataclysm and a real, shiplike Noah's ark. This book was a huge thrust to help begin the modern creationist movement.

The primary focus in *The Genesis Flood* was the size of the ark and its animal-carrying capacity. A block-shaped ark was ideal for this, easily suggesting that the ark had plenty of volume. Later studies confirmed that a ship with a rectangular cross-section 50 cubits wide and 30 cubits high was stable. Images of a rectangular ark strikingly similar to Kircher's design rendered centuries earlier began to appear in publications (see figure 3).

Figure 3. This 1985 painting by Elfred Lee was completed after multiple interviews in the early 1970s with George Hagopian, an "eyewitness" of a box-shaped ark. (Image used with permission from Elfred Lee.)

The next few decades saw another popular phenomenon — the search for Noah's ark. Documentary movies and books claimed Noah's ark was hidden on Mt. Ararat, and prime-time television broadcast some mysterious photos of dark objects jutting out from the snow. George Hagopian was one of the first modern "eyewitnesses" who purported to have seen a box-shaped ark. And so it happened — Noah's ark was illustrated worldwide as a box.

When looking at history, artists in each generation have defined Noah's ark according to the cultural setting and what they knew at the time. While we used to see variety in the shape of the ark, more recent depictions have seemingly locked into the box shape. But new insights — in keeping with the biblical specifications of the ark and conditions during the Flood — suggest that it's time we start thinking "outside the box."

Thinking Outside the Box

While the Bible gives us essential details on many things, including the size and proportions of Noah's ark, it does not necessarily specify the precise shape of this vessel. It is important to understand, however, that this lack of physical description is consistent with other historical accounts in Scripture.[1] So how should we illustrate what the ark looked like? The two main options include a default rectangular shape reflecting the lack of specific detail, and a more fleshed-out design that incorporates principles of ship design from maritime science, while remaining consistent with the Bible's size and proportions.

Genesis describes the ark in three verses, which require careful examination:

1. Other objects spoken of in Scripture lack physical details that have been discovered (through archaeology and other research) later (e.g., the walls of Jericho were actually double and situated on a hillside — one higher than the other with a significant space of several feet between them).

> 6:14—Make yourself an ark [*tebah*] of gopherwood; make rooms [*qinniym*] in the ark, and cover it inside and outside with pitch [*kofer*].
>
> 6:15—And this is how you shall make it: The length of the ark shall be three hundred cubits, its width fifty cubits, and its height thirty cubits.
>
> 6:16—You shall make a window [*tsohar*] for the ark, and you shall finish it to a cubit from above; and set the door of the ark in its side. You shall make it with lower, second, and third decks.

Most Bibles make some unusual translation choices for certain key words. Elsewhere in the Bible, the Hebrew word translated here as "rooms" is usually rendered "nests"; "pitch" would normally be called "covering"; and "window" would be "noon light." Using these more typical meanings, the ark would be something like this:

The *tebah* (ark) was made from gopher wood, it had nests inside, and it was covered with a pitch-like substance inside and out. It was 300 cubits long, 50 cubits wide, and 30 cubits high. It had a noon light that ended a cubit upward and above, it had a door in the side, and there were three decks. (For the meaning of "upward and above," see the section "2. A cubit upward and above" on the following pages.)

As divine specifications go, Moses offered more elaborate details about the construction of the tabernacle, which suggests this might be the abridged version of Noah's complete directions. On the other hand, consider how wise Noah must have been after having lived several centuries. The instructions that we have recorded in Genesis may be all he needed to be told. But in any case, 300 cubits is a big ship, not some whimsical houseboat with giraffe necks sticking out the top.

Scripture gives no clue about the shape of Noah's ark beyond its proportions — length, breadth, and depth. Ships have long been described like this without ever implying a block-shaped hull.

The scale of the ark is huge yet remarkably realistic when compared to the largest wooden ships in history. The proportions are even more amazing — they are just like a modern cargo ship. In fact, a 1993 Korean study was unable to find fault with the specifications.

All this makes nonsense of the claim that Genesis was written only a few centuries before Christ, as a mere retelling of earlier Babylonian flood legends such as the *Epic of Gilgamesh*. The *Epic of Gilgamesh* story describes a cube-shaped ark, which would have given a dangerously rough ride. This is neither accurate nor scientific. Noah's ark is the original, while the Gilgamesh Epic is a later distortion.

What about the Shape?

For many years, biblical creationists have simply depicted the ark as a rectangular box. This helped emphasize its size. It was easy to explain capacity and illustrate how easily the ark could have handled the payload. With the rectangular shape, the ark's stability against rolling could even be demonstrated by simple calculations.

Yet the Bible does not say the ark must be a rectangular box. In fact, Scripture does not elaborate about the shape of Noah's ark beyond those superb, overall proportions — length, breadth, and depth. Ships have long been described like this without implying a block-shaped hull.

Scientific Study Endorses Seaworthiness of Ark

Noah's ark was the focus of a major 1993 scientific study headed by Dr. Seon Hong at the world-class ship research center KRISO, based in Daejeon, South Korea. Dr. Hong's team compared 12 hulls of different proportions to discover which design was most practical. No hull shape was found to significantly outperform the 4,300-year-old biblical design. In fact, the ark's careful balance is easily lost if the proportions are modified, rendering the vessel either unstable, prone to fracture, or dangerously uncomfortable.

The research team found that the proportions of Noah's ark carefully balanced the conflicting demands of stability (resistance to capsizing), comfort (seakeeping), and strength. In fact, the ark has the same proportions as a modern cargo ship.

The study also confirmed that the ark could handle waves as high as 100 feet (30 m). Dr. Hong is now director general of the facility and claims "life came from the sea," obviously not the words of a creationist on a mission to promote the worldwide Flood. Endorsing the seaworthiness of Noah's ark obviously did not damage Dr. Hong's credibility.

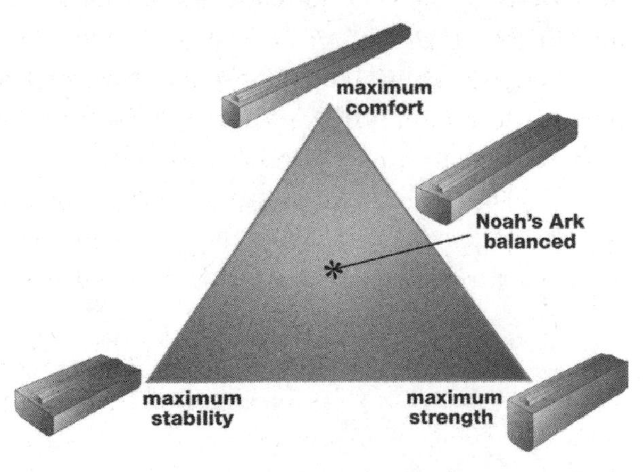

Figure 4. The proportions of the ark were found to carefully balance the conflicting demands of stability, comfort, and strength.

The word *ark* in

Hebrew is the obscure term *tebah*, a word that appears only one other time when it describes the basket that carried baby Moses (Exodus 2:3). One was a huge, wooden ship and the other a tiny, wicker basket. Both floated, both preserved life, and both were covered; but the similarity ends there. If the word implied anything about shape, it would be "an Egyptian basket-like shape," typically rounded. More likely, however, *tebah* means something else, like "lifeboat."[2]

The Bible leaves the details regarding the shape of the ark wide open — anything from a rectangular box with hard right angles and no curvature at all, to a shiplike form. Box-like has the largest carrying capacity, but a ship-like design would be safer and more comfortable in heavy seas. Such discussion is irrelevant if God intended to sustain the ark no matter how well designed and executed.

Clues from the Bible

Some people question whether the ark was actually built to handle rough seas, but the Bible gives some clues about the sea conditions during the Flood:

> The ark had the proportions of a seagoing vessel built for waves (Genesis 6:15).
>
> Logically, a mountain-covering, global flood would not be dead calm (Genesis 7:19).
>
> The ark moved about on the surface of the waters (Genesis 7:18).
>
> God made a wind to pass over the earth (Genesis 8:1).
>
> The Hebrew word for the Flood (*mabbul*) could imply being carried along.

The 1993 Korean study showed that some shorter hulls slightly outperformed the ark model with biblical proportions. The study assumed waves came from every direction, favoring shorter hulls like that of a modern lifeboat. So why was Noah's ark so long if it didn't need to be streamlined for moving through the water?

The answer lies in ride comfort (seakeeping). This requires a longer hull, at the cost of strength and stability, not to mention more wood. The ark's high priority for comfort suggests that the anticipated waves must have been substantial.

1. Something to Catch the Wind

Wind-driven waves would cause a drifting vessel to turn dangerously side-on to the weather. However, such waves could be safely navigated by making

2. C. Cohen, "Hebrew TBH: Proposed Etymologies," *The Journal of the Ancient Near Eastern Society* (JANES), April 1, 1972, p. 36–51. (The journal was at that time called The Journal of the Ancient Near Eastern Society of Columbia University.)

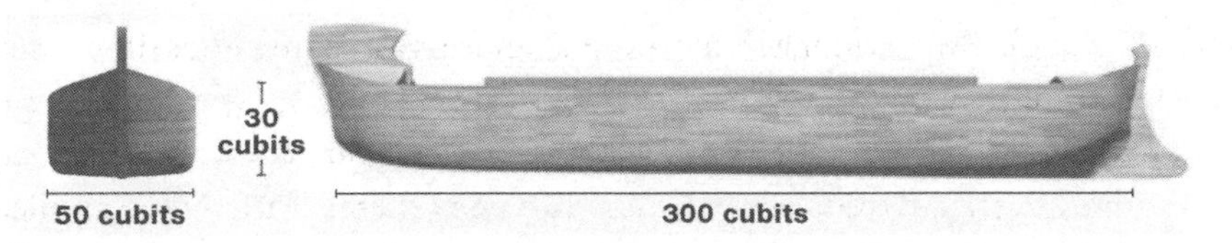

Figure 5. Scripture gives no clue about the shape of Noah's ark beyond its proportions that are given in Genesis 6:15, which reads: "And this is how you shall make it: The length of the ark shall be three hundred cubits, its width fifty cubits, and its height thirty cubits."

the ark steer itself with a wind-catching obstruction on the bow. To be effective, this obstruction must be large enough to overcome the turning effect of the waves. While many designs could work, the possibility shown here reflects the high stems which were a hallmark of ancient ships.

2. A Cubit Upward and Above

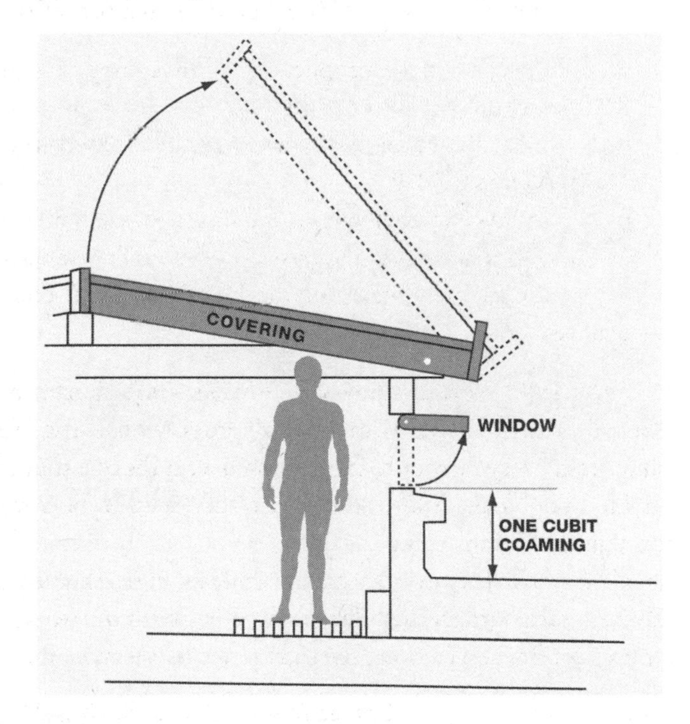

Any opening on the deck of a ship needs a wall (coaming) to prevent water from flowing in, especially when the ship rolls. In this illustration, the window "ends a cubit upward and above," as described in Genesis 6:16. The central position of the skylight is chosen to reflect the idea of a "noon light." This also means that the window does not need to be exactly one cubit. Perhaps the skylight had a transparent roof (even more a "noon light"), or the skylight roof could be opened (which might correspond to when "Noah removed the covering of the ark"). While variations are possible, a window without coaming is not the most logical solution.

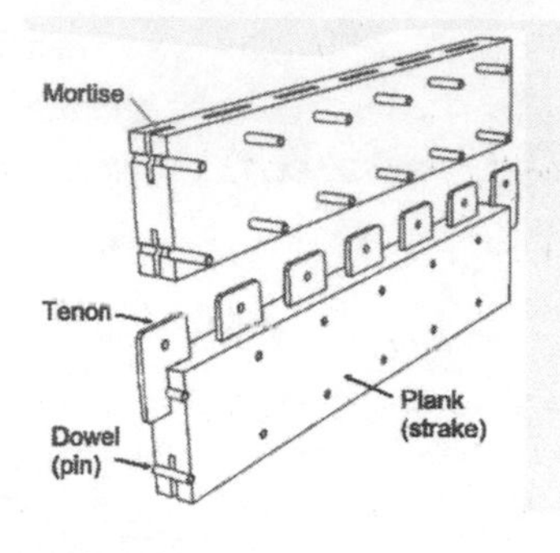

3. Mortise and Tenon Planking

Ancient shipbuilders usually began with a shell of planks (strakes) and then built internal framing (ribs) to fit inside. This is the complete reverse of the familiar European method where planking was added to the frame. In shell-first construction, the planks must be attached to each other somehow. Some used overlapping (clinker) planks that were dowelled or nailed, while others used rope to sew the planks together. The ancient Greeks used a sophisticated system where the planks were interlocked with thousands of precise mortise and tenon joints. The resulting hull was strong enough to ram another ship, yet light enough to be hauled onto a beach by the crew. If this is what the Greeks could do centuries before Christ, what could Noah do centuries after Tubal-Cain invented forged metal tools?

4. Ramps

Ramps help to get animals and heavy loads between decks. Running them across the hull avoids cutting through important deck beams, and this location is away from the middle of the hull where bending stresses are highest. (This placement also better utilizes the irregular space at bow and stern.)

5. Something to Catch the Water

To assist in turning the ark to point with the wind, the stern should resist being pushed sideways. This is the same as a fixed rudder or skeg that provides directional control. There are many ways this could be done, but here we are reflecting the "mysterious" stern extensions seen on the earliest large ships of the Mediterranean.

How Long Was the Original Cubit?

Do we really know the size of Noah's ark (Genesis 6:15), the ark of the covenant (Exodus 25:10), the altar (Exodus 38:1), Goliath (1 Samuel 17:4), and Solomon's Temple (1 Kings 6:2)? While the Bible tells us that the length of

Noah's ark was 300 cubits, its width 50 cubits, and its height 30 cubits, we must first ask, "How long is a cubit?" The answer, however, is not certain because ancient people groups assigned different lengths to the term "cubit" (Hebrew word *ammah*), the primary unit of measure in the Old Testament.

Table 1. The length of a cubit was based on the distance from the elbow to the fingertips, so it varied between different ancient groups of people. Here are some samples from Egypt, Babylon, and ancient Israel:

Culture	Inches (centimeters)
Hebrew (short)	17.5 (44.5)
Egyptian	17.6 (44.7)
Common (short)	18 (45.7)
Babylonian (long)	19.8 (50.3)
Hebrew (long)	20.4 (51.8)
Egyptian (long)	20.6 (52.3)

But when Noah came off the ark, only one cubit measurement existed — the one he had used to construct the ark. Unfortunately, the exact length of this cubit is unknown. After the nations were divided years later at the Tower of Babel, different cultures (people groups) adopted different cubits. So it requires some logical guesswork to reconstruct the most likely length of the original cubit.

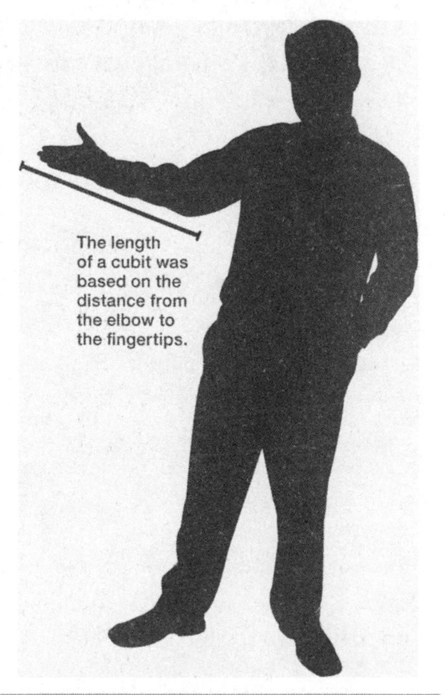

Since the Babel dispersion was so soon after the Flood, it is reasonable to assume that builders of that time were still using the cubit that Noah used. Moreover, we would expect that the people who settled near Babel would have retained or remained close to the original cubit. Yet cubits from that region (the ancient Near East) are generally either a common (short) or a long cubit. Which one is most likely to have come from Noah?

In large-scale construction projects, ancient civilizations typically used the long cubit (about 19.8–20.6 inches [52 cm]). The Bible offers some input in 2 Chronicles 3:3 which reveals that Solomon used an older (long) cubit in construction of the Temple.

Most archaeological finds in Israel are not as ancient as Solomon, and these more modern finds consistently reveal the use of a short cubit, such as confirmed by measuring Hezekiah's tunnel. However, in Ezekiel's vision, an angel used "a cubit plus a handbreadth," an unmistakable definition for the long cubit (Ezekiel 43:13). The long cubit appears to be God's preferred standard of measurement. Perhaps this matter did not escape Solomon's notice, either.

Though the original cubit length is uncertain, it was most likely one of the long cubits (about 19.8–20.6 inches). If so, the ark was actually bigger than the size described in most books today, which usually use the short cubit.

Was Noah's Ark the Biggest Ship Ever Built?

Few wooden ships have ever come close to the size of Noah's ark. One possible challenge comes from the Chinese treasure ships of Yung He in the 1400s. An older contender is the ancient Greek trireme *Tessarakonteres*.

At first, historians dismissed ancient Greek claims that the *Tessarakonteres* was 425 feet (130 m) long. But as more information was learned, the reputation of these early shipbuilders grew markedly. One of the greatest challenges to the construction of large wooden ships is finding a way to lay planks around the outside in a way that will ensure little or no leaking, which is caused when there is too much movement between the planks. Apparently, the Greeks had access to an extraordinary method of planking that was lost for centuries, and only recently brought to light by marine archaeology.

Figure 6. The ark is near the maximum size that is known to be possible for a wooden vessel. How big was the ark? To get the 510 feet (155 m) given here, we used a cubit of 20.4 inches (51.8 cm).

It is not known when or where this technique originated. Perhaps they used a method that began with the ark. After all, if the Greeks could do it, why not Noah?

Designed for Tsunamis?

Was the ark designed for tsunamis? Not really. Tsunamis devastate coastlines, but when a tsunami travels in deep water, it is almost imperceptible to a ship. During the Flood, the water was probably very deep — there is enough water in today's oceans to cover a relatively flat terrain to a consistent depth of over two miles (3.2 km). The Bible states that the ark rose "high above the earth" (Genesis 7:17) and was stranded early (Genesis 8:4), before mountaintops were seen. If the launch was a mirror of the landing — the ark being the last thing to float — it would have been a deep-water voyage from start to finish.

The worst waves may have been caused by wind, just like today. After several months at sea, God made a wind to pass over the earth. This suggests a large-scale weather pattern likely to produce waves with a dominant direction. It is an established fact that such waves would cause any drifting vessel to be driven sideways (broaching). A long vessel like the ark would remain locked in this sideways position, an uncomfortable and even dangerous situation in heavy weather.

However, broaching can be avoided if the vessel catches the wind at one end and is "rooted" in the water at the other — turning like a weather vane into the wind. Once the ark points into the waves, the long proportions create a more comfortable and controlled voyage. It had no need for speed, but the ark did "move about on the surface of the waters."

The box-like ark is not entirely disqualified as a safe option, but sharp edges are more vulnerable to damage during launch and landing. Blunt ends would also produce a rougher ride and allow the vessel to be more easily thrown around (but, of course, God could have miraculously kept the ship's precious cargo safe, regardless of the comfort factor). Since the Bible gives proportions consistent with those of a true cargo ship, it makes sense that it should look and act like a ship, too.

Coincidentally, certain aspects of this design appear in some of the earliest large ships depicted in pottery from Mesopotamia, not long after the Flood. It makes sense that shipwrights, who are conservative as a rule, would continue to include elements of the only ship to survive the global Flood — Noah's ark.

Scripture does not record direction-keeping features attached to the ark. They might have been obvious to a 500 year old, or perhaps they were common among ships in Noah's day as they were afterward. At the same time, the brief specifications in Genesis make no mention of other important details, such as storage of drinking water, disposal of excrement, or the way to get out of the ark. Obviously, Noah needed to know how many animals were coming, but this is not recorded either.

The Bible gives clear instruction for the construction of a number of things, but it does not specify many aspects of the ark's construction. Nothing in this newly depicted ark contradicts Scripture, even though it may be different from more accepted designs. But this design, in fact, shows us just how reasonable Scripture is as it depicts a stable, comfortable, and seaworthy vessel that was capable of fulfilling all the requirements stated in Scripture.

3

Should Christians Be Pushing to Have Creation Taught in Government Schools?

KEN HAM AND ROGER PATTERSON

Although this item specifically targets public schools in the United States, the principles can be applied to any school system in any country.

There have been a number of recent, highly controversial instances involving school boards discussing the topic of creation/evolution in the government-run school classroom, in science textbook disclaimers, and so on.

On the one hand, it's encouraging to see the increasing interest from citizens to put pressure on school boards deciding what is taught in the classrooms. The humanist elites are livid that this is even a topic for discussion. They want a monopoly on the teaching of molecules-to-man evolution in the public school science classrooms. On the other hand, if creation were taught in the science classrooms, would it be taught accurately and respectfully by a qualified individual?

The Issue

Public school teachers know that they can critically discuss different theories in regard to just about every issue — but not evolution. Even if a school board simply wants evolution to be critically analyzed (a good teaching technique, after all) without even mentioning creation or the Bible, the American

Civil Liberties Union and other humanists are immediately up in arms. There are the usual accusations of trying to get "religion" into schools and that it's a front for what they label as "fundamentalist Christianity."

By the way, when the public school system threw out prayer, Bible readings, creation, and the Ten Commandments, they didn't throw out religion. They replaced the Christian worldview influence with an atheistic one. The public schools, by and large, now teach that everything a student learns about science, history, etc., has nothing to do with God — it can all be explained without any supernatural reference. This is a religious view — an anti-Christian view with which students are being indoctrinated. Humanists know that naturalistic evolution is foundational to their religion — their worldview that everything can be explained without God. That is why they are so emotional when it comes to the topic of creation/evolution.

We are certainly encouraged at Answers in Genesis that there are moves in different places to stop the censorship of the anti-Christian propagandists in the public schools and allow students to, at the very minimum, question evolution. We are sure this is in part due to the influence of the creation ministries in society and the plethora of creationist and anti-evolutionist materials now available to parents and students. On the other hand, Christians have to understand that fighting the evolution issue in public schools is actually the same battle as fighting abortion, homosexual behavior, pornography, etc.

In other words, just as these issues are *symptoms* of the foundational change in our culture (i.e., from believing that God's Word is the absolute authority to that of man's opinions being the authority), so the evolution issue is also a symptom of this same foundational change.

Evolutionism as a Religion

If you were to ask the average person if evolution is a religion, he would probably say no. However, evolution is actually one of the cornerstones of the religion of humanism. (Now keep in mind that evolutionists do use real observational science such as natural selection, speciation, genetic studies, etc., as part of their overall argument. However, evolutionism in the sense of the belief aspects of evolution [life arising by natural processes, etc.] is a belief system — a religion.) Despite the vigorous objections of many humanists, humanism is a religion. Even a cursory reading of the "Humanist Manifesto I" penned in 1933 reveals that it is a religious document:

> FIRST: Religious humanists regard the universe as self-existing and not created.
>
> SECOND: Humanism believes that man is a part of nature and that he has emerged as a result of a continuous process.
>
> SEVENTH: Religion consists of those actions, purposes, and experiences which are humanly significant. Nothing human is alien to the religious. It includes labor, art, science, philosophy, love, friendship, recreation — all that is in its degree expressive of intelligently satisfying human living. The distinction between the sacred and the secular can no longer be maintained.[1]

Many other points in the document point to humanism as a religion that is to replace "the old attitudes" of traditional religions. John Dewey, considered the father of the modern American public school systems, was a signatory on the document. His application of his religious ideals to the education system cannot be denied. As a result, the public school system in America, and much of the world, is dominated by humanist philosophies.

Later versions of the manifesto also include the idea that humans have evolved as part of nature with no supernatural intervention at all.[2] Also presented are the beliefs that we can only know about the world around us by observation and experimentation — no biblical revelation is accepted — and that man is the measure of all things. All of these ideas are solidly anti-Christian in their sentiments.

Notable signatories of the "Humanist Manifesto III" include Eugenie Scott, executive director of the National Center for Science Education, and Richard Dawkins. Both of these individuals work hard to have their religious

1. American Humanist Association, "Humanist Manifesto I," www.americanhumanist.org/who_we_are/about_humanism/Humanist_Manifesto_I.
2. American Humanist Association, "Humanism and Its Aspirations: Humanist Manifesto III," www.americanhumanist.org/Who_We_Are/About_Humanism/Humanist_Manifesto_III. This article includes the tenet: "Humans are an integral part of nature, the result of unguided evolutionary change." The same idea is presented in the Humanist Manifesto II.

views presented to the students in classrooms across the world. Ultimately, we should think of their efforts to promote evolutionary teaching in schools as support for their respective religious organizations.

Many humanists would call themselves secular humanists in order to avoid the connection to the word "religion." They have adopted a similar manifesto founded on the same basic principles but avoiding the religious phrasing.

> **Separation of Church and State:** Because of their commitment to freedom, secular humanists believe in the principle of the separation of church and state. The lessons of history are clear: wherever one religion or ideology is established and given a dominant position in the state, minority opinions are in jeopardy. A pluralistic, open democratic society allows all points of view to be heard. Any effort to impose an exclusive conception of Truth, Piety, Virtue, or Justice upon the whole of society is a violation of free inquiry.[3]

Then, in the section on evolution we read:

> Today the theory of evolution is again under heavy attack by religious fundamentalists. Although the theory of evolution cannot be said to have reached its final formulation, or to be an infallible principle of science, it is nonetheless supported impressively by the findings of many sciences. There may be some significant differences among scientists concerning the mechanics of evolution; yet the evolution of the species is supported so strongly by the weight of evidence that it is difficult to reject it. Accordingly, we deplore the efforts by fundamentalists (especially in the United States) to invade the science classrooms, requiring that creationist theory be taught to students and requiring that it be included in biology textbooks. This is a serious threat both to academic freedom and to the integrity of the educational process. We believe that creationists surely should have the freedom to express their viewpoint in society. Moreover, we do not deny the value of examining theories of creation in educational courses on religion and the history of ideas; but it is a sham to mask an article of religious faith as a scientific truth and to inflict that doctrine on the scientific curriculum. If successful, creationists may seriously undermine the credibility of science itself.[4]

3. Council for Secular Humanism, "A Secular Humanist Declaration," www.secularhumanism.org/index.php?section=main&page=declaration.
4. Ibid.

The secular humanists basically believe we should not "impose an exclusive conception of truth" unless it involves suppressing religious ideas (including creation) — it is mandatory that the truth of evolution can have exclusive reign in the science classrooms. What they fail to realize is that they are simply substituting one "article of religious faith" for another in an arbitrary way that fits their agenda; Christians could assert the opposite claim.

If the documents from the humanists are not enough to be convincing about whether humanism (with the belief in naturalistic evolution as its foundation) is a religion that attempts to explain the meaning of life, the U.S. Supreme Court has also recognized humanism as a religion. In the 1961 case *Torcaso* v. *Watkins* regarding the legality of requiring a religious test for public office, the rationale for the finding includes the view that "religions in this country which do not teach what would generally be considered a belief in the existence of God, are Buddhism, Taoism, Ethical Culture, Secular Humanism, and others."[5]

Humanism, whether secular or religious, is a religion, albeit a non-theistic one for most of its adherents. One of humanism's fundamental tenets — evolution by natural processes alone — is the sole view allowed to be taught in public school science classrooms. This demonstrates that the public school systems are indeed promoting one religious view over another in the science classrooms. Again, religion was not removed from schools; Christian views were simply replaced by humanistic views. There is indeed a state religion in the American government school system — secular humanism![6]

Despite the assertion by humanists that evolution is an undeniable fact, is it really a scientific idea?

Science is generally limited to those things that are observable, testable, and repeatable. Language in the humanist documents mentioned above would affirm this notion. When we are discussing operational science, conducting experiments, and building technology based on those principles, creationists and humanists have no disagreement. It is only when we look to explain the past that the disagreements occur.

Everyone has the same evidence to examine, but we all look at the evidence in light of our pre-existing worldview. Evolutionists believe that life has evolved by natural processes, so they interpret the evidence in light of that belief. Creationists do the same, using God's Word, the Bible, as the standard.

5. *Torcaso* v. *Watkins*, 81 S. Ct. 1681 (1961).
6. The same basic case can be made for other humanist ideas such as moral relativism, situational ethics, the rejection of the supernatural, the value of human life, etc. Humanism has become the *de facto* religion in the public schools.

Since events of the past cannot be observed, tested, or repeated, we cannot ultimately call our understanding of those events scientific.[7] Christians should trust what God has revealed in Scripture and build their thinking, in every area, on that foundation.

What Are Christians Doing?

Some Christians who are teaching in the government schools sometimes find themselves in a situation where they can openly teach creation in the science classrooms. Teachers should understand what is allowed according to their state and local laws and statutes, and take advantage of those opportunities. However, there are often political implications to consider and a teacher who even legally teaches biblical creation may face other repercussions.

Some teachers choose to avoid teaching evolutionary ideas in the biology classroom. While on the surface this might sound like a wise idea, it may present some problems. Many standardized tests that students may have to take include information on evolution. Not teaching the basic concepts may lead to these students doing poorly on these exams. Also, if the curriculum requires the teaching of evolutionary ideas, teachers could be violating their contract by intentionally eliminating this subject. Avoiding the issue is not the best strategy, as it will likely lead to problems on many different levels.

What Should Christians Be Doing?

Whenever permissible, evolutionary ideas should be taught — but warts and all. There are many inconsistencies within the evolutionary framework and many disagreements about how to interpret the evidence. When appropriate, point out that many scientists, both creationists and evolutionists, do not believe that Darwinian evolution is adequate for explaining the existence of life on earth.

7. The unscientific, even anti-scientific, nature of evolution is not the focus of this article. For more information on this topic, please see "Science or the Bible?" available at www.answersingenesis.org/articles/am/v2/n3/science-or-the-bible, and "Evolution: The Anti-science" available at www.answersingenesis.org/articles/aid/v3/n1/evolution-anti-science.

Also, many states have allowances for students to be released from school for special religious instruction. Consider supporting or starting a ministry that uses this time to teach students the true history of the earth from the Bible. Providing Christian students with this instruction will equip them to share this truth with teachers and other students. Additionally, these students should be equipped to share the gospel with their fellow students and teachers. Salvation is the ultimate goal for Christians in such a ministry, not just converting evolutionists into creationists.

We need bold Christians who will become active in their communities, school boards, and other organizations who will be prompting these changes from the bottom up. In these settings, Christians can start asking challenging questions about the exclusion of Christianity from schools, the acceptance of the religion of humanism, the absence of critical thinking when it comes to teaching evolution, etc. Based on the U.S. Constitution, no single religion should be endorsed in a government-run school. If no one stands up to challenge these ideas, the schools will continue to indoctrinate students with the religious beliefs of humanists.

AiG's True Position on Teaching Creation in Public Schools

Answers in Genesis is often misrepresented as trying to get creationist teaching into the public schools.[8] AiG does not lobby any government agencies to include the teaching of biblical creation in the public schools. As we have stated many times, we do not believe that creation should be mandated in public school science classrooms. If teaching creation were mandated, it would likely be taught poorly (and possibly mockingly) by a teacher who does not understand what the Bible teaches and who believes in evolution.

At the same time, it is not right that the tenets of secular humanism can be taught at the exclusion of Christian ideas. This type of exclusivity does not promote the critical thinking skills of students demanded by most science education standards. Teachers should be allowed, at the very least, the academic freedom to present various models of the history of life on earth and teach the strengths and weaknesses of those models. Recognizing that in the current political climate we can only expect to see evolution taught, it is only reasonable to include teaching the shortcomings of evolutionary ideas.

8. For example, the prominent U.S. newspaper *Star-Tribune* of Minneapolis-St. Paul, Minnesota (August 14, 2009) falsely stated that AiG is on a "mission to get creationism into science classrooms nationwide."

Advice to Christian Teachers and Administrators

Many Christians in the public school system view themselves as missionaries in a hostile environment. Their presence there is undoubtedly valuable and provides an opportunity to be salt and light in their communities. If you are a teacher or administrator in the public schools, we encourage you to be both wise and bold as you prayerfully consider your role in this controversial creation/evolution issue.

If your state or country does not even permit the questioning of evolution or discussing creation, there are other options that will help keep a teacher from getting fired. There are many strategies that take the responsibility for any creation teaching away from the school and its administration:

1. Offer an optional course after school that is free for students (perhaps once or twice a month) to refute some of the evolution and long-age teachings. You or someone you know who enjoys teaching creation can use many of the great biblically based, creationist resources. Show the students that they are not getting all of the information from the textbooks. The books *Evolution Exposed: Biology* and *Earth Science* are designed to counter the unbiblical notions taught in the science textbooks. Get these books into the hands of the students so that they can understand both sides of the origins debate.
2. Offer to be an adult sponsor for students who wish to start a Creation Club in the school. This student-led alternative can be very effective at getting outside speakers into the school to address the club and present information. Clubs can meet at lunch or after school, just like a Chess Club or any other.
3. Have your local church youth group provide a short course to counter evolutionary claims. Students in the youth group can invite other students to attend and learn more about the issue. Use a DVD-based curriculum such as *Demolishing Strongholds* or *The Answers Academy* to communicate these ideas to students.
4. As stated above, many states offer the option of "released time." Support or start a ministry in your community that would provide biblical instruction for public school students.
5. Support local ministries like the Gideons, Fellowship of Christian Athletes, Young Life, and many others that seek to share the gospel and God's Word with students in public schools.

(Be discerning, as not all groups will have a literal view of Genesis and local chapters often hold varying views.)

6. Understand the limits a teacher has to discuss ideas with students outside of the classroom. The political climate in your district should be taken into consideration, as well as recognizing that you may face persecution.
7. Have a local church or group of churches offer to bring students to the Creation Museum where they can be presented with biblical truths about God as the Creator. Students can help pass the word around at public schools.

Conclusions

As much as we want to see students know that true science confirms the creation account in Genesis and that molecules-to-man evolution is a blind-faith belief that flies in the face of much scientific evidence, in the long run the school battle will not be successful unless society as a whole (and the Church) returns to the Bible as *the* authority. That's why at AiG, we spend so much energy to equip the Church to restore biblical authority beginning with Genesis. Then, and only then, will the secular worldview of society be successfully challenged. More important, recognize that spreading the glorious gospel of Jesus Christ is the ultimate goal.

If you are not directly involved in public schools in any way, pray for those who are and support Christian teachers and administrators who are trying to make a difference. Support and pray for families and students in the public schools. Volunteer to be a mentor or to assist in the public schools or teach a Sunday school class to help the students understand the origins issue.

4

What Are "Kinds" in Genesis?

DR. GEORGIA PURDOM AND BODIE HODGE

"Zonkeys, Ligers, and Wholphins, Oh My!" Although not exactly the same mantra that the travelers in the classic *Wizard of Oz* repeat, these names represent real life animals just the same. In fact, two of these strange-sounding animals, a zonkey and a zorse, can now be seen at the new Creation Museum petting zoo. But what exactly are these animals and how did they come to be? Are they new species? Can the Bible explain such a thing?

What Is a "Kind"?

The first thing that needs to be addressed is: "What is a kind?" Often, people are confused into thinking that a "species" is a "kind." But this isn't necessarily so. A *species* is a man-made term used in the modern classification system. And frankly, the word *species* is difficult to define, whether one is a creationist or not! There is more on this word

Figure 1. Zonkey and zorse at the Creation Museum

and its definition and relationship to "kinds" later in this chapter. The Bible uses the term "kind." The Bible's first use of this word (Hebrew: *min*) is found in Genesis 1 when God creates plants and animals "according to their kinds." It is used again in Genesis 6 and 8 when God instructs Noah to take two of every kind of land-dwelling, air-breathing animal onto the ark and also in God's command for the animals to reproduce after the Flood. A plain reading of the text infers that plants and animals were created to reproduce within the boundaries of their kind. Evidence to support this concept is clearly seen (or rather not seen) in our world today, as there are no reports of dats (dog + cat) or hows (horse + cow)! So a good rule of thumb is that if two things can breed together, then they are of the same created kind. It is a bit more complicated than this, but for the time being, this is a quick measure of a "kind."

As an example, dogs can easily breed with one another, whether wolves, dingoes, coyotes, or domestic dogs. When dogs breed together, you get dogs; so there is a dog kind. It works the same with chickens. There are several breeds of chickens, but chickens breed with each other and you still get chickens. So there is a chicken kind. The concept is fairly easy to understand.

But in today's culture, where evolution and millions of years are taught as fact, many people have been led to believe that animals and plants (that are

DOG VARIATIONS

Affenpinscher
Deerhound
Lundehund
Greyhound
Lhasa Apso
Siberian Husky
Dalmatian
Lion Dog
Karelian Bearhound
Welsh Corgi
Afghan Hound
Västgöta Spitz
Kanaan Dog
Miniature Pinscher
Chow-chow
King Charles Spaniel
Cao fila
Entlebücher Sennenhund
Collie
Kelpie
Beagle
Pointer
Pug
Belgian Sheepdog

Figure 2. Domestic dogs all belong to the same dog kind.

Figure 3. The amazing variety of chicken breeds all belong to the same kind.

classed as a specific "species") have been like this for tens of thousands of years and perhaps millions of years. So when they see things like lions or zebras, they think they have been like this for an extremely long time.

From a biblical perspective, though, land animals like wolves, zebras, sheep, lions, and so on have at least two ancestors that lived on Noah's ark, only about 4,300 years ago. These animals have undergone many changes since that time. But dogs are still part of the dog kind, cats are still part of the cat kind, and so on. God placed variety within the original kinds, and other variation has occurred since the Fall due to genetic alterations.

Variety within a "Kind"

Creation scientists use the word baramin to refer to created kinds (Hebrew: *bara* = created, *min* = kind). Because none of the original ancestors survive today, creationists have been trying to figure out what descendants belong to each baramin in their varied forms. Baramin is commonly believed to be at the level of family and possibly order for some plants/animals (according to the common classification scheme of kingdom, phylum, class, order, family, genus, species). On rare occasions, a kind may be equivalent to the genus or species levels.

Baraminology is a field of study that attempts to classify fossil and living organisms into baramins. This is done based on many criteria, such as physical

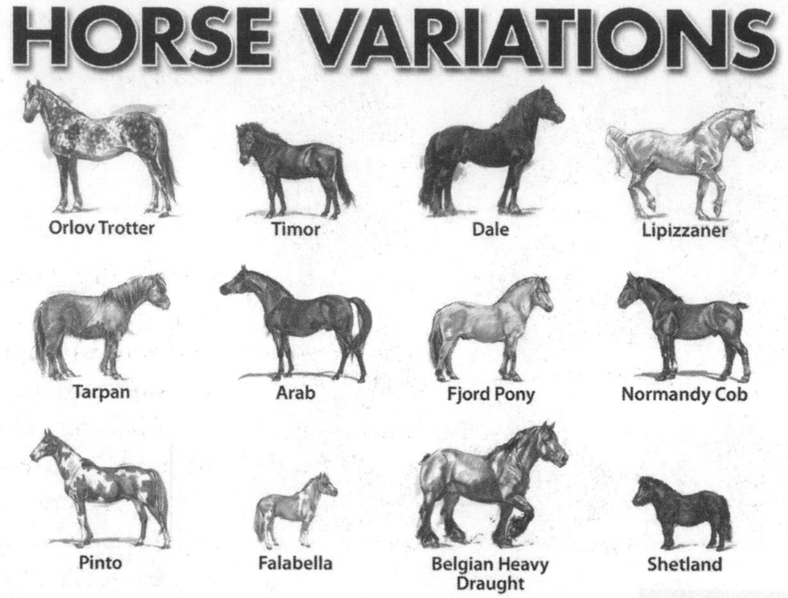

HORSE VARIATIONS

Orlov Trotter
Timor
Dale
Lipizzaner
Tarpan
Arab
Fjord Pony
Normandy Cob
Pinto
Falabella
Belgian Heavy Draught
Shetland

Figure 4. Horses of all shapes and sizes are of the same kind.

characteristics and DNA sequences. For living organisms, hybridization is a key criterion. If two animals can produce a hybrid, then they are considered to be of the same kind.[1] However, the inability to produce offspring does not necessarily rule out that the animals are of the same kind, since this may be the result of mutations (since the Fall).

Zonkeys (from a male zebra bred with a female donkey), zorses (male zebra and female horse), and hebras (male horse and female zebra) are all examples of hybrid animals. Hybrid animals are the result of the mating of two animals of the same "kind." Perhaps one of the most popular hybrids of the past has been the mule, the mating of a horse and donkey. So seeing something like a zorse or zonkey shouldn't really surprise anyone, since donkeys, zebras, and horses all belong to the horse kind.

The concept of kind is important for understanding how Noah fit all the animals on the ark. If kind is at the level of family/order, there would have been plenty of room on the ark to take two of every kind and seven of some. For example, even though many different dinosaurs have been identified, creation scientists think there are only about 50 "kinds" of dinosaurs. Even though breeding studies are impossible with dinosaurs, by studying fossils one can

1. Some might argue that if the hybrid offspring are infertile, then this indicates that the parent animals are of separate created kinds. However, fertility of the offspring has no bearing on the kind designation. Hybridization is the key.

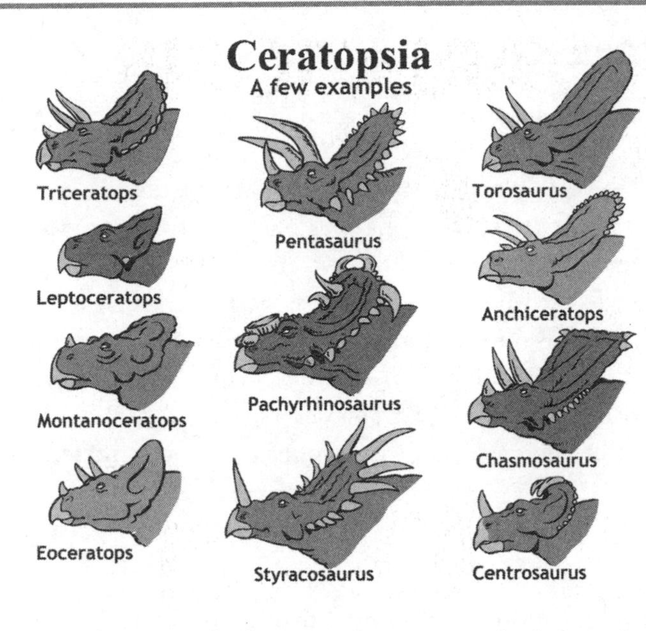

Figure 5. Using fossil evidence, we can identify kinds within the dinosaurs.

ascertain that there was likely one Ceratopsian kind with variation in that kind and so on.

After the Flood, the animals were told to "be fruitful and multiply on the earth" (Genesis 8:17). As they did this, natural selection, mutation, and other mechanisms allowed speciation within the kinds to occur. Speciation was necessary for the animals to survive in a very different post-Flood world. This is especially well illustrated in the dog kind in which current members (e.g., coyotes, dingoes, and domestic dogs) are confirmed to be descended from an ancestral type of wolf.[2]

Hybrid animals are usually the result of parent animals that have similar chromosome numbers. Many times the hybrids are infertile due to an uneven chromosome number that affects the production of eggs and sperm. However, this is not always the case, as even some mules (horse + donkey) have been known to reproduce. Consider some of the following amazing animal hybrids.

Zonkeys, Zorses, and Mules

These hybrids are the result of mating within the family Equidae. As we've said before, zonkeys are the result of mating a male zebra and a female donkey; zorses are the result of mating a male zebra and a female horse; and mules are the result of mating a male donkey and a female horse. But reverse matings (such as hinnies produced from a male horse and female donkey) are rare, although still possible. All are considered "infertile" due to uneven chromosome numbers, but fertility has been observed in some cases. Zonkeys and zorses have a mixture of their parents' traits, including the beautiful striping patterns of the zebra parents.

2. Savolainen et al., "Genetic Evidence for an East Asian origin of Domestic Dogs," *Science* 298 (2002): 1610–1613.

Ligers, Tigons, and Other Cats

These hybrids are the result of mating within the family Felidae. Ligers are the result of mating a male lion and a female tiger. Ligers are the largest cats in the world, weighing in at over 1,000 pounds (450 kg). Tigons are the result of mating a female lion and a male tiger. These matings only occur in captivity, since lions live in Africa, tigers live in Asia, and the two are enemies in the wild. Female hybrids are typically fertile while male hybrids are not.

Other hybrids in this family include bobcats that mate with domestic cats and bobcats with lynx (Blynx and Lynxcat). There have been mixes of the cougar and the ocelot, as well as many others. This shows that large, midsize, and small cats can ultimately interbreed, and therefore suggests that there is only one cat kind.

Wolphin

Turning to the ocean, this hybrid is the result of mating within the family Delphinidae. The wholphin is the result of mating a false killer whale (genus *Pseudorca*) and bottlenose dolphin (genus *Tursiops*). Such a mating occurred in captivity at Hawaii's Sea Life Park in 1985.[3] The wholphin is fertile. This hybrid shows the difficulty of determining the species designation, since a major criterion is the ability to interbreed and produce fertile offspring. Even though the whale and dolphin are considered separate genera, they may, in fact, belong to the same species. This shows how difficult it is to define the term *species*. Of course, from a biblical perspective it is easy to say they are both the same kind!

"Fixity of Species" and Changing Definitions

So what is the relationship between the *kinds* and *species* anyway? If one were to ask around to see what kind of definitions people have of the word *species* [or *genus*], most would respond by saying they have something to do with classification. In today's society, the words *genus* and *species* are synonymous with the Linnaean taxonomy system.

In the early 1700s, if someone said something about a "species" or "genus," it would have had nothing to do with classification systems. So why is this important today and what can we learn from it? The word *species*, and its changing definition, were partly responsible for the compromise of the Church in late 1800s. In fact, the Church is still struggling over this change. Let's do a brief history review.

3. Stephen Adams, "Dolphin and Whale Mate to Create a 'Wholphin,' " Telegraph.co.uk website news, April 2, 2008, Telegraph Media Group Limited, www.telegraph.co.uk/news/uknews/1582973/Dolphin-and-whale-mate-to-create-a-wolphin.html.

Species: Origin and Meaning

The English word *species* comes directly from Latin. For example, the Latin Vulgate (early Latin Bible translation), by Jerome around A.D. 400, says of Genesis 1:21:

> creavitque Deus cete grandia et omnem animam viventem atque motabilem quam produxerant aquae in *species* suas et omne volatile secundum *genus* suum et vidit Deus quod esset bonum [emphasis added].

Species is also found in the Latin version in Genesis 1:24, 25 as well. The Latin basically meant the biblical "kind." In fact, this word carried over into English (and other languages that have some Latin influence). It means a "kind, form, or sort." Another word that was commonly used for a kind in the Latin Vulgate was *genus*. This is evident in Genesis 1:11, 12, and 21. In both cases, these two words (*species* and *genus*) were used for the Hebrew word *min* or kind.

It made sense that Carl Linnaeus, a Swedish Christian, began using Latin terms for his new classification system. It was logical to use these common terms, which were a part of the commercial language throughout Europe (much in the way that English, for example, is seen as a universal language in the world today for communication and so on). Linnaeus even wrote his large treatise, *Systema Natvrae*, and other findings, in Latin in the mid to late 1700s.

Early commentators recognized that species originally meant the biblical kinds, as even John Calvin, prominent reformer in the 1500s, stated in his notes on Genesis 1:24:

> I say, moreover, it is sufficient for the purpose of signifying the same thing, (1) that Moses declares animals were created "according to their species": for this distribution carried with it something stable. It may even hence be inferred that the offspring of animals was included. For to what purpose do distinct species exist, unless that individuals, by their several kinds, may be multiplied?

Of course, Calvin originally wrote in Latin, but this early English translation by Thomas Tymme in 1578 still shows the point that the word *species* was used to mean the biblical kind. Calvin is even pointing out stability or fixity (i.e., biblical kinds). Dr. John Gill, about the same time as Linnaeus, equates species and kinds in his note under Genesis 1:22 by saying:

> With a power to procreate their kind, and continue their species, as it is interpreted in the next clause; *saying, be fruitful, and multiply, and fill the waters in the seas.*

Others, such as Basil, prior to the Latin Vulgate, discussed *species* as the biblical kind in the fourth century in his *Homilies* on Genesis 1. Matthew Henry, in the late 1600s and early 1700s, used *species* as kinds in his notes on Genesis 2:3, saying there would be no new "species" created after creation week had completed. The list could continue. The point is that *species* originally meant the biblical kind.

Species: A Change

After Linnaeus, both of these words (*species* and *genus*) were commonly used in modern biological classification systems with slightly different definitions. In the mid-to-late 1700s, *species* began taking on a new, more specific definition in scientific circles as a biological term (that definition is still being debated even today). But, by and large, the definition had changed so that, instead of there being a dog *species* (or dog kind), there were many dog *species*.

In the common and Church sense, the word *species* was still viewed as the biblical "kind." But as the scientific term gained popularity, this led to a problem. When theologians and members of the Church said "fixity of species" (meaning fixity of the biblical kinds) people readily saw that there were variations among the *species* (by the new definition). They thought, *But* species *do change!* Of course, no one ever showed something like a dog changing into something like a cat. Dogs were still dogs, cats were still cats, and so on.

However, a bait-and-switch fallacy had taken place. Christians were teaching fixity of species (kinds), but the definition of *species* changed out from under them. So Christians looked ignorant when people began observing that species — by the *new* definition — do change. Of course, in reality, this was merely variation within the created kinds. For example, dogs could be observed changing into something different — still dogs, but not looking like other "species" (by the new definition) of dogs. So it appeared that the created kinds were becoming new species (new definition), even though the animals did not change into a different kind of animal. It *appeared* that the Church was wrong.

Perhaps the most influential critique of fixity of species came from Charles Darwin, whose book *On the Origin of Species* tackled the misunderstood idea of *fixity of species* (though it never used the term "fixity"). Mr. Darwin studied many creatures during his travels and realized there was variation and not *fixity of species* (by the new definition).

The Implications

The results of this were devastating to the Church. And people began doubting the Word of God as a result, walking away from Christianity, and embracing an evolutionary philosophy. George Bentham, writing May 30, 1882, to Francis Darwin regarding his father Charles's ideas, said:

The Dog Species

Figure 6. Original definition of species: all dogs were one species.

> I have been throughout one of his most sincere admirers, and fully adopted his theories and conclusions, notwithstanding the severe pain and disappointment they at first occasioned me. On the day that his celebrated paper was read at the Linnean Society, July 1st, 1858, a long paper of mine had been set down for reading, in which, in commenting on the British Flora, I had collected a number of observations and facts illustrating what I then believed to be a fixity in species, however difficult it might be to assign their limits, and showing a tendency of abnormal forms produced by cultivation or otherwise, to withdraw within those original limits when left to themselves. Most fortunately my paper had to give way to Mr. Darwin's and when once that was read, I felt bound to defer mine for reconsideration; I began to entertain doubts on the subject, and on the appearance of the 'Origin of Species,' I was forced, however reluctantly, to give up my long-cherished convictions, the results of much labour and study, and I cancelled all that part of my paper which urged original fixity, and published only portions of the remainder in another form, chiefly in the 'Natural History Review.'[4]

Several Dog Species

Figure 7. New definition of species: several wolf species, several coyote species, etc.

4. Francis Darwin, ed., *The Life and Letters of Charles Darwin Including an Autobiographical Chapter*, Volume 2, as produced by Classic Literature Library, Free Public Book Domain, originally published in 1897, www.charles-darwin.classic-literature.co.uk/the-life-and-letters-of-charles-darwin-volume-ii/ebook-page-41.asp

Even today, an objection commonly leveled at the Bible is that it claims that species are fixed. A good response would be: "To which definition of *species* are you referring?" By the old definition (as a kind), creationists would agree, but would probably better state it in modern English as fixity of the created kinds so as not to confuse the issue. The idea of onc kind changing into another can be argued against based on the fact that no such change has ever been observed.

After Darwin's book, many churches gave up *fixity of species* (by either definition) and began taking compromised positions such as theistic evolution (basically giving up Genesis for molecules-to-man evolution and then picking up with Abraham). Realizing that the Church had been duped by a bait-and-switch fallacy provides a valuable learning tool. When people fail to understand history, they often repeat it.

A Great Place for Creation Research

All of these animals' ancestors that we have discussed above — horses, donkey, zebras, tigers, lions, whales, and dolphins — were created with genetic diversity within their various kinds (or by the older definition of *species*). Through time, the processes of natural selection, mutation, and other mechanisms have altered that original information (decreased or degenerated) to give us even more variation within a kind.

Great variety can be observed in the offspring of animals of the same kind, just as the same cake recipe can be used to make many different cakes with various flavors and colors. Hybrids have a portion of the same genetic information as their parents but combined in a unique way to give a very unique-looking animal. What an amazing diversity of life God has created for us to enjoy!

The study of created kinds is an exciting area of research, and our hope is to help encourage others to get involved. Whether studying the duck-goose kind, elephant-mammoth kind, camel-llama kind, apple-pear kind, or others, the field of baraminology is a great place for biologists, botanists, geneticists, and paleontologists (for extinct kinds) to get immersed in creation research.

5

How Could Noah Fit the Animals on the Ark and Care for Them?

JOHN WOODMORAPPE

According to Scripture, Noah's ark was a safe haven for representatives of all the kinds of air-breathing land animals and birds that God created. While it is possible that God made miraculous provisions for the daily care of these animals, it is not necessary — or required by Scripture — to appeal to miracles. Exploring natural solutions for day-to-day operations does not discount God's role: the biblical account hints at plenty of miracles as written, such as God bringing the animals to the ark (Genesis 6:20; 7:9, 15), closing the door of the ark (7:16), and causing the fountains of the deep and the windows of heaven to open on the same day (7:11). It turns out that a study of existing, low-tech animal care methods answers trivial objections to the ark. In fact, many solutions to seemingly insurmountable problems are rather straightforward.[1]

How Did Noah Fit All the Animals on the Ark?

To answer this question, we must first ask how many animals were actually on the ark. Critics have fantasized the presence of millions of animals overloading

1. For an in-depth, documented discussion of this and related topics in language that is understandable to lay people and students, see John Woodmorappe, *Noah's Ark: A Feasibility Study* (Dallas, TX: Institute for Creation Research, 2009).

the ark. In actuality, the Bible makes it clear that the cargo was limited to land-dwelling, air-breathing vertebrate animals — corresponding to modern birds, mammals, and reptiles, as well as their extinct counterparts.

Was every species on the ark? No! From chapters such as Leviticus 11, it is obvious that the created kind (*min* in Hebrew, in Genesis 1:11–12, 21, 24–25) was a much broader category than the modern term of classification, *species*. Current baraminological[2] research suggests that the created kind most closely corresponded to the *family* level in current taxonomy. However, to be conservative in this study, the *genus* was set as equivalent to the original created kind. As for the clean animals that entered the ark in seven pairs, this added a modest number of additional animals, notably bovids (cow-like mammals) and cervids (deer-like mammals). Under these conservative assumptions, there were no more than 16,000 land animals and birds on the ark.

According to the Bible, the ark had three decks (floors). It is not difficult to show that there was plenty of room for 16,000 animals, assuming they required approximately the same floor space as animals in typical farm enclosures and laboratories today. The vast majority of the creatures (birds, reptiles, and mammals) are small. The largest animals were probably only a few hundred pounds of body weight.

It is still necessary to take account of the floor spaces required by large animals, such as elephants, giraffes, rhinos, and some dinosaurs. But even these, collectively, do not require a large area. God would likely have sent to Noah young (and therefore small, but not newborn) representatives of these kinds so that they would have a full reproductive potential for life after the Flood to repopulate the earth (Genesis 7:1–3). Even the largest dinosaurs were relatively small when only a few years old.

Without tiering of cages, only 47 percent of the ark floor would have been necessary. What's more, many could have been housed in groups, which would have further reduced the required space.

What about the provisions for the animals? It can be shown that the food would have filled only 6 to 12 percent of the volume of the ark, and the potable water only an additional 9 percent of the same.[3]

What About the Dinosaurs?

There are only several hundred genera of dinosaurs known. What's more, the continuous invalidation of old names largely offsets the continuous discovery

2. Baramin is a term coined by creation scientists to describe the original created kinds. It comes from the Hebrew words bara (meaning "create") and min (meaning "kind").
3. Woodmorappe, *Noah's Ark: A Feasibility Study*, p. 17–21, 95–98.

The proposed skylight roof could be opened. This might be the covering when "Noah removed the covering of the ark" (Genesis 8:13).

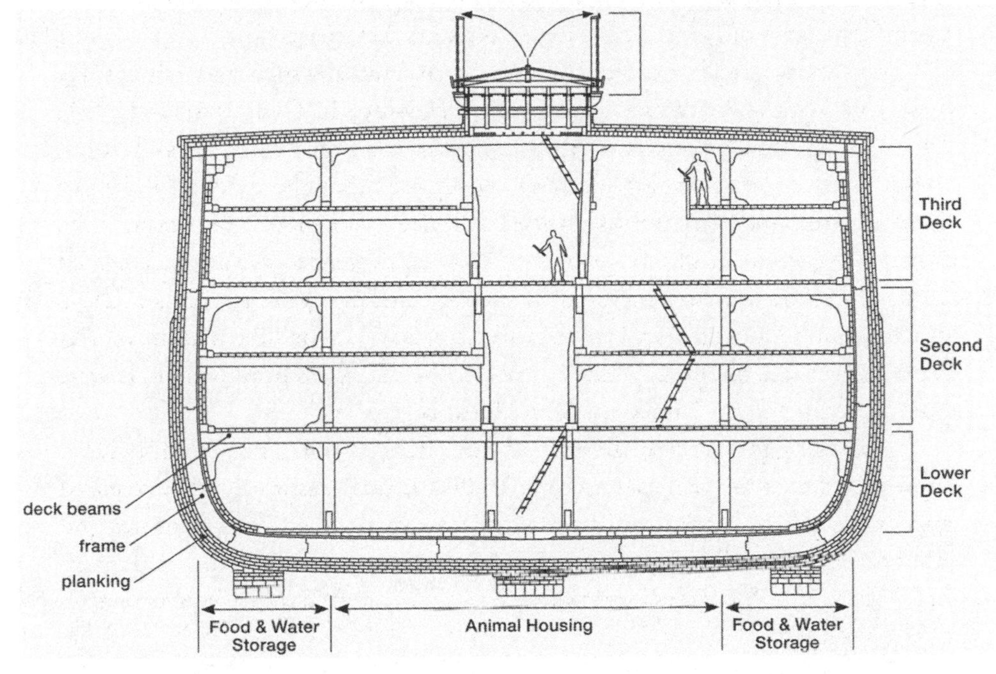

Figure 1. This is a cross-section view of a possible design of the interior of the ark.

of new kinds of dinosaur genera.[4] Only a modest fraction of all dinosaurs reached giant size. About 16 percent of dinosaur genera had an adult weight in excess of ten tons, and almost half of dinosaur genera weighed no more than a ton when mature.

However, the foregoing is academic because dinosaurs could have been represented as young. Interestingly, according to the most recent models of dinosaur maturation, even the largest sauropod dinosaurs were no more than several hundred kilograms in weight by the time they were just over a year old,[5] which could have corresponded to their time of release from the ark.

What Did the Dinosaurs Eat?

Dinosaurs could have eaten basically the same foods as the other animals. The young representatives of the large sauropods could have eaten compressed

4. M.J. Benton, "How to Find a Dinosaur, and the Role of Synonymy in Biodiversity Studies," *Paleobiology* 34 no. 4 (2008): 516–533.
5. T.M. Lehman and H.N. Woodward, "Modeling Growth Rates for Sauropod Dinosaurs," *Paleobiology* 34 no. 4 (2008): 264–281.

hay, other dried plant material, seeds and grains, and the like. Carnivorous dinosaurs — if any were meat-eaters before the Flood — could have eaten dried meat, reconstituted dried meat, or slaughtered animals. Giant tortoises would have been ideal to use as food in this regard. They were large and needed little food to be maintained themselves. There are also exotic sources of meat, such as fish that wrap themselves in dry cocoons.

How Were the Animals Cared For?

Anti-Bible critics have compared the challenges of caring for the animals with that of modern zoos. This is fallacious. We must distinguish between the long-term care required for animals kept in zoos and the temporary, emergency care required on the ark. The animals' comfort and healthy appearance were not essential for emergency survival during one stressful year, where survival was the primary goal.

Studies of non-mechanized animal care indicate that eight people could have fed and watered 16,000 creatures. The key is to avoid unnecessary walking around. As the old adage says, "Don't work harder, work smarter."

Therefore, Noah probably stored the food and water near each animal. Even better, drinking water could have been piped into troughs, just as the Chinese have used bamboo pipes for this purpose for thousands of years. The

Figures 2 and 3. With Noah being over 500 years in age, it would make sense that he had the knowledge to be able to incorporate automatic feeding and watering systems where they only had to be refilled occasionally.

use of some sort of self-feeders, as is commonly done for birds, would have been relatively easy and probably essential. Animals that required special care or diets were uncommon and should not have needed an inordinate amount of time from the handlers. Even animals with the most specialized diets in nature could have been switched to readily sustainable substitute diets. Of course, this assumes that animals with specialized diets today were likewise specialized at the time of the Flood. But that may not have been the case in the ancestral kinds that were taken on the ark.

Animals with Special Diets

Many challenges to the reliability of the biblical account of Noah's ark, based on animals' feeding requirements, are steeped in mythology. Do captive anteaters necessarily require ants? No! Neither do most insect-eating animals require insects in their diet. Nor do most animals that eat only live prey in nature necessarily require moving prey in captivity. (For the few that do, it would not have been difficult to provide a rudimentary live-animal feeder.)

Even the most "fussy" animal kinds today contain individual representatives that can depart from the foods their kind normally eats in nature. For example, although most koalas eat nothing but fresh eucalyptus leaves, there are individual koalas that will subsist on dried eucalyptus leaves. Likewise, some individual pandas will accept dried bamboo stalks.

How Did the Animals Breathe?

The ventilation of the ark was not only necessary to provide fresh air but, more important, to dissipate body heat. A basic, non-mechanical ventilation system was sufficient for the ark. The density of animals on the ark, compared to the volume of enclosed space, was much less than we find in some modern, mass animal housing used to keep stock that are raised for food (such as chicken farms), which often require no special mechanical ventilation.

The Bible is not specific as to the kind and size of window on the ark. It is reasonable to believe that one relatively small window would have adequately ventilated the ark. Of course, if there were a window running along the top center section, which the biblical description allows, all occupants would be even more comfortable. It is also interesting to note that the convective movement of air, driven by temperature differences between the warm-blooded animals and the cold interior surfaces, would have been significant enough to drive the flow of air. Plus, wind blowing into the window would have enhanced the ventilation further. However, if supplementary ventilation was necessary, it could have been provided by wave motion or even a small number of animals harnessed to slow-moving rotary fans.

What Did Noah and His Family Do with the Animal Waste?

As much as 12 U.S. tons (11 m. tons) of animal waste may have been produced daily. The key to keeping the enclosures clean was to avoid the need for Noah and his family to do the work. The right systems could also prevent the need to change animal bedding. Noah could have accomplished this in several ways. One possibility would be to allow the waste to accumulate below the animals, much as we see in rustic henhouses. In this regard, there could have been slatted floors, and animals could have trampled their waste into the pits below. Small animals, such as birds, could have multiple levels in their enclosures, and waste could have simply accumulated at the bottom of each.

The danger of toxic or explosive manure gases, such as methane, would be alleviated by the constant movement of the ark, which would have allowed manure gases to be constantly released. Second, methane, which is half the density of air, would quickly find its way out of the window of the ark. There is no reason to believe that the levels of these gases within the ark would have remotely approached hazardous levels.

Alternatively, sloped floors in animal enclosures would have allowed the waste to flow into large central gutters and then into collection pits, allowing

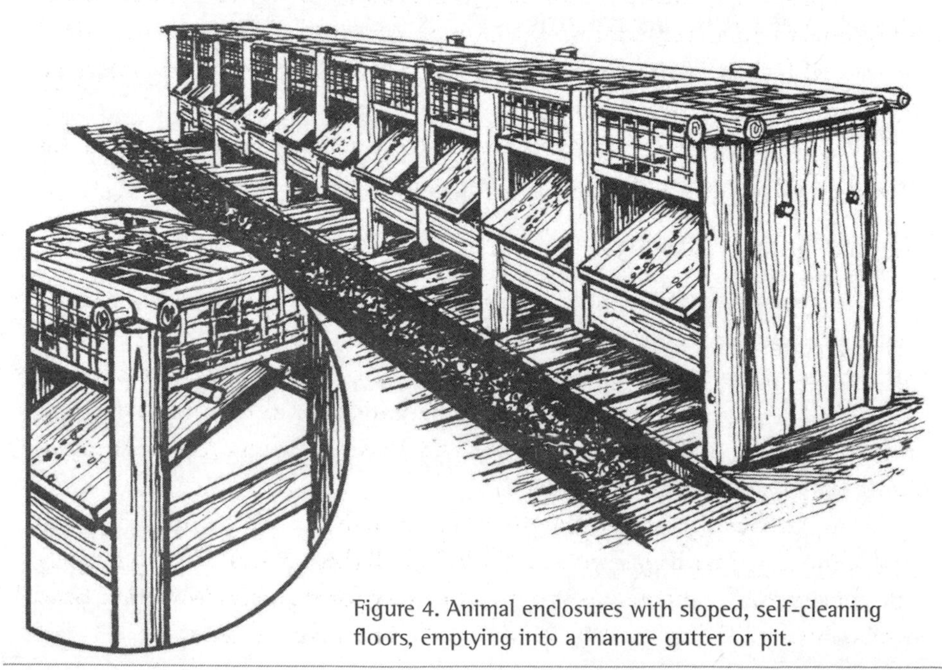

Figure 4. Animal enclosures with sloped, self-cleaning floors, emptying into a manure gutter or pit.

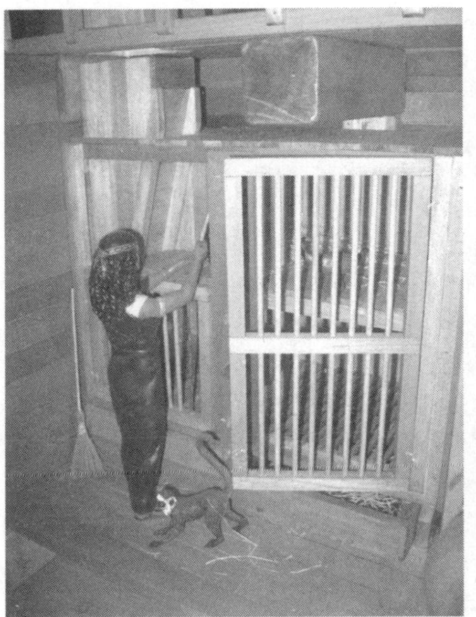

Figures 5 and 6. Some floors could allow waste to fall below and could be stocked with hay or sawdust to soak it up. It is possible that a clean-up would not even be required for the duration of the year-long Flood.

gravity to do most of the work. Noah's family could have then dumped this overboard without an excessive expenditure of manpower.

The problem of manure odor may, at first thought, seem insurmountable. But we must remember that throughout most of human history, humans lived together with their farm animals. Barns, separate from human living quarters, are a relatively recent development.

While the voyage of the ark may not have been comfortable or easy, it was certainly doable, even under such unprecedented circumstances.

Did the Animals Hibernate?

If animals hibernated, this would, of course, have greatly alleviated the need to feed, water, and remove the waste of the ark animals. Critics point out that the vast majority of animals on the ark were not of the type that hibernate. However, this ignores the possibility that hibernation (or its equivalent in tropical environments, such as aestivation) may have been much more widespread in the animal kingdom than it is today.

It is, of course, also possible that God put the animals into a sleep for most of the time that they were on the ark. But all this is moot. Whether supernatural or natural, hibernation was not necessary for the animals to have been adequately cared for on the ark. It only would have made it easier.

Were Single Pairs Sufficient?

Critics point to the fact that, when a single pair of animals is released, it usually does not lead to a lasting population. But this ignores the fact that, under modern conditions, the released pair must compete against pre-existing animals, causing it to usually lose out. In contrast, the ark-released animals were introduced to an environment free of competitors. Experience has shown that single-pair introductions usually do lead to lasting populations when there are few or no competitors. One must also keep in mind that nowhere in the Bible does it claim that all animals that were released from the ark gave rise to lasting populations. There have been and continue to be extinctions, often caused by man.

Critics have also argued that single pairs are not sufficient to be able to transmit the genetic variability of the parent, pre-Flood population. This is a half-truth. In most traits, a single pair contains the most-commonly occurring gene forms (that is, alleles) that occur in the population at large. The rare alleles, which a single pair will seldom have, are usually uncommon in the population and of little or no relevance to its survivorship or fitness. Mutations in the post-Flood world could have created a new set of rarely occurring alleles.

Consider, for example, the human blood types. The relevant possibilities are: A-only, B-only, both A and B (that is, blood type AB), and neither A nor B (that is, blood type O). There are also rare blood types, but these, again, are just that — rare, and of little relevance to human survival. They are one-step mutational derivatives of the common blood types. A single pair of individuals would very likely have the A and B alleles represented within it. Rare blood types would be re-established by mutations of the common alleles after the Flood, and would probably not be the same as their pre-Flood counterparts.

Didn't the Ark-released Animals Eat Each Other?

Those who attack the Bible say that the carnivores released from the ark would have soon eaten up the herbivores, leading to the eventual extinction of both. This falsely assumes that the only sources of meat available to the ark-released carnivores were the ark-released herbivores. Such was not the case.

The post-Flood world must have had plenty of rotting corpses of various animals that were not buried in the Flood sediments. Experience has shown that most carnivores prefer to eat carrion than to kill live animals for food. Also, the Flood must have left behind many residual pools of water and marine life. As these waters retreated or dried up, fish and other marine animals were stranded in lakes, ponds, and streams on land. This could also have served as food for the ark-released carnivores. In fact, experience shows that many normally non–fish-eating carnivores, such as lions, will eat fish if it is available, and do so in preference to hunting their usual prey.

These alternative sources of food must have diverted the attention of predators for a considerable period of time after the Flood. This would have allowed the prey populations to build up to an appreciable size before they became the main target of the predators.

How Did Marine Life Survive?

What about the animals that were not on the ark? Critics have said that the Flood must have been so destructive that nothing could possibly have survived. How could they possibly know this? As a matter of fact, fish and other marine life produce an astonishing number of larval offspring. Only a tiny number of these need to survive in order to propagate their kind. And while much of the Flood waters may have been violent, many lateral and vertical parts of the water column would have allowed sea life to survive during the Flood.

How Could Freshwater and Saltwater Fish Coexist in the Flood?

Most saltwater fish cannot live in freshwater, and most freshwater fish cannot live in saltwater. So how could both have survived the Flood? To begin with, the intolerances are not symmetrical in nature. Most ocean fish can survive considerable reductions in the salinity of water, even though they cannot go all the way to the near-zero salinity of fresh water. In contrast, most freshwater life is intolerant of more than a slight elevation of salt levels in the water.

There is a range of brackish water (about 5–10 percent the salinity of current ocean water) that would be tolerated by nearly all ocean fish as well as a significant fraction of freshwater fish. What about those organisms that cannot tolerate this? Variations in salinity according to geographic area, and the probable stratification of denser, saltier water, would have created pockets of considerable salinity and other pockets that approached freshwater qualities. Sensitive organisms could survive there.

Finally, it should be noted that organisms that are extremely intolerant of either salinity or reductions in salinity vary from species to species. The narrow range that they tolerate probably arose since the Flood by the mechanisms of natural selection of some of the great genetic variability built into the original created kinds (and still observable today) and in some cases through mutations also. In fact, there is evidence from selective breeding that tolerance or intolerance to salinity can be markedly changed in a matter of generations. (For more in this topic see chapter 20, "How Could Fish Survive the Genesis Flood?")

6

Was the Flood of Noah Global or Local in Extent?

KEN HAM AND DR. ANDREW A. SNELLING

Many Christians and their leaders believe that it is not relevant whether the Flood of Noah described in Genesis 6–8 was global or localized (in the Mesopotamian Valley of the Tigris and Euphrates Rivers). After all, they say, it's not relevant to a Christian's salvation, and the gospel message to be preached is all about Jesus.

Besides, matters about rocks and the earth's history are the domain of the geologists, because the Bible isn't a science textbook. So if the geologists say there never was a global Flood, then that settles it! Thus, Christians who advocate an old earth agree with the secular geologists, and therefore they oppose any notion that the Flood of Noah was global.

However, whether the Flood of Noah was global or local in extent *is* a crucial question. This is because ultimately what is at stake is the authority of *all* of God's Word. Indeed, if the text of Scripture in Genesis 6–8 clearly teaches that the Flood was global and we reject that teaching, then we undermine the reliability and authority of other parts of Scripture, including John 3:16. God's Word must be trustworthy and authoritative in all that it affirms.

Millions of Years or a Global Flood?

Secular geologists have interpreted the fossil-bearing sedimentary layers, such as those exposed in the walls of the Grand Canyon, as having taken millions of years to form. Countless sea creatures lived on shallow seafloors, for example, and were slowly buried, to be replaced by new sea creatures growing on the seafloors. The various sedimentary rock layers that we now see stacked up on top of one another thus supposedly slowly accumulated as sea creatures were progressively buried.

The guiding principle used by secular geologists to interpret the rock record is "the present is the key to the past," which means that the geologic processes we see operating today, at the rates they operate today, are all that are necessary to explain the rock layers (figure 1). While catastrophes such as local flooding and volcanic eruptions are allowable because they do occur today, any suggestion of a global catastrophic Flood as described in the Bible is totally ruled out before the geological evidence is even examined.

On the other hand, the description of the Flood in Genesis 6–8 is not hard to understand. We are told that the "fountains of the great deep" burst open and poured water out onto the earth's surface for 150 days (five months). Simultaneously, and for the same length of time, the "floodgates of heaven" were open, producing torrential global rainfall.[1]

Figure 1. Two views of the rock layers: the world teaches that the vast majority of the rock layers were laid down slowly over millions of years; but in light of a global Flood in Genesis 6–9, it makes more sense that bulk of the rock layers that contain fossils were laid down during this catastrophe only thousands of years ago.

The combined result was that the waters destructively rose across the face of the earth to eventually cover "*all* the high hills under the *whole* heaven." The mountains also were eventually covered, so that every creature "in whose nostrils is the breath of life" perished. Only Noah, his family, and all the air-breathing, land-dwelling creatures he took on board the ark were saved.

Based on that clear description of this real historical event, it is very rational to conclude that we should expect to find evidence today of billions

1. The reference to 40 days and 40 nights (Genesis 7:12, 17) appears to be telling us how long it was before the ark started to float, for the windows of heaven were closed on the same day (150th) as the fountains of the deep were (Genesis 7:24–8:3). For a detailed argument based on the Hebrew text see William Barrick, "Noah's Flood and its Geological Implications," in Terry Mortenson and Thane H. Ury, eds., *Coming to Grips with Genesis* (Green Forest, AR: Master Books, 2008), p. 251–282.

of dead animals and plants buried in rock layers composed of water-deposited sand, lime, and mud all around the earth. And indeed, that's exactly what we do find — billions of fossils of animals and plants buried in sedimentary rock layers stretching across every continent all around the globe.[2] So instead of taking millions of years to form, most of the fossil-bearing sedimentary rock layers, as seen in the walls of the Grand Canyon and elsewhere, could have formed rapidly during the year of this global catastrophic Flood of Noah.[3]

It should immediately be obvious that these two interpretations of the evidence are mutually exclusive! Most of these rock layers are either the sobering testimony to Noah's Flood or the record of millions of years of history on this earth. One must be true and the other must be false. We can't consistently or logically believe in both, because the millions of years can't be fitted into the 370-day length of the global cataclysmic Flood of Noah described in Genesis 6–8. That is ultimately the fundamental reason why many old-earth advocates in the Christian community oppose the clear teaching of Scripture that the Flood was global. Only a relatively insignificant local flood would fit with the secular geological interpretation of millions of years of slow and gradual geologic processes for most of the fossil record.

Biblical Problems

In order to relegate Noah's Flood to being only local in extent, and/or to being a myth, the Hebrew text of Genesis 6–8 and also the larger context have to be virtually ignored.

The Book of Genesis is clearly divided into two main sections. Chapters 1–11 deal with *universal* origins (the material universe, the plant and animal kingdoms, humans, marriage, sin, death, redemption, the nations of the earth, etc.). Chapters 12–50, on the other hand, concentrate on the *particular* origin of the Hebrew nation and its tribes, mentioning other nations only insofar as they came in contact with Abraham and his descendants.[4]

The realization of this fact of the context of the Flood account within the section of Genesis on universal origins sheds important light on the question of the magnitude of the Flood. Furthermore, the biblical account of the Flood

2. See chapter 29 in this volume: Andrew A. Snelling, "What Are Some of the Best Flood Evidences?"
3. Some localized fossil-bearing deposits may have formed after the Fall of Adam and Eve in sin and before Noah's Flood, and some of the localized fossiliferous rock layers at the top of the geological record were formed in post-Flood events. But creationist geologists are in general agreement that most of the fossil-bearing sedimentary rock record is a result of Noah's Flood.
4. W.H. Griffith Thomas, *Genesis: A Devotional Commentary* (Grand Rapids, MI: Eerdmans, 1946), p. 18–19.

catastrophe occupies more than 3 chapters of these 11 chapters on universal origins, while only 2 chapters are devoted to the creation of all things! How important, therefore, must the Flood account be! Yet nobody denies that the account in Genesis 1–2 of the creation of all things is referring to the scale of the whole earth, and indeed the whole universe. Thus the context of Genesis 6–8 demands that the scriptural narrative be understood to be describing a watery catastrophe of global proportions.

But when we read the Flood account itself, we see this conclusion confirmed. We are immediately struck with prolific usage of universal terms such as "all," "every," "under heaven," and "in whose nostrils was the breath of life." For example, Genesis 6:7–13 tells us why God sent the Flood judgment:

> The Lord said, "I will blot out man whom I have created from the face of the land, from man to animals to creeping things and to birds of the sky; for I am sorry that I have made them." . . . God looked on the earth, and, behold, it was corrupt; for all flesh had corrupted their way upon the earth. Then God said to Noah, "The end of all flesh has come before Me; for the earth is filled with violence because of them; and, behold, I am about to destroy them with the earth" (NASB).

Note in particular God's emphasis on "all flesh" and "the earth," not just some flesh or part of the earth. Also, note that the Flood came to destroy animals and birds, not just sinful humans. The Apostle Paul tells us in Romans 8:19–23 that the whole non-human creation was subjected to the Curse because of man's sin, and thus the whole of creation suffers death and decay. So also in the Flood, the non-human creation suffered, regardless of whether animals or birds had come into close contact with sinful man or not.

Then when the Flood began, we are told in Genesis 7:11–12 that "all the fountains of the great deep (were) broken up," and "the rain was upon the earth." Again, the words "all" and "the earth" are clearly intended to imply global extent. Indeed, this usage of universal terms is prolific as the Flood account reaches a crescendo in Genesis 7:18–24:

> The waters prevailed, and greatly increased on the earth. . . . And the waters prevailed exceedingly on the earth, and all the high hills under the whole heaven were covered. . . . and the mountains were covered. And all flesh died that moved upon the earth . . . every creeping thing . . . and every man: All in whose nostrils was the breath of the spirit of life, all that was on the dry land, died. So He destroyed all living things which were on the face of the ground. . . . They were

destroyed from the earth. . . . And the waters prevailed on the earth one hundred and fifty days.

Figure 2. A flood that covered the highest hills by a significant amount, yet was local does not make sense!

So frequent is this use of universal terms, and so powerful are the points of comparison ("high hills," "whole heaven," and "mountains"), that it is extremely difficult to imagine what more could have been written under the direction of the Holy Spirit to express the concept of a global Flood! In the words of a leading Hebrew scholar of the 19th century, who strongly opposed those who tried to tone down the universal terms of the Genesis Flood account:

> They have disregarded the spirit of the language, and disregarded the dictates of common sense. It is impossible to read the narrative of our chapter (Genesis 7) without being irresistibly impressed that the whole earth was destined for destruction. This is so evident throughout the whole of the description, that it is unnecessary to adduce single instances. . . . In our case universality does not lie in the words merely, but in the tenor of the whole narrative.[5]

Something else in the Flood account is irreconcilable with the Flood being localized in the Mesopotamian Valley. In Genesis 7:20 we are told that "the mountains were covered." Because water always seeks its own level, how could the mountains only be covered in one local area without also covering the mountains in all adjoining areas and even on the other side of the planet (figure 2)? This clear statement in God's Word only makes physical and scientific sense if the Flood were global in extent.

Even the renowned and theologically liberal Hebrew scholar James Barr, then Oriel Professor of the Interpretation of Holy Scripture at Oxford University in England, was prepared to admit in a letter to David C.C. Watson dated April 23, 1984:

5. M.M. Kalisch, *Historical and Critical Commentary on the Old Testament* (London: Longman, Brown, Green, et al., 1858), p. 209–210.

> . . . so far as I know, there is no Professor of Hebrew or Old Testament at any world-class university who does not believe that the writer(s) of Genesis 1–11 intended to convey to their readers the ideas that . . . Noah's Flood was understood to be world-wide and extinguish all human and animal life except for those in the Ark. Or to put it negatively, the apologetic arguments which suppose . . . the flood to be a merely local Mesopotamian flood are not taken seriously by any such Professors, as far as I know.[6]

Theological Problems

If the Flood were only a relatively recent local event of no geologic significance, then the fossil-bearing sedimentary layers that were supposedly laid down over millions of years must have preceded the appearance of man on the earth, including Adam. After all, man only appears very recently in the fossil record. For a Christian who accepts the millions of years, this would mean that animals were living, dying, suffering disease, eating each other, and being buried and fossilized prior to Adam's appearance in the Garden of Eden. In the geologic record we find the fossilized remains of fish eating other fish, animals eating other animals, animals with diseases like cancer, and much more, which indicates that these fossils are a record of disease, violence, and death.

However, theologically there is a big problem here. In Genesis 1:30–31 we are told that when God created all the animals they all were vegetarians, and that God was pleased with everything that He had created because it was "very good." This means that all of creation was perfect when measured against the goodness of God — the only standard God uses (Matthew 19:17).

Furthermore, it is not until *after* God pronounced the Curse on all of creation because of Adam and Eve's disobedience that we are told that the ground would bring forth thorns and thistles (Genesis 3:17–18). But the evolutionary geologists tell us that there are fossilized thorns in Canadian sedimentary layers that are supposedly 400 million years old.[7] The Bible-believing Christian cannot accept this age-claim however.

If the plain statements of God's Word have any authority, then these fossilized thorns could only have grown after the Curse, after Adam was created by God. So the geologic record in which these fossilized thorns are found could only have been deposited after the Curse. However, the only event after the Curse that could have been responsible for burying and fossilizing these thorns,

6. Copy of this letter on file.
7. W.N. Stewart and G.W. Rothwell, *Paleobotany and the Evolution of Plants* (Cambridge, UK: Cambridge University Press, 1993), p. 172–176.

and the billions of other plants and animals we see in the vast rock layers of the earth, is the year-long Genesis Flood. This then rules out the millions of years.

Another theological problem arises when we come to Genesis 9:11–15. God made a promise to Noah and his descendants that "never again shall there be a flood to destroy the earth." In other words, God was promising never to send another event like the one Noah experienced, where we are told specifically in Genesis 7:21 that "all flesh died."

Obviously, if the Flood of Noah were only local in extent, then because we have seen lots of local floods since the time of Noah, that have destroyed both man and animals, God has broken His promise many times over! To the contrary, this rainbow covenant God made with Noah and his descendants could only have been kept by God if the Flood were global in extent, because never since in human history has a global flood been experienced.

The Views of Jesus and the New Testament Authors

The Lord Jesus Christ, God's living Word (John 1:1–3), made special reference to Noah and the Flood in Luke 17:26–30, where He said that, "the Flood came and destroyed them all."

There is no biblical or logical reason to assume that all of pre-Flood humanity was living in the Mesopotamian Valley. Genesis 4 indicates that early man built cities, had nomadic herds of animals, invented things, and explored the earth (v. 17–22). So if all the ungodly globally on the earth will be judged when He comes again, when Jesus by way of comparison describes the Flood and all the ungodly being destroyed by it, then He was saying that the Flood also was global.

Similarly, the Apostle Peter in 2 Peter 3:3–7 warned of last-days scoffers who would wilfully forget that after the earth was created by God, it perished, "being flooded with water," and that the present earth is "reserved for fire until the day of judgment." There are three events he is thus referring to: the creation of the world (Greek *kosmos*), the destruction of that world (Greek *kosmos*) by a watery cataclysm (the Flood), and the coming destruction of the heavens and the earth by fire in the future.

In context, it is clear that Peter had to be teaching the Flood was global, because the creation of the world was global, and the future judgment by fire will also be global. Indeed, the use of the Greek term *kosmos* for both the world that was created and the world that was flooded leaves us no doubt that the Apostle Peter, under the inspiration of the Holy Spirit, was teaching that the Flood was global in extent.

Scientific Problems

If the Flood were only local in extent, why did Noah have to take birds on board the ark (Genesis 7:8), when the birds in that local flooded area could simply have flown away to safe unflooded areas? Similarly, why would Noah need to take animals on board the ark from his local area, when other representatives of those same animal kinds would surely have survived in other, unflooded areas?

Indeed, why would Noah have had to build the ark to the scale specified by God (Genesis 6:15) — 300 cubits long, 50 cubits wide, and 30 cubits high, or approximately 450 feet long, 75 feet wide, and 45 feet high? With these dimensions, the total volume of the ark would have been approximately 1.45 million cubic feet, and with three decks it would have had a total deck area of approximately 98,800 square feet, equivalent to slightly more than the area of 20 standard basketball courts! The gross tonnage of the ark would have been about 14,500 tons, well within the category of large metal ocean-going vessels today.[8]

Quite obviously, an ark of such dimensions would only be required if the Flood were global in extent, designed by God to destroy all animals and birds around the world, except for those preserved on that ark. Indeed, because the Bible implies that Noah was warned 120 years before the Flood came (Genesis 6:3), God could have simply told Noah and his family to migrate with any required animals and birds out of the area that was going to be flooded.

In Genesis 1:28 we are told that God commanded Adam and Eve to fill the earth. Adam and his descendants' life-spans were hundreds of years, in which they would have had ample time to produce many children. The chronological framework from Adam to the Flood based on the genealogies given in Genesis 5

8. For fuller details regarding the size and construction of the ark, see Tim Lovett, *Noah's Ark: Thinking Outside the Box* (Green Forest, AR: Master Books, 2008).

indicates a period of 1,656 years for the human population to grow and spread around the earth in obedience to God's command.

Depending on the assumptions used for the number of children in each family, one could easily calculate, using a standard population growth equation, that the human population at the time of the Flood could have been up to a billion or more people. If so, there is no question that they would have spread beyond some localized area, and thus have required a global Flood to destroy them all. God gave a similar command to Noah and his descendants after the Flood to fill the earth (Genesis 9:1, 7), and in a matter of about 150 years God judged them for not obeying that command. Clearly, in the 1,656 years between Adam and the Flood, with the number of people in the pre-Flood population, the earth would have been filled, which is confirmed by God's assessment in Genesis 6:13 that because the earth was filled with violence through man's sinfulness He would destroy them "with the earth," obviously necessitating that the Flood judgment was of global extent.

Conclusions

This has only been a brief survey of the problems associated with the local Flood view designed to accommodate the supposed millions of years of earth history. The Lord Jesus Christ and the Apostle Peter clearly taught that the Flood of Noah was global in extent, and both the context and the descriptive words used in Genesis 6–8 quite plainly describe the Flood as global in extent.

It wasn't until popularization of the belief in geology that only slow and gradual geological processes formed the geologic record over millions of years that the local Flood compromise became increasingly popular. Yet the Scriptures are clear that the deaths of animals and man only came into the world as a result of the Curse. So the fossils must have been produced after that tragic event. The subsequent global Flood could have produced most of the fossil-bearing sedimentary layers, including the fossilized thorns we find.

And Noah would not have needed to build an ark or take animals on board if the Flood were only local, as there was plenty of warning to escape to another region. These and many more biblical, theological, and scientific considerations make the local Flood compromise totally untenable. This is all ultimately about the authority of *all* of God's Word, which plainly teaches that the Flood of Noah was global in extent.

7

Is Man the Cause of Global Warming?

MICHAEL OARD

Global warming is big news. The media, environmentalists, and politicians, such as Al Gore,[1] continue to pound away that global warming is real, it is man-caused, and great harm will come to our world because of it. Some even say that global warming is the most significant threat to ever affect man. Bjorn Lomborg quotes respected scientist James Lovelock as saying: "Before this century is over, billions of us will die and the few breeding pairs of people that survive will be in the Arctic where the climate remains tolerable."[2] Intense storms of various sorts, drought, and heat waves will devastate the earth.[3]

Is all this true? Is global warming real? Is it all caused by man? Should we as Christians care about global warming, and if we do care, what should we do about it?

Man Is a Steward of God's Creation

We should be concerned with global warming, as well as other environmental issues, simply because God created the universe, the world, and everything in it (Exodus 20:11). It is His creation; He created it directly with a purpose and with man in mind. It did not evolve over billions of years. Man was

1. Al Gore, *An Inconvenient Truth: The Planetary Emergency of Global Warming and What We Can Do About It* (New York, NY: Rodale Press, 2006).
2. B. Lomborg, *Cool It: The Skeptical Environmentalist's Guide to Global Warming* (New York, NY: Alfred A. Knopf, 2007), p. 41.
3. N. Shute, "The Weather Turns Wild," *U.S. News & World Report*, February 5, 2001, p. 44–52.

told right away in the Garden of Eden to take dominion over the earth (Genesis 1:26–28), which means that we are to be stewards of His creation. We are to cultivate and take care of our surroundings, which at that time was the Garden of Eden: "Then the LORD God took the man and put him in the garden of Eden to tend and keep it" (Genesis 2:15).

What Should Christians Do about Global Warming?

Amidst all the hype, Christians need to first apply 1 Thessalonians 5:21: "Test all things; hold fast what is good." We are to hold fast to God's Word, the Bible, and Jesus as our Lord and Savior. Then we need to examine the evidence *carefully*. As stewards of God's creation, it will take time and energy to find out the facts. It is too easy to accept a superficial analysis of a controversial subject, in which case we might learn just enough to get into trouble. No, we need to dig deeper than the superficial level.

It is no different than evaluating the creation/evolution issue. At the superficial level, evolutionists can paint a pretty picture. It is only when you dig below the surface that you find out that evolution is unsubstantiated.

Since creationists are used to separating data from interpretation (the battle between creation and evolution is not over the data but the interpretation of the data), it is relatively easy to apply the same principles to the global warming issue. So we need to check the real data *first*. We need to be as objective as possible when examining the data, realizing that bias for man-made global warming and its harms is rampant.[4]

Evaluating the Data

When we examine the data, what can we say about global warming? This section will evaluate the facts, while the next main section will delve into additional evidence. We will then be able to evaluate global warming.

Carbon Dioxide and Other Greenhouse Gases Have Increased

First, carbon dioxide and other greenhouse gases, such as methane, have increased significantly over the past 100 years (figures 1a, b). These have been measured continuously since the middle of the 20th century and inferred from proxy indicators before that.

4. J. Pena and R. Vogel, eds., *Global Warming: A Scientific and Biblical Exposé of Climate Change* (DVD), Coral Ridge Ministries and Answers in Genesis, 2008; L. Vardiman, *Some Like It Hot* (Dallas, TX: Institute for Creation Research, 2009); M.J. Oard, "Global Warming: Examine the Issue Carefully," *Answers,* October–December 2006, p. 24–26.

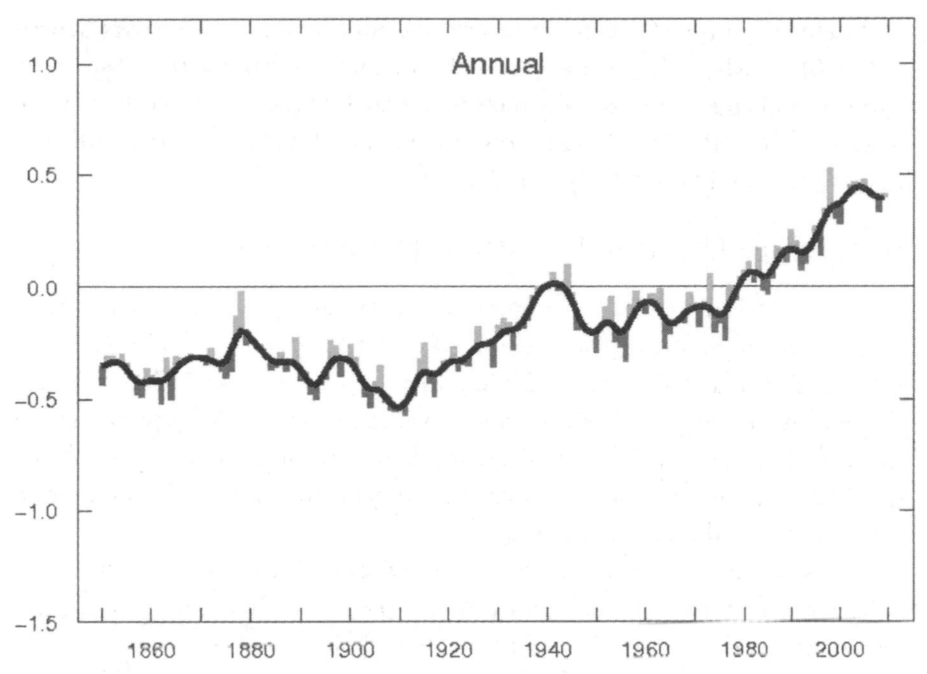

Figure 1a: Annual global temperature from 1850 to July 2009, from the U.K. Met Office Hadley Centre and the Climate Research Unit at the University of East Anglia. Note that temperatures have been cooling since about 2002.

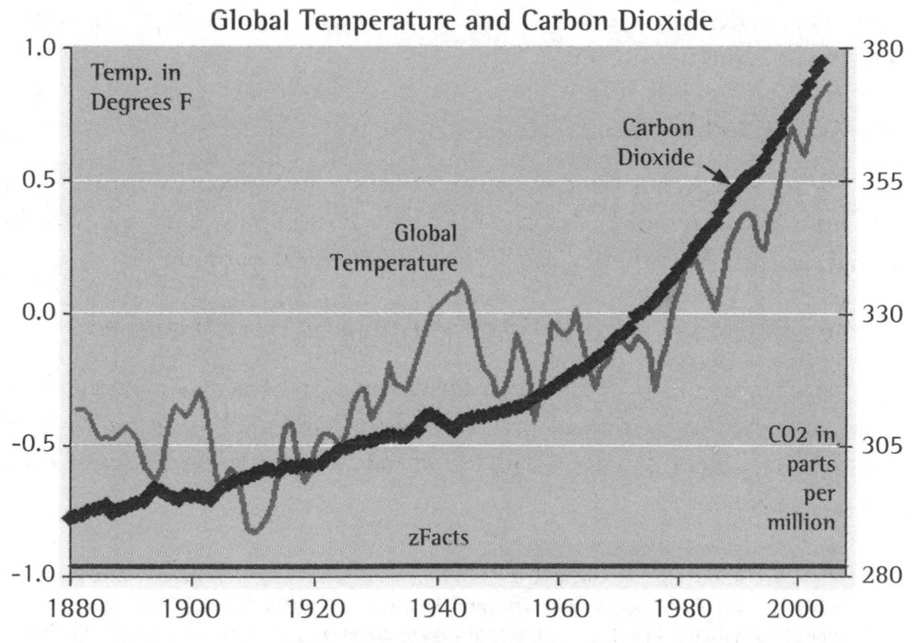

Figure 1b: The increase in carbon dioxide since 1880

Carbon dioxide has been continuously measured since 1959 and been inferred mainly from tree rings and ice cores before 1959. Note that carbon dioxide has increased more after about 1960 than before. Despite the title of the article from which this graphic is taken, the correlation of CO_2 and temperature does not demonstrate a cause-effect relationship.[5]

Carbon dioxide has been added to the air primarily because of the burning of fossil fuels since the industrial revolution. A secondary source for carbon dioxide is believed to be tropical deforestation. As trees are cut down, they rot and the carbon in the wood is oxidized to carbon dioxide. It is true that forests are being cut down in the tropics, especially in Brazil. However, forests grow back. So, it is not deforestation that counts, but the total amount of forest. When we consider the total amount of forest, the trend is unclear; we cannot be certain if it is increasing or decreasing.[6] So the rotting of tropical trees likely is not a significant source of carbon dioxide for the atmosphere.

Carbon dioxide is actually a minor gas in the greenhouse effect. The major greenhouse gas is water vapor, which accounts for 95 percent of greenhouse warming.[7] The greenhouse effect is actually good. Without these greenhouse gases the earth would be about 60°F cooler, and we would likely all freeze to death.

It is theoretically true that the increase in carbon dioxide and other greenhouse gases should cause warmer temperatures. The main question is how much.

There Are Natural Causes of Climate Change

A second fact is that there are natural causes of climate change. There are short-period natural processes that change the temperature by about a degree over several years. Two of these are a strong volcanic eruption that causes cooler global temperatures and an El Niño that causes warmer global temperatures. Volcanism causes cooling by the reflection of sunlight back to space from particles trapped in the stratosphere. The amount of carbon dioxide and water vapor given off during volcanism is insignificant over the space and time periods significant to climate change.

There are also long-period temperature changes caused by effects on the sun that can be correlated to the number of sunspots: the more sunspots, the warmer the temperature on earth and vice versa. Since sunspots are cool spots,

5. ZFacts, "Evidence that CO_2 Is Cause," www.zfacts.com/p/226.html.
6. A. Granger, "Difficulties in Tracking the Long-term Global Trend in Tropical Forest Area," *Proceedings of the National Academy of Science* 105 no. 2 (2008): 818–823.
7. P.J. Michaels and R.C. Balling Jr., *The Satanic Gases: Clearing the Air About Global Warming* (Washington, D.: Cato Institute, 2000), p. 25–28.

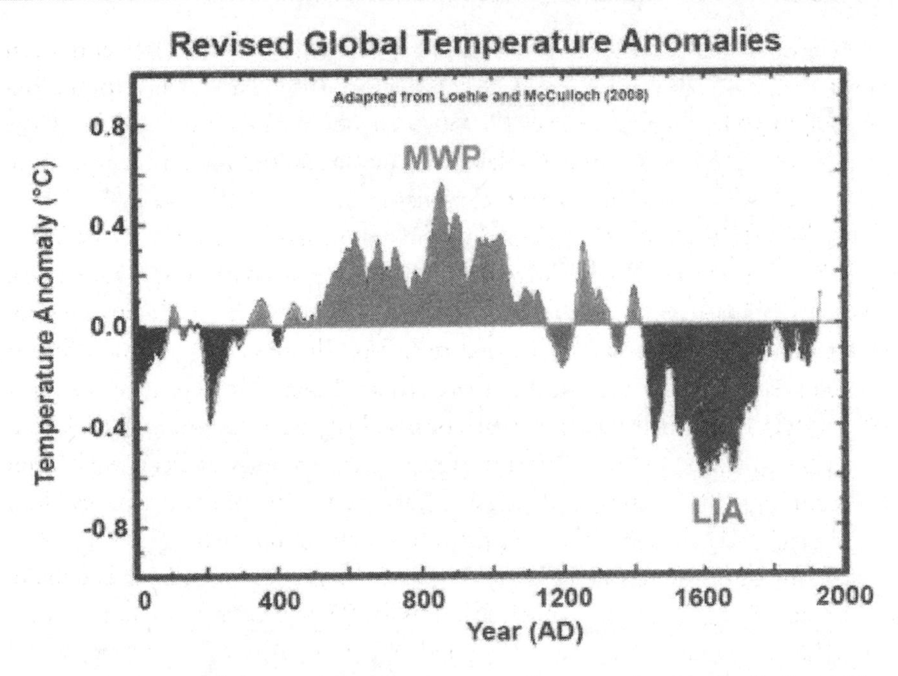

Figure 2. Average global temperature for the past 2,000 years showing the Medieval Warm Period (MWP) and the Little Ice Age (LIA). Before about the middle 1800s, there was little change in carbon dioxide to cause these fluctuations.

heating on earth seems counter intuitive. But when there are many sunspots, there are also many hot spots, called faculae, that more than make up for the cool spots. Two long period temperature changes recognized are the Medieval Warm Period (MWP) from about 800 to 1200 and the Little Ice Age (LIA) from about 1400 to 1880 (figure 2). These have been based on historical records and are well correlated to the number of sunspots using proxy data.[8] Variations in carbon dioxide levels were not responsible for these changes.

The climatic effect of natural processes is also seen during the 20th century by comparing the increase in carbon dioxide with the temperature change (figure 1b). Carbon dioxide increased slowly until after World War II and then accelerated. But the global temperature rose strongly from 1910 to 1940 (remember the dust bowl years in the 1930s), dropped a little between 1940 and 1975 (remember the coming ice age scare), and rose strongly again from 1975 to about 2002. The temperature has generally been cooling from 2002 to 2009 while carbon dioxide in the atmosphere continues to increase

8. C. Loehle and J.H. McCulloch, "Correction to a 2000-year Global Temperature Reconstruction Based on Non-tree Ring Proxies," *Energy & Environment* 19 no. 1 (2008): 93–100.

substantially. Nicola Scafetta and Bruce West stated that natural cycles from the sun account for at least 50 percent of the 20th century global warming.[9]

The increase in the amount of sunshine reaching the earth with a large number of sunspots is small. This is why many man-made global warming advocates discount the significance of the sun. It is known that higher sunspot numbers, which cause a stronger solar magnetic field, better shield the earth from cosmic rays. It is possible that fewer cosmic rays result in fewer low clouds that cause warmer surface temperatures and vice versa.[10] This hypothesis has been seriously challenged, so only time will tell if the hypothesis stands.

There Is No Consensus of Scientists

Third, although it is commonly claimed that there is a consensus of scientists that blame man for global warming, in actuality there is no consensus at all. Many prominent scientists disagree. Dr. Art Robinson has maintained a website since 1998, signed by around 20,000 scientists, saying that, as of 2009, there is no convincing scientific evidence that greenhouse gases are causing or will cause catastrophic heating of the earth's atmosphere and disruption of the earth's climate.[11] Of these, over 2,500 are physicists, geophysicists, climatologists, meteorologists, oceanographers, and environmental scientists, who are particularly qualified to evaluate global warming.

Climate Simulations Exaggerate Carbon Dioxide Warming

Fourth, dozens of computer climate simulations have attempted to quantify the relationship between increased carbon dioxide and temperature change. In the simulations, the scientists double carbon dioxide and leave every other variable alone. The resulting temperature changes range from 3°F to 11° F warming, usually by the year 2100.

But these simulations are crude, since the computer models cannot accurately simulate the many types of clouds and their effects, solar and infrared radiation processes, ocean processes, ice processes, etc.[12] The strengths and weaknesses of computer models need to be understood, but it seems that those who want runaway global warming believe these models *without question*.

9. N. Scafetta and B. West, "Is Climate Sensitive to Solar Variability?" *Physics Today* 61 no. 3 (2008): 50–51.
10. H. Svensmark, "Cosmoclimatology: A New Theory Emerges," *Astronomy and Geophysics* 48 no. 1 (2007): 18–24; L. Vardiman, "A New Theory of Climate Change," *Acts & Facts* 37 no. 11 (2008): 10–12.
11. Global Warming Petition Project, www.petitionproject.org.
12. Michaels and Balling, *The Satanic Gases: Clearing the Air About Global Warming*, p. 55–73.

It is interesting that nature has partially run the experiment for us. Carbon dioxide has increased a little more than 30 percent since the industrial revolution. Other greenhouse gases, not including water vapor, also have increased about 30 percent in "carbon dioxide equivalency units," for a total increase of about 60 percent in "carbon dioxide."[13] Global warming is claimed to be 1.2°F (yes, you heard right, the warming has been very small so far), but at least half is from natural causes. So if a 60 percent increase in "carbon dioxide" causes only a 0.6 degree Fahrenheit warming (man's share), a doubling of carbon dioxide should cause a 1°F warming. The models are therefore 3 to 11 times too sensitive to a doubling of carbon dioxide and should not be believed.

Some Benefits of Global Warming

Fifth, despite all the well-publicized harms, there are benefits to global warming. The media typically exaggerate the harms. Take for example the supposed decreasing polar bear populations as a result of less sea ice in the Northern Hemisphere. This was the theme behind the popular movie *Arctic Tale*.[14] Lomborg documents that the polar bear populations actually have increased.[15]

Some net benefits are that global warming will save the lives of more people, since many more people die of the cold than die of the heat. For instance, in Europe, seven times as many people die of the cold than die of the heat.[16] Other benefits include more plant growth due to higher carbon dioxide levels, aiding farming and ranching; crops able to be grown at higher latitudes; and shipping through ice-free areas of the Arctic Ocean, which will save much fuel and money. At this point it is difficult to tell whether there will be a net benefit or a net harm. Only objective research will determine this.

The Cost to "Fight" Global Warming Is Horrendous

Sixth, if certain environmentalists and politicians get their way, the cost to "fight" global warming will be horrendous, if the attempt is successful and doesn't produce even worse side effects. Lomborg estimates the cost of fighting global warming at many trillions of dollars.[17] Although Lomborg actually believes in the temperature rises suggested by the computer models, he makes a strong case that this money is best spent elsewhere, and that the earth will adapt to warming.

13. Ibid., p. 27.
14. M.J. Oard, movie review: "Arctic Tale — Exaggerating the Effects of Global Warming," www.answersingenesis.org/articles/aid/v2/n1/arctic-tale.
15. Lomborg, *Cool It: The Skeptical Environmentalist's Guide to Global Warming*, p. 3–9.
16. Ibid., p. 17.
17. Ibid, p. 32–38.

Figure 3: Athabasca Glacier, Canadian Rockies, was near the sign in 1890. It has since melted back to its current location due to global warming.

Additional Evidence

In any analysis of such a controversial subject, there is bound to be uncertainty in some variables. Only four of the most important will be evaluated.

Global Warming Is Real

First, global warming is real. Although some claim there is no global warming or we cannot measure it, the evidence for global warming is compelling. The claimed warming since 1880 is only 1.2°F. But we see the effects of the warming in that practically all glaciers have

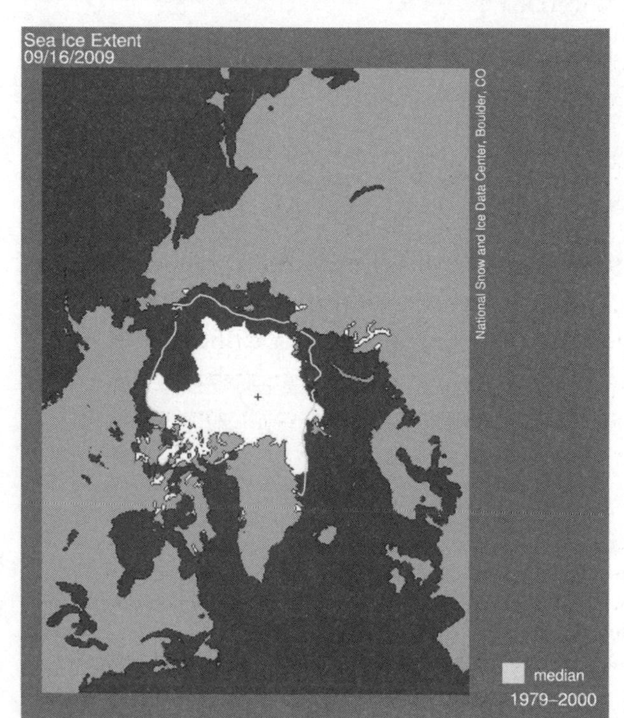

Figure 4: Minimum sea ice extent mid-September 2009, compared with the 1979 to 2000 average minimum (courtesy of the National Snow and Ice Data Center). However, the amount of sea ice has recovered 15 percent over 2008, which was about 10 percent greater than the record low in 2007, possibly due to global cooling as shown in figure 1a.

receded since about 1880 (figure 3), and the sea ice in the Arctic Ocean has decreased (figure 4).

The recent global warming is not caused by the earth breaking out of the Ice Age[18] about 4,000 years ago, because the atmosphere responds very fast to changes that affect climate. The change in seasons is one example of how fast the temperature can change when the angle of the sun changes. The earth has been more or less in steady state since the end of the Ice Age.

However, there is a question of whether the amount of claimed warming is accurate, since there are many biases (mostly favoring warming) in the long-term temperature records. Although those who analyze global temperatures have mostly purged the record of these errors, the claimed warming likely is too warm. Professor Robert Balling has studied these biases for a long time and has concluded:

> But as this chapter makes clear, major problems remain. First, the temperature records are far from perfect and contain contaminations from urbanization, distribution of measurement stations, instrument changes, time of observation biases, assorted problems in measuring near-surface temperatures in ocean areas, and on and on. This could introduce a total bias of 0.2°C to 0.3°C, or about one-third of the observed warming.[19]

This means that global warming since 1880 may be only about 0.8°F, which is closer to the satellite and weather balloon data of the lower atmosphere.

The Lower Atmosphere is Warming Less than 1.2°F

Second, satellites have been measuring the amount of temperature change in the atmosphere since 1979. Weather balloons have been probing the atmosphere for longer than that. At first, it was thought that the satellite temperatures showed a cooling trend. However, there were some errors in the measurements. Now, it appears that the satellite and weather balloon data both show less warming in the lower atmosphere than the claimed 1.2°F surface warming.[20]

---

18. M.J. Oard, *Frozen In Time: The Woolly Mammoth, the Ice Age, and the Biblical Key to Their Secrets* (Green Forest, AR: Master Books, 2004).
19. R.C. Balling Jr., "Observational Surface Temperature Records Versus Model Predictions," in P.J. Michaels, ed., *Shattered Consensus: The True State of Global Warming* (New York, NY: Rowman & Littlefield Publishers, Inc, 2005), p. 67.
20. J. Christy, "Temperature Changes in the Bulk of the Atmosphere," in P.J. Michaels, ed., *Shattered Consensus: The True State of Global Warming* (New York, NY: Rowman & Littlefield Publishers, Inc, 2005), p. 72–105.

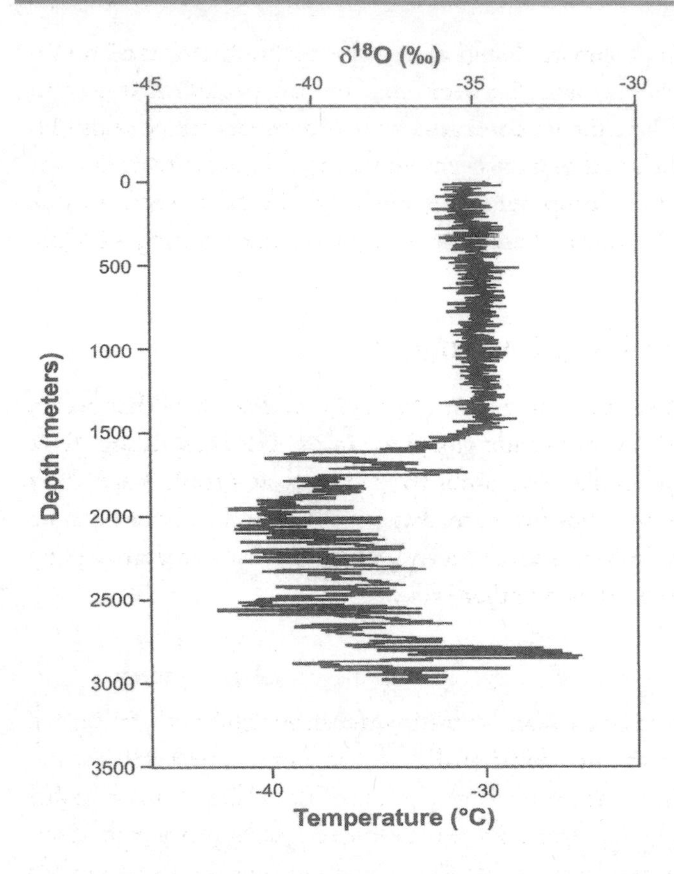

Figure 5: The oxygen isotope ratio from bedrock to the top of the GISP2 ice core at Summit on the Greenland Ice Sheet (plot courtesy of Dr. Larry Vardiman). The oxygen isotope ratio is generally proportional to temperature with cooler temperatures to the left.

The Climate Likely Cannot Jump to a More Catastrophic Mode

Third, some scientists have concluded that the atmosphere goes through thresholds to different climatic states. They believe that although our climate has been steady, global warming may bring the temperature up to the "tipping point" that will cause a shift to a much different climate, possibly leading to an ice age. The threshold idea is based on Greenland ice cores showing large, abrupt changes in temperature during the Ice Age portion (figure 5).

Some suggest that global warming will halt the Gulf Stream that transports warm water into the high North Atlantic Ocean. Temperatures then plummet in Europe and an ice age can occur. This is the basis of the movie *The Day After Tomorrow*,[21] taken from the preposterous book *The Coming Global Superstorm*.[22] Despite Hollywood fantasy, some scientists believe that such a scenario is possible over a time frame of a decade or two.

21. M.J. Oard, "The Greenhouse Warming Hype of the Movie The Day After Tomorrow," *Acts & Facts Impact*, 373 (Dallas, TX: Institute for Creation Research, 2004).
22. A. Bell and W. Strieber, *The Coming Global Superstorm* (New York, NY: Pocket Books, 2000).

The idea of an abrupt climate change after the temperature passes a "threshold" is where the worldview issue between creation and evolution is crucial. Evolutionary scientists date the ice cores at hundreds of thousands of years old, and the ice sheets are believed to have been more or less the same thickness for millions of years. But these abrupt temperature changes in the ice cores are due to a rapid, post-Flood Ice Age and are only related to changes during a unique Ice Age.[23]

Storms and Droughts Likely Unchanged

Fourth, it seems like every large storm, drought, or heat wave that occurs in the world is blamed on man-made global warming. But these things have been happening for millennia. The problem is that most people have short memories about past events. Furthermore, damage is greater now because more people and property lie in harm's way. But overall, there do not seem to be any long-term trends in any of these weather events.[24]

Summary

In the face of claims that man is causing disastrous global warming, an objective look at the facts and additional evidence show otherwise. Natural processes on the sun account for over 50 percent of the claimed 1.2°F global warming, which is likely too warm. Since the climate simulations greatly exaggerate the temperature rise from an increase in carbon dioxide, these models cannot be trusted. Thus, man is likely responsible for only about 0.5°F warming — miniscule and likely impossible to mitigate.

What is really needed is unbiased research in climate change. Climate disaster is not just around the corner; we have sufficient time for careful research.

Acknowledgment

I thank Drs. Larry Vardiman and Jason Lisle for reviewing the manuscript and offering valuable improvements.

23. M.J. Oard, *The Frozen Record: Examining the Ice Core History of the Greenland and Antarctic Ice Sheets* (Dallas, TX: Institute for Creation Research, 2005).
24. P.J. Michaels, *The Predictable Distortion of Global Warming by Scientists, Politicians, and the Media* (Washington DC: CATO Institute, 2004).

8

Did Bible Authors Believe in a Literal Genesis?

DR. TERRY MORTENSON

Anyone who has read the Bible very much will recognize that there are different kinds of literature in the Old and New Testaments. There are parables, poetry, prophetic visions, dreams, epistles, proverbs, and historical narrative, with the majority being the latter. So, how should we interpret Genesis 1–11? Is it history? Is it mythology? Is it symbolic poetry? Is it allegory? Is it a parable? Is it a prophetic vision? Is it a mixture of these kinds of literature or some kind of unique genre? And does it really matter anyway?

We will come back to the last question later, but suffice it to say here that the correct conclusion on genre of literature is foundational to the question of the correct interpretation. If we interpret something literally that the author intended to be understood figuratively, then we will misunderstand the text. When Jesus said "I am the door" (John 10:9), He did not mean that He was made of wood with hinges attached to His side. Conversely, if we interpret something figuratively that the author intended to be taken literally, we will err. When Jesus said, "The Son of Man is about to be betrayed into the hands of men, and they will kill Him, and the third day He will be raised up" (Matthew 17:22–23), He clearly meant it just as literally as if I said to my wife, "Margie, I'm going to fill up the gas tank with gas and will be back in a few minutes."

There are many lines of evidence we could consider to determine the genre of Genesis 1–11, such as the internal evidence within the Book of Genesis and how the Church has viewed these chapters throughout church history. But in this chapter we want to answer the question, "How did the other biblical authors (besides Moses, who wrote Genesis[1]) and Jesus interpret them?" From my reading and experience it appears that most people who consider the question of how to interpret the early chapters of Genesis have never asked, much less answered, that question.

Moses as depicted in the Creation Museum's biblical authority room.

To begin, consider what God says about the way He spoke to Moses in contrast to the way He spoke to other prophets. In Numbers 12:6–8 we read:

> Then He said, "Hear now My words: if there is a prophet among you, I, the LORD, make Myself known to him in a vision; I speak to him in a dream. Not so with My servant Moses; he is faithful in all My house. I speak with him face to face, even plainly, and not in dark sayings; And he sees the form of the LORD. Why then were you not afraid to speak against My servant Moses?"

So God says that He spoke "plainly" to Moses, not in "dark sayings," that is, not in obscure language. That strongly suggests that we should not be looking for mysterious, hard-to-understand meanings in what Moses wrote. Rather, we should read Genesis as the straightforward history that it appears to be. An examination of how the rest of the Bible interprets Genesis confirms this.

1. That Moses was the author of the first five books (called the Pentateuch) of the Old Testament is clear from Scripture itself. The Pentateuch explicitly claims this in Exodus 17:14, 24:4, 34:27; Numbers 33:1–2; Deuteronomy 31:9–11. Other OT books affirm that Moses wrote these books, which by the time of Joshua became known collectively as "the Law," "the book of the Law," or "the Law of Moses": Joshua 1:8, 8:31–32; 1 Kings 2:3; 2 Kings 14:6 (quoting Deuteronomy 24:16), 21:8; Ezra 6:18; Nehemiah 13:1; Daniel 9:11–13; Malachi 4:4. The New Testament agrees in Matthew 19:8; John 5:46–47, 7:19; Acts 3:22 (quoting from Deuteronomy 18:15); Romans 10:5 (quoting from Leviticus 18:5), and Mark 12:26 (referring to Exodus 3:6). Jewish tradition also ascribes the Pentateuch to Moses. Also, the theories of liberal theologians who deny the Mosaic authorship of these books are fraught with false assumptions and illogical reasoning. See Gleason L. Archer Jr., *A Survey of Old Testament Introduction* (Chicago, IL: Moody Press, 1985), p. 109–113.

Old Testament Authors and Their Use of Genesis

When we turn to other Old Testament authors, there are only a few references to Genesis 1–11. But they all treat those chapters as literal history.

The Jews were very careful about genealogies. For example, in Nehemiah 7:61–64 the people who wanted to serve in the rebuilt temple needed to prove that they were descended from the priestly line of Aaron. Those who could not prove this could not serve as priests. First Chronicles 1–8 gives a long series of genealogies all the way back to Adam. Chapter 1 (verses 1–28) has no missing or added names in the genealogical links from Adam to Abraham, compared to Genesis 5 and 11. The author(s) of 1 Chronicles obviously took these genealogies as historically accurate.

Outside of Genesis 6–11, Psalm 29:10 contains the only other use of the Hebrew word *mabbul* (translated "flood").[2] God literally sat as King at the global Flood of Noah. If that event was not historical, the statement in this verse would have no real force and the promise of verse 11 will give little comfort to God's people.

David, the writer of many of the psalms, from a Creation Museum display.

Psalm 33:6–9 affirms that God created supernaturally by His Word, just as Genesis 1 says repeatedly. Creatures came into existence instantly when God said, "Let there be. . . ." God did not have to wait for millions or thousands of years for light or dry land or plants and animals or Adam to appear. "He spoke and it was done; He commanded and it stood fast" (Psalm 33:9).

Psalm 104:5 and 19 speak of events during creation week.[3] But verses 6–9 in this psalm give additional information to that provided in Genesis 8, which describes how the waters receded off the earth at the end of the Flood.[4] The Psalmist is clearly describing historical events.

2. There are four other Hebrew words that are used in the OT to describe lesser, localized floods.
3. Most of this psalm is referring to aspects of God's creation as it existed at the time the Psalmist was writing. Contrary to what some old-earth creationists assert, Psalm 104 is not a "creation account."
4. That these verses do not refer to creation week is evident from the promise reflected in verse 9, which echoes the promise of Genesis 9:11–17. God made no such promise on the third day of creation week when He made dry land appear.

In beautiful poetic form, Psalm 136 recounts many of God's mighty acts in history, beginning with statements about some of His creative works in Genesis 1.

Isaiah recorded God's Word, not mythical tales.

In Isaiah 54:9 God says (echoing the promise of Psalm 104:9) to Israel, "For this is like the waters of Noah to Me; for as I have sworn that the waters of Noah would no longer cover the earth, so have I sworn that I would not be angry with you, nor rebuke you." The promise of God would have no force if the account of Noah's Flood was not historically true. No one would believe in the Second Coming of Christ if the promise of it (as recorded in Matt. 24:37–39) was given as, "Just as Santa Claus comes from the North Pole in his sleigh pulled by reindeer on Christmas Eve and puts presents for the whole family under the Christmas tree in each home, so Jesus is coming again as the King of kings and Lord of lords." In fact, the analogy would convince people that the Second Coming is a myth.

In Ezekiel 14:14–20 God refers repeatedly to Noah, Daniel, and Job and clearly indicates that they were all equally historical and righteous men. There is no reason to doubt that God meant that everything the Bible says about these men is historically accurate.

New Testament Authors' View of Genesis

The New Testament has many more explicit references to the early chapters of Genesis.

The genealogies of Jesus presented in Matthew 1:1–17 and Luke 3:23–38 show that Genesis 1–11 is historical narrative. These genealogies must all be equally historical or else we must conclude that Jesus was descended from a myth and therefore He would not have been a real human being and therefore not our Savior and Lord.[5]

Paul built his doctrine of sin and salvation on the fact that sin and death entered the world through Adam. Jesus, as the Last Adam, came into the world to bring righteousness and life to people and to undo the damaging work of the first Adam (Romans 5:12–19; 1 Corinthians 15:21–22, 45–47). Paul affirmed that the serpent deceived Eve, not Adam (2 Corinthians 11:3; 1 Timothy 2:13–14). He took Genesis 1–2 literally by affirming that Adam was created first and Eve was made from the body of Adam (1 Corinthians 11:8–9). In Romans 1:20, Paul indicated that people have seen the evidence of God's existence and some of His attributes since the creation of the world.[6] This means that Paul believed that man was right there at the beginning of history, not billions of years after the beginning.

Paul relied heavily on Genesis as plainly written.

Peter similarly based some of his teachings on the literal history of Genesis 1–11. In 1 Peter 3:20, 2 Peter 2:4–9, and 2 Peter 3:3–7, he referred to the Flood. He considered the account of Noah and the Flood just as historical as

5. In Matthew 1:1–17, Matthew has clearly left out some names in his genealogy (for a literary purpose), as seen by comparing it to the Old Testament history. But all the people are equally historical all the way back to Abraham, who is first mentioned in Genesis 11. Luke 3:23–38 traces the lineage of Jesus back to Adam. There is no reason to think there are any missing names in Luke's genealogy, because 1) he was concerned about giving us the exact truth (Luke 1:4), and 2) his genealogy from Adam to Abraham matches 1 Chronicles 1:1–28 and Genesis 5 and 11, and there is no good reason for concluding that Genesis has missing names. See Ken Ham and Larry Pierce, "Who Begat Whom? Closing the Gap in Genesis Genealogies," www.answersingenesis.org/articles/am/v1/n2/who-begat-whom, and Travis R. Freeman, "Do the Genesis 5 and 11 Genealogies Contain Gaps?" in Terry Mortenson and Thane H. Ury, eds., *Coming to Grips with Genesis* (Green Forest, AR: Master Books, 2008), p. 283–314.
6. The New King James and the King James Version translate the Greek in this verse as "from the creation of the world." The word "from" in English has a similar range of meanings as the Greek word (*apo*) that it translates here. There are a number of reasons to take it in a temporal sense, meaning "since" as the NAS, NIV, and ESV translate it. For a fuller discussion of this important verse, see Ron Minton, "Apostolic Witness to Genesis Creation and the Flood," in Terry Mortenson and Thane H. Ury, eds., *Coming to Grips with Genesis* (Green Forest, AR: Master Books, 2008), p. 351–354.

The words of John and Peter demonstrate their trust in the historicity of the Genesis accounts.

the account of the judgment of Sodom and Gomorrah (Genesis 19). He affirmed that only eight people were saved and that the Flood was global, just as the future judgment at the Second Coming of Christ will be. He argued that scoffers will deny the Second Coming because they deny the supernatural creation and Noah's Flood. And Peter told his readers that scoffers will do this because they are reasoning on the basis of the philosophical assumption that today we call uniformitarian naturalism: "all things continue as they were from the beginning of creation" (2 Peter 3:4).[7]

It has been objected that the apostles did not know the difference between truth and myth. But this is also false. In 1 Corinthians 10:1–11 Paul refers to a number of passages from the Pentateuch where miracles are described and he emphasizes in verses 6 and 11 that "these things happened." In 2 Timothy 4:3–4 Paul wrote:

> For the time will come when they will not endure sound doctrine, but according to their own desires, because they have itching ears, they will heap up for themselves teachers; and they will turn their ears away from the truth, and be turned aside to fables.

The Greek word translated here as "fables" is *muthos*, from which we get our English word "myth." In contrast to "truth" or "sound doctrine," the same Greek word is used in 1 Timothy 1:4, 4:7; Titus 1:14; and 2 Peter 1:16. In a first-century world filled with Greek, Roman, and Jewish myths, the apostles clearly knew the difference between truth and myth. And they constantly affirmed that the Word of God contains truth, not myth.

7. For more discussion of this, see Terry Mortenson, "Philosophical Naturalism and the Age of the Earth: Are They Related?" *The Master's Seminary Journal* 15 no. 1 (2004): 71–92, online at www.answersingenesis.org/docs2004/naturalismChurch.asp.

Christ and His Use of Genesis

In John 10:34–35 Jesus defended His claim to deity by quoting from Psalm 82:6 and then asserting that "Scripture cannot be broken." That is, the Bible is faithful, reliable, and truthful. The Scriptures cannot be contradicted or confounded. In Luke 24:25–27 Jesus rebuked His disciples for not believing all that the prophets have spoken (which He equates with "all the Scriptures"). So in Jesus's view, all Scripture is trustworthy and should be believed.

Another way that Jesus revealed His complete trust in the Scriptures was by treating as historical fact the accounts in the Old Testament, which most contemporary people think are unbelievable mythology. These historical accounts include Adam and Eve as the first married couple (Matthew 19:3–6, Mark 10:3–9), Abel as the first prophet who was martyred (Luke 11:50–51), Noah and the Flood (Matthew 24:38–39), the experiences of Lot and his wife (Luke 17:28–32), the judgment of Sodom and Gomorrah (Matthew 10:15), Moses and the serpent in the wilderness wanderings after the exodus from Egypt (John 3:14), Moses and the manna from heaven (John 6:32–33, 49), the miracles of Elijah (Luke 4:25–27), and Jonah in the big fish (Matthew 12:40–41). As Wenham has compellingly argued,[8] Jesus did not allegorize these accounts but took them as straightforward history, describing events that actually happened, just as the Old Testament describes. Jesus used these accounts to teach His disciples that the events of His own death, resurrection, and Second Coming would likewise certainly happen in time-space reality. Jesus also indicated that the Scriptures are essentially perspicuous (or clear): 11 times the gospel writers record Him saying, "Have you not read. . . ?"[9] And 30 times He defended His teaching by saying "It is written."[10] He rebuked His listeners for not understanding and believing what the text plainly says.

Besides the above-mentioned evidence that Jesus took Genesis 1–11 as straightforward, reliable history, the gospel writers record three important statements that reveal Jesus' worldview. Careful analysis of these verses (Mark 10:6; Mark 13:19–20; Luke 11:50–51) shows that Jesus believed that Adam and Eve were in existence essentially at the same time that God created everything else (and Abel was very close to that time), not millions or billions of years after God

8. John Wenham, *Christ and the Bible* (Downers Grove, IL: InterVarsity Press, 1973), p. 11–37.
9. In these instances Jesus referred to Genesis 1–2, Exodus 3–6, 1 Samuel 21:6, Psalm 8:2 and 118:22, and to unspecified Levitical law — in other words, to passages from the historical narrative, the Law, and the poetry of Scripture.
10. Passages He specifically cited were from all five books of the Pentateuch, Psalms, Isaiah, Jeremiah, Zechariah, and Malachi. Interestingly, in the temptation of Jesus, Satan used Scripture literally and, in response, Jesus did not imply that the literal interpretation of Satan was wrong. Rather, He corrected Satan's misapplication of the text's literal meaning by quoting another text, which He took literally (see Matthew 4:6–7).

made the other things.[11] This shows that Jesus took the creation days as literal 24-hour days. So everything Jesus said shows that we can justifiably call Him a young-earth creationist.

It has been objected that in these statements Jesus was just accommodating the cultural beliefs of His day. But this is false for four reasons. First, Jesus was the truth (John 14:6), and therefore He always spoke the truth. No deceitful or misleading words ever came from His mouth (1 Peter 2:22). Even his enemies said, "Teacher, we know that You are truthful and defer to no one; for You are not partial to any, but teach the way of God in truth" (Mark 12:14; NASB). Second, Jesus taught with authority on the basis of God's Word, which He called "truth" (John 17:17), not as the scribes and Pharisees taught based on their traditions (Matthew 7:28–29). Third, Jesus repeatedly and boldly confronted all kinds of wrong thinking and behavior in his listeners' lives, in spite of the threat of persecution for doing so (Matthew 22:29; John 2:15–16, 3:10, 4:3–4, 9; Mark 7:9–13). And finally, Jesus emphasized the foundational importance of believing what Moses wrote in a straightforward way (John 5:45; Luke 16:31, 24:25–27, 24:44–45; John 3:12, Matthew 17:5).

Why Is This Important?

We should take Genesis 1–11 as straightforward, accurate, literal history because Jesus, the Apostles, and all the other biblical writers did so. There is absolutely no biblical basis for taking these chapters as any kind of non-literal, figurative genre of literature. That should be reason enough for us to interpret Genesis 1–11 in the same literal way. But there are some other important reasons to do so.

Only a literal, historical approach to Genesis 1–11 gives a proper foundation for the gospel and the future hope of the gospel. Jesus came into the world to solve the problem of sin that started in real, time-space history in the real Garden of Eden with two real people called Adam and Eve and a real serpent that spoke to Eve.[12] The sin of Adam and Eve resulted in spiritual and physical

---

11. See Terry Mortenson, "Jesus' View of the Age of the Earth," in Terry Mortenson and Thane H. Ury, eds., *Coming to Grips with Genesis* (Green Forest, AR: Master Books, 2008), p. 315–346.
12. Why Christians have trouble believing Genesis 3 when it speaks of a talking serpent is a mystery to me. We have talking parrots today, which involves no miracles. And if the Christian believes in any miracles of the Bible, then he must believe that Balaam's donkey was used by God to speak to the false prophet (Numbers 22:28). Since Satan is a supernatural being who can do supernatural things (e.g., 2 Corinthians 11:11–13; Matthew 4:1–11; 2 Thessalonians 2:8–9), it is not difficult at all to understand or believe that he could speak through a serpent to deceive Eve (cf. 2 Corinthians 11:3; Revelation 12:9).

death for them, but also a divine curse on all of the once "very good" creation (see Genesis 1:31 and 3:14–19). Jesus is coming again to liberate all Christians and the creation itself from that bondage to corruption (Romans 8:18–25). Then there will be a new heaven and a new earth, where righteousness dwells and where sin, death, and natural evils will be no more. A non-literal reading of Genesis destroys this message of the Bible and ultimately is an assault on the character of God.[13]

Genesis is also foundational to many other important doctrines in the rest of the Bible, such as male, loving headship in the home and the church.

Conclusion

The Bible is crystal clear. We must believe Genesis 1–11 as literal history because Jesus, the New Testament Apostles, and the Old Testament prophets did, and because these opening chapters of Genesis are foundational to the rest of the Bible.

As we and many other creationists have always said, a person doesn't have to believe that Genesis 1–11 is literally true to be saved. We are saved when we repent of our sins and trust solely in the death and Resurrection of Jesus Christ for our salvation (John 3:16, Romans 10:9–10). But if we trust in Christ and yet disbelieve Genesis 1–11, we are being inconsistent and are not faithful followers of our Lord.

God said through the prophet Isaiah (66:1–2):

> Thus says the LORD: "Heaven is My throne, and earth is My footstool. Where is the house that you will build Me? And where is the place of My rest? For all those things My hand has made, and all those things exist, says the LORD. But on this one will I look: on him who is poor and of a contrite spirit, and who trembles at My word."

Will you be one who trembles at the words of God, rather than believing the fallible and erroneous words of evolutionists who develop hypotheses and myths that deny God's Word? Ultimately, this question of the proper interpretation of Genesis 1–11 is a question of the authority of God's Word.

---

13. See James Stambaugh, "Whence Cometh Death? A Biblical Theology of Physical Death and Natural Evil," and Thane H. Ury, "Luther, Calvin, and Wesley on the Genesis of Natural Evil: Recovering Lost Rubrics for Defending a Very Good Creation," in Terry Mortenson and Thane H. Ury, eds., *Coming to Grips with Genesis* (Green Forest, AR: Master Books, 2008), p. 373–398 and 399–424, respectively.

9

Do Fossils Show Signs of Rapid Burial?

DR. JOHN D. MORRIS

Uniformitarianism (or gradualism) is the secular belief that rock layers were laid down slowly over millions of years. This view was prominently taught by Charles Lyell through much of the 19th century and strongly influenced Charles Darwin, as well as much of modern geology.

But is uniformitarianism really a true understanding of the rock and fossil records? Did it really take long ages to lay down all these rock layers? Today, that view is being seriously questioned, and rightfully so! Consider a modern geology professor's comments:

> Furthermore, much of Lyell's uniformitarianism, specifically his ideas on identity of ancient and modern causes, gradualism, and constancy of rate, has been explicitly refuted by the definitive modern sources, as well as by an overwhelming preponderance of evidence that, as substantive theories, his ideas on these matters were simply wrong.[1]

When we look at the geologic record in light of the Bible, however, a whole new way of understanding the formation of rock layers and their contained fossils opens up. Earth history as described in the Bible was dominated by several great, world-changing events. First, the earth resulted totally from the six-day creation event (Genesis 1). It was subsequently altered by the Curse on

1. James H. Shea, "Twelve Fallacies of Uniformitarianism," *Geology* 10 no. 9 (1982): 456.

all creation due to Adam's rebellion (Genesis 3). This was soon followed by the great Flood of Noah's day (Genesis 6–9). The Flood is described as nothing less than a tectonic and hydraulic restructuring of the planet, particularly its surface layers. No place on earth escaped its terror. All land-dwelling, air-breathing life not on the ark was drowned by the Flood waters (Genesis 7:22).

What Would a Major, Catastrophic, Global Flood Do?

A global Flood would have done what major floods do. Such a Flood would have eroded and dissolved both soil and rock. Fragments would have been transported and redeposited elsewhere as sediments full of dead plants and animals, the creatures that died in Noah's Flood. Now we observe those sediments hardened into sedimentary rock layers, while the dead things have hardened into fossils.

We can be certain the great majority of earth's sedimentary rock layers and their contained fossils are the result of that great Flood. Evolutionists often wrongly use rocks and fossils to support long ages of evolutionary change, but since Noah's Flood really occurred, it must have laid down the rock layers and fossils. Take rocks and fossils away from evolutionists and evolution's story, and they have no evidence remaining!

Don't think of the Flood as a time when things were merely carried along and then settled out of moving water. Rather, the sediments were deposited in dynamic episodes, one following the other until thick sequences of layers had accumulated, triggered by a combination of consecutive tidal waves (tsunamis), tides, pulses of gravity-driven underwater mud flows, and other processes. The whole sediment package amassed quickly, within the Flood year, not over the hundreds of millions of years claimed by evolutionists. The fossils are evidence of this rapid accumulation.

The conventional secular idea about sediment and fossil deposition involves long ages of slow and gradual accumulation in calm and placid seas. However, fossils are almost never found today in the sea. Life abounds in the sea, but fossils of sea creatures do not. Fossils are hardly ever preserved in an oceanic context. Great deposits of fossils are found in marine sediments, but always on the land! They show evidence of dynamic marine forces destroying life on the continents. What can we make of the myriads of marine fossils found in Kansas, but none in the south Pacific?

How to Make a Fossil

An oft-repeated series of textbook illustrations shows a hypothetical animal dying alongside a stream. Before nature's degradative influences have full sway, the stream overflows, burying the carcass in mud, protecting it from ruin. Over the years, the mud accumulates around the remains, and eventually the entire region subsides, allowing even greater thicknesses of lake bottom or ocean bottom mud to blanket the area, mineralizing the bones and consolidating the mud into rock. Eventually, the region rises again, and erosion exposes the now-fossilized remains.

This scenario would, no doubt, be applicable in rare cases, but it ignores significant advances in sedimentation theory made in recent decades. Geologists now recognize that most rock units are the result of widespread, high-intensity processes, accomplishing in minutes what has traditionally been attributed to slow and gradual processes.

Clams

Most animal fossils are of marine invertebrates, especially shellfish — animals with a hard outer shell, such as clams. Clam fossils are found by the millions, perhaps billions. Clams are surprisingly agile creatures, able to burrow in the sand in their search for food and shelter. The muscle that connects the clam's two halves relaxes at death. The dead clam opens up, and scavengers eat the insides. But often the fossils retain both shell halves, tightly closed — all "clammed" up (figure 1). This is how a clam protects itself from danger.

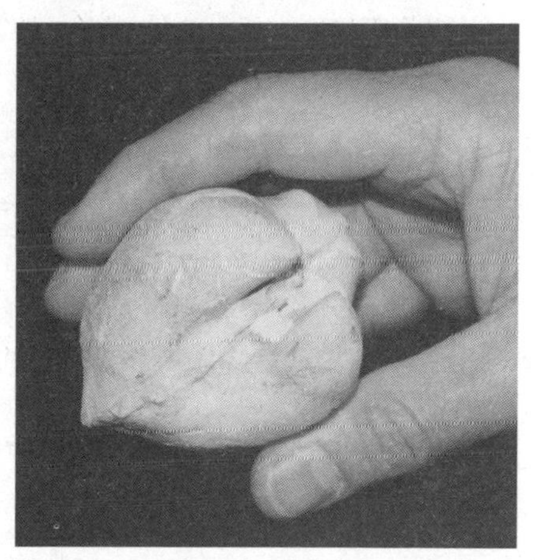

Figure 1. A clam fossilized in the closed position

Usually when we find clam fossils they are jammed together in great numbers, not at all how they live in their life zones today. Thus, we discern the clams felt themselves in danger as they were transported and deposited along with other clams of roughly the same density and shape with many others, buried so deeply they couldn't burrow out. They speak of a rapid depositional process, requiring only a short time.

Fish

Sometimes the fossilized animals appear to have been caught suddenly and buried in life poses — true "action shots." For instance, occasionally a fish fossil is found in the process of eating another fish! How long does it take for a fish to

Figure 2 (left). A fish fossilized in the process of eating another fish.

Figure 3 (below). Rapid fossils such as an ichthyosaur trapped in sediment at the moment of giving birth

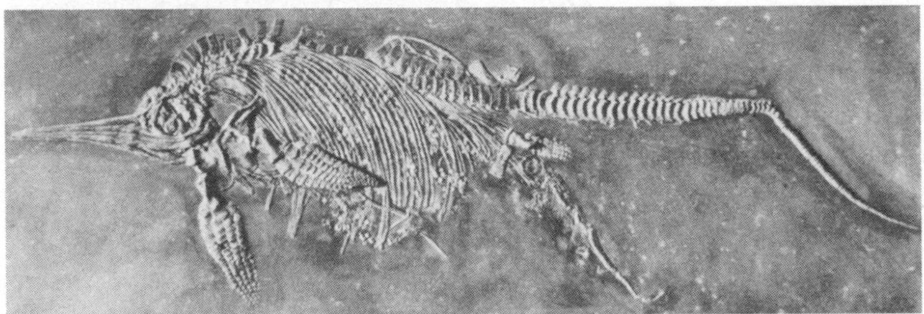

swallow his lunch? It might take a few seconds, but in that brief interval it was trapped and buried (figure 2). Sometimes we see animals such as the ichthyosaur (an extinct marine reptile) pictured in the process of giving birth (figure 3). No great time required here — only a mighty and rapid process.

Jellyfish

Another remarkable fossil is the jellyfish (figure 4). Jellyfish are made mostly of water, and when they get washed up on shore, they quickly dry out. Within a very short time there is nothing left. Yet huge jellyfish fossil graveyards have been found, requiring rapid deposition, burial, and fossilization.[2] Fossil jellyfish graveyards refute the favorite evolutionist excuse

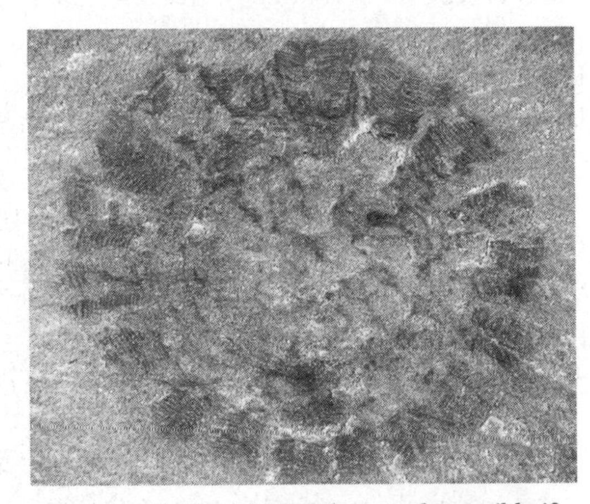

Figure 4. Fossilized jellyfish are only possible if they were buried catastrophically.

2. Reginald Sprigg, "Early Cambrian (?) Jellyfishes from the Flinders Ranges, South Australia," *Transactions of the Royal Society of South Australia* 71 no. 2 (1947): 212–224.

for the lack of transitional fossils, with the claim that only hard parts of fossils are preserved. Instead, we don't expect to find transitional fossils, because none existed. Under the right conditions, any fossil can be preserved.

Right Conditions

Just what are the "right conditions"? Obviously, animals or plants must be quickly buried to avoid the action of scavengers. Many animals are specifically designed to clean the environment of dead and rotting carcasses, and they do a marvelous job. Our world would be a stinking garbage dump without the action of ants, termites, and dung beetles, as well as hyenas, etc.

To become a fossil, a living thing must be out of the reach of other creatures and processes which would destroy it. This includes not only scavengers, but also decomposers, like bacteria. Where can you hide from microscopic bacteria? Likewise, the dead body must be kept from oxidation. Only by undergoing rapid burial, away from scavengers, bacteria, and oxygen, can an organism be fossilized. Yet we find fossils in almost every rock type. Surely catastrophic processes are displayed in the fossils.

Polystrate Fossils

Usually, fossils are found in only one particular layer, but sometimes fossils are discovered straddling two or more geologic layers, each thought to have required long ages to accumulate in conventional thinking. For instance, in the coal regions of Kentucky, trees are often found standing upright in growth position, with their base in one layer, but extending up through several more layers, including, in some cases, layers of coal.

Figure 5. Polystrate fossils, like this tree trunk, cross several geologic layers and cannot be explained by processes that require millions of years of deposition.

Geologists are taught that coal is the metamorphosed remains of plant material, which slowly accumulated as peat in peat swamps. Eventually, as the story goes, the layers of peat were submerged under the ocean and great thicknesses of sediments were deposited on top of them. "Millions of years" of heat and pressure altered the peat into coal. Later, the entire areas emerged from the water to receive more peat and the cycle repeated. But if so, how could one tree stand upright through whole sequences of layers, especially under the sea, while awaiting several cycles of deposition of overlying sediment layers and the necessary heat and pressure? "Polystrate" trees are a good example of rapid deposition (figure 5).

The same argument goes for a fossilized animal whose body thickness extends from one layer into the next. For instance, a whale fossil was found in California that spanned several layers. The entire rock unit could not have required more time to accumulate than is required for a whale carcass to decay.[3]

How Long Does it Take to Fossilize Something?

Figure 6. This hat was turned to stone after being left in an abandoned mine.

It does not take long ages for buried creatures and plants to petrify. Much has been made of a miner's hat found after having been lost for several years. When it was re-located, it had completely petrified — a real "hard" hat (figure 6). Similarly, wood can petrify quickly. A farmer laid a fence in the mid 1800s, and over the years the portion above ground rotted away. But around the year 2000, a fence line of stumps was found totally petrified.[4] It doesn't take a long time to petrify something; it just takes the right conditions. Those right conditions would have often been available during the great Flood of Noah's day.

And how about animal tracks? These are found in many places and many different types of geologic layers. Sometimes the deep trails of large animals like dinosaurs were "fossilized," but often the animal was a small lizard or salamander. Worm trails and burrows were often fossilized.

When an animal makes a track, the sediment layer must be in a soft, unconsolidated condition. Later, as the sediment hardens, the track's shape is preserved. But while it was still soft, the track was fragile and subject to

3. Andrew A. Snelling, "The Whale Fossil in Diatomite, Lompoc, California," *Technical Journal* 9 no. 2 (1995): 244–258.
4. John D. Morris, "Are Human Artifacts Ever Petrified?" Institute for Creation Research, www.icr.org/article/are-human-artifacts-ever-petrified.

erosion. The question must then be raised, how long does it take for sediments to harden into sedimentary rock? Not long at all. A concrete sidewalk is essentially a man-made rock. The presence of a proper "cementing agent" is necessary, but when present, the soft cement can rapidly harden into solid "rock." Many examples of rapid solidification could be cited. It doesn't take a long time, but it does take the right conditions.

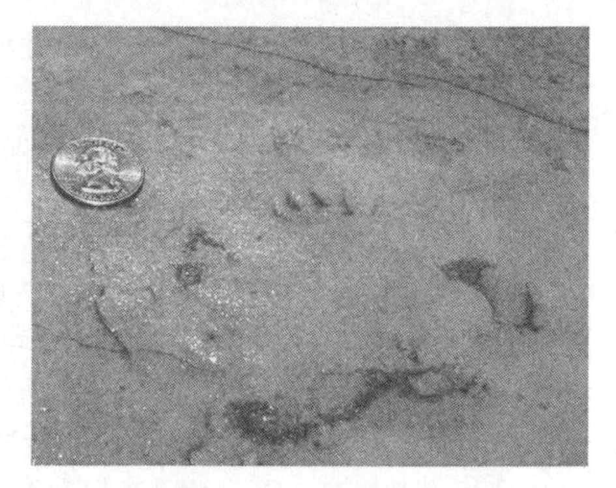

Figure 7. This fossil footprint provides trace evidence of the animal that made it.

And that's the point. Things don't necessarily take a long time to fossilize; they just take the right conditions. The conditions for rapid burial would have occurred globally across the continents at the time of the great Flood of Noah's day. Continual erosion provided the sediment to bury organisms. The proper cementing agents would also be present in the waters that transported the sediments that buried the organisms. It doesn't take long for sediments to harden if the cement is provided. The Flood also provided lots of heat, which spurs on some types of hardening. The fact that the fossils are found in profusion as they are is evidence that such conditions were often met.

Conclusion

This brief look at fossilization and these few examples are a great confirmation of the Scriptures, specifically the Flood of Noah's day. These examples can also be problematic for uniformitarianism (gradualism), which sadly, many today are taught as fact. We can have confidence in Scripture. Not only does it speak with authority about spiritual things, but when it speaks of scientific things, even fossils, it can be trusted.

> Thy word is true from the beginning: and every one of thy righteous judgments endureth for ever (Psalm 119:160; KJV).

10

What about the Similarity Between Human and Chimp DNA?

DR. DAVID A. DEWITT

The first thing I want to do is clear up a common misconception — especially among many within the Church. Many falsely believe that in an evolutionary worldview humans evolved from chimpanzees. And so they ask, "If humans came from chimps, then why are there still chimps?" However, this is not a good question to ask because an evolutionary worldview does not teach this. The evolutionists commonly teach that humans and chimpanzees are both basically "cousins" and have a common ancestor in our past. If you go back far enough, *all* life likely has a single common ancestor in the evolutionary view. This, of course, does not mesh with Genesis 1–2.

Evolutionists frequently assert that the similarity in DNA sequences provides evidence that all organisms (especially humans and chimps) are descended from a common ancestor. However, DNA similarity could just as easily be explained as the result of a common Creator.

Human designers frequently reuse the same elements and features, albeit with modifications. Since all living things share the same world, it should be expected that there would be similarities in DNA as the organisms would have similar needs. Indeed, it would be quite surprising if every living thing had completely different sequences for each protein — especially ones that carried out the same function. Organisms that have highly similar functionality and physiological needs would be expected to have a degree of DNA similarity.

What Is DNA?

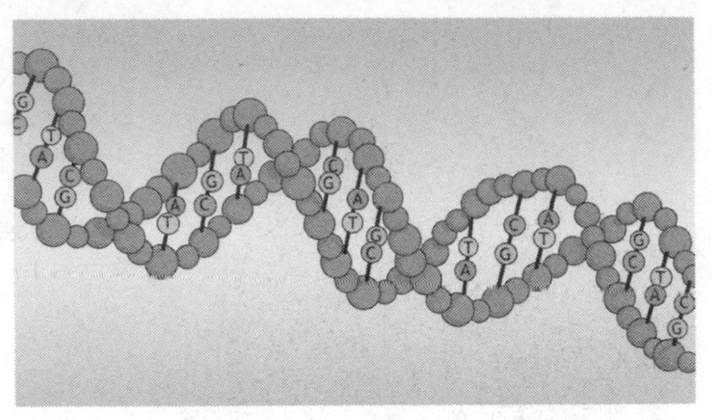

Figure 1. The double-stranded DNA molecule forms with an A opposite a T and a G opposite a C. This sequence determines the structure of proteins.

Every living cell contains DNA (deoxyribonucleic acid), which provides the hereditary instructions for living things to survive, grow, and reproduce. The DNA is comprised of chemicals called bases, which are paired and put together in double-stranded chains. There are four different bases, which are represented by the letters A, T, C, and G. Because A is always paired with T and C is always paired with G, one strand of DNA can serve as a template for producing the other strand.

The DNA is transcribed into a single chain of nucleotides called RNA (ribonucleic acid), which is then translated into the amino acid sequence of a protein. In this way, the sequence of bases in DNA determines the sequence of amino acids in a protein which in turn determines the protein structure and function.

In the human genome (total genetic information in the nucleus of the cell), there are roughly three billion base pairs of DNA with about 20,000 genes (regions that code for proteins). Surprisingly, only about 1 percent of the DNA actually codes for proteins. The rest is non-coding DNA. Some of this DNA comprises control areas — segments of DNA responsible for turning genes on and off, controlling the amount and timing of protein production. There are also portions of DNA that play structural roles. Still other regions of DNA have as yet unknown functions.

What Is the Real Percent Similarity between Humans and Chimpanzees?

Ever since the time of Darwin, evolutionary scientists have noted the anatomical (physical/visible) similarities between humans and the great apes, including chimpanzees, gorillas, and orangutans. Over the last few decades, molecular biologists have joined the fray, pointing out the similarities in DNA sequences. Previous estimates of genetic similarity between humans and chimpanzees suggested they were 98.5–99.4 percent identical.[1]

1. For example:, D.E. Wildman et al., "Implications of Natural Selection in Shaping 99.4% Nonsynonymous DNA Identity between Humans and Chimpanzees: Enlarging Genus Homo," *Proc. Natl. Acad. Sci.* 100 no. 12 (2003): 7181–7188.

Figures 2 and 3: Evolutionists believe that the similarity in the DNA sequence of gorillas, chimpanzees, and humans is proof that they all share a common ancestor (Photos: Shutterstock)

Because of this similarity, evolutionists have viewed the chimpanzee as "our closest living relative." Most early comparative studies were carried out only on genes (such as the sequence of the cytochrome c protein), which constituted only a very tiny fraction of the roughly three billion DNA base pairs that comprise our genetic blueprint. Although the full human genome sequence has been available since 2001, the whole chimpanzee genome has not. Thus, much of the previous work was based on only a fraction of the total DNA.

In the fall of 2005, in a special issue of *Nature* devoted to chimpanzees, researchers reported the draft sequence of the chimpanzee genome.[2] At the time, some researchers called it "the most dramatic confirmation yet"[3] of Darwin's theory that man shared a common ancestor with the apes. One headline read: "Charles Darwin Was Right and Chimp Gene Map Proves It."[4]

Figure 4: The journal *Nature* often trumpets the common ancestry of humans and chimps.

So what is this great and overwhelming "proof" of chimp-human common ancestry? Researchers found

2. The Chimpanzee Sequencing and Analysis Consortium 2005, "Initial Sequence of the Chimpanzee Genome and Comparison with the Human Genome," *Nature* 437 (2005): 69–87.
3. Alan Boyle, "Chimp Genetic Code Opens Human Frontiers," MSNBC, www.msnbc.msn.com/id/9136200.
4. The Medical News, "Charles Darwin Was Right and Chimp Gene Map Proves It," www.news-medical.net/news/2005/08/31/12840.aspx.

96 percent genetic similarity and a difference between us of 4 percent. This is a very strange kind of proof because it is actually *double* the percent difference that evolutionists have claimed for years![5] Even so, no matter what the actual percent difference turned out to be, whether 2, 4, or 10 percent, they still would have claimed that Darwin was right to support their worldview.

Further, the use of percentages obscures the magnitude of the differences. For example, 1.23 percent of the differences are single base pair substitutions (figure 5).[6] This doesn't sound like much until you realize that it represents about 35 million differences! But that is only the beginning. There are 40–45 million bases present in humans that are missing from chimps and about the same number present in chimps that are absent from man. These extra DNA nucleotides are called "insertions" or "deletions" because they are thought to have been added to or lost from the original sequence. (Substitutions and insertions are compared in figure 5.) This puts the total number of DNA differences at about 125 million. However, since the insertions can be more than one nucleotide long, there are about 40 million total separate mutation events that would separate the two species in the evolutionary view.

To put this number into perspective, a typical 8½ x 11-inch page of text might have 4,000 letters and spaces. It would take 10,000 such pages full of text to equal 40 million letters! So the difference between humans and chimpanzees includes about 35 million DNA bases that are different, about 45 million in the human that are absent from the chimp, *and* about 45 million in the chimp that are absent from the human.

Creationists believe that God made Adam directly from the dust of the earth just as the Bible says in Genesis 2. Therefore, man and the apes have never had an ancestor in common. Assuming they did, for the sake of analyzing the argument, then 40 million separate mutation events would have had to take place and become fixed in the population in only 300,000 generations. This is an average of 133 mutations locked into the genome every generation. Locking

5. Studies of chimp-human similarity have typically ignored insertions and deletions although these account for most of the differences. A study by Roy Britten included these insertions and deletions and obtained a figure that is close to the 4 percent reported for the full sequence. See Roy J. Britten, "Divergence Between Samples of Chimpanzee and Human DNA Sequence Is 5% Counting Indels," *Proc. Nat. Acad. Sci.* 99 no. 21 (2002): 13633–13635.
6. Individuals within a population are variable and some chimps will have more or fewer nucleotide differences with humans. This variation accounts for a portion of the differences. 1.06 percent are believed to be fixed differences. Fixed differences represent those that are universal. In other words, all chimpanzees have a given nucleotide and all humans have a different one at the same position.

<table>
<tr><td>A</td><td>G</td><td>T</td><td>C</td><td>G</td><td>T</td><td>A</td><td>C</td><td>C</td></tr>
<tr><td>|</td><td>|</td><td>|</td><td>|</td><td></td><td>|</td><td>|</td><td>|</td><td>|</td></tr>
<tr><td>A</td><td>G</td><td>T</td><td>C</td><td>A</td><td>T</td><td>A</td><td>C</td><td>C</td></tr>
</table>

Substitution

<table>
<tr><td>A</td><td>G</td><td>T</td><td>C</td><td>G</td><td>T</td><td>A</td><td>C</td><td>C</td></tr>
<tr><td>|</td><td>|</td><td>|</td><td>|</td><td></td><td>|</td><td>|</td><td>|</td><td>|</td></tr>
<tr><td>A</td><td>G</td><td>T</td><td>C</td><td></td><td>T</td><td>A</td><td>C</td><td>C</td></tr>
</table>

Insertion/deletion

Figure 5: Comparison between a base substitution and an insertion/deletion. Two DNA sequences can be compared. If there is a difference in the nucleotides (e.g., an A instead of a G) at a given position, this is a substitution. In contrast, if there is a nucleotide base that is missing it is considered an insertion/deletion. It is assumed that a nucleotide has been inserted into one of the sequences or one has been deleted from the other. It is often too difficult to determine whether the difference is a result of an insertion or a deletion and thus it is called an "indel." Indels can be of virtually any length.

in such a staggering number of mutations in a relatively small number of generations is a problem referred to as "Haldane's dilemma."[7]

The Differences Make the Difference

There are many other differences between chimpanzee and human genomes that are not quantifiable as percentages.[8] Specific examples of these differences include:

> At the end of each chromosome is a string of repeating DNA sequences called telomeres. Chimpanzees and other apes have about 23,000 base pairs of DNA at their telomeres. Humans are unique among primates with much shorter telomeres only 10,000 long.[9]

While 18 pairs of chromosomes are virtually identical, chromosomes 4, 9, and 12 show evidence of being "remodeled."[10] In other words, the genes and markers on these chromosomes are not in the same order in the human and

7. Walter J. ReMine, "Cost Theory and the Cost of Substitution — A Clarification," *TJ* 19 no. 1 (2005): 113–125. Note also: This problem is exacerbated because most of the differences between the two organisms are likely due to neutral or random genetic drift. That refers to change in which natural selection is not operating. Without a selective advantage, it is difficult to explain how this huge number of mutations could become fixed in both populations. Instead, many of these may actually be intrinsic sequence differences present from the beginning of creation.
8. Discussed in D.A. DeWitt, "Greater than 98% Chimp/Human DNA Similarity? Not Any More," *TJ* 17 no. 1 (2003): 8–10.
9. S. Kakuo, K. Asaoka, and T. Ide, "Human Is a Unique Species Among Primates in Terms of Telomere Length," *Biochem. Biophys. Res. Commun.* 263 (1999): 308–314.
10. Ann Gibbons, "Which of Our Genes Make Us Human?" Science 281 (1998): 1432–1434.

chimpanzee. Instead of being "remodeled," as the evolutionists suggest, these could also be intrinsic differences as each was a separate creation.

Even with genetic similarity, there can be differences in the amount of specific proteins produced. Just because DNA sequences are similar does not mean that the same amounts of the proteins are produced. Such differences in protein expression can yield vastly different responses in cells. Roughly 10 percent of genes examined showed significant differences in expression levels between chimpanzees and humans.[11]

Gene families are groups of genes that have similar sequences and also similar functions. Scientists comparing the number of genes in gene families have revealed significant differences between humans and chimpanzees. Humans have 689 genes that chimps lack and chimps have 86 genes that humans lack. Such differences mean that 6 percent of the gene complement is different between humans and chimpanzees, irrespective of the individual DNA base pairs.[12]

Thus, the percentage of matching DNA is only one measure of how similar two organisms are, and not really a good one at that. There are other factors besides DNA sequence that determine an organism's phenotype (how traits are physically expressed). Indeed, even though identical twins have the same DNA sequence, as they grow older, twins show differences in protein expression.[13] Therefore, there must be some interaction between the genes and the environment.

Importantly, not all of the data support chimp-human common ancestry as nicely as evolutionists typically suggest. In particular, when scientists made a careful comparison between human, chimpanzee, and gorilla genomes, they found a significant number of genetic markers where humans matched gorillas more closely than chimpanzees! Indeed, at 18–29 percent of the genetic markers, either humans and gorillas or chimpanzees and gorillas had a closer match to each other than chimpanzees and humans.[14]

These results are certainly not what one would expect according to standard evolutionary theory. Chimpanzees and humans are supposed to share a more recent common ancestor with each other than either have with the gorilla. Trying to account for the unexpected distribution of common markers that would otherwise conflict with evolutionary predictions, the authors

11. Y. Gilad et al., "Expression Profiling in Primates Reveals a Rapid Evolution of Human Transcription Factors," *Nature* 440 (2006): 242–245.
12. J.P. Demuth et al., "The Evolution of Mammalian Gene Families," PLoS ONE 1 no. 1 (2006): e85, www.plosone.org/article/info:doi%2F10.1371%2Fjournal.pone.0000085.
13. M.F. Fraga et al., "Epigenetic Differences Arise During the Lifetime of Monozygotic Twins," *Proc. Natl. Acad. Sci.* 102 no. 30 (2005): 10,604–10,609.
14. N. Patterson et al., "Genetic Evidence for Complex Speciation of Humans and Chimpanzees," *Nature* 441 (2006): 315–321.

of this study made the bizarre suggestion: Perhaps chimpanzees and humans split off from a common ancestor, but later descendants of each reproduced to form chimp-human hybrids. Such an "explanation" appears to be an attempt to rescue the concept of chimp-human common ancestry rather than to provide the data to confirm this hypothesis.

All Similarities Are Not Equal

A high degree of sequence similarity does not equate to proteins having exactly the same function or role. For example, the FOXP2 protein, which has been shown to be involved in language, has only 2 out of about 700 amino acids which are different between chimpanzees and humans.[15] This means they are 99.7 percent identical. While this might seem like a trivial difference, consider exactly what those differences are. In the FOXP2 protein, humans have the amino acid asparagine instead of threonine at position 303 and then a serine that is in place of an asparagine at 325. Although apparently a minor alteration, the second change can make a significant difference in the way the protein functions and is regulated.[16] Thus, a very high degree of sequence similarity can be irrelevant if the amino acid that is different plays a crucial role. Indeed, many genetic defects are the result of a single change in an amino acid. For example, sickle cell anemia results from a valine replacing glutamic acid in the hemoglobin protein. It does not matter that every other amino acid is exactly the same.

Usually people think that differences in amino acid sequence only alter the three-dimensional shape of a protein. FOXP2 demonstrates how a difference in one amino acid can yield a protein that is regulated differently or has altered functions. Therefore, we should not be too quick to trivialize even very small differences in gene sequences. Further, slight differences in regions that don't code for proteins can impact how protein levels are regulated. This alteration can change the amount of protein that is produced or when it is produced. In such cases, the high degree of similarity is meaningless because of the significant functional differences that result from altered protein levels.

What about Similar "Junk DNA" in Human and Chimp DNA?

Evolutionists have suggested that there are "plagiarized mistakes" between the human and chimpanzee genome and that these are best explained by a

15. W. Enard et al., "Molecular Evolution of FOXP2, a Gene Involved in Speech and Language," *Nature* 418 (2002): 869–872.
16. This difference in amino acid sequence opens up a potential phosphorylation site for protein kinase C. Phosphorylation is a major mechanism for regulating the activity of enzymes as well as transcription factors.

common ancestor. A teacher who found identical errors on two students' papers would be rightly inclined to believe that the students cheated. The best explanation for two papers with an identical error is that they are both from the same original source. In the same way, some evolutionists have suggested that differences or deactivated genes shared by humans and chimps are best explained by common ancestry. They claim that the only alternative is a Creator who put the same error in two different organisms — a claim they would call incredible.

Evolutionists may consider something to be an error when there is a perfectly good reason that is yet unexplained. They conclude that the error is the result of an ancient mutation based on evolutionary assumptions. Further, when it comes to DNA, there may be genetic hotspots that are prone to the same mutation. For example, humans and guinea pigs share alleged mistakes in the vitamin C pseudogene without sharing a recent common ancestor.[17]

Examples of the alleged "plagiarized mistakes" are endogenous retroviruses (ERVs) — part of the so-called "junk DNA." ERVs are stretches of DNA that can be spliced (cut out), copied, and inserted into other locations within the genome. There are many different types of these mobile pieces of DNA.[18]

The ERVs are not always consistent with evolutionary expectations. For example, scientists analyzed the complement component C4 genes (an aspect of the immune system) in a variety of primates.[19] Both chimpanzees and gorillas had short C4 genes. The human gene was long because of an ERV. Interestingly, orangutans and green monkeys had the same ERV inserted at exactly the same point. This is especially significant because humans are supposed to have a more recent common ancestor with both chimpanzees and gorillas and only more distantly with orangutans. Yet the same ERV in exactly the same position would imply that humans and orangutans had the more recent common

17. Y. Inai, Y. Ohta, and M. Nishikimi, "The Whole Structure of the Human Nonfunctional L-Gulono-Gamma-Lactone Oxidase Gene — the Gene Responsible for Scurvy — and the Evolution of Repetitive Sequences Theron," *J Nutr Sci Vitimol* 49 (2003): 315–319.
18. Humans have many more short interspersed elements (SINEs) than chimps, but chimps have two novel families of retroviral elements, which are absent from man. Comparing endogenous "retroviral elements" yielded 73 human-specific insertions and 45 chimpanzee-specific insertions. Humans have two SINE (Alu) families that the chimpanzees lack and humans have significantly more copies (approximately 7,000 human-specific copies versus approx. 2,300 chimpanzee-specific ones). There are also approximately 2,000 lineage specific L1 elements. All of these lineage specific changes would be required to take place sometime between the last chimp/human common ancestor and the most recent common ancestor for all people on the planet. Importantly, these are modifications for which there is no known selective advantage.
19. A.W. Dangel et al., "Complement Component C4 Gene Intron 9 Has a Phylogenetic Marker for Primates: Long Terminal Repeats of the Endogenous Retrovirus ERV-K(C4) Are a Molecular Clock of Evolution," *Immunogenetics* 42 no. 1 (1995): 41–52.

ancestor. Here is a good case where ERVs do not line up with the expected evolutionary progression. Nonetheless, they are still held up as evidence for common ancestry.

Additional evidence has suggested that ERVs may in fact have functions.[20] One very important function has to do with implantation during pregnancy.[21]

What about the Alleged Fusion of Human Chromosome 2?

Humans normally have 23 pairs of chromosomes while chimpanzees have 24. Evolutionary scientists believe that human chromosome 2 has been formed through the fusion of two small chromosomes in an ape-like ancestor in the human lineage instead of an intrinsic difference resulting from a separate creation. While this may account for the difference in chromosome number, a clear and practical mechanism for how a chromosomal abnormality becomes universal in such a large population is lacking. The fusion would have occurred once in a single individual. Every single human being on earth would have to be a descendant of that one individual. Because there is no selective advantage to a fused chromosome, this becomes even more difficult for evolutionists to explain since natural selection would not be a factor.

Evolution proponents who insist that the chromosome 2 fusion event proves that humans and chimpanzees shared a common ancestor are employing a logical fallacy known as affirming the consequent. Affirming the consequent follows the pattern:

> If P, then Q
> Q
> Therefore, P

In other words,

> If humans and chimpanzees share a common ancestor, then there will be evidence of chromosome fusion.
>
> There is evidence of chromosome fusion.
>
> Therefore, humans and chimpanzees share a common ancestor.

Here is why it is a logical fallacy: For the sake of the argument, let us assume that humans are descended from ancestors that had 48 chromosomes just like the apes, and that there was a common ancestor five million years ago.

20. Georgia Purdom, "Human Endogenous Retroviruses (HERVs) —Evolutionary "Junk" or God's Tools?" www.answersingenesis.org/docs2006/1219herv.asp.
21. K.A. Dunlap et al., "Endogneous Retroviruses Regulate Periimplantation Placental Growth and Differentiation," Proc. Nat. Acad. Sci. 103 no. 29 (2006): 14,390–14,395.

The alleged chromosome 2 fusion would have occurred after the human line split from that of chimpanzees and been passed to all humans on the planet. Even in an evolutionary scenario, the chromosome fusion does not provide evidence for continuity between humans and chimps because it only links those individuals that share the fusion.[22]

In other words, there is no extra evidence for humans having an ancestor in common with chimpanzees provided by the fusion of chromosome 2. It is no more compelling than it would be if humans and chimpanzees had the same number — 48. One could even argue that common ancestry with chimpanzees is less compelling because of the alleged fusion on chromosome 2.

Conclusion

The similarity between human and chimpanzee DNA is really in the eye of the beholder. If you look for similarities, you can find them. But if you look for differences, you can find those as well. There are significant differences between the human and chimpanzee genomes that are not easily accounted for in an evolutionary scenario.

Creationists expect both similarities and differences, and that is exactly what we find. The fact that many humans, chimps, and other creatures share genes should be no surprise to the Christian. The differences are significant. Many in the evolutionary world like to discuss the similarities while brushing the differences aside. Emphasis on percent DNA similarity misses the point because it ignores both the magnitude of the actual differences as well as the significance of the role that single amino acid changes can play.

Please consider the implications of the worldviews that are in conflict regarding the origin of mankind. The Bible teaches that man was uniquely formed and made in the image of God (Genesis 1 and 2). The Lord directly fashioned the first man Adam from dust and the first woman Eve from Adam's side. He was intimately involved from the beginning and is still intimately involved. Keep in mind that the Lord Jesus Christ stepped into history to become a man — not a chimp — and now offers the free gift of salvation to those who receive Him.

22. There is debate among creationists as to whether the evidence for a chromosome 2 fusion event in humans is compelling. Some believe it is an intrinsic difference; others are open to it occurring early in human history, perhaps shortly before Noah. In both cases, evidence linking humans to chimpanzees based on chromosome fusion is lacking.

11

Was There Death Before Adam Sinned?

KEN HAM

Annie's cruel death destroyed Charles's tatters of beliefs in a moral, just universe. Later he would say that this period chimed the final death-knell for his Christianity. . . . Charles [Darwin] now took his stand as an unbeliever."[1]

When Charles Darwin wrote his famous book *On the Origin of Species*, he was in essence writing a history concerning death. In the conclusion of the chapter entitled "On the Imperfections of the Geological Record," Darwin wrote, "Thus, from the war of nature, from famine and death, the most exalted object which we are capable of conceiving, namely, the production of the higher animals, directly follows."[2]

From his evolutionary perspective on the origin of life, Darwin recognized that death had to be a permanent part of the world. Undoubtedly, he struggled with this issue as he sought to reconcile some sort of belief in God with the death and suffering he observed all around him, and which he believed had gone on for millions of years.

This struggle came to a climax with the death of his daughter Annie — said to be "the final death-knell for his Christianity."

Belief in evolution and/or millions of years necessitates that death has been a part of history since life first appeared on this planet. The fossil layers

1. A. Desmond and J. Moore, *Darwin: The Life of a Tormented Evolutionist* (New York, NY: W.W. Norton & Company, 1991), p. 387.
2. C. Darwin, *On the Origin of Species* (Cambridge, MA: Harvard University Press, 1964), p. 490.

(containing billions of dead things) supposedly represent the history of life over millions of years. As Carl Sagan is reported to have said, "The secrets of evolution are time and death."[3]

Time and Death

This phrase sums up the history of death according to those who believe in evolution and/or millions of years. In this system of belief:

- death, suffering, and disease over millions of years led up to man's emergence;
- death, suffering, and disease exist in this present world; and
- death, suffering, and disease will continue on into the unknown future. Death is a permanent part of history.

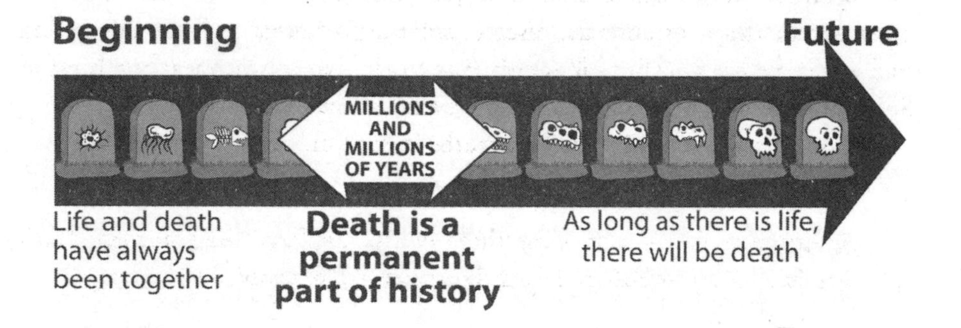

Sin and Death

Rather than "time and death," the phrase "sin and death" sums up the history of death according to the Bible. From a perspective of the literal history

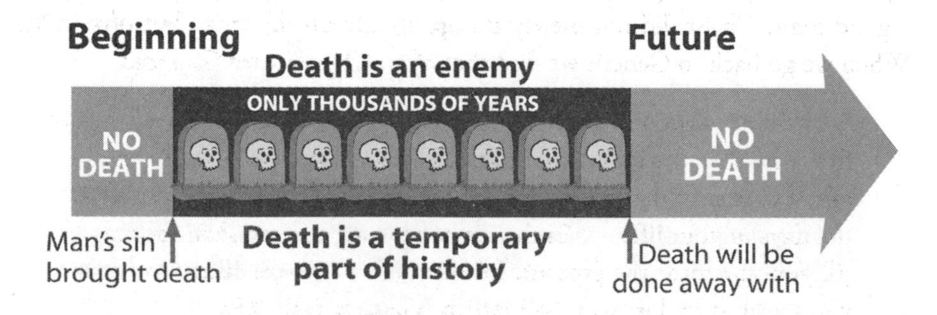

3. C. Sagan, *Cosmos, Part 2: One Voice in the Cosmic Fugue*, produced by Public Broadcasting Company, Los Angeles, with affiliate station KCET, and first aired in 1980 on PBS stations throughout the United States.

of the Book of Genesis, there was a perfect world to start with — described by God as "very good" (Genesis 1:31) — but it was marred because of Adam's rebellion. Sin and its consequence of death entered the world that was once a paradise (Romans 5:12 ff., 8:20–22; 1 Corinthians 15:21–22).

In 1 Corinthians 15:26, Paul describes death as the "last enemy." And that's the point — death is an enemy — it's an intrusion. The death of man and the animals was not part of the original creation. And even though death reigns in this present world, one day in the future there will be no more death: "And God shall wipe away all tears from their eyes; and there shall be no more death, neither sorrow, nor crying, neither shall there be any more pain: for the former things are passed away" (Revelation 21:4; KJV).

The idea of millions of years came from the belief that most of the fossil-bearing layers were laid down millions of years before man existed. Those Christians who accept the idea of millions of years and try to fit it into the Bible also must accept death of animals, disease, suffering, thorns, and animals eating each other before sin. But all of this flies in the face of the clear teaching of Scripture that such things could not have existed until after sin.

Consider the following biblical truths in support of that conclusion.

Human Death

Scripture makes it very clear there could not have been human death (physical death) before Adam sinned. For example, Romans 5:12 states:

> Therefore, just as through one man sin entered the world, and death through sin, and thus death spread to all men, because all sinned. . . .

This "death" referred to in Romans 5 cannot have just been "spiritual" death, but also included physical death. The context confirms this. In verses 6–11 the Apostle Paul speaks repeatedly of Christ dying for us, and of someone dying for a good man. Christ did not merely die spiritually on the cross, but physically. When we go back to Genesis we find that after Adam sinned God said:

> Because you have heeded the voice of your wife, and have eaten from the tree of which I commanded you, saying, "You shall not eat of it": Cursed is the ground for your sake; in toil you shall eat of it all the days of your life. . . . In the sweat of your face you shall eat bread till you return to the ground, for out of it you were taken; for dust you are, and to dust you shall return (Genesis 3:17, 19).

God decreed that our bodies would return to dust (physical death) as a result of sin. There is no doubt there could not have been human death before sin.

Animal Death

Unlike the case of Romans 5:12, there is no verse of Scripture that specifically teaches that there was no animal death before sin. However, there are passages of Scripture that, when taken together, lead us to conclude this.

First, it should be noted that the Bible is not about animals — it is about man and his relationship with God. Thus, we would not expect as much specific teaching concerning animals as there is about man. However, consider the following passages:

> A. Genesis 1:29–30 — And God said [to Adam and Eve], "See, I have given you every herb that yields seed which is on the face of all the earth, and every tree whose fruit yields seed; to you it shall be for food. Also, to every beast of the earth, to every bird of the air, and to everything that creeps on the earth, in which there is life, I have given every green herb for food"; and it was so.

These verses seem to clearly teach that man and the animals were to be vegetarian originally. This is confirmed by the fact that in Genesis 9:3 after the Flood, concerning the diet of man, God said to Noah, "Every moving thing that lives shall be food for you. I have given you all things, even as the green herbs."

In other words, it is clear that originally man was to be vegetarian, but now God changed that diet so that man could eat the flesh of animals. As Genesis 1:30 concerns the diet of animals, and it is connected to Genesis 1:29, it is a strong indication that the animals were to be vegetarian originally (before sin).

Problem: For those Christians who believe in millions of years, the fossil record that is claimed by secularists to be millions of years old has in it numerous examples of animals having eaten other animals — supposedly millions of years before man! This is contrary to the Bible's clear teaching that animals were vegetarian originally (before sin).

> B. Genesis 1:31 — Then God saw everything that He had made, and indeed it was very good. So the evening and the morning were the sixth day.

At the end of the sixth day of creation, God described the entire creation as "very good." However, in the fossil record, there are many examples of diseases in the bones of animals (e.g., tumors [cancer]; arthritis; abscesses etc). Such diseases could not be described as "very good," when in the rest of the Bible diseases are always viewed as bad and a result of sin and the curse. These diseases simply could not have existed before sin, if the Bible is true (and it is).

Problem: Those Christians who believe in millions of years for most of the fossil layers to form must accept that diseases like cancer were in the bones of animals before sin, and that God described such diseases as "very good."

> C. Romans 8:20–22 — For the creation was subjected to futility, not willingly, but because of Him who subjected it in hope; because the creation itself also will be delivered from the bondage of corruption into the glorious liberty of the children of God. For we know that the whole creation groans and labors with birth pangs together until now.

Paul makes it clear in Romans 8 that the "whole creation" groans because of sin. Most commentators on this passage in the history of the Church have interpreted this "whole creation" to refer to the whole non-human creation (including the animals).[4] That is the only interpretation that makes sense. First, Paul already established the connection between sin and human death in Romans 5. Second, the reference to "birth pangs" (8:22) seems to be an allusion to the judgment on Eve in Genesis 3:16. Also, the groaning of the creation is linked in this passage (Romans 8:18–25) to the groaning of believers in this sinful world. Furthermore, the liberation of the whole creation will happen with the future final redemption of believers (when they get their resurrection bodies) at the Second Coming of Jesus Christ (Romans 8:23–25). Since the Christian's and the creation's liberation are linked, it is most reasonable theologically to conclude that they came into bondage to corruption at the same time also.

Finally, if we reject that conclusion and imagine that the whole creation was in bondage to corruption as soon as God created it (Genesis 1), then what kind of God would He be to call that corruption "very good"? So the whole originally perfect creation was put into bondage to corruption by God's curse recorded in Genesis 3.

Problem: Christians who believe in millions of years have to accept animals eating each other, diseases like cancer, and animals dying and going extinct over the course of millions of years before man, and then on into the present. This would mean that the Fall of man didn't change anything, and that God described all this death and disease as "very good." In this case, the creation is not "groaning" because of sin. But as we have seen, Paul makes it

4. Douglass Moo, *The Epistle to the Romans* (Grand Rapids, MI: Eerdmans, 1996), p. 514; Thane H. Ury, "Luther, Calvin, and Wesley on the Genesis of Natural Evil: Recovering Lost Rubrics for Defending a *Very Good* Creation," in Terry Mortenson and Thane H. Ury, eds., *Coming to Grips with Genesis* (Green Forest, AR: Master Books, 2008), p. 399–423.

clear the creation is groaning because of sin. This only makes sense if a "very good" creation (perfect creation — no death, disease, suffering, etc.) was subject to "futility" and now "groans" because sin changed everything.

> D. Acts 3:21 — . . . whom heaven must receive until the times of restoration of all things, which God has spoken by the mouth of all His holy prophets since the world began.

The Bible teaches that there will one day be a "restoration" of "all things." This is because something happened (sin) to cause a problem (the whole creation groans). We look forward to a new heaven and new earth where there will be no death (which the Bible describes as an enemy) or suffering, because there will be no more Curse (Revelation 21:3–5, 22:3). It will be a perfect place — just as everything was once perfect before sin.

Problem: For those Christians who believe in millions of years, and thus must accept death, disease, and suffering of animals before sin, what will this restoration look like? More death and suffering and disease for millions of years or forever? That would be a horrible prospect. No, the restoration will look like things were before sin — all was "very good." And that indeed is something to look forward to!

From the above and other passages of Scripture (including Colossians 1:15–20, which speaks of Jesus Christ as the Creator and Redeemer of "all things"), we have good reasons to believe that animals could not have eaten other animals and died of diseases before sin. The only other ways animals could have died would be from old age (wearing out) or accidents (catastrophes, etc.) — but these would not fit with everything originally being "very good," and would not fit with Paul's teaching in Romans 8 that the whole creation groans now because of sin.

We can therefore conclude with confidence there was no animal death before sin.

Plant Death

Some people argue that there was death before sin, because plants were given for food for man and the animals (Genesis 1:29–30), thus plants died before sin.

However, this objection fails to note carefully what the Bible says about life and death. Biblically speaking, plants do not have a life, as animals and man do. At the end of Genesis 1:30 we see that humans and animals have "life," but plants do not. The word "life" is a translation of two Hebrew words there: *nephesh chayyah*. *Nephesh* is the word usually translated "soul" or "creature" depending on context, and *chayyah* is the noun form of the verb "to live." *Nephesh* or *nephesh chayyah* is never used to describe plants in the Old Testament. They only describe people and animals. Just as plants are not "alive" in the same sense as animals and man are, so also they do not "die" in the same sense. In only one place does the Old Testament use the Hebrew word for "die" (*mut*) when referring to plants, and in that passage (Job 14:7–12) it is very clear that the death of a plant (tree) is categorically different from the death of a man. So when animals and people ate plants in the world before sin, it did not involve death, because plants do not "die" in the sense that man and animals do.

Implications

If the Bible makes it clear there was no animal death and disease and no carnivorous animals before sin, then we cannot add millions of years into the Bible — to do so undermines the authority of Scripture, and comes with severe implications.

In reality, the battle between creation and evolution, between young-earth and old-earth views, is in fact a battle between two totally different histories of death.

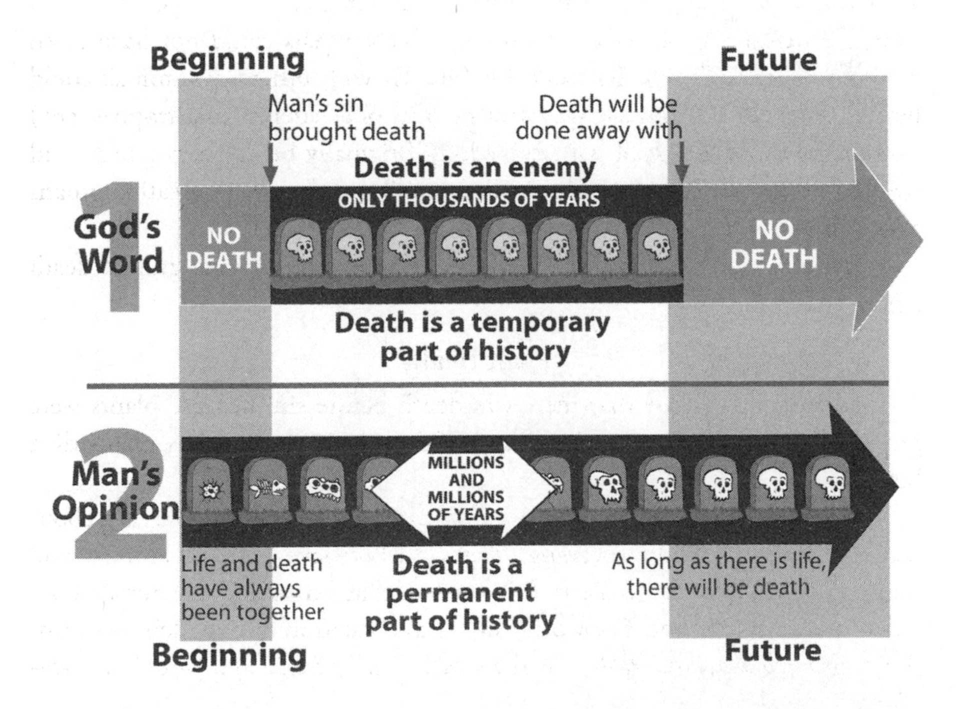

For the Christian, which history of death you accept has major theological implications.

1. If a Christian accepts the history of death over millions of years, then when God stated in Genesis 1:31 that everything He had made was "very good," this would mean that death, suffering, violence, and diseases like cancer (as represented in the fossil record) were also "very good." This situation is represented in the following diagram:

This view of history, if consistently applied, would lead to the situation summed up by the heretical Bishop John Shelby Spong:

> But Charles Darwin says that there was no perfect creation because it is not yet finished. It is still unfolding. And there was no perfect human life which then corrupted itself and fell into sin. . . . And so the story of Jesus who comes to rescue us from the fall becomes a nonsensical story. So how can we tell the Jesus story with integrity and with power, against the background of a humanity that is not fallen but is simply unfinished?[5]

Bishop Spong accepts the history of death over millions of years. As a result of this, he cannot accept a perfect creation that was marred by sin. Thus, the groaning (death and suffering, etc.) we observe today has continued for millions of years. This is also true of all "long-age creationists." These are those who accept the secular belief in an old world, while opposing evolution in favor of "progressive creation" or "intelligent design."

2. However, if a Christian accepts the history of death as given by a literal reading of the Genesis account, then this history can be represented by the following diagram:

5. Australian Broadcasting Corporation TV "Compass" interview with Bishop John Shelby Spong, by Geraldine Doogue, in front of a live audience at the Eugene Groosen Hall, ABC Studios, Ultimo, Sydney, July 8, 2001. From a transcript at www.abc.net.au/compass/intervs/spong2001.htm.

The perfect creation with no death, disease, or suffering is described as "very good." The Bible makes it clear that God does not delight in death. We read in Ezekiel 33:11, "Say to them, 'As I live,' says the Lord GOD, 'I have no pleasure in the death of the wicked, but that the wicked turn from his way and live. Turn, turn you from your evil ways! For why should you die, O house of Israel?' " God takes no pleasure in the afflictions and calamities (death, etc.) of people.

The Bible makes it obvious that death is the penalty for our sin. In other words, it is really our fault that the world is the way it is — God is a loving, merciful God. When we sinned in Adam, we effectively said that we wanted life without God. All of us also sin individually (Romans 3:23). God had to judge sin, as He warned Adam He would (Genesis 2:17, cf. 3:19). In doing so, God has given us a taste of life without Him — a world that is running down — a world full of death and suffering. As Romans 8:22 says, "The whole creation groans and labors with birth pangs." Man, in essence, forfeited his right to live.

However, even though we are sinners, those who have turned from their sin and trusted Christ for forgiveness will spend eternity with their Creator in a place where righteousness dwells — and there will be no more crying, suffering, or death.

The true history of death, as understood from a literal Genesis, enables us to recognize a loving Creator who hates death, the enemy that will one day be thrown into the lake of fire (Revelation 20:14).

Which history of death do you accept? Is it one that makes God an ogre responsible for millions of years of death, disease, and suffering? Or is it one that correctly places the blame on our sin, and correctly represents our Creator God as a loving, merciful Savior who wept at the tomb of dead Lazarus (John 11:35)?

12

Abortion: Is It Really a Matter of Life and Death?

PAUL F. TAYLOR

The whole subject of abortion[1] produces very strong emotions on both sides of the argument. The two primary sides are:

Pro-life: The pro-life position is that life begins at fertilization, and that all human life is precious and made in the image of God.

Pro-choice (or more so "anti-life"): The pro-choice position is that it is the woman's right to choose whether or not to have an abortion, because an unborn child is considered to be a part of the woman's body. Under this definition, the unborn child is not considered to be fully human.

You would think that pro-choice meant that someone would allow the baby to choose whether he or she should live or die (miscarry), but that is not the case. Even while the baby is choosing to live and continuing to develop, some do not respect *that* choice. And that has brought us to the heat of a debate that rages around the world.

1. If you need help and support as a result of the issues raised in this chapter, please contact one of the following organizations: UK: CARE (Christian Action Research and Education) (www.care.org.uk), IMAGE (www.imagenet.org.uk), Society for the Protection of the Unborn Child (www.spuc.org.uk), LIFE (www.lifeuk.org), US: Heartbeat International (www.heartbeatinternational.org), Care Net (www.care-net.org), National Right to Life (www.nrlc.org). Or feel free to contact one of these organizations to find something closer to home as well.

Such emotions are understandable and can cloud the debate, hiding the truth of what the Bible teaches. However, as this chapter will hopefully make clear, emotional responses to the subject of abortion are not necessarily inappropriate — indeed, such responses may be the most appropriate. Also, an acknowledgment that emotional issues cloud both sides of the debate should not be taken to imply that this chapter will steer a "middle ground" between the two positions. It will not — because the Bible does not do so.

The emotional arguments against abortion include a disgust at the nature of the procedure being discussed. Emotional arguments in favor of abortion focus on an anger that suggests that no one has the right to undermine a woman's right to choose what she does with her own body.

Although this essay is not designed to steer a middle way, it will be necessary to examine some issues dispassionately. This is not because I believe the subject does not demand one's emotions, but because I want to start by cutting through the emotional charge and examining the issues from a "first-principles" biblical perspective. Only when this foundation is laid can we return to the issue of which emotional responses may be appropriate.

Life Before Birth

Of crucial importance to the debate is the status of the embryo, fetus, or baby before birth. Please forgive the coldness of the question — but what exactly is it? Should we refer to it as it, or is it a he or she?

The Bible does not directly refer to abortion. There are many other issues about which the Bible does not give specific comment. However, in many cases, it is clear what the biblical position is. And the Bible does have a great deal to say about the status of life before birth. In Jeremiah 1:4–5 we read:

> Then the word of the LORD came to me, saying:
> "Before I formed you in the womb I knew you;
> Before you were born I sanctified you;
> I ordained you a prophet to the nations."

The Lord is giving a number of pieces of information to the prophet. First, God says that He knew Jeremiah when he was in the womb. Second, He makes clear that He knew Jeremiah even before He was formed in the womb. Third, He tells Jeremiah that his growth in the womb was as a result of being "formed" by God Himself.

Today, we have a great deal of knowledge of how a baby develops in his or her mother's womb. In this passage, God is making clear that this is not an arbitrary process. It is a direct act of formation by God. The Hebrew word that

is translated as formed is *yatsar*, and refers to being formed or shaped in the same sort of manner that a potter shapes clay. This analogy is interesting, because the image of God as a potter is closely associated with the Book of Jeremiah. Jeremiah 18 is the famous chapter that talks about the potter and the clay. It is significant that a similar image is being used of an unborn child in Jeremiah 1:5.

The passage implies that there is a personhood associated with the unborn Jeremiah. Therefore, the unborn child should be considered as a full human being, with all the implications that the fact entails. We need to examine whether other passages of Scripture make a similar assumption of personhood for other characters, and, hence, whether we can determine if the Bible counts unborn babies as human beings.

Jesus and John

Scripture makes clear that both Jesus and John the Baptist were human before their birth. Jesus was given a name, and His birth was foretold to Mary, at the time of His conception, as recorded in Luke 1:26–38. Some might want to argue, however, that Jesus was a special case. However, no special case argument can be made to apply to John, the account of whose birth is closely wound up with the account of Jesus' birth.

In Luke 1:41 we note that Elizabeth was "filled with the Holy Spirit." She was immediately able to ascertain that Mary was pregnant with the Messiah.

> Why is this granted to me, that the mother of my Lord should come to me? (Luke 1:43).

What is interesting about this passage is that the unborn John joins in the celebration.

> For indeed, as soon as the voice of your greeting sounded in my ears, the babe leaped in my womb for joy (Luke 1:44).

John does not just leap — he leaps for joy! Under the inspiration of the Holy Spirit, this Scripture has been recorded in order to emphasize that John's prophetic work in "preparing the way of the Lord" was beginning before his birth. Therefore, John must have been fully human before his birth.

Mosaic Law

There is an interesting account in the Mosaic Law about the various penalties for different types of murders.

> If men fight, and hurt a woman with child, so that she gives birth prematurely, yet no harm follows, he shall surely be punished accordingly as the woman's husband imposes on him; and he shall pay as the judges determine. But if any harm follows, then you shall give life for life, eye for eye, tooth for tooth, hand for hand, foot for foot, burn for burn, wound for wound, stripe for stripe (Exodus 21:22–25).

When examining Mosaic Law, it is important to remember that the penalties prescribed do not necessarily apply to today, because these laws were civil laws for the children of Israel. For example, because the Church does not hold the sword of the state today, we are not entitled to legislate stoning for adultery. Nevertheless, the fact that stoning is the punishment prescribed for adultery in the Mosaic theocracy illustrates to us how seriously God views that particular sin.

So when we analyze the passage from Exodus 21 quoted above, we see that there are differing sanctions, based on differing circumstances. In the first case analyzed, we have a pregnant woman who is hurt and gives birth prematurely. In this case, however, the baby is not harmed. So the offense is treated in the same manner as it would if the woman had not been pregnant.

The situation changes notably if harm comes to the baby. On this occasion, there is to be recompense of the "eye for an eye" model. This is not to suppose that we are entitled to use the same sanctions today. Nevertheless, the concept of "life for life" illustrates that God considers the death of the unborn to be equivalent to the death of the living. Accordingly, a society should reflect this value in its laws, even if the sanction prescribed is different.

What we have seen from this analysis of Bible passages is that the Bible considers the unborn baby to be human and to have personality, and that God views the value of the life of the unborn, when it is prematurely harmed, to be of equal value to that of any other human being.

Amazingly, this passage has actually been used by some to attempt to condone abortion. This is because of a mistranslation in certain modern versions of the Bible. For example, the Message Bible has:

> When there's a fight and in the fight a pregnant woman is hit so that she *miscarries* but is not otherwise hurt . . . [emphasis added]

The Message Bible puts the emphasis on the harm to the woman, whereas other editions emphasize the harm to both mother and baby. The Hebrew term translated either as premature birth or miscarriage is *yatsa*. This word, which means "to come out," is used many times in the Old Testament, and in each case always refers to a whole birth. It usually refers to a live birth, though one passage refers to a still birth. In no other place, however, is the term used for a miscarriage.[2]

Fearfully and Wonderfully Made

The most famous passage referring to the life of the unborn must be from Psalm 139.

> For You formed my inward parts; You covered me in my mother's womb. I will praise You, for I am fearfully and wonderfully made; Marvelous are Your works, And that my soul knows very well. My frame was not hidden from You, When I was made in secret, And skillfully wrought in the lowest parts of the earth. Your eyes saw my substance, being yet unformed. And in Your book they all were written, The days fashioned for me, When as yet there were none of them (Psalm 139:13–16).

This is a pictorial account of the development of an unborn baby. It refers to the formation of flesh (covering), internal organs (inward parts), and bones (frame). None of these developments was hidden from God, though they were "secret" from people, indicating that we cannot directly see the formation of the unborn. The concept of the "lowest parts of the earth" is a euphemism for the female reproductive system. Even in this unborn state, it is clear that the baby is human, as God has already determined "the days fashioned" for the baby.

What these passages from Scripture show us is that the unborn baby has personality and sensitivity before birth. It is therefore human, and subject to all the protections of the moral laws that protect other humans. If the unborn baby was an integral part of the woman's body, then it would not have the separate actions and reactions outlined in these scriptural passages. Viewing the evidence that shows that unborn babies can react to external stimuli, such as light and sound, is a further confirmation of their unique life apart from the mother.

Caring for the Mother

An argument frequently used in favor of abortion is that we need to have concern for the mother. Abortion was supposedly legalized in the UK and the United States to alleviate the suffering of women undergoing crisis pregnancies.

Such crises in pregnancies are very real. Women can be in very real distress

2. G. Butner, "Exodus 21:22–25: Translations and Mistranslations", www.errantskeptics.org/Exodus2122.htm.

during times of pregnancy, particularly if the pregnancy is not planned, or is going wrong because of illness, etc.

Nevertheless, a lot of the difficult cases become clearer once we have determined from Scripture, as above, that the unborn baby is human. Both the UK's Abortion Act of 1967, and the famous U.S. case of Roe v. Wade, were supposed to eliminate dangerous backstreet abortions, and reduce difficult cases, without being used as a general abortion-on-demand measure. Nevertheless, the practical outworking of these laws on both sides of the Atlantic has been startling.

David Reardon has suggested that many women get abortions because they feel under pressure to do so.[3] Some such pressures he identifies as circumstantial — women concerned about how they might cope, financially, emotionally, etc. But many more pressures come from other people. He particularly notes that the pressures frequently come from men — husbands, boyfriends, fathers, etc. Women are often coming under pressure to "do the right thing," even if they have severe doubts. This is one of the factors, Reardon notes, which has made Post-Abortion Trauma such a major psychological illness among women in the last 20 years or so. Reardon's studies suggested that 53 percent of women felt coerced into abortion by other people, and 65 percent by circumstances (obviously some overlap here). Only 33 percent had felt that their abortion was a "free" choice.

In the case of coercion by others, it can be seen that abortion is frequently not even an answer to this coercion. Many women have had abortions because of pressure from male partners in the hope of saving their relationships, only to find that the partner leaves anyway.

In the case of coercion by circumstances, it is my belief that pro-life Christians need to be pro-active in providing help and care for mothers undergoing crisis pregnancies. Is the proposed abortion happening because the mother cannot afford baby equipment and care? Then Christians should be providing that equipment and care. Will the mother be thrown out of her home if she proceeds with the pregnancy? Then Christians must provide emergency refuge and shelter.

Reardon's study, which examined women whose abortions had been about ten years previous to the study, also noted that adolescent women (aged 20 or under) were frequently likely to leave abortions to later in gestation, due to reduced ability to make decisions. This immaturity among younger women led to a greater likelihood of post-abortion trauma, and also physical issues, such as a high rate of subsequent infertility. The work of Christian post-abortion counselors, such as Image (see reference 1), has shown that women can be most helped through the application of God's forgiveness, when the woman repents.

3. D.C. Reardon, "Women at Risk of Post-Abortion Trauma," www.afterabortion.org/women_a.html.

Reasons for Abortion

In 2007, 205,598 abortions were carried out in England and Wales,[4] and 13,703 in Scotland.[5] This UK total[6] of 219,301 compares with 23,641 in 1968. There are currently more than 600 abortions performed per day in the UK. Of these figures, 82 percent were performed on single women. About 1 percent of abortions were performed because of suspected handicap in the unborn child. One in five pregnancies in the UK ends in abortion. Abortion law was further liberalized under the 1990 Human Fertilization and Embryology Bill, with the result that, in certain cases, abortion can be carried out up to full term. Statistics like these seem to run counter to the generally held mythology that legalized abortions are not carried out for social reasons. Indeed, one top surgeon has recently criticized the "cavalier" way that young surgeons carry out abortions, complaining, "I know of no case where the Department of Health has questioned the legality of abortions."[7]

Social justifications for abortion would seem to be of secondary importance, if the unborn baby is defined as human. Yet the overwhelming majority of abortions carried out in the UK are for "social reasons" — government statistics suggest that 98 percent of all abortions are for social reasons.[8] The earlier sections have shown that abortions are not even in the interest of the mother, when one considers the violence that can be done to the body, the risk for young adolescent pregnant women, and the dangers of post-abortion trauma. However, many difficult cases continue to be cited, so it is worth examining the practical outcome of a couple of these.

Anecdotal evidence suggests that abortions are often offered to mothers when Down's Syndrome is suspected. Indeed, in the UK, nine out of ten babies

4. It is common in the UK for England and Wales statistics to be grouped, with the other states' figures quoted separately.
5. Abortion in Britain, Image (an evangelical, pro-life organization), www.imagenet.org.uk/pages/abortionfactsheet.php.
6. Abortion is illegal in Northern Ireland, though 1,343 women traveled to the mainland for abortions in 2007.
7. "Top Surgeon Tells Court that Junior Doctors Are 'Cavalier' Over Abortions," Christian Concern For Our Nation, www.ccfon.org/view.php?id=751.
8. Abortion Statistics, England and Wales 2006, Dept of Health June 2007, para 4.2.2.

suffering from Down's Syndrome are aborted.[9] The attitude frequently seems to be that it is "kinder" in some way for such a child not to live, because of its "quality of life." But the people concerned — the "sufferers" of Down's Syndrome — may have very different opinions about their quality of life. The issue of "quality of life" is an evolutionary concept and has no place in a biblical worldview, which sees all human life as being in the image of God.

Anya Souza — a Down Syndrome sufferer — was allowed to address the 2003 International Down Syndrome Screening Conference in London. She said:

> I can't get rid of my Down's Syndrome, but you can't get rid of my happiness. You can't get rid of the happiness I give others either. It's doctors like you that want to test pregnant women and stop people like me being born. Together with my family and friends I have fought to prevent my separation from normal society. I have fought for my rights. . . . I may have Down's syndrome but I am a person first.[10]

Another set of difficult cases often cited in support of abortion "rights" is what to do about pregnancies resulting from incest or rape. In these cases, it is clear that a crime has taken place — and that crime could well have been a very violent crime. The woman concerned has been violated, and is clearly already going to be suffering as a result of what has happened to her.

Abortion itself is an act of violence on the unborn baby (and the mother). It is not clear that the difficulties of undergoing an abortion could be in any way a comfort to the woman who has suffered the crimes of incest or rape. Moreover, the unborn baby is an innocent party to the event. It does not make sense to end the life of the innocent party because of another act of violence. Add to this the dangers that the mothers themselves may suffer, as stated above — such as infertility and post-abortion trauma.

The Life of the Mother

All human life is valuable. The unborn baby's life is precious — and so is the mother's. There are certainly a precious few occasions when, tragically, there is a choice between the life of the baby and the life of the mother. It may be necessary, under these extreme conditions, to consider saving the life of the mother or the child. These tragic situations arise because we live in a fallen world.

One example of the above would be an ectopic pregnancy, where the unborn baby has started to develop in the fallopian tube, rather than in the

9. D. Mutton et al., "Trends in Prenatal Screening for, and Diagnosis of, Down's Syndrome: England and Wales, 1989–97," British Medical Journal, October 3, 1998.
10. "Ability and Disability or Eugenic Abortion," Society for the Protection of the Unborn Child, www.spuc.org.uk/students/abortion/disability.

uterus. It may not be possible to move the baby, and the baby would, in any case, die in such circumstances, as would the mother. Sadly, it may be necessary for the baby to be removed surgically, which will result in his death. With this situation though, it is a matter of trying to save a life or two, as opposed to forcing death on one or both of them.

Other circumstances can be more complicated. When there is a tragic choice between saving either the baby or the mother, but it is impossible to do both, then individual families will need, prayerfully, to come to their own decisions on this matter, and no one would be able to criticize their painful choice. It is fortunate that such events are very rare — about 0.004 percent of all cases involve the possible death of the mother.[11]

Language of Abortion

The issue of the personhood of Ms. Souza leads us to examine the use of terminology in the abortion debate. The terminology is important, because language that denies the humanity of the unborn child makes it easier for abortionists to make their case.

The unborn baby is often referred to using two terms. *Embryo* indicates the fertilized product of conception from implantation to eight weeks. *Fetus* (or *foetus*) indicates the baby from the eighth week to birth. Such terms are often easier to use, if the baby is to be terminated, as they do not sound human. The etymology of the latter term is interesting — *fetus* means "little one."

There is also the word *conception*. It always has been, and to most people still is, the combination of the sperm and egg — or fertilization. But *Stedman's Medical Dictionary* now defines *conception* as implantation of the combined sperm and egg (that must be over 4–5 days old [blastocyte]) when it attaches to the lining of the uterus (endometrium). This has now led to people aborting children with "morning after pills," cloning of humans, and embryonic stem cell research all the while declaring that it is "before conception."

The Real Issue

As with so many cases, we find that abortion is not the real problem. The real problem is much deeper, and abortion is a symptom of the deeper problem. A society that permits abortion does not do so by chance. It is a society that has neglected the fundamentals of God's law. The basis for our objection to abortion has been the biblical position that the unborn baby is human. However, in an evolutionary view, why should any human be accorded special

11. Dr. Michael Jarmulowicz, cited in "The Physical and Psycho-Social effects of Abortion on Women: A Report by the Commission of Inquiry into the Operation and Consequences of The Abortion Act," June 1994, p. 5.

status, compared with, for instance, the welfare of animals? To put it crudely, if an animal is sick or injured, we will often take it to the vet to be "put down."

The difference between the welfare of humans and animals stems back to Genesis. Humans were not made *ex nihilo* in the way that animals were. The first man was fashioned out of the dust, and God breathed into him the breath of life (Genesis 2:7). The first chapter of the Bible reminds us that God made us in His image (Genesis 1:26). This statement was not made of any other animal.

Evolutionary beliefs have influenced us to think that we are simply evolved animals — that we share a common ancestor with the apes — indeed, further back, we are supposed to share a common ancestor with all mammals. As one modern and rather base pop song puts it — "you and me baby ain't nothin' but mammals." If that is the case, then the arguments against abortion become hollow. Even if the unborn baby is human, such humans are dispensable if we are just mammals. The dignity of human life means nothing if humans have evolved by millions of years of death, disease, and bloodshed.

The Bible's position is vastly different. We did not evolve by millions of years of death, disease, and bloodshed; we are not just animals. We are special because we are made in the image of God. We are fallen from that image, certainly, but that image still sets us apart from the animals. Our certainty of the truth of Genesis provides us with the assurance that we are human, and that our humanity began at the moment of conception. It is for that reason that we oppose abortion, because it is a denial of the humanity of the unborn baby.

Further Study

Because this short chapter can only cover so much, I want to encourage you to do further study. I suggest the following resources:

www.answersingenesis.org/get-answers/topic/abortion-euthanasia

David Menton, *Fearfully and Wonderfully Made*, DVD, Answers in Genesis, 2005.

Mike Riddle, *Cloning, Stem Cells, and the Value of Life*, DVD, Answers in Genesis, 2007.

Tommy Mitchell, "When Does Life Begin," *The New Answers Book 2* (Green Forest, AR: Master Books, 2008), p. 313–323.

13

Is the Christian Worldview Logical?

DR. JASON LISLE

Many people have the impression that Christians live in two "worlds" — the world of faith and the world of reason. The world of faith is the realm that Christians live in on Sunday morning, or the world to which they refer when asked about spiritual or moral matters. However, it would seem that Christians live in the world of reason throughout the rest of the week, when dealing with practical, everyday matters. After all, do we really need to believe in the Bible to put gasoline in the car, or to balance our checkbook?

Misconceptions of Faith

The notion of "faith versus reason" is an example of a *false dichotomy*. Faith is not antagonistic to reason. On the contrary, biblical faith and reason go well together. The problem lies in the fact that many people have a misunderstanding of *faith*. Faith is not a belief in the absurd, nor is it a belief in something simply for the sake of believing it. Rather, faith is having confidence in something that we have not perceived with the senses. This is the biblical definition of faith, and follows from Hebrews 11:1. Whenever we have confidence in something that we cannot see, hear, taste, smell, or touch, we are acting upon a type of faith. All people have faith, even if it is not a saving faith in God.

For example, people believe in laws of logic. However, laws of logic are not material. They are abstract and cannot be experienced by the senses. We can write down a law of logic such as the law of non-contradiction ("It is impossible to have **A** and **not A** at the same time and in the same relationship."), but the sentence is only a physical representation of the law, not the law itself.[1] When people use laws of logic, they have confidence in something they cannot actually observe with the senses; this is a type of faith.

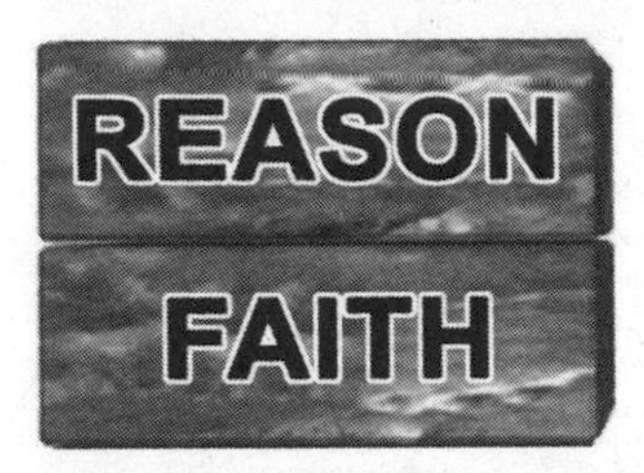

When we have confidence that the universe will operate in the future as it has in the past, we are acting on faith. For example, we all presume that gravity will work the same next Friday as it does today. But no one has actually observed the future. So we all believe in something that goes beyond sensory experience. From a Christian perspective, this is a very reasonable belief. God (who is beyond time) has promised us that He will uphold the universe in a consistent way (e.g., Genesis 8:22). So we have a good reason for our faith in the uniformity of nature. For the consistent Christian, reason and faith go well together.

It is appropriate and biblical to have a good reason for our faith (1 Peter 3:15). Indeed, God encourages us to *reason* (Isaiah 1:18). The apostle Paul *reasoned* with those in the synagogue and those in the marketplace (Acts 17:17). According to the Scriptures, the Christian faith is not a "blind faith." It is a faith that is rationally defensible. It is logical and self-consistent. It can make sense of what we experience in the world. Moreover, the Christian has a moral obligation to think rationally. We are to be imitators of God (Ephesians 5:1), patterning our thinking after His revelation (Isaiah 55:7–8; Psalm 36:9).

The Mark of Rationality

There are those who would challenge the rationality of the biblical worldview. Some say that the Christian worldview is illogical on the face of it. After all, the Bible speaks of floating ax heads, the sun apparently going backward, a universe created in six days, an earth that has pillars and corners, people walking on water, light before the sun, a talking serpent, a talking donkey, dragons, and a senior citizen taking two of every land animal on a big boat! The critic suggests that no rational person can possibly believe in such things in our modern age of scientific enlightenment. He claims that to believe in such things would be *illogical.*

The Bible does make some extraordinary claims. But are such claims truly *illogical*? Do they actually violate any laws of logic? Although the above biblical examples go beyond our ordinary, everyday experiences, none of them are

1. Otherwise, when you erase the sentence, the law would cease to exist!

contradictory. They do not violate any laws of logic. Some biblical criticisms involve a misuse of language: taking figures of speech (e.g., "pillars of the earth") as though these were literal, when this is clearly not the case. This is an error on the part of the critic, not an error in the text. Poetic sections of the Bible, such as the psalms, and figures of speech should be taken as such. To do otherwise is academically dishonest.

Most of the criticisms against the Bible's legitimacy turn out to be nothing more than a subjective opinion of what is possible. The critic arbitrarily asserts that it is not possible for the sun to go backward in the sky, or for the solar system to be created in six days. But what is his evidence for this? He might argue that such things cannot happen based on known natural laws. With this we agree. But who said that natural laws are the limit of what is possible? The biblical God is not bound by natural laws. Since the Bible is indeed correct about the nature of God, then there is no problem at all in God reversing the direction of the planets, or creating the solar system in six days. An infinitely powerful, all-knowing God can do anything that is rationally possible.

Non-Christian circles of reasoning are ultimately self-defeating. They do not pass their own test.

When the critic simply dismisses those claims of the Bible that do not appeal to his personal, unargued sense of what is possible, he is being irrational. He is committing the logical fallacy known as "begging the question." Namely, he has decided in advance that such things as miracles are impossible, thereby tacitly assuming that the Bible is not true because it contains miracles. But this is the very assumption with which he began his reasoning. The critic is reasoning in a vicious circle. He has decided in advance that there is not an all-powerful God who is capable of doing the things recorded in Scripture, and then argues on this basis against the biblical God. Such reasoning is not cogent at all. So, when the critic accuses the Bible of being illogical because it goes against his subjective assessment of what is possible, it turns out that it is the critic — not the Bible — who is being illogical.

When people argue that something in the Bible seems strange or unreasonable, we must always ask, "strange or unreasonable *by what standard*?" If it is merely the critic's personal, arbitrary opinion, then we must politely point out that this has no logical merit whatsoever. Personal feelings are not the limit of what is true or possible. In fact, since all the treasures of knowledge are in Christ (Colossians 2:3), it turns out that God Himself is the limit of what is possible. His Word is therefore the standard of what is reasonable, and we have no independent (and non-arbitrary) standard by which we can judge the Word of God.

The Laws of Logic

The extraordinary claims of Scripture cannot be dismissed merely on the basis that they are extraordinary. If indeed the biblical God exists, and if indeed He has the characteristics attributed to Him by the Bible (all-knowing, all-powerful, beyond time, etc.) then the critic has no basis whatsoever for denying that the miraculous is possible. Clearly, an all-powerful God can make a donkey talk, can create the universe in six days, can bring two of every animal to Noah, etc. These are simply not problems in the biblical worldview. When the critic dismisses the miraculous solely on the basis that it is miraculous, he is simply begging the question.

Everyone has an ultimate standard, whether he realizes it or not. If it is not the Bible, it will be something else.

However, sometimes the critic asserts that the Bible has actually violated a law of logic; he claims that two passages in the Scriptures are contradictory. This is a more serious challenge, because two contradictory statements cannot both be true — even in principle. If the Bible actually endorsed two contradictory statements, then necessarily one of them would have to be false, and the Bible could not be totally inerrant. In reality, most alleged contradictions turn out to be nothing of the kind. They simply reveal that the critic does not truly understand what a contradiction is. A contradiction is "**A** and **not A** at the same time and in the same relationship" where **A** is any proposition. To contradict is to both affirm and deny the same proposition. And this is not the nature of most alleged biblical contradictions. (See the contradictions series on the Answers in Genesis website for more information on this.) Here's an example:

The fact that Christ has two genealogies is not contradictory. Indeed, all people have (at least) two genealogies — one through their dad, and one through their mom. Some people have more than two because their biological father may not be their legal father. The fact that Jesus was born in Bethlehem, but is nonetheless "of Nazareth" is no contradiction since Jesus did grow up in Nazareth. The fact that Matthew (8:28) mentions two demon-possessed men does not contradict the fact that Mark (5:2) and Luke (8:27) chose to mention only one of the two. Perhaps one was much more violent than the other; in any case, there is no contradiction.

Alleged Contradictions Demonstrate That the Bible Is True!

Amazingly, when the critic asserts that the Bible contains contradictions, he has unwittingly refuted his own position, and has demonstrated that the Bible is true. The reason is this: the truth of the Bible is the only cogent reason to believe in the law of non-contradiction. Virtually everyone believes in the law of non-contradiction. We all "know" that two contradictory statements cannot both be true. But have you ever thought about *why* this is?

The law of non-contradiction stems from the nature of the biblical God. God does not deny Himself (2 Timothy 2:13), and all knowledge is in God (Colossians 2:3), thus true knowledge will not contradict itself. The law of non-contradiction (as with all laws of logic) is a universal, invariant law because God Himself upholds the entire universe (Hebrews 1:3), and God does not change with time (Hebrews 13:8). We know these things because God has revealed them in His Word. Thus, the Bible is the only objective basis for knowing that the law of non-contradiction is universally and invariantly true in all situations.

Therefore, when the unbeliever applies the law of non-contradiction, he is implicitly standing upon the Christian worldview. Even when he argues against the Bible, the critic must use God's standard of reasoning in order to do it. The fact that the critic is able to argue at all demonstrates that he is wrong. God alone is the correct standard for reasoning because all truth is in Him. We must therefore start with God as revealed in His Word in order to have genuine knowledge (Proverbs 1:7), whether we admit this truth or suppress it (Romans 1:18). So while it may seem at first that we do not need to believe the Bible in order to put gasoline into the car or to balance our checkbook, implicitly we must indeed rely upon the Bible. Without God as revealed in the Bible, there would be no rational basis for the laws of logic upon which we depend in order to function in our everyday life.

Since rationality itself stems from the nature of the biblical God, it follows that the Christian worldview is necessarily rational. This isn't to say that all Christians are rational all the time. We do not always follow God's standard in practice, even though God has saved us by His grace. Nonetheless, the Christian worldview as articulated in the Scriptures is fully logical and without error. This must be the case since the Bible is the inspired Word of the infallible God. It also follows that non-biblical worldviews are inherently illogical; they deny implicitly or explicitly the revelation of the biblical God in whom are deposited all the treasures of wisdom and knowledge (Colossians 2:3).

Although non-biblical worldviews may have "pockets" of rationality within them, they must ultimately appeal to Scripture as a basis for laws of logic, which they then deny as the one and only inspired Word of God. So not only is the Christian worldview logical, it is the *only* worldview that is ultimately, consistently logical. The Christian has faith — he believes in things (such as the accounts of Scripture) that he has not personally observed by sensory experience. But he has a very good reason to believe in the Scriptures; the biblical God alone makes reason possible. So a good reason for my faith is that my faith makes reason possible.

The unbeliever must use Christian principles to argue against the Bible. The fact that he is able to argue at all proves that he is wrong.

The non-Christian does not have a good reason for his beliefs. He has a type of faith, too, but his faith is "blind." He is without an apologetic (a defense of his faith) such that he has no excuse for his beliefs (Romans 1:20). In the essay, "My Credo," Cornelius Van Til cogently argued that "Christianity alone is reasonable for men to hold. It is wholly irrational to hold any other position than that of Christianity. Christianity alone does not slay reason on the altar of 'chance.' "

Yes, the Christian worldview is logical. But what's more, only the Christian worldview is logical. Competing systems of thought cannot account for laws of logic and their properties, the ability of the human mind to access and use laws of logic, or the moral obligation to reason logically. Such truths are entirely contingent upon Almighty God as objectively revealed in the Bible.

14

What about Cloning and Stem Cells?

DR. TOMMY MITCHELL AND DR. GEORGIA PURDOM

There are few issues in our society that raise as many emotional and ethical concerns as cloning and stem cells. Scientists, journalists, special interest groups, and even patients themselves regularly bombard us with their particular views on this issue. How are we to know what to think regarding these issues? How do we separate fact from fiction? Since cloning and stem cells are two separate (but related) issues, we will deal with them individually.

What Is Cloning?

Cloning is a process by which a genetically identical copy of a gene, an entire cell, or even an organism is produced. For this chapter, we will confine the discussion primarily to the cloning of an entire organism. This is a topic about which there is much misinformation. It is also a subject that raises some very serious ethical issues.

Cloning as usually understood is an artificial process, meaning it is carried out in a laboratory setting. It can and does, however, occur regularly in nature. There are organisms (e.g., bacteria, protists, and some plants) that typically reproduce by asexual reproduction. Here a genetically identical copy of the parent is produced by the splitting of a single cell (the parent cell).

Identical twins are also clones. In fact, identical twins have been called "natural clones" since splitting of a fertilized egg causes this, producing two copies of the same organism.

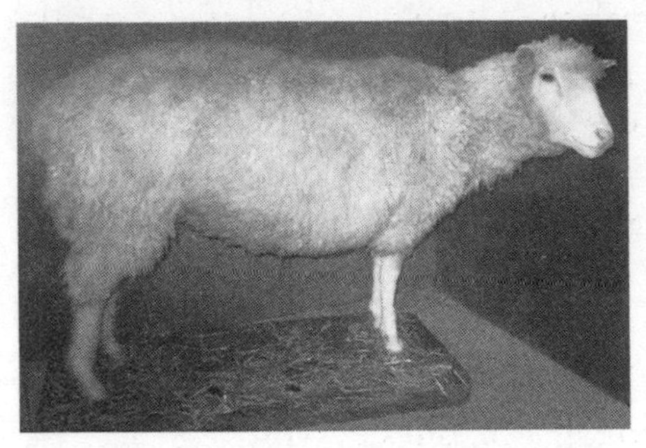

Dolly was the result of cloning a mammary cell from a mature sheep, but at what cost?

It is the issue of artificial cloning that has captured the interest of so many in our society. This process has garnered much attention in recent years, especially with the birth of the famous sheep, Dolly. Actually, many different types of animals have been cloned including tadpoles, mice, cats, sheep, cattle, a horse, and others.

How Is a Clone Made?

The simplest method for making a clone is to remove the nucleus (containing the organism's DNA) from a somatic (body) cell in the animal you want to clone. You then take an egg cell (from the same type of animal) that has had its own nucleus removed, and you place the donor nucleus into the egg cell. This is called somatic cell nuclear transfer (SCNT). This egg is grown briefly in a test tube and then implanted into the womb of an adult animal. If there are no complications, at the end of gestation an animal is born with an identical genetic makeup of the donor animal. As one might imagine, the process is technically quite difficult. Let's use the aforementioned Dolly as an example. It took 277 eggs that ultimately produced 29 embryos and only one living sheep to create Dolly.[1] This is consistent with the failure rate for other animals. As can be seen, many embryos are wasted in these attempts.

It should also be noted that Dolly died at age six. She apparently died of a respiratory infection. Some have suggested that she exhibited signs of premature aging, but others have disputed these reports. The strongest speculation is that her early death was due to shortening of telomeres. Telomeres are segments of DNA that exist on the ends of chromosomes. They progressively shorten with age due to repeated cell division until they reach a point that no further replication of the chromosome can occur. Since Dolly was cloned from a 6-year-old sheep, it could be said that Dolly's DNA when she died was actually 12 years old. The telomere issue remains a significant problem for those involved in cloning research.

How Can Cloning Be Used?

There are two main purposes for cloning: to produce an identical organism (reproductive cloning) or to produce a cloned embryo for the purpose of obtaining embryonic stem cells (therapeutic cloning). There are those who promote reproductive cloning in many different areas. For example, cloning of

1. www.en.wikipedia.org/wiki/Cloning

certain animals used for food or for animals used in specific work environments has been suggested. This has also been proposed as a possible solution for the rescue of many endangered species. Although it is far beyond our present technology, some have theorized that the extinct woolly mammoth or even dinosaurs might in the future be produced through reproductive cloning!

Therapeutic cloning is aimed at producing cloned embryos from which embryonic stem cells may be obtained. This is done ostensibly to use the stem cells to treat disease or illness. While this is laudable in one sense, there are serious ethical issues that arise (see the following stem cell section).

The obvious next step would be to consider cloning a human being. There are those who advocate therapeutic cloning of humans to provide an adequate supply of embryonic stem cells. It has even been suggested by some that humans should be reproductively cloned in order to provide a ready reserve of tissues and organs should they ever be needed. The clone would simply be "spare parts," to be used at the discretion of the "parent" human.

So What's the Problem?

If man is just another animal, just a higher form of pond scum, there really is no problem. Cloning a person is totally justifiable. Just make copies of ourselves and chop them up as we please. People are nothing special.

But those of us who trust in God's Word know there is a problem here. We are not just a higher form of pond scum. We are not just animals. We are made in the image of the Creator.

> And God said, "Let us make man in our image, after our likeness . . ." (Genesis 1:26; ASV).

Therefore, humans are not to be created at man's whim. Rather, we are a special creation of our Father in heaven.

What Is a Stem Cell?

Simply put, a stem cell is a cell in the body (or in an embryo) that has the capability of turning into many specialized cell types. At the time of conception, when the sperm and egg unite, we consist of only one cell. Ultimately, as this cell divides into two cells, then four, then eight, and so on, the roughly 200 different cell types in the body must be produced. This process can occur because of stem cells.

The very earliest cells produced after fertilization are called *totipotent* because they have the capability of turning into any other cell type in the body as well as extra-embryonic cell types such as those which form the placenta. As cells divide and begin to specialize (a process called differentiation), the stem cells along these pathways lose the ability to produce certain types of cells. At this point they are called *pluripotent* in that they can still develop into all the tissue types of the body but not the extra-embryonic tissue types. After further differentiation, the cells become *multipotent*, meaning the number of potential cell types that can be derived from them has been reduced. This process continues until cells are only able to produce cells of one type.

Along the way, some stem cells stop differentiating and merely reproduce themselves, thereby giving the body a reservoir of stem cells. These cells then provide a source of new cells for tissue replacement and repair.

Why Are Stem Cells Important?

Medical researchers are interested in stem cells for their potential to treat various diseases. For example, stem cells that could be induced to change into insulin-secreting cells could help cure those with diabetes. Patients with damage to the spinal cord could benefit from new nerve tissue generated from stem cells. Those suffering from heart muscle damage after a heart attack might be able to have new heart muscle derived from stem cells. Think about Parkinson's disease, multiple sclerosis, Alzheimer's disease . . . the list of potential interventions based on stem cell therapy seems almost endless.

This research is very important. It is certainly one of the most exciting medical advances in our lifetime. Physicians strive to relieve the suffering of their patients. Who among them would not want to have available a means to cure many horrible diseases? This research has so much potential. However, that potential comes with a grave concern. That concern revolves around how we obtain these stem cells.

How Are Stem Cells Obtained?

In order to understand the basis of the debate over stem cell research, one must understand that there are two basic types of stem cells: embryonic stem cells (ESC) and adult stem cells (ASC).

Embryonic stem cells are, as you would expect from their name, derived from embryos. Four to five days after fertilization, the embryo consists of a hollow ball of cells called a blastocyst. It is from this ball of cells that all the body's tissues are ultimately derived. To harvest embryonic stem cells, the embryo is disrupted (killed) and the cells collected. As this cell harvest occurs very early in development, very little differentiation of the stem cells would have taken place. These cells would be considered pluripotent.

Adult stem cells, on the other hand, are not necessarily derived from "adults." This is somewhat confusing to many as adult stem cells can be obtained from any fully formed person, whether newborn, infant, child, or adult. These cells can be found in many tissues in the body: bone marrow, skin, teeth, liver, brain, intestines, blood vessels, skeletal muscle, among others.

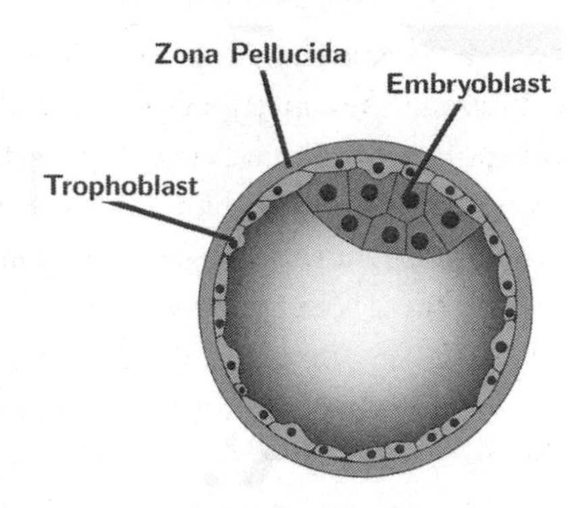

While an embryo must be killed in order to harvest embryonic stem cells, harvesting adult stem cells does not lead to the death of the donor.

The concern regarding adult stem cells is that these cells could have limitations on the types of tissues that could be obtained from them. In theory, these stem cells are further down the path of differentiation (they would be multipotent rather than pluripotent), thus limiting their potential usefulness in medical research and intervention.

How Are Stem Cells Used?

After being isolated, stem cells are then grown in laboratory culture. They are placed in dishes containing a special culture medium. The cells divide and multiply. The initial phase of the process would be designed to grow an adequate supply of the stem cells themselves.

So how are different tissue types generated from stem cells? There are many different methods used to cause a stem cell to differentiate into a specific cell type. Manipulation of the culture medium can guide this process. Other research techniques include hormonal stimulation or genetic modification of the stem cells. This is still an area of intensive investigation, with new techniques becoming available seemingly every few months.

As an example, let's select a patient who has suffered a heart attack. A portion of the heart muscle has been damaged or killed as a result of this event. It would certainly be to the patient's benefit to be able to repair the heart muscle. In this situation, the patient's medical team might choose to intervene with stem cell therapy. Stem cells could be induced to differentiate into heart muscle cells. These cells could then be administered to the patient in hopes of improving the function of the damaged heart. This type of intervention is, in fact, taking place at this time.[2] The results have been very promising thus far.

2. Medical News Today, "First Human Receives Cardiac Stem Cells in Clinical Trial to Heal Damage Caused By Heart Attacks," July 1, 2009, www.medicalnewstoday.com/articles/155915.php.

Depending on the particular situation, the stem cells might be given intravenously,[3] by injection or direct deposit of the cells into the target site, given by intracoronary injection (for cardiac intervention), or injection into the spinal fluid (for neurologic problems). The hope for the future is that by using stem cells, entire organs might be grown for transplant. Again, research in this area is promising.

Are There Problems with Stem Cell Treatments?

As with any new research endeavor, there are pitfalls associated with stem cell research. While we tout the successes, we should also be aware of the problems and limitations.

Several major issues have limited embryonic stem cell therapy. First of all, in laboratory animals, embryonic stems cell have shown a tendency to form tumors. The reasons for this are unclear, although some have speculated that ESC can form tumors due to their tendency to associate with each other rather than with the target tissue.[4] Obviously, this is an area of intense investigation at present.

The other major issue is that of tissue rejection. As with any transplant, foreign tissue is recognized by the body as "non self." So an embryonic stem cell transplant from a random donor would be no different than a heart or a kidney transplant. After all, these embryonic stem cells would come from another person. These cells would be seen as foreign tissue by the body. Thus, anti-rejection drugs would be needed to prevent rejection of the new tissue. However, it should be noted that therapeutic cloning using a person's own cells would avoid this problem.

Adult stem cells apparently do not have the problem of tumor formation. Therapy with ASC would also not have the problem of tissue rejection as long as the stem cells are harvested from the patients themselves.[5]

That is not to say that intervention with adult stem cells is without problems. The main problem is that even though ASC can be found in many body tissues, they occur in very small numbers and can be quite difficult to isolate. Thus, obtaining an adequate supply of ASC for a given therapeutic intervention can be difficult. The most often claimed problem with adult stem cells is the supposed limitation on the number of tissue types that can be derived from them. Since embryonic stem cells have undergone less initial differentiation, there is the potential to derive all needed cell types from ESC. Thus, it would

3. This has the problem of the so-called "first pass effect" where the cells given are filtered out of the circulation by the lungs.
4. Joseph Panno, *Stem Cell Research* (New York, NY: Facts on File, 2005), p. 9.
5. ASC therapy using cells from another person would encounter that same rejection potential as ESC.

stand to reason that ASC are more limited.

However, actual research does not bear out these claims. Adult stem cells have, to date, been used to generate almost every different cell type in the body.[6] It has been shown that adult stem cells of one cell lineage can be induced to produce cells in another. For example, blood-forming stem cells in bone marrow can differentiate into cardiac muscle cells, etc.[7] Some multipotent adult stem cells have been induced to revert to an apparent pluripotent state, and have subsequently produced many more cell types than would have been predicted. So while this may have seemed a problem in theory, it has not been a problem in practice.

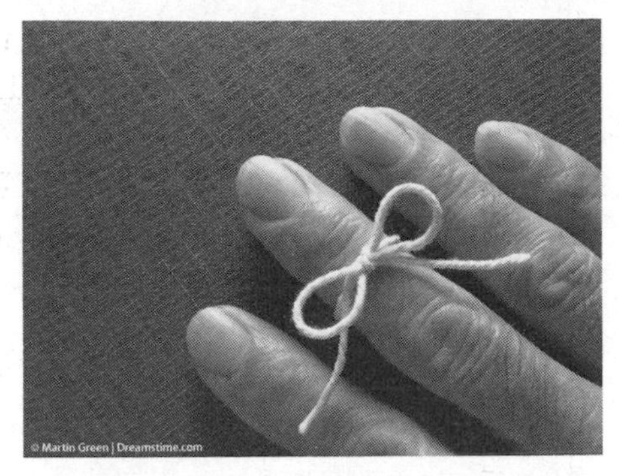

Although adult stem cells have their problems, they have produced far more success than embryonic trials. Alzheimer's and other degenerative diseases are prime candidates for such research.

Should Both ESC and ASC Research and Treatments Be Pursued?

So should we not pursue any avenue we can to help the sick and the dying? Do we not want stem cell therapy to succeed? Certainly we want to help the sick. We want medical science to progress. But we must also examine the facts and ask the question, "At what cost?"

First of all, what can be said for adult stem cell research? Simply this: adult stem cell therapy has been used to treat over 70 diseases to date. Some stem cell therapies have been used for over 40 years.[8] ASC have a proven track record with the hope of greater successes to come. Thus far the only significant clinical interventions available are from using adult stem cells. For some reason the media, when reporting on these issues, has consistently downplayed these successes and even implied that these successes are the result of embryonic stem cell research rather than adult stem cell research.

Embryonic stem cells, on the other hand, despite the regularly reported theoretical benefits, have yet to achieve any significant clinical success. Those in favor of ESC argue that given time these advances will come. Perhaps this is so, but again we need to ask, "At what cost?"

6. "Adult Stem Cell Pluripotency," www.stemcellresearch.org/facts/ASCRPlasticity.pdf.
7. "Stem Cell Basics," National Institutes of Health, Stem Cell Information, www.stemcells.nih.gov/info/basics/basics4.asp.
8. Specifically those involving blood-forming stem cells for bone marrow diseases.

What Is the Cost of Embryonic Stem Cell Research?

Although one could point to the lack of success of embryonic stem cell research, in spite of the years and countless dollars invested in it, and say, "It hasn't been worth the cost," the biggest cost is yet to be counted. The cost is that of human life.

As has been noted, embryonic stem cells are obtained by the destruction of an embryo. An embryo is fully human. So in order to get these stem cells to help one person, another person must be killed. This is simply morally unacceptable.

Scripture tells us that life begins at conception (here defined as the moment of fertilization). In His Word, God tells us:

> Then the word of the LORD came to me, saying: " Before I formed you in the womb I knew you; Before you were born I sanctified you; I ordained you a prophet to the nations" (Jeremiah 1:4–5).

> Behold, I was brought forth in iniquity, And in sin my mother conceived me (Psalm 51:5).

> For You formed my inward parts; You covered me in my mother's womb. I will praise You, for I am fearfully and wonderfully made; Marvelous are Your works, And that my soul knows very well. My frame was not hidden from You, When I was made in secret, And skillfully wrought in the lowest parts of the earth (Psalm 139:13–15).

We are told that the Lord knew us before we were conceived. We have a sin nature in the womb. How could this be if we are not fully human at the time of fertilization?

What's the Ethical Solution?

As has been shown, stem cell therapy has the potential to alleviate much suffering. It is an avenue of medical research that should be pursued in hopes of building on the successes already achieved. However, in our haste to help the sick, we must not neglect those who cannot speak for themselves. Adult stem cell therapy can allow us to fight disease without the destruction of human life.

Although everyone wants to see such devastating diseases come to an end, we all must realize our work will only lead to a temporary alleviation. Jesus Christ, the true conqueror of disease and death, will create a new heaven and a new earth where the effects of sin have been removed. That is the cure we eagerly await.

15

How Old Does the Earth Look?

DR. ANDREW A. SNELLING

Insisting that the earth and the universe are young, only 6,000 years old or so, does not make the biblical view popular in today's enlightened "scientific" culture. It would be so easy just to go along with the view believed and followed by the overwhelming majority of scientists — and taught in nearly all universities and museums around the world — that the universe is 13–14 billion years old and the earth 4.5 billion years old.

After all, many Christians and most scientists who are Christians believe in such a vast antiquity for the earth and universe. Consequently, they even insist the days in Genesis 1 were not literal days, but were countless millions of years long. Also, they claim the Genesis account of creation by God is just poetic and/or figurative, so it is not meant to be read as history.

Why a Young Age for the Earth?

Of course, the reason for insisting on a young earth and universe is because other biblical authors took Genesis as literal history and an eyewitness account provided and guaranteed accurate by the Creator Himself (2 Timothy 3:16a; 2 Peter 1:21). Jesus also took Genesis as literal history (Mark 10:6–9; Matthew 19:4–5; Luke 17:27). So, the outcome of letting Scripture interpret Scripture is a young earth and universe.

The Hebrew language and context used in Genesis 1 can only mean literal (24 hour) days.[1] Furthermore, as history, the genealogies in Genesis 5 and 11 provide an accurate chronology, so that from the creation of the first man, Adam, to the present day is only about 6,000 years. Since the earth was only created five literal days before Adam, then on the authority of God's Word, the earth is only about 6,000 years old.

Does the Earth Look Old?

Nevertheless, most people, including Christians, would still claim dogmatically that the earth *looks* old. But why does the earth supposedly look old? And how old does the earth really look? If we rightly ask such questions, then we are likely to get closer to the right answers.

The use of the word *looks* gives us the necessary clue to finding the answers. Looking at an object and making a judgment about it requires two operations by the observer. There is first the observation of the object with one's eyes. Light impulses then go from the eyes to be processed by one's brain. How one's brain interprets what has been seen through one's eyes is dependent on what information is already stored in the brain. Such information has been progressively acquired and stored in our brains since birth. So, for example, as a child we learn what a rock is by being shown a rock.

We observe that a sandstone is made of sand cemented together, and we see a trilobite fossil inside the sandstone (figure 1), so we wonder how the trilobite came to be fossilized in the sandstone and how both the sandstone and the trilobite fossil formed. However, we never actually observed either the trilobite being buried by sand and fossilized or the deposition of the sand and its cementation into sandstone. Therefore, we don't really know how and when

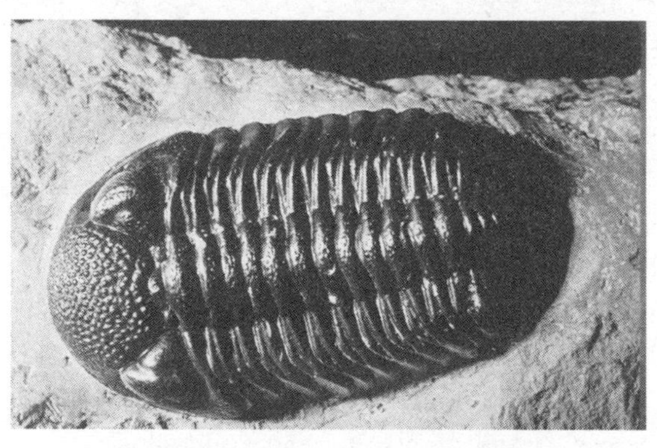

Figure 1. A trilobite fossil in a piece of sandstone

1. S.W. Boyd, "Statistical Determination of Genre in Biblical Hebrew: Evidence for an Historical Reading of Genesis 1:1–2:3," *Radioisotopes and the Age of the Earth: Results of a Young-Earth Creationist Research Initiative*, L. Vardiman, A.A. Snelling, and E.F. Chaffin, eds. (El Cajon, CA: Institute for Creation Research and Chino Valley, AZ: Creation Research Society, 2005), p. 631–734.

the trilobite fossil and the sandstone formed — so just by looking at them we really don't know how old they are.

How, then, can we work out how old they might be and how they formed? Because we can't go back to the past, it *seems* logical to think in terms of what we see happening around us today — in the present. Today, rivers slowly erode land surfaces and gradually transport the sand downstream to their mouths, where they build deltas. The sediments also are eventually spread gradually out on the seafloor, where bottom-dwelling creatures like trilobites could perhaps be occasionally buried and then fossilized.

So with this apparently logical scenario in our minds, based on our everyday experience, when we look at that piece of sandstone with the trilobite fossil in it, it seems totally reasonable to conclude that, because it took such a long time to erode and transport the sand and then deposit it to bury and fossilize the trilobite, the sandstone and trilobite fossil must be very old. Perhaps they may even be millions of years old. However, it needs to be remembered that there are no particular intrinsic features of the sandstone and the trilobite fossil that are incontestably diagnostic of any supposed great age. The conclusion that they must be old wasn't because they actually look old, but because it was assumed they took a long time to form based on present-day experience.

Long Age Reasoning Questioned

Now let's extend this reasoning to the earth itself. Why is it that most people think the earth looks old? Isn't it because they *assume* it took a long time to form based on their present-day experience of geological processes? After all, volcanic eruptions only occur sporadically today, so the vast, thick lava flows stacked on top of one another — for example, in the USA's Pacific Northwest — *must* have taken a long time to accumulate. However, this reasoning is wrong for three very valid reasons:

First, it ignores the fact that we *cannot* go back to the past to actually verify by direct observations that vast, thick stacks of lava flows — and sandstones with trilobite fossils — took a long time to form millions of years ago. The inference that the present is the key to the past is only an assumption, not a fact.

Second, that assumption deliberately ignores the fact that we do have direct eyewitnesses from the past who have told us what did happen to the earth and how old it really is. The Bible claims to be the communication to us of the Creator God who has always existed. Its authenticity is overwhelmingly verified by countless exactly fulfilled predictions, archeological and scientific evidences, corroborating eyewitness accounts, and the changed lives and testimonies of Bible-believing Christians. In Genesis 1–11, it is revealed how to calculate the age of the earth, and how rock layers and fossils were rapidly and recently formed in the year-long, global, catastrophic Flood.

And third, there is now abundant scientific evidence that rock layers and fossils can only form rapidly due to catastrophic geological processes not usually seen today, and not on the scale they must have occurred at in the past.[2]

Catastrophism Today

Geologists are always studying present-day geological processes, including rare catastrophic events, such as floods, earthquakes, and violent volcanic eruptions. Such processes have been observed to produce and change geological features very rapidly; so geologists have learned not to ignore such currently rare catastrophic events when interpreting how the earth's features were produced in the past.

Further examples of why most people think the earth looks old are river valleys and canyons. Because the rivers in most valleys and canyons today seem to only slowly and imperceptibly erode their channels, even during occasional floods, most people assume it must have taken millions of years to erode valleys and canyons.

However, the observational realities are more instructive than such an erroneous assumption. For example, since the Colorado River today does not erode its channel, the only truly viable explanation for the carving of Grand Canyon is rapid catastrophic erosion on an enormous scale by dammed waters left over from the global Genesis Flood.[3] Such rapid catastrophic erosion carving canyons has even been observed. As a result of the 1980 and subsequent eruptions at Mount St. Helens, up to 600 feet of rock layers rapidly accumulated nearby. A mudflow on March 18, 1982, eroded a canyon system over 100 feet deep in these sediment layers, resulting in a one-fortieth scale model of the real Grand Canyon (figure 2).[4]

2. S.A. Austin, "Interpreting Strata of Grand Canyon," in *Grand Canyon: Monument to Catastrophe*, S. A. Austin, ed. (Santee, CA: Institute for Creation Research, 1994), p. 21–56; A.A. Snelling, "The World's a Graveyard," *Answers*, April–June, p. 76–79; J.H. Whitmore, "Aren't Millions of Years Required for Geological Processes?" *The New Answers Book 2*, Ken Ham, ed. (Green Forest, AR: Master Books, 2008), p. 229–244.
3. S.A. Austin, "How was Grand Canyon Eroded?" in *Grand Canyon: Monument to Catastrophe*, S.A. Austin, ed. (Santee, CA: Institute for Creation Research, 1994), p. 83–110. See also chapter 18 in this volume, "When and How Did the Grand Canyon Form?"
4. S.A. Austin, "Mount St. Helens and Catastrophism," *Proceedings of the First International Conference on Creationism*, vol. 1 (Pittsburgh, PA: Creation Science Fellowship, 1986), p. 3–9.

Figure 2. This canyon system, with 100-foot high cliffs, was eroded adjacent to Mount St. Helens in less than a day!

Uniformitarianism Predicted

In 2 Peter 3, we read a prediction that Peter made around A.D. 62 that scoffers would arise who would challenge and deny that God created the earth and subsequently destroyed the earth by the cataclysmic global Flood. Peter says they would be "willingly ignorant" and deliberately reject the evidence for a created earth and the year-long global Flood. They would claim instead that the present is the key to the past, that present-day geological processes have always operated at today's snail's pace, and that they alone are necessary to explain how rock layers and fossils formed and how old the earth is.

This prediction was actually fulfilled about 200 years ago — about 1,750 years after the prediction was made. James Hutton, a doctor and farmer-turned-geologist, claimed in his 1785 Royal Society of Edinburgh paper and 1795 book *Theory of the Earth* that he saw "no vestige of a beginning" for the earth because present-day geological processes have slowly recycled rock materials over vast eons of time. This was a deliberate rejection of the biblical account of the recent, catastrophic global Flood, up until that time accepted by most scholars to be the explanation for fossil-bearing rock layers. Indeed, Hutton insisted that "the past history of our globe *must* be explained by what can be seen happening now"[5] (emphasis added).

It was Charles Lyell, a lawyer-turned-geologist, with his two-volume *Principles of Geology* (1830–33), who eventually convinced the geological establishment to abandon the biblical Flood in favor of this "principle" he called uniformitarianism. Lyell openly declared that he wanted to remove the influence of Moses (the human author of Genesis) from geology, revealing his motivation was spiritual, *not* scientific.[6] He insisted on the uniformity through time of natural processes only at today's rates — a belief that was later encapsulated in the phrase "the present is the key to the past."

This is the belief that now underpins virtually all modern geological explanations about the earth and its rock layers. And it is a *belief* because it cannot be proved that *only* today's geological processes can explain the earth's history and determine its age. No one has ever observed past geological processes, except for God — and Noah and his family — during the Flood when these processes were definitely catastrophic on a global scale. Yet most people today, even Christians, have unwittingly imbibed this uniformitarian belief, having been brainwashed by the constant barrage of teaching over many decades by the world's education systems (schools, colleges, and universities), museums, and media (newspapers, magazines, television, and even Hollywood). Indeed, most people automatically see the earth as old because they have accepted it is a proven scientific fact that it is old!

Using the Right Glasses

However, based on the authority of God's Word, we can dogmatically say they are absolutely wrong. Looking at the world through "glasses" that are based on human reasoning alone (man's word) makes people wrongly think the earth looks really old. On the other hand, when we as Christians see the world through the biblical "glasses" provided by God's inerrant Word — so that we

5. A. Holmes, *Principles of Physical Geology*, second ed. (London: Thomas Nelson and Sons, 1965), p. 43–44, 163.
6. R.S. Porter, "Charles Lyell and the Principles of the History of Geology," *British Journal for the History of Science*, IX, 32 no. 2 (1976): 91–103.

see the world as God sees it — we can assert unashamedly that the earth does not really look that old at all, being only about 6,000 years old (which, of course, is young). Indeed, the earth we see today is the way it looks because it is the destroyed remains of the original earth God created, still marred by the subsequent Curse.

Furthermore, not only should we understand that the Bible provides the true history of the earth, but that history tells us the earth only looks the way it does today because of what happened in the past. In other words, the past is the key to the present!

Conclusion

Paul, in 2 Corinthians 11:3, warns us about the way Satan subtly beguiled the mind of Eve in the Garden of Eden by questioning and twisting God's Word. Today, Satan has subtly beguiled so many people, including Christians, by twisting the clear testimony of God's Word that "the past is the key to the present" into "the present is the key to the past." And just as he used the appealing look of the fruit on that tree to entice Eve, so he uses the snail's pace of geological processes today to make people doubt or deny what God has told us about the young age of the earth and His eyewitness account of the formation of the rock layers and fossils.

It also must be emphasized that even though we must trust God and His Word by faith alone (Hebrews 11:3), it is neither an unreasonable nor a subjective faith. This is because God is not a man that He should lie, so the evidence we see in God's world will always ultimately be consistent with what we read in God's Word. Thus, when we put on our biblical "glasses," we should be able to immediately see and recognize the overwhelming evidence that the earth looks (and is) young and that the earth's fossil-bearing rock layers are a product of the global, catastrophic Flood.

After all, if the Genesis Flood really did occur, what evidence would we look for? Genesis 7 says all the high hills and mountains under the whole heaven were covered by the water from the fountains of the great deep and the global torrential rainfall so that all land-dwelling, air-breathing creatures not on the ark perished. Wouldn't we, therefore, expect to find the remains of billions of plants and creatures buried in rock layers rapidly laid down by water all around the earth? Yes, of course! And that's exactly what we find — billions of rapidly buried fossils in rock layers up on the continents, rapidly deposited by the ocean waters rising up and over the continents all around the earth. This confirms that the rocks and fossils aren't millions of years old — and neither is the earth.

So how old does the earth look? If we look at the earth through the "glasses" of human reasoning — that only snail-paced present geological processes can explain the past — then the earth does indeed look old. However, that autonomous human reasoning blatantly denies what God's Word clearly tells us about the true age of the God-created earth and about what happened in the recent past during the global, cataclysmic Flood, which is the key to understanding why the earth looks the way it does today.

16

Does Evolution Have a . . . *Chance*?

MIKE RIDDLE

> One has only to contemplate the magnitude of this task to concede that the spontaneous generation of a living organism is impossible. Yet we are here — as a result, I believe, of spontaneous generation.[1] — George Wald, Nobel Laureate

In today's culture, molecules-to-man evolution is being taught as a fact, even though it is known to "go against the odds." But few realize the odds they are up against! And they are immense!

The Bible teaches that God is the Creator of all things (Genesis 1; Colossians 1:16; John 1:1–3; Revelation 4:11). While these passages rule out any possibility of Darwinian evolution, they do allow for variation within a created kind. But there is much opposition to what the Bible teaches. People holding to evolution would argue that random chance events, natural selection, and billions of years are sufficient to account for the universe and all life forms.

Do You Believe in "Magic"?

Most people recognize "magic" as an illusionary feat or trickery by sleight of hand. But how far are you willing to go to believe something can happen by

1. George Wald [biochemist and winner of Noble Prize in Physiology or Medicine, 1967], "The Origin of Life," *Scientific American* 191 no. 48 (1954): 46.

"dumb luck" or chance? For example, if I were to roll a die and have it come up six three times in a row, would you consider that lucky? How about if I rolled six ten times in a row? Now you might suspect that I am using some trickery or that the die is weighted.

How far are we willing to go to accept something as a chance occurrence or before we recognize that it was just an illusion? We can test this by measuring our *credulity factor*. Credulity is the willingness to believe something on little evidence.

Measuring Our Credulity Factor against Evolution

Evolutionists state that life originated by natural processes about 3.8 billion years ago. Is there any evidence for this happening? Freeman Dyson, theoretical physicist, mathematician, and member of the U.S. National Academy of Sciences states:

> Concerning the origin of life itself, the watershed between chemistry and biology, the transition between lifeless chemical activity and organized biological metabolism, there is no direct evidence at all. The crucial transition from disorder to order left behind no observable traces.[2]

Since the origin of life has never been observed, this is a major hurdle! We are left with the question, "Is the origin of life by naturalistic processes possible?" This can, in part, be tested by examining two areas:

1. The success of scientists in creating life or the components of a living cell.
2. The probability that such an event could occur.

The Structural Unit of Living Organisms – The Cell

Cells are made up of thousands of components. One of these components is protein. Proteins are large molecules made up of a chain of amino acids. In order to get a protein useful for life, the correct amino acids must be linked together in the right order. How easy is this and does it happen naturally? It turns out that this is not an easy process. There are large hurdles that evolutionary processes must overcome in order to build a biological protein.

2. Freeman Dyson, *Origins of Life* (New York, NY: Cambridge University Press, 1999), p. 36.

Protein molecules contain very specific arrangements of amino acids. Even one missing or incorrect amino acid can lead to problems with the protein's function.

Making Mathematics Painless

Before applying mathematics and probability to the origin of life, we need to consider seven parameters that will affect the formation of a single protein.

First, there are over 300 different types of amino acids. However, only 20 different amino acids are used in life. This means that in order to have life, the selection process for building proteins must be very discriminating.

Second, each type of amino acid molecule comes in two shapes commonly referred to as left-handed and right-handed forms. Only left-handed amino acids are used in biological proteins; however, the natural tendency is for left- and right-handed amino acid molecules to bond indiscriminately.

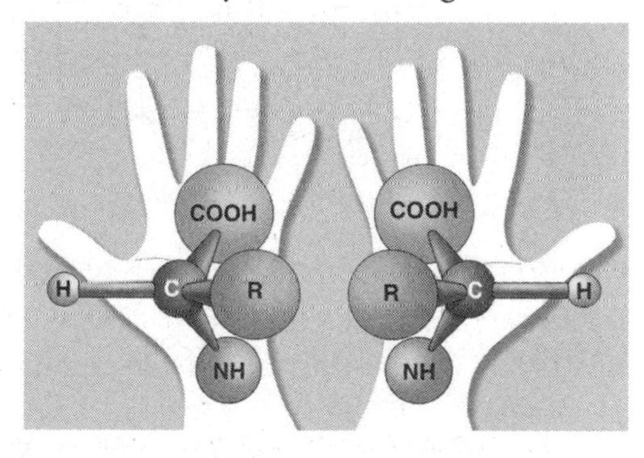

Third, the various left-handed amino acids must bond in the correct order or the protein will not function properly.[3]

Fourth, if there was a pond of chemicals ("primordial soup"), it would have been diluted with many of the wrong types of amino acids and other chemicals available for bonding, making the proper amino acids no longer usable. This means there would have been fewer of the required amino acids used to build a biological protein.

Fifth, amino acids require an energy source for bonding.[4] Raw energy from the sun needs to be captured and converted into usable energy. Where did the

3. "The order of the amino acids in a protein determines its function and whether indeed it will have a function at all." Lee Spetner, *Not By Chance* (New York, NY: Judaica Press, 1997), p. 31.
4. "The important fact that amino acids do not combine spontaneously, but require an input of energy, is a special problem." Charles Thaxton, Walter Bradley, and Roger Olsen, *The Mystery of Life's Origin* (Dallas, TX: Lewis and Stanley, 1992), p. 55.

energy converter come from? It would require energy to build this biological machine. However, before this energy converter can capture raw energy, it needs an energy source to build it — a catch-22 situation.[5]

Sixth, proteins without the protection of the cell membrane would disintegrate in water (hydrolysis), disintegrate in an atmosphere containing oxygen, and disintegrate due to the ultraviolet rays of the sun if there was no oxygen present to form the protective ozone layer.[6]

Seventh, natural selection cannot be invoked at the pre-biotic level. The first living cell must be in place before natural selection can function.

Considering all seven of these hurdles, how probable is it that a single protein could have evolved from a pool of chemicals? Probability outcomes are measured with a value ranging from zero through one. The less likely an event will happen, the smaller the value (closer to zero). The more likely an event will occur, the larger the value (closer to one).

Let's practice this using a coin. What are the chances of getting a heads when we flip a penny? The answer is 50 percent, or one chance in two (written 1/2). What is the chance of getting two heads in a row? Since each toss is 1/2 we can multiply each occurrence to get the final probability. This would be 1/2 x 1/2 which would equal 1/4 (or one chance in four). Now let's use some bigger numbers.

When we flip a coin we have two possible outcomes, heads or tails. In this problem, we want to calculate the probability of getting all heads every time we flip a coin. We can use this exercise to test our credulity factor. How many heads in a row are we willing to accept as a chance occurrence? At what point would we suspect an illusion or some form of magic (trickery)?

The objective of using probabilities is to demonstrate the probability or chance of getting a certain result. On average, how many times and how often will we need to flip the coin to achieve 100 heads in a row? *Over 300 million times a second for over one quadrillion years!*

The chances of getting all heads 100 times in a row is similar to the chance of getting 100 left-handed amino acids to form a biological protein. Proteins range in size from about 50 to over 30,000 amino acids. To get a small protein of 100 left-handed amino acids from an equal mixture of left- and right-handed amino acids, the probability would then be 10^{30} or 1 followed by 30 zeros (1,0

5. "A source of energy alone is not sufficient, however, to explain the origin or maintenance of living systems. The additional crucial factor is a means of converting this energy into the necessary useful work to build and maintain complex living systems." Thaxton, Bradley, and Olsen, *The Mystery of Life's Origin*, p. 124.
6. "What we have then is a sort of 'catch 22' situation. If we have oxygen we have no organic compounds, but if we don't have oxygen we have none either." Michael Denton, *Evolution: A Theory in Crisis* (Bethesda, MD: Adler and Adler, 1985), p. 262.

Number of desired heads in a row	Probability	Number of flips	Credulity factor (chance)
1	1/2 have	2	Yes / No
2	1/4 ($1/2^2$)	4	Yes / No
3	1/8 ($1/2^3$)	8	Yes / No
4	1/16 ($1/2^4$)	16	Yes / No
5	1/32 ($1/2^5$)	32	Yes / No
8	1/256 ($1/2^8$)	256	Yes / No
10	1/1024 ($1/2^{10}$)	1024	Yes / No
20	1/1,048,576 ($1/2^{20}$)	1,048,576	Yes / No
100	$1/10^{30}$ ($1/2^{100}$)	1 followed by 30 zeros	Yes / No

00,000,000,000,000,000,000,000,000,000). How believable (credulity factor) is it that this could happen by random chance? Also, consider that this has never been observed! Chance protein formation has always been accepted as a matter of faith by evolutionists.

But wait, there is more! This number, 10^{30}, only measures the possibility of getting all left-handed amino acids. It does not say anything about their order. In our example, we have a chain of 100 amino acids. Each position can be occupied by any 1 of 20 different amino acids common to living things, and these must be in a specific order to form a functional protein. What is the probability that the correct amino acid will be placed in position number 1 of the chain? It will be 1/20. What is the probability that the first two positions will be correct? This can be calculated by multiplying the two probabilities together ($1/20 \times 1/20 = 1/20^2$). Therefore, the probability of getting all 100 amino acids in the correct position would be 1/20 multiplied by itself 100 times or $1/20^{100}$ (this equates to $1/10^{130}$). This is 1 followed by 130 zeros!

Large numbers can be hard to visualize or even comprehend. To put this in picture format we can use a smaller number 10^{21} (1 followed by 21 zeros). If we were to take 10^{21} silver dollars and lay them on the face of the earth; they would cover the entire land surface to a depth of 120 feet.[7]

Are there upper limits for which we can logically expect an event will not occur by random chance? The mathematician Emile Borel proposed $1/10^{50}$ as

7. Peter Stoner, *Science Speaks* (Wheaton, IL: Van Kampen Press, 1952), p. 75.

a universal probability bound. This means that any specified event beyond this value would be improbable and could not be attributed to chance.[8]

As we can see, the probability of getting a single small protein ($1/10^{130}$) far exceeds this limit. Even if the protein can interchange amino acids at various positions (such as in the case of the protein cytochrome a),[9] the resulting probability still exceeds the limit of $1/10^{50}$. So far we have only looked at the probability of getting a single small protein by random chance. What are the chances of getting all the proteins necessary for life?

> No matter how large the environment one considers, life cannot have had a random beginning . . . there are about two thousand enzymes, and the chance of obtaining them all in a random trial is only one part in $(10^{20})^{2000} = 10^{40,000}$, an outrageously small probability that could not be faced even if the whole universe consisted of organic soup.[10]

This number is so large (1 followed by 40,000 zeros) that it staggers the imagination how life could have evolved by natural, random processes. Yet, people continue to hold onto their belief that life did evolve by random chance (high credulity factor).

> Time is in fact the hero of the plot. . . . What we regard as impossible on the basis of human experience is meaningless here. Given so much time, the "impossible" becomes possible, the possible probable, and the probable virtually certain. One has only to wait: time itself performs the miracles.[11]

This statement attributes supernatural qualities to *time*! It also allows for anything to happen. This means we are no longer bound by the laws of science or any other natural limits. The statement thus becomes meaningless.

8. Emile Borel, *Probabilities and Life* (New York, NY: Dover, 1962), p. 28.
9. A transport protein involved in the transfer of energy (electrons) within cells.
10. Sir Fred Hoyle and Chandra Wickramasinghe, *Evolution from Space* (London: Dent, 1981), p. 148, 24.
11. George Wald, "The Origin of Life," p.48.

Tricks of the Trade

Since scientists have been unable to create life, they are forced to speculate through research and sometimes "sleight of hand" how it might have arrived on earth. Below are some of the tricks of the trade used to avoid the obvious — that God is the Creator of all things (Colossians 1:16).

1. It happens naturally

"The formation of biological polymers from monomers is a function of the laws of chemistry and biochemistry, and these are decidedly *not* random."[12]

Explanation

This is an incorrect statement. If it happens naturally, then why can't scientists duplicate this in the lab? Amino acids do not spontaneously bond together to make proteins. First, it takes a source of energy to do this. Second, the natural tendency is to bond left- and right-handed amino acids, but life requires all left-handed amino acids. Third, they must be in the correct order or the protein will not function properly. Fourth, it requires the instructions of DNA to get the right amino acids. Where did DNA come from? Fifth, protein molecules tend to break down in the presence of oxygen or water.

2. The deck of 52 cards

In a deck of 52 playing cards there are almost 10^{68} possible orderings of the cards. If we shuffle the deck we can conclude that the possible ordering of the cards having occurred in the order we got is 1 chance in 10^{68}. This is certainly highly improbable, but we did come up with this exact order of cards. Therefore, no matter how low the probability, events can still occur and evolution is not mathematically impossible.

Explanation

In this example the math is correct but the interpretation is wrong. If the arrangement had been specified beforehand, then the actual outcome would be surprising. By shuffling the cards, the probability is one that a sequence will occur. The fallacy is that the order is predicted after the fact.

3. All the people

We are in a room of 100 people. What is the probability that all 100 people would be here in this room at this exact time? The probability is enormous, but yet we are all here.

12. Ian Musgrave, "Lies, Damned Lies, Statistics, and Probability of Abiogenesis Calculations," TalkOrigins, www.talkorigins.org/faqs/abioprob/abioprob.html.

Explanation

Two things are wrong with this reasoning. First, the people were not prespecified. This is another example of an after-the-fact prediction. Second, each person made a decision to attend; therefore, this is not a chance gathering. This turns out to be a misunderstanding between a chance event and intelligent choice.

4. Probability is not involved

Probability has nothing to do with evolution because evolution has no goal or objective.

Explanation

This statement disagrees with modern biology textbooks.

When there is more than one possible outcome and the outcome is not predetermined, probability can become a factor. In the case of evolution there is no pre-assigned chemical arrangement of amino acids to form a protein. Therefore, the formation of a biological protein is based on random chance. Scientists know today that it is only because of the instructions (information) in DNA that only left-handed amino acids are linked in the proper order.

> Cells link amino acids together into proteins, but only according to instructions encoded in DNA and carried in RNA.[13]

Both creationists and evolutionists agree that DNA is essential for linking the correct amino acids in a chain to form a protein. The unanswered question is, "Where and how did DNA acquire the enormous amount of information (instructions) to form a protein?" There is no known natural explanation that can adequately explain the origin of life, or even a single protein. The evolutionists are then left to rely on the odds (chance) that such a tremendous, improbable event occurred. Molecular biologist Michel Denton puts the event in perspective:

> Is it really credible that random processes could have constructed a reality, the smallest element of which — a functional protein or gene — is complex beyond our own creative capacities, a reality which is the very antithesis of chance, which excels in every sense anything produced by the intelligence of man?[14]

But wait, there is still more!

13. G.B. Johnson, Biology: *Visualizing Life* (Austin, TX: Holt, Rinehart, and Winston, 1998), p. 193.
14. Denton, *Evolution: A Theory in Crisis*, p. 342.

The Human Body, Time, and Evolution

It is estimated that the human body is made up of 60 trillion cells (60,000,000,000,000).[15] How long would it take to just assemble this many cells, one at a time and in no particular order at the rate of:

One per second	1.9 million years
One per minute	114 million years
One per hour	6.8 billion years

These ages assume no mistakes! However, the evolutionary mechanism is based upon random errors (mistakes) in the DNA. Also included in assembling all the 60 trillion cells is that they have to make the right organs which all have to interact.

The human body contains more than 40 billion capillaries extending over 25,000 miles, a heart that pumps over 100,000 times a day, red blood cells that transport oxygen to tissues, white blood cells that rush to identify enemy agents in the body and mark them for destruction, eyes and ears that are more complex than any man-made machine, a brain that contains over 100 trillion interconnections, plus many other parts such as the nervous system, skeleton, liver, lungs, skin, stomach, and kidneys.

The complexity and dimensions of the human body are staggering. The probability of assembling 60 trillion cells that form specific organs that all work together to form a single human being in the evolutionary time scale of 3.8 billion years is a giant leap of faith. However, an all-knowing, all-powerful Creator has told us in His Word that He is the designer.

> The hearing ear and the seeing eye, The LORD has made them both (Proverbs 20:12).

Every human body is a testimony to a purposeful Creator. As Malcolm Muggeridge said:

> One of the peculiar sins of the twentieth century which we've developed to a very high level is the sin of credulity. It has been said that when human beings stop believing in God they believe in nothing. The truth is much worse: they believe in anything.[16]

15. Boyce Rensberger, *Life Itself* (New York, NY: Oxford University Press, 1996), p. 11.
16. Malcolm Muggeridge, "An Eighth Deadly Sin," *Woman's Hour* radio broadcast, March 23, 1966. Quoted in Malcolm Muggeridge and Christopher Ralling, *Muggeridge Through the Microphone: B.B.C. Radio and Television* (London: British Broadcasting Corporation, 1967).

Conclusion

Probability arguments can present a strong argument for the existence of a Creator God. However, even when such evidence is presented to an evolutionist there is no guarantee that he or she will be persuaded. The real issue is not about evidence; it is a heart issue. As Christians we are called to have ready answers and break down strongholds that act as stumbling blocks to the unbeliever. It is the Holy Spirit that changes lives.

> But sanctify the Lord God in your hearts, and always be ready to give a defense to everyone who asks you a reason for the hope that is in you, with meekness and fear (1 Peter 3:15).

> For the weapons of our warfare are not carnal but mighty in God for pulling down strongholds, casting down arguments and every high thing that exalts itself against the knowledge of God, bringing every thought into captivity to the obedience of Christ (2 Corinthians 10:4–5).

17

What about Eugenics and Planned Parenthood?

DR. GEORGIA PURDOM

In 1915 a baby boy was born to Anna Bollinger. The baby had obvious deformities, and medical doctor Harry Haiselden decided the baby was not worth saving.[1] The baby was denied treatment and died. The story became national news and the cruelty of eugenic practices became public knowledge.

The year 1915 seems far removed from our modern times, but the concept of eugenics is alive and well. In 2005, two doctors from the Netherlands published "The Groningen Protocol — Euthanasia in Severely Ill Newborns."[2] This protocol was published to help doctors decide whether or not a newborn should be actively killed based on the newborn's disease and perceived quality of life.[3]

In this chapter we will explore historical and modern perspectives of eugenics, how Planned Parenthood has played a role in furthering the cause of

1. "A friend of Anna's asked the doctor, 'If the poor little darling has one chance in a thousand won't you operate and save it?' The doctor laughed and replied, 'I'm afraid it might get well.' " Edwin Black, *War against the Weak* (New York, NY: Four Walls Eight Windows, 2003), p. 252.
2. Eduard Verhagen and Pieter J. J. Sauer, "The Groningen Protocol — Euthanasia in Severely Ill Newborns," *New England Journal of Medicine* 352 no. 10 (2005): 959–962.
3. The doctors analyzed 22 cases of newborns with severe spina bifida that had been euthanized. What is the typical outcome for individuals with spina bifida? The March of Dimes web page on spina bifida states, "With treatment, children with spina bifida [all forms] usually can become active individuals. Most live normal or near-normal life spans." March of Dimes, "Spina Bifida," www.marchofdimes.com/pnhec/4439_1224.asp. And yet these children were considered by the doctors to not have a life worth living.

eugenics in the past and present, and what the proper biblical perspective on these issues should be.

What Is Eugenics?

The term *eugenics* was first coined in 1883 by Francis Galton, father of eugenics and cousin of Charles Darwin. The term comes from the Greek roots *eu* (good) and *genics* (in birth) to communicate the idea of being well-born.

The ultimate goal of eugenics was to create a superior race of humans.[4] Many adherents believed in evolution by natural selection, but that natural selection was moving too slowly in favoring the best and eliminating the worst.[5] They also believed that charity in the form of taking care of the poor and sick was prohibiting natural selection from working properly and thus the need to intervene with artificial selection.[6]

Artificial selection was accomplished through two types of eugenics — positive and negative. Positive eugenics focused on increasing the "fit" through promoting marriages among the well-born and promoting those fit couples to have multiple children. Negative eugenics focused on decreasing the number of the "unfit" through prohibiting birth (birth control and sterilization) and segregation (e.g., institutionalization of the unfit, marriage restriction laws, and immigration restriction).

4. Dr. John Harvey Kellogg, founder of the Race Betterment Foundation, stated, "We have wonderful new races of horses, cows, and pigs. Why should we not have a new and improved race of men?" Black, *War against the Weak*, p. 88.
5. Leading eugenicist Paul Popenoe in his 1915 paper entitled, "Natural Selection in Man," stated, "Science knows no way to make good breeding stock out of bad, and the future of the race is determined by the kind of children which are born and survive to become parents in each generation. There are only two ways to improve the germinal character of the race, to better it in a fundamental and enduring manner. One is to kill off the weaklings born in each generation. That is Nature's way, the old method of natural selection which we all agreed must be supplanted. When we abandon that, we have but one conceivable alternative, and that is to adopt some means by which fewer weaklings will be born in each generation. The only hope for permanent race betterment under social control is to substitute a selective birth-rate for Nature's selective death-rate. That means — eugenics." Steven Selden, *Inheriting Shame: The Story of Eugenics and Racism in America* (New York, NY: Teachers College Press, 1999), p. 11.
6. In her 1922 book *Pivot of Civilization*, Margaret Sanger, founder of Planned Parenthood, stated, "Organized charity itself is the symptom of a malignant social disease. Those vast, complex interrelated organizations aiming to control and to diminish the spread of misery and destitution and all the menacing evils that spring out of this sinisterly fertile soil, are the surest sign that our civilization has bred, is breeding and is perpetuating constantly increasing numbers of defectives, delinquents and dependents. My criticism, therefore, is not directed at the 'failure' of philanthropy, but rather at its success." Black, *War Against the Weak*, p. 129

History of Eugenics

Although many people associate eugenics with the late 1800s and early 1900s, it is an ancient idea that was in practice long before it was called eugenics. The Law of the Twelve Tables (449 B.C.), which served as the foundation of Roman Law, states "*Cito necatus insignis ad deformitatem puer esto,*" which means, "An obviously deformed child must be put to death."[7] Both Plato and Aristotle supported this practice[8] and it was not uncommon for infants to be exposed or left outside the home for a period of time to determine if they were fit enough to survive. The Romans wanted only the most fit for their future warriors.

Francis Galton, upon reading his cousin Charles's book *Origin of Species,* [9] decided to apply the mechanisms of natural and artificial selection to man. He stated, "Could not the undesirables be got rid of and the desirables multiplied?"[10] Galton promoted the ideas that human intelligence and other hard-to-measure traits such as behaviors were greatly influenced by heredity (not the environment, which was the popular mindset of the day).[11] He advocated for a program of positive eugenics. His book *Hereditary Genius* (1869) was well liked by Charles[12] and had a great influence on the ideas presented in his book *Descent of Man* (1871).[13]

7. Wikipedia, "Twelve Tables," www.en.wikipedia.org/wiki/Twelve_Tables.
8. Christian Medical and Dental Association, "A History of Eugenics," www.cmda.org/AM/Template.cfm?Section=Home&CONTENTID=4214&TEMPLATE=/CM/ContentDisplay.cfm.
9. Galton writing to Darwin stated, "I have laid [*Origin of Species*] down in the full enjoyment of a feeling that one rarely experiences after boyish days, of having been initiated into an entirely new province of knowledge, which, nevertheless, connects itself with other things in a thousand ways." Correspondence between Charles Darwin and Francis Galton, Letter 82, www.galton.org/letters/darwin/correspondence.htm.
10. Black, *War against the Weak*, p. 16.
11. Galton wrote, "I have not patience with the hypothesis occasionally expressed, and often implied, especially in tales written to teach children to be good, that babies are born pretty much alike and that the sole agencies in creating differences between boy and boy, and man and man, are steady application and moral effort. It is in the most unqualified manner that I object to pretensions of natural equality." Donald DeMarco and Benjamin Wiker, *Architects of the Culture of Death* (San Francisco, CA: Ignatius Press, 2004), p. 94.
12. Darwin, writing to Galton, stated, "Exhale myself [*sic*], else something will go wrong with my inside. I do not think I ever in all my life read [*Hereditary Genius*] anything more interesting and original — and how well and clearly you put every point!" DeMarco and Wiker, *Architects of the Culture of Death*, p. 92.
13. "But some remarks on the action of natural selection on civilised nations may be here worth adding. This subject has been ably discussed by Mr. W.R. Greg, and previously by Mr. Wallace and Mr. Galton. Most of my remarks are taken from these three authors. With savages, the weak in body or mind are soon eliminated; and those that survive commonly exhibit a vigorous state of health. We civilised men, on the other hand, do our utmost to check the process of elimination; we build asylums for the imbecile, the maimed, and the

In the early 1900s the eugenics movement became well established in the United States. The movement was well-funded by men like Carnegie, Rockefeller, and Kellogg. Eugenic societies, conferences, research institutions, and journals gave a façade of real science to the study of eugenics. This was further promoted by eugenic departments and courses at the university level.

Francis Galton, Darwin's cousin, promoted eugenic beliefs.

The American eugenics movement focused heavily on negative eugenics.[14] Ten classes of social misfits were determined upon which programs of negative eugenics were applied.

> First, the feebleminded; second, the pauper class; third, the inebriate class or alcoholics; fourth, criminals of all descriptions including petty criminals and those jailed for nonpayment of fines; fifth, epileptics; sixth, the insane; seventh, the constitutionally weak class; eighth, those predisposed to specific diseases; ninth, the deformed; tenth, those with defective sense organs, that is, the deaf, blind, and mute.[15]

All of these traits were thought to be inheritable.[16] Ten percent of the American population was thought to fit into these broad, ill-defined categories (sometimes known as the "submerged tenth").[17] Many of those people were forcibly institutionalized in asylums for the "feebleminded and epileptic." Although not stated in

---

sick; we institute poor-laws; and our medical men exert their utmost skill to save the life of every one to the last moment. There is reason to believe that vaccination has preserved thousands, who from a weak constitution would formerly have succumbed to small-pox. Thus the weak members of civilised societies propagate their kind. No one who has attended to the breeding of domestic animals will doubt that this must be highly injurious to the race of man. It is surprising how soon a want of care, or care wrongly directed, leads to the degeneration of a domestic race; but excepting in the case of man himself, hardly any one is so ignorant as to allow his worst animals to breed." Charles Darwin, *The Descent of Man, and Selection in Relation to Sex*, 1st edition (London: John Murray, 1871), p.168–169.

14. Positive eugenics was also encouraged but to a lesser degree. Fitter family contests were held at many county fairs to disseminate information about eugenics and to encourage with prizes and recognition of the "fittest" families to reproduce.
15. Black, *War against the Weak*, p. 58.
16. Leading eugenicist Charles Davenport stated, "When we look among our acquaintances we are struck by their diversity in physical, mental, and moral traits . . . they may be selfish or altruistic, conscientious or liable to shirk . . . for these characteristics are inheritable." Ibid., p. 105–106.
17. Ibid., p. 52.

the list, those of "races" other than the Caucasian "race" would also, by the mere fact of ethnic background, be placed into one or more of these categories. Unfortunately, the eugenics movement in the United States heavily influenced Hitler and his scientists and, in return, many eugenicists and eugenic publications supported the horrifying practices of Hitler's Nazi regime. Negative eugenic practices were even sanctioned by the American government.

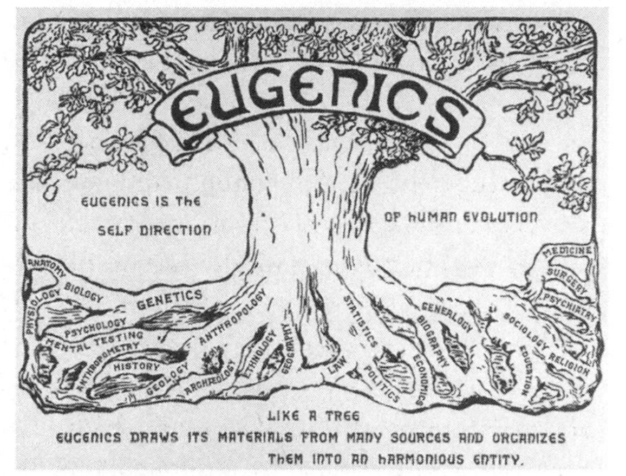

Logo of the Second International Congress of Eugenics, 1921

Forced Sterilization

In 1907, Indiana enacted the first forced sterilization law. The law would be applied to "mentally impaired patients, poorhouse residents, and prisoners."[18] Over 30 states enacted sterilization laws, and between 60,000 and 70,000 people were forcibly sterilized between 1900 and 1970.[19] Most forced sterilizations were performed after 1927. In 1927 the Supreme Court ruled in favor of the forced sterilization of Carrie Buck[20] (in *Buck* v. *Bell*) with justice Oliver Wendell Holmes stating, "It is better for all the world, if instead of waiting to execute degenerate offspring for crime . . . society can prevent those who are manifestly unfit from continuing their kind. . . . Three generations of imbeciles are enough."[21]

Immigration Restriction

The Immigration Act of 1924 set quotas on the number of people allowed into the United States from other countries. Lawmakers were heavily influenced

18. Ibid., p. 67.
19. Joan Rothschild, *The Dream of the Perfect Child* (Bloomington, IN: Indiana University Press, 2005), p. 45; Black, *War against the Weak*, p. 398.
20. Carrie's widowed mother, Emma, was considered feebleminded and institutionalized at the Colony for Epileptics and Feebleminded in Virginia. Carrie was raped as a teenager and subsequently institutionalized at the same colony. Carrie's baby, Vivian, who was eight months old when evaluated, was said to not look quite right. Thus, "three generations of imbeciles" as declared by Holmes. Black, *War against the Weak*, p.108–123.
21. Robert Marshall and Charles Donovan, *Blessed are the Barren: The Social Policy of Planned Parenthood* (San Francisco: Ignatius Press, 1991), p. 277.

by "scientific data" presented to them by high-ranking members of the eugenics movement.[22]

Marriage Restriction Laws

These laws (which varied by state) were designed to keep the Caucasian "race" pure. The laws prohibited "mixed race" marriages (i.e., Negro and Caucasian) but also marriages with those considered defective (e.g., blind).

What Was the Christian Response to Eugenics?

The Christian response to eugenics was mixed. The Christian apologist G.K. Chesterton condemned eugenics in his 1922 book *Eugenics and Other Evils*. He saw how eugenics was being used in Germany to support Nazi ideals.[23]

However, some pastors used their pulpits to promote eugenics. The American Eugenics Society sponsored a sermon contest in 1926. Of the five sermons I read online, all were filled with popular rhetoric from the eugenics movement with little scriptural support given for eugenics. The pastors seemed to have accepted the "science" of eugenics without analyzing it in light of the Bible.[24] This is very similar to the modern situation in which many Christian pastors accept the "science" of evolution, promote the idea in their churches, and don't analyze the conflicts between evolution and Scripture.

History of Planned Parenthood and Its Relationship to Eugenics

The name most commonly associated with Planned Parenthood is that of its founder Margaret Sanger. Margaret was born in 1879, the 6th of 11 children in a poor family, in New York.[25] She was initially quite committed to the Catholic faith but eventually became very cynical in part due to the influence of her

22. Black, *War against the Weak*, p. 202.
23. George Grant, *Grand Illusions: The Legacy of Planned Parenthood* (Franklin, TN: Adroit Press, 1992), p. 94.
24. Scriptural supports for eugenics were often verses taken out of context. For example: "Of a certain moral weakling Jesus said: 'It would be better for him if he had not been born' [referring to Judas Iscariot, Mark 14:21; NIV]. The same thing might be said of millions of weaklings today. . . . And if these millions might be prevented from reproduction so that succeeding generations might appear without their handicaps what a great step would be taken toward the realization of a better order of society of which Jesus dreamed! . . . And the Christian eugenicist believes that in the spirit and purpose of his work he would have the unqualified approval of Jesus." "Eugenics," Sermon #36 excerpt, American Eugenic Society Sermon Contest, 1926, www.eugenicsarchive.org/eugenics/topics_fs.pl?theme=32&search=&matches. However, Paul wrote, "for all have sinned and fall short of the glory of God" (Romans 3:23). Nothing we do on earth can bring about the perfect "new heaven and new earth" (Revelation 21:1) that will someday be brought into existence by God Himself.
25. Grant, *Grand Illusions: The Legacy of Planned Parenthood*, p. 47.

"free thinking" father.[26] Margaret married into money and eventually became an active member of the Socialist Party. She was attracted to the party's fight for "women's suffrage, sexual liberation, feminism, and birth control."[27] Sanger also became a fan of the concepts promoted by Thomas Malthus (who also heavily influenced Charles Darwin in the development of the concept of evolution by natural selection). Malthus was concerned that the human population was growing too rapidly (especially the poor, diseased, and racially inferior) and would outgrow natural resources. The solution proposed by his followers, like Sanger, was to decrease and eliminate the "inferior" population through birth control (including sterilization and abortion).[28] Sanger stated, "The most merciful thing a large family can do to one of its infant members is to kill it."[29]

Margaret Sanger, founder of Planned Parenthood, promoted birth control as a means of controlling the "unfit" in society.

Sanger became one of the foremost champions of birth control and not just for the benign reason of helping poor women who could not afford large families, but also for "the liberation of sexual desire and the new science of eugenics."[30] In 1921 she organized the American Birth Control League. In 1922 she published the book *The Pivot of Civilization* which "unashamedly called for the elimination of 'human weeds,' for the cessation of charity, for the segregation of 'morons, misfits, and the maladjusted' and for the sterilization of 'genetically inferior races.' "[31] Sanger stated:

> The emergency problem of segregation and sterilization must be faced immediately. Every feeble-minded girl or woman of the hereditary type, especially of the moron class, should be segregated

26. Ibid., p. 48.
27. Ibid., p. 50.
28. Ibid., p. 56.
29. Ibid., p. 63.
30. DeMarco and Wiker, *Architects of the Culture of Death*, p. 291.
31. Grant, *Grand Illusions: The Legacy of Planned Parenthood*, p.59. Sanger, in *Pivot of Civilization*, stated, "Birth control, which has been criticized as negative and destructive, is really the greatest and most truly eugenic method, and its adoption as part of the program of Eugenics would immediately give a concrete and realistic power to their science. As a matter of fact, Birth Control has been accepted by the most clear thinking and far seeing of the Eugenicists themselves as the most constructive and necessary of the means to racial health." Black, *War against the Weak*, p. 129.

> during the reproductive period. Otherwise, she is almost certain to bear imbecile children, who in turn are just as certain to breed other defectives. . . . Moreover, when we realize that each feeble-minded person is a potential source of an endless progeny of defect, we prefer the policy of immediate sterilization, of making sure that parenthood is absolutely prohibited to the feeble-minded.[32]

Her magazine, *The Birth Control Review*, contained many articles authored by leading eugenicists of her day. Sanger openly endorsed the concepts and methods of race purification carried out by the Nazis.[33] Sanger believed sex was an evolutionary force that should not be prohibited because of its ability to create genius.[34] In 1942, the American Birth Control League became the Planned Parenthood Federation of America (PPFA).

Modern Perspectives on Eugenics and Planned Parenthood

Eugenics became associated with the horrors of the Nazi regime in the 1940s and so its popularity in the public arena began to fade. In addition, much of the so-called "science" of eugenics was shown to be false by increased knowledge in the field of genetics. It became almost laughable to think that the eugenic-defined trait of "sense of humor" (no pun intended!) could be associated with a particular gene and/or somehow quantified.

However, eugenic concepts and the eugenic ideals of PPFA didn't die. Edwin Black states, "While human genetics was becoming established in America, eugenics did not die out. It became quiet and careful."[35] The eugenic agenda today is not different in principle or goal but only in name and methods. Eugenicist Frederick Osborn in 1965 stated, "The term medical genetics has taken the

32. Ibid., p.131.
33. Grant, *Grand Illusions: The Legacy of Planned Parenthood*, p. 61.
34. DeMarco and Wiker, *Architects of the Culture of Death*, p. 295. Sanger, in *Pivot of Civilization*, stated, "Modern science is teaching us that genius is not some mysterious gift of the gods. . . . Nor is it. . . the result of a pathological and degenerate condition. . . . Rather it is due to the removal of physiological and psychological inhibitions and constraints which makes possible the release and channeling of the primordial inner energies of man into full and divine expression." Ibid. Sanger, in *Pivot of Civilization*, stated, "Slowly but surely we are breaking down the taboos that surround sex; but we are breaking them down out of sheer necessity. The codes that have surrounded sexual behavior in the so-called Christian communities, the teachings of the churches concerning chastity and sexual purity, the prohibitions of the laws, and the hypocritical conventions of society, have all demonstrated their failure as safeguards against the chaos produced and the havoc wrought by the failure to recognize sex as a driving force in human nature — as great as, if indeed no greater than, hunger. Its dynamic energy is indestructible." Ibid., p. 295–296.
35. Black, *War against the Weak*, p.421.

place of the term negative eugenics."[36] Genetic databases filled with individual genetic identities could now generate precise family genetic profiles as opposed to the subjective determination of non-measurable traits by self or other family members stored on millions of index cards that filled eugenic institutions in the early 20th century. In recent years, many feared the adverse use of genetic identities and profiles when applying for jobs and insurance.[37]

James Watson, co-discoverer of the structure of DNA, stated in 2003, "If you are really stupid, I would call that a disease. The lower 10 percent who really have difficulty, even in elementary school, what's the cause of it? A lot of people would like to say, 'Well, poverty, things like that,' It probably isn't. So I'd like to get rid of that, to help lower the 10 percent."[38] The idea of the "submerged tenth" is still alive and well in the 21st century.

Preimplantation genetic diagnosis (PGD) allows parents who have embryos created for use in in vitro fertilization (IVF) to check for genetic disorders and chromosomal abnormalities before the embryos are implanted. The "defective" embryos are destroyed. PGD is also being used for sex selection (only babies of the desired sex are used for IVF), disability selection (e.g., deafness), and predisposition or late-onset disease selection (i.e., predispositions to cancer and late-onset diseases like Alzheimer's).[39] Embryos are destroyed if they are not the desired sex, will have a disability, or may have cancer or disease later in life. PPFA endorses prenatal diagnosis procedures and genetic counseling.[40] Eugenic concepts of prohibiting the birth of the "unfits" is still popular in the 21st century.

Planned Parenthood still endorses many eugenic ideas. This should not be surprising as the PPFA website "History and Successes" page clearly states, "Margaret Sanger, the founder of Planned Parenthood, is one of the movement's great heroes. Sanger's early efforts remain the hallmark of Planned Parenthood's mission. . . ."[41] Sanger's efforts advocated sterilization, abortion, and infanticide of "defectives" in the name of eugenics. Further indicative of the promotion of eugenics, PPFA endorses abortion of deformed babies:

---

36. Ibid., p. 424.
37. The Anti-Genetic Discrimination Bill was passed into U.S. law in 2008. The law states that genetic information cannot be used against an individual for insurance or job purposes. Many countries have no such law.
38. Black, *War Against the Weak*, p. 442.
39. Susannah Baruch, David Kaufman, and Kathy L. Hudson, "Genetic Testing of Embryos: Practices and Perspectives of US in vitro Fertilization Clinics," *Fertility and Sterility* 89 no. 5 (2008): 1053–1058.
40. DeMarco and Wiker, *Architects of the Culture of Death*, p. 301.
41. Planned Parenthood, "History and Successes," www.plannedparenthood.org/about-us/who-we-are/history-and-successes.htm.

> From 1956 to 1962, hundreds of women in the U.S. and Europe who took the drug thalidomide while pregnant give birth to children missing arms and legs. Sherri Finkbine, an American mother of four who used thalidomide, is refused an abortion. More than 60 percent of Americans disapprove of the refusal. Mrs. Finkbine flees to Sweden for a safe, legal abortion. (The fetus is gravely deformed.) Her case and others involving women who have taken thalidomide convince many Americans that anti-abortion laws need reform.[42]

Thus, those infants who are "gravely deformed" should have been permitted to be eliminated according to PPFA. According to the American Life League, in 2006 PPFA was directly responsible (through its clinics) for 289,750 abortions.[43] Thus, PPFA was responsible for almost 25 percent of the abortions estimated to have occurred in the U.S. in 2006.[44]

PPFA also still advocates for sexual liberation by encouraging the concept that sex and sexual desire is part of a normal, healthy lifestyle.[45] These concepts are in line with Sanger's view of sex, which she wrote about in a letter to her 16-year-old granddaughter: "Kissing, petting, and even intercourse are alright as long as they are sincere."[46] Alan Guttmacher, former president of PPFA stated, "We are merely walking down the path that Mrs. Sanger carved out for us."[47] How true!

Biblical Perspectives on Eugenics and Planned Parenthood

When we start with the truth of God's Word, we see that eugenics and the ideas promoted by Planned Parenthood do not align with the Bible.

The Bible shows that God considers all people equal.

> There is neither Jew nor Greek, there is neither slave nor free, there is neither male nor female; for you are all one in Christ Jesus (Galatians 3:28).

42. Ibid.
43. American Life League, "Abortion and Planned Parenthood Statistics," www.all.org/article.php?id=10123.
44. The estimated number of abortions that occurred in the US in 2006 is 1,206,200. National Right to Life, "Abortion in the United States: Statistics and Trends," www.nrlc.org/ABORTION/facts/abortionstats.html.
45. "A basic understanding of sex and sexuality can help us sort out myth from fact and help us all enjoy our lives more." and ". . . the more we know about sex and sexuality, the better we are able to take charge of our sex lives and our sexual health." Planned Parenthood, "Sex and Sexuality," www.plannedparenthood.org/health-topics/sexuality-4323.htm.
46. DeMarco and Wiker, *Architects of the Culture of Death*, p. 294.
47. Grant, *Grand Illusions: The Legacy of Planned Parenthood*, p. 63.

> And He has made from one blood every nation of men to dwell on all the face of the earth (Acts 17:26a).

God doesn't care whether people have dark brown skin or light brown skin, whether they are deaf or have perfect hearing — God does not show partiality.

The Bible shows that life is precious to God.

> Then God said, "Let Us make man in Our image, according to Our likeness; let them have dominion over the fish of the sea, over the birds of the air, and over the cattle, over all the earth and over every creeping thing that creeps on the earth." So God created man in His own image; in the image of God He created him; male and female He created them (Genesis 1:26–27).

> For You formed my inward parts;
> You covered me in my mother's womb.
> I will praise You, for I am fearfully and wonderfully made;
> Marvelous are Your works,
> And that my soul knows very well.
> My frame was not hidden from You,
> When I was made in secret,
> And skillfully wrought in the lowest parts of the earth.
> Your eyes saw my substance, being yet unformed.
> And in Your book they all were written,
> The days fashioned for me,
> When as yet there were none of them (Psalm 139:13–16).

> For God so loved the world that He gave His only begotten Son, that whoever believes in Him should not perish but have everlasting life (John 3:16).

God created each of us individually and we are His image-bearers on earth. He loved us so much that He sent His Son Jesus to die for us so that we might have eternal life.

The Bible shows the importance of caring for the needy.

> You shall neither mistreat a stranger nor oppress him, for you were strangers in the land of Egypt. You shall not afflict any widow or fatherless child. If you afflict them in any way, and they cry at all to Me, I will surely hear their cry (Exodus 22:21–23).

> Then the King will say to those on His right hand, "Come, you blessed of My Father, inherit the kingdom prepared for you from the foundation of the world: for I was hungry and you gave Me food; I was thirsty and you gave Me drink; I was a stranger and you took Me in; I was naked and you clothed Me; I was sick and you visited Me; I was in prison and you came to Me" (Matthew 25:34–36).

God commands us to care for people no matter what their affliction.

Conclusion

My friends John and Tina were told after 19 years of marriage that they were going to have a baby.[48] They were very excited and then the news came that the baby might have a chromosomal abnormality. Tina shared with me:

> Our doctor advised us multiple times to abort our baby because she was considered high risk for chromosomal issues. We were never swayed because we knew that this surprise little bundle was a gift from God. We experienced sheer ecstasy when our eyes beheld Eden Lanay for the first time. Our seven days with her will no doubt be the highlight of our entire lives [Eden was born with Trisomy 18, Edward's Syndrome]. We are so grateful to God for blessing us beyond measure with our beautiful baby girl.[49]

John said:

> As difficult as Eden's death was, we cherish our time with her. My heart breaks for those who lose their child before birth due to miscarriage or abortion. They have missed out on a marvelous experience with a new life.
>
> The seven days we had with Eden were more glorious than I can describe. I will hold on to those precious memories for the rest of my life.[50]

Life is precious — no matter how short or how impaired that life may be. Contrary to the ideas supported by eugenics and Planned Parenthood, all human life has value because it comes from the Life Giver.

48. To read more about their amazing journey and testimony, see their blog, "Baby Graves," www.babygravesdownunder.blogspot.com.
49. John and Tina Graves, email message to author, August 26, 2009.
50. Ibid.

18

When and How Did the Grand Canyon Form?

DR. ANDREW A. SNELLING AND TOM VAIL

The Grand Canyon is one of the world's most awesome erosional features. It is 277 miles (446 km) long, including the 60 miles (96 km) of Marble Canyon upstream. The depth of the main segment of the Grand Canyon varies between 3,000 and 6,000 feet (900 and 1,800 m), with the rim-to-rim width between 4 and 18 miles (6 and 29 km). Its origin has plagued geologists since the time of John Wesley Powell's first courageous voyage down the Colorado River in 1869. Despite an increase in knowledge about its geology, evolutionary geologists have yet been unable to explain the canyon.[1]

Into What Was the Grand Canyon Carved?

Before discussing when and how the Grand Canyon was formed, it is first important to understand where and through what geologic feature it was carved. Located in northern Arizona, the Grand Canyon has been eroded through the southern end of the Colorado Plateau. Carved through sedimentary layers of sandstone, limestone, and shale and into the basement formations of mostly metamorphic schists and igneous granites, the Grand Canyon is a testimony to the erosive power of water.

1. J.W. Powell, *Grand Canyon: Solving Earth's Grandest Puzzle* (New York, NY: PI Press, 2005); W. Ranney, *Carving Grand Canyon: Evidence, Theories and Mystery* (Grand Canyon, AZ: Grand Canyon Association, 2005); R. Young and E. Spamer, eds., *Colorado River Origin and Evolution: Proceedings of a Symposium held at Grand Canyon National Park in June 2000* (Grand Canyon, AZ: Grand Canyon Association, 2001).

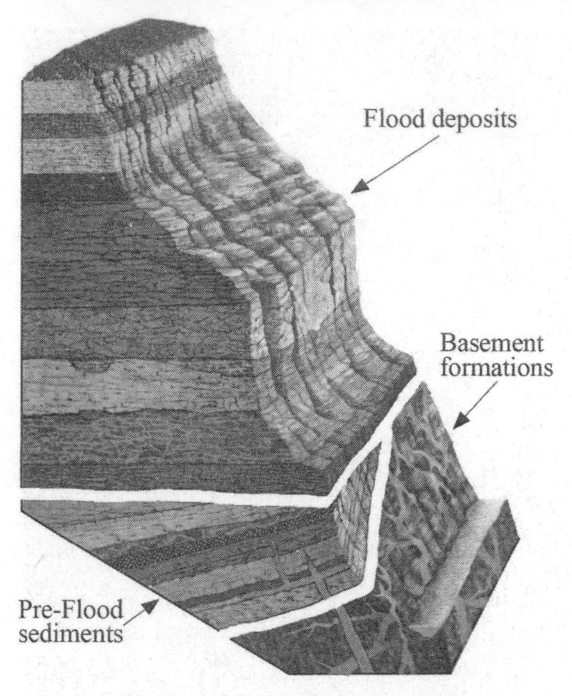

Figure 1. Grand Canyon strata diagram

But how did these rock layers first form? They can be divided into three groups as shown in figure 1. The crystalline basement formations are believed by most creation geologists to have been set in place on day 3 of the creation week. The tilted pre-Flood sediment layers are up to 14,000 feet (4,260 m) in thickness, but are only exposed in the eastern canyon and in a few other areas. The upper layers — the horizontal Flood deposits — cover the entire plateau and, in some cases, the vast majority of the North American continent.[2]

Three Undisputed Observations

The Enormous Scale of Erosion

A simple calculation of the volume of the Grand Canyon reveals almost 1,000 cubic miles (4,000 cubic km) of material have been removed from northern Arizona to produce just the topographic shape of the canyon itself. However, that is not all the erosion which occurred. The Grand Canyon has been carved into a broad elevated area known as the Colorado Plateau (figure 2). The Colorado Plateau covers an area of about 250,000 square miles (647,000 square km) and consists of several smaller plateaus, which today stand at slightly varying elevations. The Kaibab Plateau, which reached more than 9,000 feet (2,740 m), forms part of the North Rim of the Grand Canyon. The sequence of sedimentary rock layers that forms these plateaus consists of many more layers than those exposed in the walls of the Grand Canyon today. In addition, to the north of the canyon there is a sequence of ascending cliffs called the Grand Staircase in which a further 10,000 feet (3,000 m) of sedimentary layers are exposed (figure 3). However, in the Grand Canyon region, most of these layers have been eroded away leaving just a few remnants, such as Red Butte (figure

2. L.L. Sloss, "Sequences in the Cratonic Interior of North America," *Geological Society of America Bulletin* 74 (1963): 93–114.

Figure 2. The extent of the Colorado Plateau

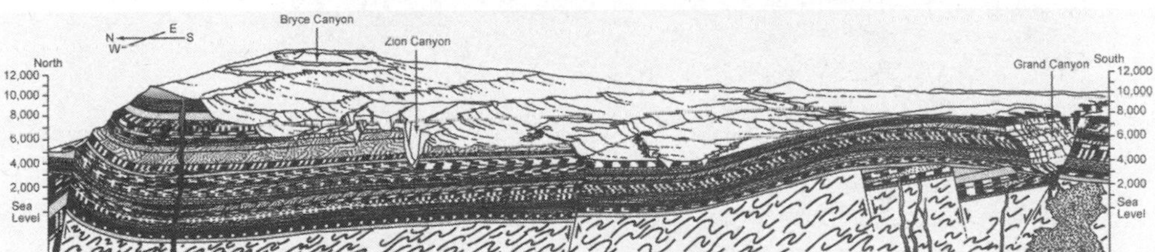

Figure 3. Cross-section through the Grand Canyon-Grand Staircase region showing the extent of the rock layers

Figure 4. Red Butte

4), about 16 miles (25 km) south of the South Rim of the canyon.[3] The layers eroded from the Grand Staircase south to the Grand Canyon area represent an enormous volume of material, removed by sheet-like erosion over a vast area. It

3. T. Vail, M.J. Oard, J. Hergenrather, and D. Bokovoy, *Your Guide to the Grand Canyon: A Different Perspective* (Green Forest, AR: Master Books, 2008), p. 54.

has been estimated that this volume of sediments eroded from the plateau was around 100,000 cubic miles (400,000 cubic km)![4]

The Grand Canyon Was Cut Through the Plateau

Perhaps the most baffling observation, even to evolutionary geologists, is that the Grand Canyon cuts through, not around, a great plateau. Ranney, in his 2005 book *Carving Grand Canyon: Evidence, Theories and Mystery*, said:

> Oddly enough, the Grand Canyon is located in a place where it seemingly shouldn't be. Some twenty miles east of Grand Canyon Village, the Colorado River turned sharply ninety degrees, from a southern course to a western one and into the heart of the uplifted Kaibab Plateau. . . . It appears to cut right through this uplifted wall of rock, which lies three thousand feet above the adjacent Marble Platform to the east.[5]

Indeed, the headwaters of the Colorado River are at a lower elevation than the top of the Kaibab Plateau through which the Grand Canyon has been cut (figure 5).

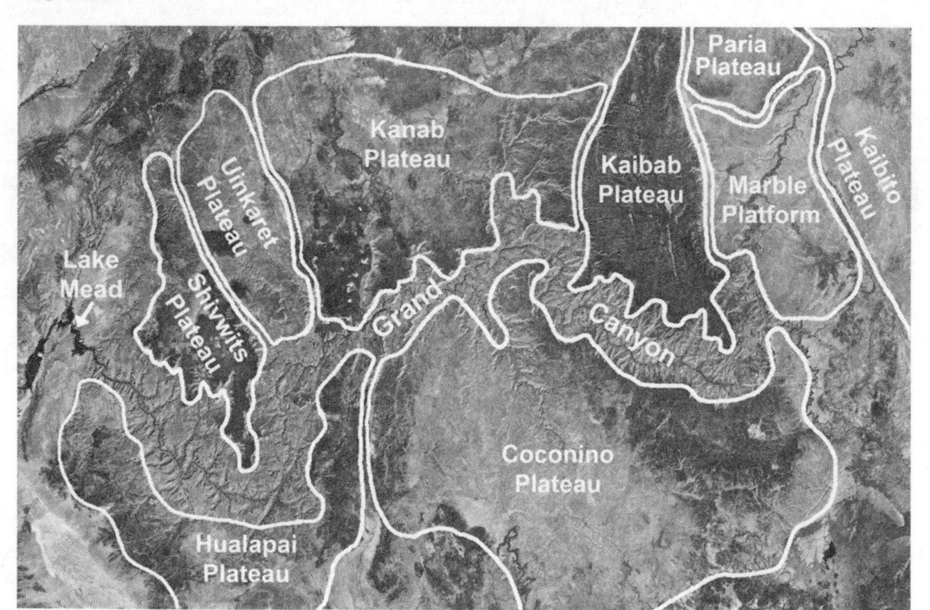

Figure 5. NASA satellite image of the Grand Canyon area, with outline of the different plateaus through which the canyon cuts.

4. M.J. Oard, T. Vail, J. Hergenrather, and D. Bokovoy, "Formation of Rock Layers in the Grand Staircase," in *Your Guide to Zion and Bryce Canyon National Parks: A Different Perspective* (Green Forest, AR: Master Books, 2010), p. 140.
5. Ranney, *Carving Grand Canyon: Evidence, Theories and Mystery*, p. 20.

Uplift of This Plateau Occurred Before Erosion of the Grand Canyon

This third observation also has profound implications concerning the origin of the Grand Canyon. At the eastern edge of the Kaibab Plateau, the sedimentary rock layers were bent, or as a geologist would say "folded," along the East Kaibab Monocline at the time the plateau was uplifted. The uppermost folded layers have been beveled by erosion and overlaid by the flat-lying Wasatch Formation, which is younger.[6] Furthermore, gravel deposits (from the Paleocene and Eocene epochs and thus younger than the folded Cretaceous layers) occur within channels eroded into the surface of the Kaibab Plateau, indicating the major uplift of the plateau and the accompanying erosion of its surface coincided with the uplift of the whole Colorado Plateau.[7] Therefore, in evolutionary thinking the plateau is geologically "old," and most evolutionary geologists believe its uplift occurred before erosion of the canyon into and through the plateau. But that leaves the headwaters of the Colorado River at a lower elevation than the top of that plateau, which indicates the Colorado River could not have carved the Grand Canyon!

The Secular Controversy Over When the Grand Canyon Was Eroded

Over the last 30 years, the time frame for the carving of the Grand Canyon has gone full circle. Thirty years ago, most evolutionists believed the canyon was about 70 million years old. But that estimate changed as radioisotope dating was utilized to show the plateau to be much older than the canyon itself. Basalts found on the North Rim near the western end of the canyon were estimated to be only 6 million years old, but these same basalts are also found on the South Rim![8] This means these lavas had to flow across from one rim to the other, a process which could not have occurred had the canyon been in place at the time. The age of at least the western Grand Canyon was thus reduced to 6 million years, but many continued to believe the central and eastern canyon was 70 million years old, based on the stream-capturing theory outlined below.

6. P.L. Babenroth and A.N. Strahler, "Geomorphology and Structure of the East Kaibab Monocline, Arizona and Utah," *Geological Society of America Bulletin* 56 (1945): 107–150.
7. D.P. Elston, R.A. Young, E.M. McKee, and M.L. Dennis, "Paleontology, Clast Ages, and Paleomagnetism of Upper Paleocene and Eocene Gravel and Limestone Deposits, Colorado Plateau and Transition Zone, Northern and Central Arizona," in *Geology of Grand Canyon, Northern Arizona (with Colorado River Guides)*, D.P. Elston, G.H. Billingsley, and R.A. Young, eds. (Washington, DC: American Geophysical Union, 1989), p. 155–173.
8. I. Lucchitta, "History of the Grand Canyon and of the Colorado River in Arizona," in *Grand Canyon Geology*, second edition, S.S. Beus, and M. Morales, eds. (New York, NY: Oxford University Press, 2003), p. 270–272.

Subsequently, the 70-million-year date was gradually reduced to 17 million years, based on several pieces of the puzzle indicating a younger canyon.[9]

New findings continue to question the age of the canyon. Some scientists still suggest 70 million years as the correct age, while others place it at less than 6 million years.[10] The debate goes on, with none of the accepted dating methods providing a clear-cut answer to the age of the Grand Canyon.[11]

The Secular Claims About How the Canyon Was Eroded

John Wesley Powell was the first to attempt an explanation of how the Grand Canyon was formed. Known as the "antecedent river" theory, Powell theorized an ancient river eroded down into the Colorado Plateau at the same rate the plateau was being uplifted.[12] Although this slow, gradual process fit nicely into the ruling uniformitarian thinking, over the next 50 to 75 years it was rejected by most geologists. The fatal blow against it came with radioisotope dating of the rim rocks.

The antecedent river theory was replaced by the idea of "stream capturing." Stream capturing suggests that through a process called headward erosion, the Grand Canyon was cut from the west through the plateau to "capture" the river, which ran a different direction at the time.[13] This is the theory many evolutionary geologists hold today, but it has seen significant changes over the last 30 years.

The initial stream capturing model had the ancestral Colorado River running through Marble Canyon to the Little Colorado River drainage, where the river then took a southeasterly direction, draining east into the Rio Grande River (figure 6). Another drainage existed to the west of the plateau cutting back through the plateau. However, its headward erosion then cut eastward through about 200 miles (320 km) of the Colorado Plateau and captured the ancestral Colorado River, which then changed its flow to a westerly direction. Subsequent to this capture, the area to the southeast was uplifted so the Little Colorado River now flows *into* the Colorado River. This idea met its demise in part because the necessary erosional debris could not be found anywhere east of the canyon.

9. V. Polyak, C. Hill, and Y. Asmerom, "Age and Evolution of the Grand Canyon Revealed by U-Pb Dating of Water Table-type Speleotherms," *Science* 319 (2008): 1377–1380.
10. K.E. Karlstrom et al., "^{40}Ar/^{39}Ar and Field Studies of Quaternary Basalts in Grand Canyon and Model for Carving Grand Canyon: Quantifying the Interaction of River Incision and Normal Faulting Across the Western Edge of the Colorado Plateau," *Geological Society of America Bulletin* 119 (2007): 1283–1312; K.E. Karlstrom et al., "Model for Tectonically Driven Incision of the Younger than 6 Ma Grand Canyon," *Geology* 36 (2008): 835–838.
11. A.A. Snelling, "Radiometric Dating: Problems with the Assumptions," *Answers*, October–December 2009, p. 70–73.
12. J.W. Powell, "Exploration of the Colorado River of the West and its Tributaries," *Smithsonian Institution Annual Report*, 1875.
13. E.D. McKee et al., "Evolution of the Colorado River in Arizona," *Museum of Northern Arizona Bulletin* 44, 1967.

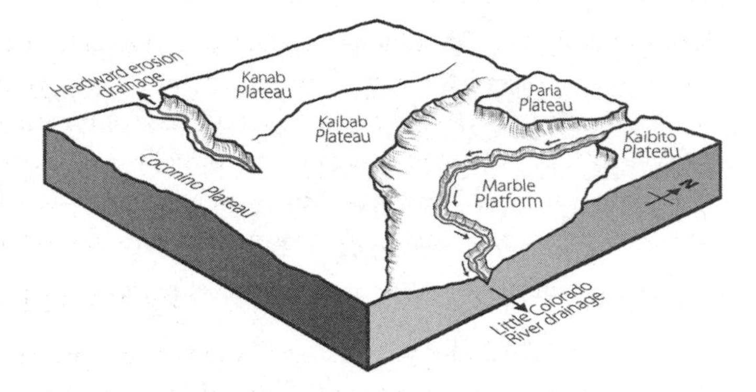

Figure 6. Ancestral Colorado River drainage flowing southeastward toward the Rio Grande

Still having the problem of the basalts on both rims of the western plateau, the theory was modified. The now widely accepted theory has the stream capturing taking place at one of the northwest-tending drainages believed to have existed prior to the plateau uplift.[14] The ancestral Colorado River was thought to have taken a turn to the north, draining into the Great Salt Lake region (figure 7). Again, once the capture took place, the plateau was uplifted, causing the northwest-tending drainages to flow *into* the Colorado River. This modified model seems to be the predominant theory among evolutionary geologists today.

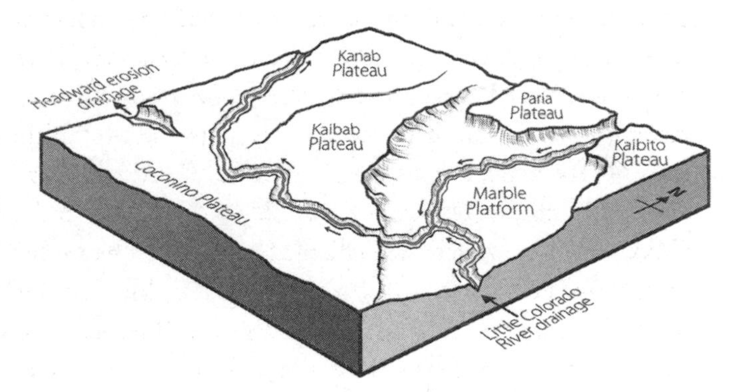

Figure 7. Ancestral Colorado River drainage flowing northwestward toward the Great Salt Lake

Evidences that Canyon Erosion Was Recent and Rapid

There are several pieces of evidence which suggest the Grand Canyon is a recent or "young" canyon. When considered individually, they are significant challenges to the uniformitarian (long-age) model; when taken as a whole, they become catastrophic. Following is a brief outline of some of those challenges.

14. Lucchitta, "History of the Grand Canyon and of the Colorado River in Arizona," in *Grand Canyon Geology*, p. 263.

Debris Not in the Present River Delta

Almost 1,000 cubic miles (4,000 cubic km) of material has been eroded to form the Grand Canyon. Where did it go? If the canyon was eroded by the Colorado River, an enormous delta should be found at the mouth of the river where it empties into the Gulf of California. But the delta contains only a small fraction of this eroded material.[15] This same problem is found with most river deltas; they only contain enough material to represent thousands, not millions, of years of erosion.

Stable Cliffs

One of the most striking features of the Grand Canyon is the massive sheer cliffs of sedimentary rocks. It is the difference in the rocks' makeup that gives the canyon its color and progressive stair-stepped profile of cliffs above broad slopes. The cliffs are made mostly of limestone and sandstone, with some formations reaching 500 feet (150 m) in thickness. The dark, almost black, color of large sections of the sheer cliffs is due to a coating of desert varnish, which develops slowly over many years[16] and is indicative of their stability. Where recent rockfalls occur, the desert varnish is missing. The fact that the cliffs maintain their desert varnish color indicates they are rarely experiencing even minor rockfalls; thus they are very stable. This is only consistent with their formation by recent catastrophic erosion, not millions of years of slow erosion.

No Talus

The lack of debris, or talus, at the base of the cliffs is also a challenge to the evolutionary model. Over millions of years of erosion, one would expect to find large amounts of talus at the base of the cliffs within the Grand Canyon.[17] The most obvious areas of this lack of talus is within the side canyons ending in broad U-shaped amphitheaters. Some of these amphitheaters are hundreds of feet deep and extend back as much as a mile (1.6 km) from the river. The majority have no water source to remove material, yet the bases of most of these cliffs are relatively "clean," with very little talus. Within the evolutionary model, there is no mechanism for the removal of this material.

---

15. P. Lonsdale, "Geology and Tectonic History of the Gulf of California," in E.L. Winteren, D.M. Hussong, and R.W. Decker, eds., *The Eastern Pacific Ocean and Hawaii, The Geology of North America*, vol. N (Boulder, CO: Geological Society of America, 1989), p. 499–521.
16. T. Liu and W.S. Broecker, "How Fast Does Rock Varnish Form?" *Geology* 28 no. 2 (2000): 183–186.
17. E.W. Holroyd III, "Missing Talus," *Creation Research Society Quarterly* 24 (1987): 15–16.

Relict Landforms

The stability of the Grand Canyon cliffs and the lack of talus at their bases are indicative of the canyon being a relict landform. In other words, the Grand Canyon has changed very little since it was carved. It is a relatively unchanged remnant or relict of the event that eroded it, which therefore could not have been today's slow river processes extrapolated back into the past.

There are several remnants, or relict landforms, of the material that now makes up the Grand Staircase to the north of the Grand Canyon. The two most noticeable ones are Red Butte, 16 miles (25 km) south of the South Rim (see figure 4), and Cedar Mountain just east of Desert View Overlook on the South Rim. These remnants, and others like them, are mostly capped with volcanic basalt, which has protected the sedimentary layers from being eroded away. These same sedimentary layers also form the base of the San Francisco Peaks just north of Flagstaff, Arizona.

These relicts testify to a massive erosional event, which in the biblical model is explained by the receding waters of the catastrophic global Genesis Flood.

Examples of Catastrophic Erosion

Catastrophic geologic events are not generally part of the uniformitarian geologist's thinking, but rather include events that are local or regional in size. One example of a regional event would be the 15,000 square miles (39,000 square km) of the Channeled Scablands in eastern Washington. Initially thought to be the product of slow gradual processes, this first came into question in 1923 when J. Harlen Bretz presented a paper to the Geological Society of America suggesting the Scablands were eroded catastrophically.[18] For the next 30 years Bretz was ridiculed for his theory, but in 1956 additional information was presented supporting the idea. Over the next 20 years, the evidence was pieced together to show the Scablands were, in fact, catastrophically eroded by the "Spokane Flood."[19] This Spokane flood was the result of the breaching of an ice dam that had created glacial Lake Missoula. Today, the United States Geological Survey estimates the flood released 500 cubic miles (2,000 cubic km) of water, which drained in as little as 48 hours, gouging out millions of tons of solid rock.

A more recent example of the power of catastrophic processes was observed at Mount St. Helens in 1980. Two hundred million cubic yards (153 million cubic meters) of material was catastrophically deposited by volcanic flows at

18. J.H. Bretz, "Glacial Drainage of the Columbia Plateau," *Geological Society of America Bulletin* 34 (1923): 573–608.
19. J.E. Allen, M. Burns, and S.C. Sargent, *Cataclysms of the Columbia* (Portland, OR: Timber Press, 1986).

the base of the mountain in just a matter of hours. Less than two years later, a minor eruption caused a mudflow, which carved channels through the recently deposited material.[20] These channels, which are 1/40th the size of the Grand Canyon, exposed flat contacts between the catastrophically deposited layers, contacts similar to those seen between the layers exposed in the walls of the Grand Canyon.

Both these events were relatively minor compared to a global flood. For example, the eruption of Mount St. Helens contained only 0.27 cubic miles (1.1 cubic km) of material compared to other eruptions, which have been as much as 950 cubic miles (3,960 cubic km). That is over 2,000 times the size of Mount St. Helens!

If Noah's Flood laid down the layers rapidly, one on top of another as was observed at Mount St. Helens, the boundaries between the layers would be flat and smooth, just as they are so magnificently displayed in the Grand Canyon. And the Channeled Scablands present a clear example of how the layers of the Grand Canyon could have easily been eroded catastrophically, possibly in a matter of just a few days.

An example of how quickly water can erode through the formations of the Grand Canyon region took place on June 28, 1983, when the pending overflow of Lake Powell required the use of the Glen Canyon Dam's 40-foot (12-m) diameter spillway tunnels for the first time. As the volume of water increased, the entire dam started to vibrate and large boulders spewed from one of the spillways. The spillway was immediately shut down and an inspection revealed catastrophic erosion had cut through the three-foot-thick reinforced concrete walls and eroded a hole 40 feet (12 m) wide, 32 feet (10 m) deep, and 150 feet (46 m) long in the sandstone beneath the dam.[21]

Catastrophic erosion such as this often starts when vacuum bubbles form and implode with jackhammer-like power, eating away anything in their way. This is called cavitation.[22] As volumes increase, whirlpool-like vortexes form, sucking material from the bottom in a process called kolking. That material then enters the flow and acts as projectiles, removing even more material. The erosive power of these forces continues almost exponentially as the volume of water increases. These same forces would have had a major role in the formation of the Grand Canyon.

20. S.A. Austin, "Rapid Erosion at Mount St. Helens," *Origins* 11 (1984): 90–98.
21. *Challenge at Glen Canyon Dam*, VHS, directed by W.L. Rusho (Denver, CO: U. S. Department of Interior, Bureau of Reclamation, 1983).
22. H.L. Barnes, "Cavitation as a Geological Agent," *American Journal of Science* 254 (1956): 493–505.

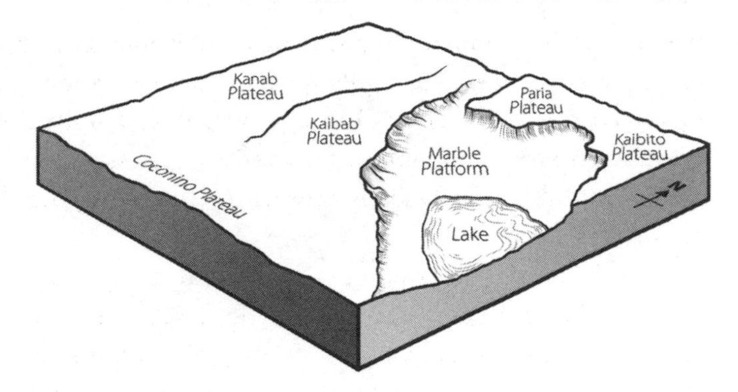

Figure 8. Natural dams trap receding Flood waters creating large lake(s).

Erosion of Grand Canyon Within the Biblical Account of Earth History

Not long after all the fossil-bearing sedimentary layers of the Colorado Plateau had been deposited by the rising Flood waters, those same waters began to recede. We are told in Psalm 104:8 that at the end of the Flood, the mountains rose and the valleys sank down, causing the waters to drain off the continents back into new ocean basins. Massive sheet erosion occurred across the plateau while it was being uplifted, carving the Grand Staircase and leaving behind the colored cliffs, canyons like Zion Canyon, and isolated remnants like Red Butte. As the Flood receded, water would have become trapped behind natural dams north and east of what is now the Grand Canyon area. Some estimate these lakes could have contained as much as 3,000 cubic miles (12,500 cubic km) of water (about three times the volume of today's Lake Michigan).[23] Figure 8 shows where one of these lakes may have been, with additional lake(s) potentially north of the Paria-Kaibito Plateau.

The warming of the oceans caused by the opening of the fountains of the great deep during the Flood would also have resulted in increased rainfall in this region immediately after the Flood. Storms potentially dumped as much as 100 inches (2.5 m) of rain at a time in the area just north of the canyon.[24] This rainfall would have increased the water level in the impounded lakes and would have been a powerful erosional force of its own.

23. S.A. Austin, "How Was Grand Canyon Eroded?" in *Grand Canyon: Monument to Catastrophe*, S.A. Austin, ed. (Santee, CA: Institute for Creation Research, 1994), p. 83–110; W. Brown, *In the Beginning: Compelling Evidence for Creation and the Flood*, sixth edition (Phoenix, AZ: Center for Scientific Creation, 1995), p. 92–95, 102–105.
24. L. Vardiman, "Hypercanes Following the Genesis Flood," in *Proceedings of the Fifth International Conference on Creationism*, R.L. Ivey, Jr., ed. (Pittsburgh, PA: Creation Science Fellowship, 2003), p. 17–28.

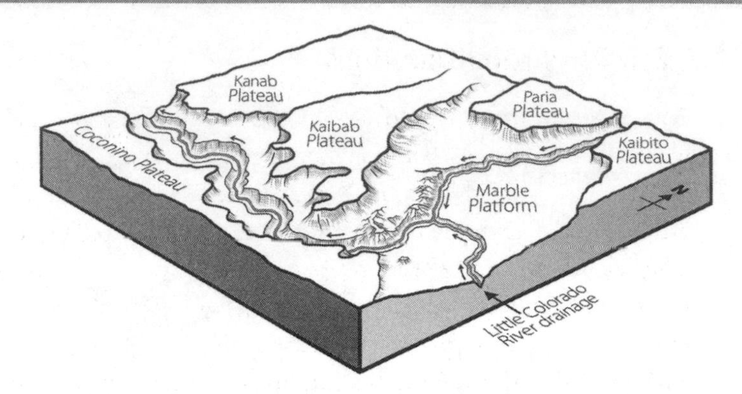

Figure 9. Current drainage of the Colorado and Little Colorado Rivers

As the Flood waters continued to recede, the sheet erosion across the rising Colorado Plateau would have diminished and the water would have started to channelize. This channelization would have then cut the initial path of the canyon.

The Kaibab Plateau now stands some 3,000 feet (900 m) above the adjacent Marble Platform, both part of the Colorado Plateau (figure 5). But the lack of erosional cliffs on the north and eastern sides of the Kaibab Plateau suggests that the southern end of the plateau continued to be uplifted after the rest of the region had stabilized. If this uplifting occurred just prior to, or even during, the channelization phase of the receding Flood waters, it would account for the lack of cliffs. It would also account for the direction of the side canyons eroded into the Kaibab Plateau. For example, some of the side canyons carved into the Marble Platform that join to form Marble Canyon, drain to the northeast, which seems to be the wrong direction. But that would have been the direction in which the receding waters flowed as the Kaibab Plateau was uplifted. Since the Kaibab Plateau is higher at its southern rim, this would also account for the longer and deeper side canyons carved into the North Rim of the Grand Canyon, which also follows along that southern edge of the plateau. Thus the South Rim of the canyon follows the northern edge of the Coconino Plateau (figure 5).

Within the uplifted Colorado Plateau are several limestone layers susceptible to being dissolved by surface and ground waters, as evidenced today by all the caves in the Redwall Limestone, from many of which streams flow. Because of all the volcanic activity during the Flood, the waters could have been slightly acidic, increasing their ability to dissolve limestone. So no sooner had these leftover Flood waters been dammed than they would have begun to find and exploit weaknesses in the limestone and other layers making up the plateau.

Whether it happened as the Flood year ended, or soon thereafter, the lakes would have soon breached their dams, washing over the plateau and exploiting any channels already there, rapidly carving through the plateau resulting in a deep canyon very similar to what we see today (figure 9).

A Few Perplexing Questions

As creationists, we do not have all the answers. In fact, there are many unanswered questions when it comes to the formation of the Grand Canyon. For example, exactly when the Kaibab Plateau was uplifted during the formation of the Grand Canyon is uncertain. Another question relates to the erosional evidence associated with the breaching of the natural dams. It is unclear as to why the waters would have eroded the course they appear to have taken, and why the remaining landscape has some of the features shown today. Also, unknown is what effect the increased rainfall in the region had on carving the canyon.

Some creationists attribute the formation of the canyon almost solely to the breaching of the dams, while others see the receding of the Flood waters to be the main carving mechanism. It is suggested here that combining the strengths of both models best explains the evidence and what we see in the Grand Canyon today.

These issues, however, do not weaken the evidence for the catastrophic carving of the Grand Canyon and its relationship to the Flood. It only shows there is still research to be done in order to better understand the canyon's formation.

Conclusion

Although we cannot be certain of the sequence and timing of these events, the evidence shows the Grand Canyon was formed rapidly, as were the layers into which it is carved. Thus, rather than slow and gradual erosion by the Colorado River over eons of time, the Grand Canyon was carved rapidly by a lot of water in a little bit of time! The reason the Colorado River exists today is because the Grand Canyon was eroded first, soon after the end of the Genesis Flood.

19

Does Astronomy Confirm a Young Universe?

DR. DON B. DEYOUNG AND DR. JASON LISLE

One of the common objections to biblical creation is that scientists have supposedly demonstrated that the universe is much older than the Bible teaches. The first chapter of Genesis clearly teaches that God created all things in six days ("ordinary" days as defined by an evening and morning) and that human beings were created on the sixth day. This is confirmed and clarified in the other Scriptures as well (e.g., Exodus 20:8–11; Mark 10:6). And since the Bible records about four thousand years between Adam and Christ (Genesis 5:3–32), the biblical age of the universe is about 6,000 years. This stands in stark contrast with the generally accepted secular age estimate of 4.6 billion years for the earth, and three times longer still, 13.7 billion years, for the universe beyond.

This fundamental time discrepancy is no small matter. It is obvious that if the secular age estimate is correct, then the Bible is in error and cannot be trusted. Conversely, if the Bible really is what it claims to be, the authoritative Word of God (2 Timothy 3:16), then something is seriously wrong with the secular estimates for the age of the universe. Since the secular time scale challenges the authority of Scripture, Christians must be ready to give an answer — a defense of the biblical time scale (1 Peter 3:15).

The Assumptions of Age Estimates

Why such a difference? What is really going on here? It turns out that all secular age estimates are based on two fundamental (and questionable) assumptions.

These are *naturalism* (the belief that nature is all there is),[1] and *uniformitarianism* (the belief that present rates and conditions are generally representative of past rates and conditions).

In order to estimate the age of something (whose age is not known historically), we must have information about how the thing came to be, and how it has changed over time. Secular scientists assume that the earth and universe were *not* created supernaturally (the assumption of naturalism), and that they generally change in the slow-and-gradual way that we see today (the assumption of uniformitarianism).[2] If these starting assumptions are not correct, then there is no reason to trust the resulting age estimates.

But notice something about the assumptions of naturalism and uniformitarianism: they are *anti-biblical* assumptions. The Bible indicates that the universe was created *supernaturally* by God (Genesis 1:1) and that present rates are *not* always indicative of past rates (such as the global Flood described in Genesis 7–8). So, by assuming naturalism and uniformitarianism, the secular scientist has already assumed that the Bible is wrong. He then estimates that the universe is very, very old, and concludes that the Bible must be wrong. But this is what he assumed at the start. His argument is circular. It's the logical fallacy called "begging the question." But all old-earth (and old-universe) arguments assume naturalism and uniformitarianism. Therefore, they are all fallacious circular arguments. That's right — all of them.

Refuting an Old Earth and Universe

A much better way to argue for the age of the universe is to hypothetically assume the opposite of what you are trying to prove, and then show that such an assumption leads to inconsistencies. In other words, we temporarily assume naturalism and uniformitarianism for the sake of argument, and then show that even when we use those assumptions, the universe appears to be much younger than secular scientists claim. This technique is called a *reductio ad absurdum* (reduction to absurdity). So the secular worldview is unreasonable since it is inconsistent with itself. In the following arguments, we will temporarily assume (for the sake

1. Some scientists hold to a softer form of naturalism called "methodological naturalism." This is the concept that a supernatural realm may indeed exist, but should not be considered when doing scientific study. For all intents and purposes, the naturalist does not accept that there is anything beyond nature — at least when he or she is doing science.
2. Uniformitarianism is a matter of degree. Some secular scientists are willing to accept that catastrophes play a major role in the shaping of the earth's features. However, virtually all of them deny the worldwide Flood, which would have been the most significant geological event in earth's history since its creation. In this sense, virtually all secular scientists embrace uniformitarianism to a large extent.

of argument) that naturalism and uniformitarianism are true, and then show that the evidence still indicates a solar system much younger than the secular estimate of 4.6 billion years, and a universe much younger than 13.7 billion years.

Moon Recession

Our nearest neighbor, the moon, has much to contribute to the recent creation worldview. A parade of lunar origin theories has passed by over the decades. These include fission of the moon from the earth (1960s), capture of the moon by earth's gravity from elsewhere in space (1970s), and formation of the moon from the collapse of a dust cloud or nebula (1980s). The currently popular model calls for lunar origin by an ancient collision of the earth with a Mars-size space object. All such natural origin theories are unconvincing and temporary; a recent supernatural creation remains the only credible explanation. Inquiry into origins need not be limited to natural science alone, as often assumed. The historical definition of science is the search for truth. If God is indeed the Creator, then scientists should not arbitrarily dismiss this fact. Many feel that modern science has been impoverished by its artificial limitation to naturalism, or secularism.

The moon reveals multiple design features. Lunar tides keep our oceans healthy, protecting marine life. The moon's (roughly circular) orbit stabilizes the earth's tilt and seasons. The moon also provides us with a night light, compass, clock, and calendar. The extent to which the moon controls the biorhythms of plants and animals, both on land and in the sea, is not well understood but is surely essential to life.

The moon also instructs us concerning the age of the earth. Consider the gravitational tide force between the earth and moon. This interaction also results in a very gradually receding moon, and slowing of the earth's rotation. These changes are highly dependent on the earth-moon separation, and are in direct conflict with the evolutionary time scale. Figure 1 shows the spinning earth and orbiting moon. A slight delay in the earth's high tides (the dark bumps) results in a forward pull on the moon, causing it to slowly spiral outward from the earth. In turn, the moon's gravity pulls back on the earth, slightly decreasing its spin.

Currently, the moon is moving outward from the earth by 3.82 cm/yr (1.5 in/yr). However, this recession is highly nonlinear and would have been greater in the past. If one assumes unlimited extrapolation back in time, gravity theory shows the moon in direct physical contact with earth about 1.55 billion years ago.[3] This is not to say that the moon was ever this near or this old.

3. Don B. DeYoung, "Tides and the Creation Worldview," *Creation Research Society Quarterly*, 45 no. 2 (2008): 100–108.

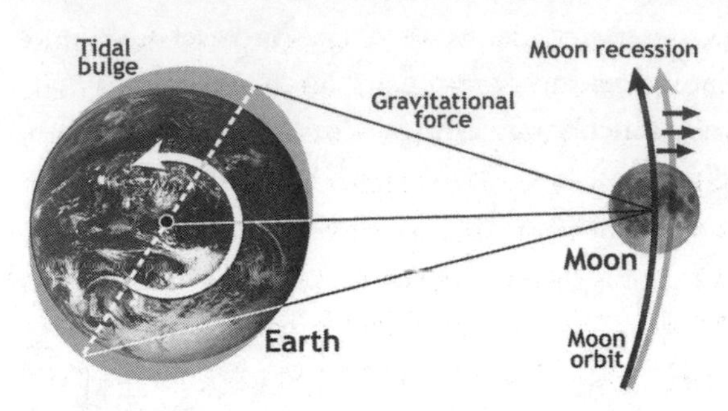

Figure 1. The moon is slowly drifting away from the earth, but the rate of recession would have been much faster in the past.

In fact, a moon located anywhere in the vicinity of the earth would be fragmented, resulting in a Saturn-like ring of debris encircling the earth. This follows because the earth's gravity force would overcome the moon's own cohesive force. The tides lead to a limited time scale for the moon, far less than 1.55 billion years. However, evolutionists assume that the moon and solar system are 4.6 billion years old. Also, life is said to have originated on earth about 3.5 billion years ago. The fundamental problem with the evolutionary time scale is obvious.

On a much shorter time scale, 6,000 years, the moon has moved outward by only about 755 feet (230 m) since its creation. Therefore, the creationist suggestion is that the moon was placed in orbit close to its present earth distance. Due to the earth's rotational slowing, the length of a day 6,000 years ago is calculated to be just 0.12 seconds shorter than at present.

Comets

Comets silently orbit the sun and put on occasional majestic displays in our night sky. Each year, dozens of comets loop the sun. About one-half of them have been named and studied on previous orbits. These comets don't last forever. Sooner or later they may be ejected from the solar system, may collide with the sun or planets, or they may break into fragments like a poorly packed snowball. There are clouds of dusty debris in the solar system, ghosts of disintegrated comets from the past. When the earth happens to pass through such a cloud, it sweeps up some of this comet dust. Then we see "shooting stars," an echo of the comet's original light show. In a spectacular 1994 display, comet Shoemaker-Levi was destroyed when it collided with Jupiter. The gravity of the massive outer planets protects the earth from similar comet collisions.

The question arises, why do comets still exist in the solar system? On a time scale of multiple billions of years, should they not all be long gone, either by escape, collision, or disintegration? The average number of solar revolutions before a comet dissipates is estimated to be about 40 trips. Comet Halley has already been observed through at least 28 orbits, dating back to 240 B.C. Its remaining years are numbered.

Astronomers recognize two comet varieties with respectively short and long revolving periods. The short-period comets have orbit times less than about 200 years. Halley's Comet is such an example with a period of about 76 years. Meanwhile, the long-period comets may require thousands of years for each solar pass. The origin of both kinds of comets remains a mystery to secular astronomers. Based on the rate at which comets are destroyed today, it is surprising (from an old-universe perspective) that either long-period or short-period comets are still present. The supply should have been depleted billions of years ago. How then do secular astronomers explain these apparently "young" comets in a solar system that they believe to be billions of years old?

To account for this paradox, secular astronomers have proposed that myriads of icy, comet-sized objects formed early in the solar system and continue to orbit at a tremendous distance from the sun where they remain permanently frozen for billions of years. It is suggested that every now and then one of these objects is dislodged from its distant orbit and injected into the inner solar system to become a new comet. According to this idea, as old comets are destroyed, new ones replace them.

Two present-day comet reservoirs are suggested by astronomers: one to supply short-period comets, the other to account for long-period comets. The Kuiper belt is thought to exist on the outer fringe of the known solar system, named for astronomer Gerald Kuiper (1905–1973). More than one hundred large, icy objects have been observed beyond planet Neptune, and multitudes more are assumed. It is thought that these trans-Neptunian objects (TNOs) are the largest members of the Kuiper belt. It is assumed that the unseen smaller members of the Kuiper belt occasionally fall inward toward the sun to become short-period comets. Hundreds of times further outward from Neptune is an assumed, vast Oort cloud of icy masses, named for Jan Oort (1900–1992). It is further assumed that a passing star may disturb this remote cloud from time to time, deflecting some of these icy objects toward the inner solar system, thereby replenishing the supply of long-period comets.

So far, the only objects detected at these great distances are much larger than any known comet. The existence of vast Kuiper and Oort clouds of actual comet-sized objects is not verifiable with current technology. The simplest explanation would appear to line up with the biblical time scale: the presence of comets may be evidence that the solar system is not nearly as old as is often assumed. Comets teach us two valuable lessons. First, their eventual loss is a reminder of the temporary nature of the solar system and universe. As Psalm 102:25–26 describes it:

> . . . the heavens are the work of Your hands. They will perish, but You will endure; Yes, they will all grow old like a garment.

As a second lesson, the exact motions of comets, planets, and stars are elegant evidence of God's controlling presence throughout the physical universe.

Faint Young Sun Paradox

Astronomers use the term *stellar evolution* for the aging process of stars. Our sun is assumed to be in its midlife stage, 4.6 billion years of age, as it gradually converts its hydrogen to helium via nuclear fusion reactions in its core. However, a basic time problem arises. Computer modeling of the sun on an evolutionary time scale predicts that the sun must gradually brighten. If true, the sun would be 30 percent dimmer during the period 3.8–2.5 billion years ago. The early earth would have been locked in a global ice age, with the crust and seas frozen solid. This in turn precludes the development of early life on earth.

In conflict with the icy prediction of solar models, geologic evidence points to an earth that was warmer in the past (irrespective of the time scale). This means that there is a fundamental problem with the unlimited extrapolation back in time of solar energy output. The creationist alternative is that the sun was placed in the heavens, on day 4 of the creation week, with a temperature very close to that of the present day.

Rapid Star Aging

Stellar evolution might better be called star decay or degeneration. Current models predict very gradual changes in the nature of stars. The sun, for example, is predicted to pass through several stages in coming ages. At present it is called a "main sequence" star. In the distant future, it is predicted to expand in size and grow cooler as it becomes a red giant star. Following this, the sun reverts to a small, hot white dwarf star. Each stage is assumed to last for millions of years.

Observations suggest that some stars may age much more rapidly than generally believed. For example, consider Sirius, the brightest nighttime star. At a distance of 8.6 light years from earth, it is known as the Dog Star, prominent in the Canis Major constellation. Sirius has a dwarf companion star, and there is intriguing evidence that this dwarf may have formed from a red giant in just the past 1,000 years. Historical records, including those of Ptolemy, describe Sirius as red or pink in color. The suggestion is that the red giant companion dominated the pair at this early time. Today, Sirius is a brilliant blue-white color and its dwarf companion is basically invisible. Other stars also occasionally show unexpected color changes, indicating possible rapid aging processes. Such events call into question the fundamental time scale of current stellar evolution models.

Spiral Galaxies

Spiral galaxies also pose a problem for the secular time scale. Spiral galaxies contain blue stars in their arms. But blue stars are very luminous and expend their fuel quickly. They cannot last billions of years. Secular astronomers realize this and so they simply assume that new blue stars form continuously (from collapsing clouds of gas) to replenish the supply. However, star formation is riddled with theoretical problems. It has never been observed, nor could it truly be observed since the process is supposed to take hundreds of thousands of years. Gas in space is very resistant to being compressed into a star. Compression of gas causes an increase in magnetic field strength, gas pressure, and angular momentum, which would all tend to prevent any further compression into a star. Although these problems may not be insurmountable, we should be very skeptical of star formation — especially given the lack of observational support.

Perhaps even more compelling is the fact that spiral arms cannot last billions of years. The spiral arms of galaxies rotate differentially — meaning the inner portions rotate faster than the outer portions. Every spiral galaxy is essentially twisting itself up — becoming tighter and tighter with time. In far less than one billion years, the galaxy should be twisted to the point where the arms are no longer recognizable. Many galaxies are supposed to be ten billion years old in the secular view, yet their spiral arms are easily recognizable. The spiral structure of galaxies strongly suggests that they are much younger than generally accepted.

There is a common misunderstanding here because people sometimes confuse *linear* velocity with *angular* velocity. Many people have heard or read that spiral galaxies have a nearly "flat" rotation curve — meaning that stars near the edge have about the same linear speed as stars near the core. This is true — but it doesn't alleviate the problem. In fact it is the *cause*. A star near the core makes a very small circle when it orbits, whereas a star near the edge makes a very large circle — which takes much longer if the star travels at the same speed. So in physics terminology we say that the stars have the same speed, but the inner star has a greater angular velocity because it completes an orbit in far less time than the outer star. This is why spiral galaxies rotate differentially.

Additionally, some people are under the mistaken impression that dark matter was hypothesized to alleviate the spiral wind-up problem. But this is not so. Dark matter explains (possibly) why the stars have a flat rotation curve to begin with. It does not explain how a spiral structure could last billions of years.

To get around the spiral galaxy wind-up problem, secular astronomers have proposed the "spiral density wave hypothesis." In this model, as the spiral arms become twisted and homogenized, new spiral arms are formed to replace the old ones. The new arms are supposed to form by a pressure wave that travels around the galaxy, triggering star formation. If this idea were true, then galaxies could be ten billion years old, whereas their arms are constantly being merged and reformed.

However, the spiral density wave hypothesis may create more problems than it solves. There are difficulties in creating such a pressure wave in the first place. The spiral density wave hypothesis cannot easily explain why galactic magnetic fields are aligned with the spiral arms (since magnetic fields move with the material — not with pressure waves); nor can it easily account for the tight spiral structure near the core of some galaxies such as M51. Perhaps most significantly, the spiral density wave hypothesis presupposes that star formation is possible. We have already seen that this is a dubious assumption at best. The simplest, most straightforward explanation for spiral galaxies is the biblical one: God created them thousands of years ago.

Conclusion

Many more such evidences for a young earth, solar system, and universe could be listed. Space does not permit us to discuss in detail how planetary magnetic fields decay far too quickly to last billions of years, or how the internal heat of the giant planets suggests they are not as old as is claimed. In all cases, the age estimates are far too young to be compatible with an old universe. It should be noted that all these age estimates are an upper limit — they denote the *maximum possible age*, not the actual age. So they are all compatible with the biblical time scale, but challenge the notion of an old universe.

It should also be noted that in all cases we have (for argument's sake) based the estimate on the assumptions of our critics. That is, we have assumed hypothetically that both naturalism and uniformitarianism are true, and yet we still find that the estimated ages come out far younger than the old-universe view requires. This shows that the old-universe view is internally inconsistent. It does not comport with its own assumptions. However, the biblical view is self-consistent. As with other fields of science, the evidence from astronomy confirms that the Bible is true. The answer to the title of this chapter is a resounding *yes* — the heavens declare a recent, supernatural creation!

References and Resources for Further Study

Don B. DeYoung, *Astronomy and Creation* (Winona Lake, IN: BMH Books, 2010).
Danny Faulkner, *Universe by Design* (Green Forest, AR: Master Books, 2004).
Jason Lisle, *Taking Back Astronomy* (Green Forest, AR: Master Books, 2006).
Jason Lisle, *The Ultimate Proof of Creation* (Green Forest, AR: Master Books, 2009).

20

How Could Fish Survive the Genesis Flood?

DR. ANDREW A. SNELLING

Some skeptics and long-age Christians lampoon the biblical account of the global Genesis Flood cataclysm by insisting that it was impossible for Noah to have a giant aquarium aboard the ark to preserve all the marine creatures, including trilobites.[1] However, this accusation is of course easily dismissed, because a careful reading of the relevant biblical text (Genesis 7:13–16, 21–23) clearly shows that God only brought to the ark representatives of all the created kinds of air-breathing, land-dwelling creatures. After all, the water-dwelling creatures would surely have been able to survive in the Flood waters.

Obviously, the air-breathing, land-dwelling creatures could not have lived through the earth-covering global Flood, but one would think the aquatic animals would have been right at home in all that water. Perhaps not, however, if during the Flood there was mixing of fresh and salt waters. Yet even that is uncertain, because we don't know how much mixing of fresh and salt waters would have occurred during the Flood. What we do know is that many of today's fish species, for example, are specialized, so they do not survive in water of radically different saltiness from their usual habitats. So how did freshwater and saltwater fish survive the Flood?

1. Ian R. Plimer, *Telling Lies for God: Reason vs. Creationism* (Sydney, Australia: Random House, 1994), p. 111; H. Ross, *A Matter of Days* (Colorado Springs, CO: NavPress, 2004), p. 123.

Saltiness of the Pre-Flood Ocean

To begin with, we do not know how salty the oceans were before the Flood, although early in the fossil record of the Flood we find echinoderms that could have only lived in a salty pre-Flood ocean. What we do know is that if at creation the oceans originally were totally freshwater, then at the current estimated rate of salt build-up in the oceans, all the salt in the oceans would have accumulated in only about 62 million years.[2] Of course, this assumes that the salt accumulation has always been at today's rate.

However, in the biblical account of earth history we are told that the Flood was initiated by the breaking up of the "fountains of the great deep" (Genesis 7:11), which likely were huge outpourings of hot water and steam that burst from inside the earth, associated with cataclysmic volcanic eruptions.[3] Such waters today are very salty, because of dissolved minerals in them. Furthermore, toward the end of the Flood there was massive erosion of the new continental land surfaces as the flood waters drained back into the new ocean basins, thereby carrying a lot more salt with them.

So the oceans before the Flood were a lot less salty than they are now. And since salt has not been added to the oceans uniformly through earth history at today's estimated rate, their current saltiness accumulated in far less than 62 million years.

However, this is still assuming freshwater oceans to begin with! We cannot, of course, be sure, because the Bible is silent about the salinity of the ocean waters at the conclusion of the creation week. We are told that when God created the earth on day 1, it was covered in water, which He divided on day 2. It may be safe to assume this was all freshwater because Genesis 1:2 reveals this water was formless and "empty" (perhaps meaning void or pure).

However, on day 3 God raised the land, and the covering waters were gathered together to form the seas.[4] Thus the earth's land surface was shaped

2. S.A. Austin and D.R. Humphreys, "The Sea's Missing Salt: A Dilemma for Evolutionists," in *Proceedings of the Second International Conference on Creationism*, R.E. Walsh and C.L. Brooks, eds. (Pittsburgh, PA: Creation Science Fellowship, 1990), p. 17–33.
3. S.A. Austin et al., "Catastrophic Plate Tectonics: A Global Flood Model of Earth History," in *Proceedings of the Third International Conference on Creationism*, R.E. Walsh, ed. (Pittsburgh, PA: Creation Science Fellowship, 1994), p. 609–621.
4. There are three major possibilities regarding Genesis 1:9. One possibility has the ocean basins dropping, a second possibility has the continents lifted up through the waters, and the other possibility leaves open the miraculous — that the waters were instantly gathered into one place and dry land merely appeared. However, the focus of this chapter is not to debate these possibilities, but instead to show that that some possibilities would help add salt to the oceans.

by erosion by these retreating waters, no doubt carrying salts with them. So it's possible a lot of salt may have been introduced to the pre-Flood oceans by this means.

Then God created marine creatures on day 5 to live and thrive in those ocean waters, so they must have been created with the ability to tolerate the salty oceans, just as marine creatures are able to today. Thus salt tolerance was not an outcome of the biological changes we are told occurred as a result of the Curse, being instead an ability given marine creatures at their creation by the Creator. Indeed, it was much more likely that God created animals suitable for mild salinity, but with the information available to survive in both extremes (freshwater and even more saline water).

Water Conditions in Which Fish Survive

Living in water requires specific physiological and ecological capabilities, different to those of terrestrial organisms.[5] Thus, for example, freshwater fish tend to absorb water because the saltiness of their body fluids draws water into their bodies (by osmosis), whereas saltwater fish tend to lose water from their bodies because the surrounding water is saltier than their body fluids.

The global scale of the Flood cataclysm produced gigantic problems affecting the very survival of many species. Indeed, the fossil record contains many groups of aquatic organisms that became extinct during the Flood deposition of the sedimentary rock layers.[6] Some organisms would have simply succumbed to the trauma of the turbulence, being swept away and effectively buried alive.[7]

Others would have found their suitable living spaces destroyed, and hence died for lack of appropriate habitats. Too much freshwater for marine-dependent organisms or vice versa would have killed those unable to adapt. However, not only are there such salt versus freshwater problems for aquatic organisms, but also problems of temperature, light, oxygen, contaminants, and nutritional conditions.

To simplify this discussion, only the three main factors affecting survival will be highlighted, primarily with respect to fish — salinity, temperature, and turbidity.

5. M.M. Ellis, "Detection and Measurement of Stream Pollution," in *Biology of Water Pollution*, L.E. Keup, W.M. Ingram, and K.M. Mackenthun, eds., US Department of Interior, Federal Water Pollution Control Administration, p. 129–155, 1967.
6. S.M. Stanley, *Extinction* (New York, NY: Scientific American Books, 1987); J.C. Briggs, "A Cretaceous-Tertiary Mass Extinction?" *BioScience* 41 (1991) 619–724; D.J. Bottjer et al., eds., *Exceptional Fossil Preservation: A Unique View on the Evolution of Marine Life* (New York, NY: Columbia University Press, 2002).
7. A.A. Snelling, "The World's a Graveyard," *Answers*, April–June 2008, p. 76–79.

Salinity

Many of today's marine organisms are able to survive large salinity changes, especially estuarine and tidal pool organisms. For example, starfish can tolerate indefinitely seawater with salt concentrations as low as 16–18 percent of the normal level.[8] Barnacles can withstand exposure to less than 10 percent the usual salt concentration of seawater.

Fish, as with all other marine organisms, however, have a problem balancing the fluids outside their bodies with those inside. Freshwater fish are constantly adding too much fresh water to their bodies from food, drinking water, and tissue transfer. On the other hand, marine fish get too little fresh water to maintain their fluid balance, due to the large salt input in their drinking water and the constant osmotic pressure to draw fresh water out of their tissues into the surrounding sea water.[9]

The kidneys and gills are used by fish to manage this balance. If a freshwater fish takes in too much water, then its kidneys secrete as much water as possible, while retaining the circulating salts. Marine bony fish get rid of excess salts largely through their gills, and conserve internal water through resorption. Saltwater sharks have high concentrations of urea in their blood to retain water in the saltwater environment, whereas freshwater sharks have low concentrations of urea to avoid accumulating water. When sawfish move from saltwater to freshwater they increase their urine output 20-fold, and their blood urea concentration decreases to less than one-third.[10]

There are migratory fish that travel between salt and freshwater. For example, salmon, striped bass, sea-run trout, and Atlantic sturgeon move from seawater to freshwater to spawn, but they return to seawater to mature. Eels do just the opposite, reproducing in saltwater but growing to maturity in freshwater streams and lakes. Obviously, all these fish are able to reverse their removal of water and salt by osmotic regulation according to the amount of salt in their environment. On the other hand, sunfishes and cod remain in freshwater and seawater, respectively, for their whole life cycles. Such fish have very narrow limits of salt tolerance, beyond which the environmental conditions are lethal to them.[11]

Within many families of fish there is much evidence of hybridization, suggesting that these families may represent the biblical created "kinds." In most families

8. D.J. Batten, "How Did Fresh- and Saltwater Fish Survive the Flood?" in *The Answers Book: Updated and Expanded*, D.J. Batten, K.A. Ham, J. Sarfati, and C. Wieland, eds. (Brisbane, Australia: Answers in Genesis, 1999), p. 175–178.
9. E. Florey, *An Introduction to General and Comparative Animal Physiology* (Philadelphia, PA: W.B. Saunders, 1966), p. 97–110.
10. Batten, "How Did Fresh- and Saltwater Fish Survive the Flood?" *The Answers Book*.
11. E.P. Odum, *Fundamentals of Ecology* (Philadelphia, PA: W.B. Saunders, 1971), p. 328, 354.

of fish alive today there are also both freshwater and saltwater varieties[12] ("species" in the man-made classification system) — for example, toadfish, gar-pike, bowfin, sturgeon, herring/anchovy, salmon/trout/pike, catfish, clingfish, stickleback, scorpion-fish, and flatfish. This suggests that the ability to tolerate and adjust to large changes in water salinity was probably present in most fish at the time of the Flood.

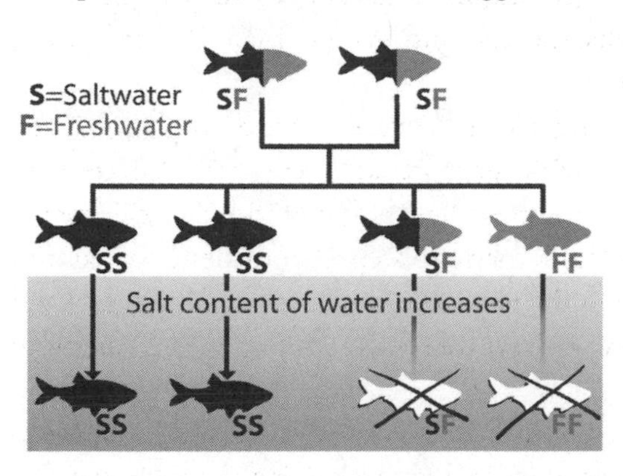

We have to also remember that there has been some post-Flood specialization in some fish "kinds." For example, the Atlantic sturgeon is a migratory salt and freshwater species, but the Siberian sturgeon (a different species in the same "kind") lives only in freshwater. Natural selection has probably resulted in the loss of the ability to tolerate saltwater.

Furthermore, hybrids of freshwater trout and migratory salmon are known, suggesting the differences between freshwater and marine fish may be quite minor. Indeed, the physiological differences may only be largely differences in degree rather than in kind. Many of today's fish species have the capacity to adapt to both fresh and salt water within their own lifetimes. This is why major aquariums are able to house freshwater and saltwater fish together, by using this ability of fish to adapt to water of different salinity from their normal habitats.

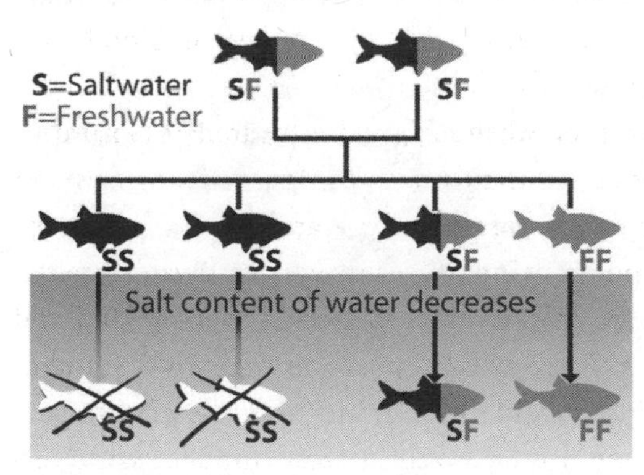

Temperature

The range of temperatures tolerated by fish varies from species to species and their habitats. Some fish have a very narrow range of temperature tolerance in cold, warm, or hot water. Other fish tolerate a wide range of temperatures, from freezing to hot waters (0–32°C, 32–90°F). Stages in the development of juvenile fish are frequently limited by the same narrow range of temperatures required by the adult fish.

12. Batten, "How Did Fresh- and Saltwater Fish Survive the Flood?" *The Answers Book.*

Most fish species, including cold-water types, can tolerate at least brief exposure to warm water at 24°C (75°F) and colder water approaching 2°C (36°F), as long as there are prolonged acclimation periods (several days to weeks). The preferred temperature ranges for some representative adult fish are: trout 16–21°C (61–70°F), sunfish 16–28°C (61–82°F), catfish 21–29°C (70–84°F), eel 16–28°C (61–82°F), and codfish 12–16°C (54–61°F).[13]

It should be emphasized that these abilities pertain to fish today. These fish species have probably been naturally selected within their kinds since the Flood and may have lost much of their original ability to survive in more extreme temperature ranges.[14] It makes more sense to postulate that God created fish to survive in moderate temperatures, with the genetic information available to subsequently select for survival in various more extreme environments.

Turbidity

Organic particles, dust and fine silt, bacteria, and plankton that are usually in suspension in natural waters are measured photoelectrically as turbidity. Such materials adversely affect fish by sinking to the seafloor, lake floor, etc., and covering it with a smothering layer that adversely affects spawning sites and kills organisms that the fish eat. Additionally, the abrasiveness of silt particles damages the gills of fish.

Turbidity also screens out light, decreasing the photic zone where photosynthesis can occur, and thus reduces the available oxygen for fish. The turbidity ranges can be described as clear (less than 10 parts per million, ppm or mg/l of particles in the water), turbid (10–250 ppm), and very turbid (greater than 250 ppm). It has been found that many fish species can survive in water with turbidities of 100,000 ppm for a week or more.[15]

Survival Strategies During the Flood

The heavy rainfall over the land would have quickly filled river basins with torrential flows. Such flooded rivers would have emptied these torrential flows

13. A. Calhorn, *Inland Fisheries Management* (The Resources Agency of California, Department of Fish and Game, 1966), p. 194, 375, 348; W.A. Anikouchine and R.W. Sternberg, *The World Ocean: An Introduction to Oceanography* (Englewood Cliffs, NJ: Prentice-Hall, 1973), p. 215, 233.
14. Batten, "How Did Fresh- and Saltwater Fish Survive the Flood?" *The Answers Book*; G. Purdom, "Is Natural Selection the Same Thing as Evolution?" in *The New Answers Book*, K.A. Ham, ed. (Green Forest, AR: Master Books, 2006), p. 271–282.
15. I.E. Wallen, "The Direct Effect of Turbidity on Fishes," *Oklahoma Agriculture and Mechanics College Bulletin* 48 (1951): 18–24.

out into the oceans as freshwater blankets. Such massive freshwater outflows from the continents would combine with the rainfall over the oceans to form freshwater layers sitting on top of the salty ocean waters, technically known as haloclines that are stable for extended time periods. In such highly stratified, strong density gradients or salt-wedge estuary situations,[16] fish flushed out from land aquatic systems could have continued to survive in freshwater environment pockets. In similar situations today, both marine and freshwater organisms are found living in the same water column, but within their preferred water conditions.

Stratification of water layers like this might even have survived strong winds if the depths of the freshwater layers were great enough to prevent internal current mixing. Turbulence may also have been sufficiently low at high latitudes for such layering to persist. Thus, situations are quite likely to have occurred during the Flood where freshwater and marine fish could have survived in water suited to them, in spite of being temporarily displaced from their normal habitats.

Different levels of salinity in pockets of water during the flood

On the other hand, very turbid water carrying silt and sediment particles, and water flows with enormous sediment bedloads, would have also moved off the continents out into the oceans. There the silt and sediment particles would have settled in the deeper water, "raining" down on the seafloor, across which ground-hugging slurries and debris flows traversed. Heavier sediment particles would have fallen out in the slower-moving coastal waters to be deposited near the landward-advancing coastlines as the sea level rose, whereas the mudflows and debris flows would deposit their loads out over the deeper seafloors.

Although there would have obviously been turbulence at the interfaces between the freshwater and saltwater layers, the silt and sediment particles would probably have settled without appreciable mixing of the waters, especially given the predominance of the powerful horizontal currents during the Flood. With the range of tolerance already cited above, many fish would have been able to survive the extended exposure to high water turbidities.

As already noted above, the hydridization within many fish kinds today suggests that the ability to tolerate and adjust to large changes in water salinity

16. Odum, *Fundamentals of Ecology*.

and turbidity was probably present in most fish at the time of the Flood. If fish were thus capable of such hydridization during the Flood, then they definitely had the ability to cope with the wide fluctuations and ranges of temperatures and turbidities of the Flood waters. Perhaps what fish we have today are more extreme examples of selection and thus are less apt to survive now compared to the fish during the Flood.

Another possibility is that the eggs of marine organisms survived the Flood to then develop into the adults that re-populated the post-Flood ocean waters. These might have done better than full-grown fish, for example, at surviving the harsh water conditions during the Flood, because the "skin" of the eggs would maintain the necessary conditions within the eggs for embryo survival.

Another Lesson from Mount St. Helens

The recovery of animals and plants at Mount St. Helens after the May 18, 1980, eruption both demonstrates and documents rapid and widely ranging restoration after a geologic catastrophe.[17] Obviously, the Flood was several orders of magnitude greater than a catastrophe, but such an eruption event does show us how the biosphere recovers and re-establishes itself.

With regard to the three key water properties of interest, significant changes were recorded in the affected areas. Salinity increased from 0.01 ppm (mg/l) before the eruption to 150.5 ppm after it. Similarly, the surface water temperatures increased from 4°C (39°F) to 22.4°C (72°F), and turbidity increased from 0.75 ppm (mg/l) to 24.6 ppm.[18]

A little more than a month after the eruption (June 30), the lake most exposed to the catastrophic event, Spirit Lake, had tolerable salinity, ambient temperature, and low turbidity. All endemic fish had obviously been killed by the catastrophe, and probably could not have survived if re-introduced in those waters at that time, due to the large demand for oxygen from the water for the decaying tree debris, and the seeps of methane and sulfur dioxide. But within ten years this lake was able to support fish, with many other aquatic species back and well established.

Perhaps the most significant post-eruption observation, though, was that a variety of habitats within and adjacent to the blast zone survived the

17. K.B. Cumming, "How Could Fish Survive the Genesis Flood?" *Impact* #222, (Dallas, TX: Institute for Creation Research, 1991).
18. R.C. Wissmar et al., "Chemical Changes of Lakes Within the Mount St. Helens Blast Zone," *Science* 216 (1982): 175–178; R.C. Wissmar et al., "Biological Responses of Lakes in the Mount St. Helens Blast Zone," *Science* 216 (1982): 178–181.

catastrophe with minimal impact on continuity of the ecosystems. Meta Lake, within the blast zone, for example, had an ice cover at the time of the searing blast, which protected the dormant ecosystem underneath from experiencing much disruption from the heat, oxygen depletion, and air-fall volcanic ash. Fish and support systems picked up where they left off before the onset of the winter season.

Similar observations were made in Swift Reservoir, in spite of massive mud and debris flows into the lake. Fish were displaced into adjacent unaffected watersheds or downstream into lower reservoirs. However, within two years massive plankton blooms had occurred and ecosystem recovery was well underway with migrant "recruits."

Such a confined catastrophe (500 square miles around Mount St. Helens) does enable projection of expectations to a major catastrophe such as the global Flood. First, in spite of the Flood's enormous magnitude there would have been refuges for survival even in close proximity to the most damaging action spots. Second, biological recovery can be incredibly fast — from one month to ten years. Third, recruitment into the recovery zones from nearby minimally affected zones can occur with normal migratory behavior of organisms. Thus, even though some animal and plant populations, or even species, might be annihilated in catastrophic events, remnant individuals can re-establish new populations.

Conclusion

Many aquatic creatures were killed in the Flood because of the turbidity of the water and changes in salinities and temperatures. Indeed, the geologic record testifies to the massive destruction of marine life, with shallow-water marine invertebrates alone accounting for an estimated 95 percent by number of the fossil record.[19]

Many marine creatures, such as trilobites and ichthyosaurs, probably became extinct as a result of the Flood. However, many fish must have survived in the Flood waters, as they were not taken aboard the ark, and yet they are in today's oceans, lakes, and rivers. As discussed here, there are many simple, plausible explanations for how freshwater and saltwater fish could have survived in spite of the water conditions during the Flood.

Furthermore, if the hydridization within many fish kinds today suggests that the ability to tolerate and adjust to large changes in water salinity and turbidity was

19. K.P. Wise, in a recorded lecture, c.1992, as quoted in J.D. Morris, *The Young Earth: The Real History of the Earth-Past, Present, and Future*, second edition (Green Forest, AR: Master Books,2007), p. 74.

probably present in most fish at the time of and during the global Flood, then they definitely had the ability to cope with the wide fluctuations and ranges of temperatures and turbidities of the Flood waters. Indeed, there are more species of fish today than any other group of vertebrates, which possibly attests to their ability to hybridize and diversify. Thus, there is no reason to doubt the reality of a global Flood as described in God's Word.

21

What about Cosmology?

DR. DANNY FAULKNER

Since the late 1960s, the dominant cosmology has been the big-bang model. The big bang is a hypothetical event in which the universe suddenly appeared 13.71 billion years ago. Initially much smaller, denser, and hotter, the universe expanded and cooled to the one that we see today. The big-bang theory is a radical departure from more than two millennia of thinking on cosmology, for since ancient times many Western scientists and philosophers had assumed that the universe was eternal. It ought to be obvious that an eternal universe does not square with Genesis 1:1, which declares that "in the beginning God created the heavens and the earth," collectively referring to the creation of all that exists in the physical world.

Many Christians have embraced the big-bang cosmology, distilling the theory down to the fact that the big bang represents a beginning of the universe, apparently in some concordance with Genesis 1:1. However, closer examination reveals that the big bang does not agree with the details of the biblical creation account at all.

Big Bang Background

Before delving into that, we ought to mention a little background on the big-bang model. The big-bang model relies upon the expansion of the universe, first confirmed by Edwin Hubble in 1928. The expansion of the universe had been predicted by Einstein's theory of gravity, general relativity, more than a decade earlier. Einstein had realized the implication of an expanding universe possibly requiring a beginning, so he introduced the cosmological constant into his solution of the universe to produce a cosmology that was not expanding, and hence could exist eternally.

This static universe was no longer tenable once Hubble showed that the universe was expanding. However, proponents of an eternal universe did not give in. Prior to 1965, the most popular cosmology was the steady state theory. The steady state model acknowledges that expansion occurs, but hypothesizes that as the universe expands, more matter spontaneously comes into existence to preserve a constant density. This steady state model is eternal — without beginning and without end.

The steady state model had tremendous philosophical appeal well into the 1960s as people had difficulty thinking about the universe in any other way than being eternal. All this changed with the 1965 discovery of the cosmic microwave background (CMB), a low-level, nearly uniform radiation permeating the universe from all directions. Since the CMB had been predicted by the big-bang model as early as 1948, and the steady state theory could not account for the CMB, most scientists adopted the big-bang model shortly after 1965.

Variations on the steady state model have not entirely gone away — there are a few adherents around today. A notable variation of the steady state theory today is plasma cosmology. However, the big-bang theory is so dominant today that these steady state variations are virtually irrelevant, so we will concentrate on the big-bang model.

Genesis and the Big Bang

As previously mentioned, some Christians adopt the big-bang model as part of their apologetic. If the universe had a beginning in agreement with the creation account, then they reason that this offers a tool to somehow prove that the Bible is true. Since the modern big-bang model hypothesizes that the universe began 13.71 billion years ago, belief in the big bang requires belief in a universe much older than the few thousand years calculated from the Old Testament chronologies. How do people reconcile this colossal difference?

The gap theory, day-age theories, allegory, and the framework hypothesis are all different ways that people have attempted to reconcile the discrepancy. All of these attempts have been discussed elsewhere, but suffice it to say here that each poorly handles Scripture. And these solutions raise thorny questions as well. What is the origin of sin? What is the penalty of sin? Did death precede the Fall of mankind? While many old-age creationists attempt to hold onto some semblance of orthodoxy on these questions, regrettably many do not, opting to allegorize much of the first few chapters of Genesis.

Other Issues

But there are other problems as well. For instance, the big-bang model posits that stars and galaxies formed within a billion years of the beginning of the universe, and that star formation continues today. Since the solar system is supposedly 4.6 billion years old, this would mean at least eight billion years of star formation preceded the creation of the earth. However, the Genesis 1 text tells us that earth preceded the stars; the earth was made on day 1 and the stars on day 4. Furthermore, in no way could one say that the creation has been completed if it is an ongoing process now.

The naturalistic origin of stars itself is a problem. Astronomers have theories of how stars form, but each one requires that stars first exist. Current cosmological theories suggest that star formation in the early universe was very intense, with stars forming at a rate many orders of magnitude faster than today. How this came about is unknown. Astronomers generally agree that some unknown mechanism triggered star formation at a prodigious rate. Is this science?

With the largest telescopes we can see distant galaxies that presumably formed in the early universe, and hence are very young. We see that these distant galaxies have the same structure that nearby, supposedly much older, galaxies have. However, physics would seem to dictate that galaxies change with age, but this does not appear to be the case in a big-bang universe.

Additionally, the big-bang model requires that the universe begin with all matter in the universe in the form of hydrogen and helium (and a trifling bit of lithium). All other heavier elements, such as oxygen, calcium, and iron, were gradually forged through nucleosynthesis in later generations of stars. However, the spectra of distant (and supposedly younger) galaxies are rich in heavier elements. This would seem to violate a basic tenet of the big-bang model, instead allowing for heavier elements to exist from the beginning.

An Evolving Model

The big-bang model itself has undergone quite an evolution since its widespread acceptance. It is interesting to compare the big-bang model at the time of the writing of this chapter, 2009, to the big-bang model of 1984, just 25 years earlier. From about 1960 to the early 1990s, the best measure of the expansion rate of the universe (the Hubble constant) was about 50 km/s/Mpc (kilometers per second per megaparsec). In the early 1990s, that rate was increased to nearly 80 km/s/Mpc. Around 1980 some astronomers had attempted to raise the Hubble constant to nearly 100 km/s/Mpc, but their work was largely rejected at the time as most astronomers thought that the lower value was firmly established.

Of course, now astronomers think that the higher value is firmly established. With a faster expansion rate, the inferred age of the universe has diminished. With the earlier value of the Hubble constant, the age was solidly thought to be 16–18 billion years old. Now cosmologists think that the universe is 13.71 billion years, give or take 1 percent. Notice that the error bars on those two figures do not overlap, so they both cannot be correct.

Several physical effects now taken as a given in big-bang models were not largely accepted in 1984. One example is inflation, first proposed by Alan Guth in 1980. Inflation was invoked to explain several problems with the big bang, such as the flatness and horizon problems. While inflationary big-bang models were being developed in 1984, these models were not widely accepted until a few years later. Other effects include string theory, dark matter, and dark energy.

Among theoretical physicists, string theory is the current explanation of how elementary particles of matter work. String theory is the idea that elementary particles are a sort of vibration in at least six additional dimensions of space. These six dimensions occur in two sets of three each. Today, these additional dimensions are rolled up beyond our ability to detect them, but in the hot cauldron of the early big bang the high temperatures would have made these extra dimensions manifest. So any serious big-bang model now must incorporate them, though in 1984 few, if any, models did. Dark matter is a mysterious substance that reveals itself by its gravitational influence. While dark matter was first proposed in the 1930s, good data to support it began to arise in the 1970s. Yet dark matter generally was not included in big-bang models of 1984.

Finally in 1999, an extensive study combined data from several different programs to produce what was then the definitive description of some parameters of the big bang. Much to the amazement of all, the data showed what appeared to be an increase in the rate of expansion of the universe. Normally, gravity ought to be sufficient to rein in expansion, but this effect was as if space were repelling itself. This effect is very similar to Einstein's cosmological constant, though the re-christened "dark energy" was intentionally named to underscore the more modern approach to how such a thing might happen. We ought to add that some of these effects, such as string theory and inflation, have no data to support them — they are included only because theoretical physicists and cosmologists think that they describe the way the world works.

So let us compare the big-bang model of today and 25 years earlier. Then, the expansion rate and hence the inferred age of the universe were remarkably different from the rate and age today. Then, there was no inflation, while today one would not think of leaving inflation out of a big-bang model. Then, string theory had not yet been developed, but now it must be included in a big-bang model. Then, dark matter, though known, was not included in cosmological models, but today it is a must to include it. Einstein's cosmological constant was thrown out by 1930, but it came roaring back 70 years later to be included in today's model.

In short, the big-bang model of 25 years ago bears almost no resemblance to the big-bang model of today. How confident of the big-bang model were cosmologists 25 years ago? They had complete confidence. How confident are today's cosmologists of the current big-bang model? They have complete confidence. If cosmologists were right then, they cannot be right today; if cosmologists are right today, they could not have been right 25 years ago. We have no idea what the big-bang model will be like 25 years hence, but we can be certain of two things: the model will be very different then from now, and cosmologists will have complete confidence in that model.

Some of these changes to the big-bang model were driven by changes in theoretical physics, as with string theory. Others were driven by new data, such as dark energy and a revised expansion rate and age. However, some, such as inflation, were invoked merely to salvage the big-bang model. This reveals a deep philosophical problem with the big-bang model. The model has become very plastic. That is, any unexpected new observation or problem can be solved by the appropriate addition of some new effect or some new field.

Some view this as constraining the model and providing physical rigor, but at some point one has to question whether the big-bang model is falsifiable. That is, is there some new result or data that could disprove the model? It would appear that with proper corrections to the model allowed, this will never happen. If this indeed is the situation, then is the big-bang model a scientific model in any way?

Nearly two millennia ago, Claudius Ptolemy published his famous geocentric model of the solar system with planets moving along epicycles that in turn orbited about the earth. In terms of longevity, the Ptolemaic model is the most successful scientific theory of all time, lasting 15 centuries. Throughout the middle ages, scientists found that when the theory did not match observations, they could fix the problem by adding additional epicycles. Unlimited modification allowed for the model to explain everything and anything that happened to arise.

Ultimately, most people realized that the Ptolemaic model became far too complex for its own good, and it collapsed under its own weight in favor of the much simpler heliocentric model. A model that can explain anything and everything is not a good theory. The big-bang model has already demonstrated that it, too, can endure modification *ad infinitum*. At some point we must question whether the big-bang model really is a good theory in the sense that it could be falsified by some new hypothetical result.

Conclusion

The history of science is filled with examples of theories once thought to be unassailable but later discarded. If the history of science is any teacher, then we would expect that the big bang will also be discarded. If we have wedded our apologetic to the big-bang model, then the rejection of the big-bang model will logically lead to the rejection of our apologetic. Many in the Roman Catholic Church four centuries ago embraced the Ptolemaic model, attempting to make it part of Christianity, and it brought discredit to them and their church when that model fell. Those who wish to make the big bang part of the biblical creation model ought to take this lesson to heart. More importantly, the big bang (in any of its versions) is not compatible with a natural reading of the Bible. The Christian should have confidence that God's Word is reliable, regardless of whether it is fashionable for fallible men to agree.

22

Did Life Come from Outer Space?

DR. GEORGIA PURDOM

The simple answer is NO! The Bible states that God created all living things on earth by His spoken word on days 3, 5, and 6 of the creation week. However, the concept that life originated in outer space and was then transferred to earth is popular in today's society. Some believe that bacteria (considered "primitive" life) or organic molecules necessary for life came from other planets, meteors, or comets. Some even suggest that intelligent extraterrestrial aliens sent life to earth. Many people are eager to believe in any ideas concerning the origin of life as long as they exclude the Creator God and the truth of His Word.

Why Life from Outer Space?

Why do scientists want to push the origin of life into outer space rather than believe that life originated on earth? The answer: complexity and time.

Complexity

Life on earth is very complex. Bacteria are considered to be the simplest life form. However, several examples from the bacterial world make it clear that the word "simple" is a relative term. Some of the "simplest" are endosymbionts — organisms that live entirely within other organisms. *Candidatus Carsonella rudii*, a bacterium that lives within the cells of the psyllid insect *Pachypsylla venusta*, is considered to have the smallest genome of any endosymbiotic bacteria.[1] It has 159,662 base pairs (DNA), which encode approximately 182 genes. The genes encode proteins for amino acid (components of protein) biosynthesis, which the host insect cannot get from its diet. The host insect provides necessary proteins that are not encoded by the bacterial genome.

Nanoarchaeum equitans, an archaeal (single-celled microorganism similar to bacteria) symbiont of the archaea *Ignicoccus*, has 490,885 base pairs, which encode approximately 552 genes. Although many of the gene functions are currently unknown, the authors of the paper that sequenced the genome stated that "the *complexity* of its information processing systems and the simplicity of its metabolic apparatus suggests an unanticipated world of organisms to be discovered" (emphasis mine).[2]

Mycoplasma genitalium has 580,076 base pairs, which encode approximately 521 genes.[3] Because of its small genome size, *M. genitalium* was the bacteria of choice for determination of the minimal genome (or minimum number of genes) needed to sustain life. However, determination of the minimal genome has been hampered by the finding that many bacterial genomes encode backup or alternative pathways, which are used when the main pathway is removed. Scientists have stated that this may lead up to a 45 percent *underestimation* of the minimal genes needed to sustain life.[4] As can be seen from these examples, life in even its "simplest" forms is very complex!

Time

According to secular timelines, the earth is 4.5 billion years old. Other parts of outer space are much older (up to 15 billion years old according to big-bang models). Since evolution works by random chance and even the simplest bacteria isn't very simple, a lot of time would be required for life to evolve. Many secular scientists suggest the earth is simply not old enough to allow for the evolution of living organisms. Thus, many scientists push the origin of life into outer space to gain the time needed for life to evolve.

1. Atsushi Nakabachi et al., "The 160-Kilobase Genome of the Bacterial Endosymbiont Carsonella," *Science* 314 no. 5797 (2006): 267.
2. Elizabeth Waters et al., "The Genome of Nanoarchaeum equitans: Insights Into Early Archaeal Evolution and Derived Parasitism," *Proceedings of the National Academy of Sciences USA* 100 no. 22 (2003): 12984–12988.
3. JCVI Comprehensive Microbial Resource, "*Mycoplasma genitalium* G-37 Genome Page," www.cmr.jcvi.org/cgi-bin/CMR/GenomePage.cgi?org=gmg.
4. Csaba Pál et al., "Chance and Necessity in the Evolution of Minimal Metabolic Networks," *Nature* 440 no. 7084 (2006): 667–670.

Does Life Exist in Outer Space?

If life came to earth from outer space, then many scientists suggest that we should be able to find evidence for living things on nearby planets, meteors, and comets. Although billions of dollars have been spent in the search for extraterrestrial life, none has been found.

Mars

Several unmanned exploration probes, rovers, and landers have been sent to Mars to determine if our closest rocky neighbor supports life or may have harbored it in the past. NASA's Phoenix lander identified water in a sample of martian soil.[5] Another NASA space probe identified specific minerals that suggested liquid water had been present on the martian surface for a longer period of time then previously estimated.[6] Scott Murchie of Johns Hopkins University stated, "This is an exciting discovery because it extends the time range for liquid water on Mars, and the places where it might have supported life."[7] Although water is certainly needed for life to exist, water alone does not result in life.

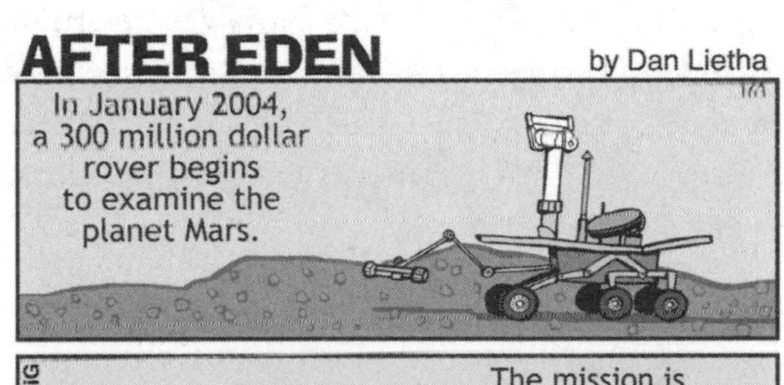

Other components of martian rocks and soil make the likelihood of finding life very unlikely. NASA's Opportunity rover produced evidence that rocks had once been in an environment that was very salty and acidic.[8] Dr. Andrew Knoll, biologist at Harvard University, stated, "It was really salty — in fact, it was salty enough that only a

5. BBC News, "Nasa's Lander Samples Mars Water," www.news.bbc.co.uk/2/hi/science/nature/7536123.stm.
6. BBC News, "New Minerals Point to Wetter Mars," www.news.bbc.co.uk/2/hi/science/nature/7696669.stm.
7. Ibid.
8. BBC News, "Early Mars 'Too Salty' for Life," www.news.bbc.co.uk/2/hi/science/nature/7248062.stm.

handful of known terrestrial organisms would have a ghost of a chance of surviving there when conditions were at their best."[9]

Methane, a gas associated with biological activity (think belching cows!), has been found in the martian atmosphere. Colin Pillinger, planetary scientist at the Open University (UK), stated, "The most obvious source of methane is organisms. So if you find methane in an atmosphere, you can suspect there is life. It's not proof, but it makes it worth a much closer look."[10] However, Nick Pope, formerly associated with the British Government's UFO project at the Ministry of Defense, thinks methane is proof, calling this discovery "the most important discovery of all time," and saying further, "We've really only scratched the surface — it's an absolute certainty that there is life out there and we are not alone."[11]

The biological source of methane is believed to be bacteria living deep underground. However, it could also be due to volcanism or an unknown geological process on Mars since "plumes" of methane were identified in 2003 and the distribution of methane was found to be patchy.[12] If the methane is of geological origin then it would actually make the martian surface very inhospitable for life.[13]

Moons of Jovian Planets

Several moons of Jupiter and Saturn, including Europa, Titan, and Enceladus, are thought to be possible sources of extraterrestrial life. All are thought to have interior oceans that might harbor bacterial life. Plumes containing water vapor erupting from Enceladus have been shown to contain organic molecules such as methane, formaldehyde, ethanol, and other hydrocarbons.[14]

Europa's underground oceans are predicted to be violent.[15] The waves generated in these oceans are postulated to provide an energy source necessary for life. Robert Tyler, an oceanographer at the University of Washington, stated, "The big thing is to have liquid water — and to the extent that this new paper [on violent

9. Ibid.
10. Fox News, "Clouds of Methane May Mean Life on Mars," www.foxnews.com/story/0,2933,479997,00.html.
11. Ibid.
12. Judith Burns, "Martian Methane Mystery Deepens," BBC News, www.news.bbc.co.uk/2/hi/science/nature/8186314.stm.
13. Ibid.
14. Lori Stiles, "Evidence for Ocean on Enceladus: Tiny Saturn Moon Could Be Targeted in Search for Extraterrestrial Life," PhysOrg, www.physorg.com/news167498118.html.
15. Anne Minard, "Jupiter Moon Has Violent, Hidden Oceans, Study Suggests," National Geographic News, www.news.nationalgeographic.com/news/2008/12/081210-europa-oceans.html.

oceans in Europa] adds an energy source, all the better for life's prospects."[16] But water plus organic molecules plus energy does not equal life. Life requires information (DNA), and information requires an intelligent source (God).

Comets

Scientists have made calculations (based on cosmological time frames of billions of years) that in the past, comets had liquid water interiors.[17] NASA's Stardust spacecraft collected samples from the dust of comet Wild 2 and found the amino acid glycine (the simplest of all amino acids).[18] Carl Pilcher, director of the NASA Astrobiology Institute, stated, "The discovery of glycine in a comet supports the idea that the fundamental building blocks are prevalent in space, and strengthens the argument that life in the universe may be common rather than rare."[19] This seems to be an overstatement since only 1 amino acid of the 20 required for life was found and other components for life such as DNA, fats, and sugars have not been found. Again, the formula of water plus amino acids (or other organic molecules) does not equal life.

Life has not yet been found in outer space and it is unlikely to exist because conditions appear too hostile for even the hardiest forms of life to exist. Even if the ingredients necessary for life (organic molecules like amino acids) were transported to earth and added to water and an energy source, life would not miraculously emerge. Life only comes from life, and life only from the Life-Giver.

If Life Did Exist in Outer Space, Could it Have Been Transferred to Earth?

Panspermia is the common name given to the concept that life originated in outer space and then migrated or was transported to earth. Panspermia is not a new idea. Lord Kelvin in 1871 suggested that life came to earth on meteors. Svante Arrhenius coined the term in 1908 and is considered the father of panspermia. We will look at the three categories mentioned in the previous section and determine if transfer of life from these sources to earth is plausible.

Mars

Several meteors of suspected martian origin have been discovered on earth. It is estimated that 5–10 percent of martian ejecta (derived from impacts by

16. Ibid.
17. PhysOrg, "Evidence of Liquid Water in Comets Reveals Possible Origin of Life," www.physorg.com/news168179623.html.
18. Bill Steigerwald, "First Discovery of Life's Building Block in Comet Made," PhysOrg, www.physorg.com/news169736472.html.
19. Ibid.

comets or asteroids) would reach earth in 100 million years (with the minimum amount of time being seven months).[20] Small ejecta (> 1 cm) could arrive on earth as meteorites with a burnt outer area but an inner cool area where bacteria could presumably survive.[21] But of the known martian meteorites, M.J. Burchell of the Centre for Astrophysics and Planetary Sciences at the University of Kent (UK), says that "given their size and transfer times (estimated from exposure to radiation in space), all will have received a sterilizing radiation dose during their transit to earth."[22]

Moons of Jovian Planets

Impacts of these moons by comets or asteroids are also thought to generate ejecta that could then travel to other locations (but not directly to earth).[23] The ejecta are postulated to travel farther into space and possibly be transferred to comets or asteroids.[24] The bacteria would presumably survive in the icy interior of the comets/asteroids.[25] The comets/asteroids could then travel to earth and so indirectly bring life from the Jovian moons.

Comets

During their travel close to a planet, comets could leave behind dust grains that would fall into planetary atmospheres.[26] If life existed in the dust grains and could survive travel through the atmosphere, then presumably a comet could transfer life to earth.

The transfer of material from Mars, Jovian moons, and comets is plausible and in some cases has been documented. However, dust and rocks are not affected by the extreme cold and radiation of outer space, whereas life would be and would probably not survive the journey to earth. Since life has not been found to exist in outer space it is doubtful life was transferred to earth from these locations.[27]

---

20. M.J. Burchell, "Panspermia Today," International Journal of Astrobiology 3 no. 2 (2004): 73–80.
21. Ibid.
22. Ibid.
23. Ibid.
24. Ibid.
25. Ibid.
26. Ibid.
27. If bacterial life is ever discovered on Mars or anywhere else in outer space, we must recognize that it might be contamination from our own space exploration. Just as it is possible for material from outer space to be transferred to earth, the reverse transfer (from earth to outer space) is also possible. Precautions are taken to ensure that spacecrafts are sterile, but none are completely sterile.

Could Life Have Been Brought to Earth by Intelligent Extraterrestrial Aliens?

The concept that aliens brought life to earth is called directed panspermia. The term was first coined by the co-discoverer of the structure of DNA, Francis Crick, and Leslie Orgel in 1973.[28] They postulated that since earth is relatively young compared to the rest of the universe that it was conceivable that a technologically advanced society in outer space developed even before earth existed (since it only took 4.5 billions years for a technological society to form on earth). Crick and Orgel believe that this alien society then seeded or "infected" other parts of outer space including earth with primitive forms of life (like bacteria). In their 1973 paper they propose the spaceship payload, the mechanisms needed to protect the bacteria for their long trip to earth, and possible motivations by the alien society for seeding life in outer space.

One of their main evidences to support this possibility comes from the similarity of the genetic code in all living things. They stated, "The universality of the genetic code follows naturally from an 'infective' theory of the origins of life. Life on earth would represent a clone derived from a single extraterrestrial organism."[29] The universality of the genetic code only follows "naturally" from their theory because of their presuppositions or starting point that their ideas about the past are supreme to God's Word concerning the history of the origin of life on earth. When we begin with God's Word we see that the universality of the genetic code follows naturally from a common Designer who created all living things by His Word.

The concept of directed panspermia is still advocated by many scientists today. In the movie *Expelled*, Ben Stein asked Richard Dawkins, a very prominent evolutionary biologist, the question, "What do you think is the possibility that . . . intelligent design might turn out to be the answer to some issues in genetics or in evolution?"[30]

Dawkins's reply:

> Well it could come about in the following way: it could be that at some earlier time somewhere in the universe a civilization evolved by, probably by, some kind of Darwinian means to a very, very high level of technology and designed a form of life that they seeded onto perhaps this this [*sic*] planet. Now that is a possibility and an intriguing possibility. And I suppose it's possible that you might find

28. F.H.C. Crick and L.E. Orgel, "Directed Panspermia," *Icarus* 19 (1973): 341–346.
29. Ibid.
30. *Expelled*, DVD, directed by Nathan Frankowski (Premise Media, 2008).

> evidence for that if you look at the, at the detail . . . details of our chemistry molecular biology you might find a signature of some sort of designer.

Burchell stated, "At present, Panspermia can neither be proved nor disproved. Nevertheless, Panspermia is an intellectual idea which holds strong attraction."[31] Sadly, this is true for many who want to exclude God and the history presented in His Word in deference to their own ideas about the past — no matter how outlandish.

Could God Have Created Life on Planets Other than Earth?

Yes, but why? Remember that God spent the vast majority of the creation week preparing the earth for the crowning glory of His creation — man. Everything God created was for man's benefit and enjoyment. Even those things which we don't often consider, like bacteria, were created to benefit man. Bacteria can accomplish this directly through symbiotic relationships in our guts, which help us digest food, and indirectly through cycling of nutrients and chemicals in the environment.[32] Man would seem to gain no benefit or enjoyment from bacteria that exist in outer space. Although we can't rule out that some form of non-intelligent life, such as bacteria, was created on another planet, it seems unlikely knowing the purposes of living organisms and their relationship to man on earth set forth by the Creator God.

31. Burchell, "Panspermia Today."
32. Joseph Francis, "The Organosubstrate of Life," Answers in Genesis, www.answersingenesis.org/articles/aid/v4/n1/organosubstrate-of-life, originally published in *Proceedings of the Fifth International Conference on Creationism*, Robert L. Ivey Jr., ed. (Pittsburgh, PA: Creation Science Fellowship, 2003), p. 433–444.

23

Did the Continents Split Apart in the Days of Peleg?

DR. ANDREW A. SNELLING AND BODIE HODGE

In Genesis chapter 10, two-thirds of the way through the genealogies of the post-Flood patriarchs, we read in verse 25:

> To Eber were born two sons: the name of one was Peleg, for in his days the earth was divided; and his brother's name was Joktan.

The same phrase, "for in his days the earth was divided," also appears in the repetition of this genealogical entry in 1 Chronicles 1:19.

Many find these genealogical lists very boring to read. So they skip over the details and often miss this phrase. However, there are some Christians who get excited about this phrase, and latch on to it, suggesting that maybe this is where continental drift, which secular scientists have proposed, fits into the Bible!

It seems odd that this little "nugget" should appear in this genealogy of Noah's three sons and their descendants after the Flood. But, does this phrase, "for in his days the earth was divided," suggest that continents drifted apart in the days of Peleg as a result of God dividing and separating the continents?

Have the Continents Shifted?

In today's secular society, people have been taught as fact that the continents were once joined together in a supercontinent that spilt apart

Figure 1. The Mid-Atlantic Ridge is strong support for the concept of plate movement.

and then the resultant continents drifted over millions of years into their present positions. One primary piece of conclusive evidence usually presented to support this idea is the jigsaw-puzzle fit of Europe and Africa matching closely with North and South America, respectively. If the North and South Atlantic Ocean basins are closed, these continents fit together at approximately the Mid-Atlantic Ridge, a range of mountains on the ocean floor centrally located in the Atlantic Ocean basins (figure 1).

It was this reconstruction that led to the idea of the earlier supercontinent called Pangea. The secular concept for this continental drift, now known as plate tectonics, goes further and suggests that there were supercontinents even earlier than Pangea, including Pannotia, and before that Rodinia, encompassing the earth's proposed multi-billion year geologic history.

Creation scientists and Flood geologists do not deny that these continents may have been connected to one another in the past as a single supercontinent in light of Genesis 1:9. Actually, it was a Christian geologist named Antonio Snider in 1859 who was the first person to publicly comment on this jigsaw puzzle fit of all the continents, except that he believed the spreading apart and separation of the continents occurred catastrophically during the Genesis Flood.

Creation scientists believe, along with their secular colleagues, that there is good observational evidence that is consistent with an original supercontinent in the past that was split apart, and that today's continents moved to their present positions on the earth's surface. However, the main difference is the timing!

Whereas our secular colleagues believe these processes were slow and gradual over millions of years, creation scientists insist it all took place by catastrophic means, involving continental *sprint* rather than continental *drift*. However, many Christians who see the specific mention of the earth being divided in the days of Peleg, as quoted from Genesis 10:25, appeal to this particular time for the biblical explanation for continental shifting.

What Happened in the Days of Peleg?

The Context of Genesis 10

A careful search of the context of Genesis 10:25 clearly reveals that the division of the earth refers to the dividing up of the post-Flood people on the basis of languages and families, and moving them into different geographical locations. In fact, all of Genesis 10 is dedicated to dividing up Noah's family into its three major divisions based on Noah's three sons and their families, and then to further list the sub-family groups.

Because these genealogical lists encompassed all the people on the post-Flood earth, the division referred to in verse 25 must have affected the entire post-Flood human population. Several other verses dotted throughout Genesis chapter 10 indicate that it was these people who were being split up by language and moved across the earth to different geographical locations or lands:

> ". . . separated into their land . . ." (Genesis 10:5).
> ". . . the families of the Canaanites were dispersed" (Genesis 10:18).
> ". . . according to their families, according to their languages, in their lands and in their nations" (Genesis 10:20).

Even the culminating verse to the chapter states:

> These were the families of the sons of Noah, according to their generations, in their nations; and from these the nations were divided on the earth after the Flood (Genesis 10:32).

The chronological sequence of events on what happened at the Tower of Babel is given in Genesis chapter 11, where we are told in verse 8 that "the LORD scattered them abroad from there over the face of all the earth. . . ." But it's actually in Genesis chapter 10 where we are told about the different groups of people who were divided up into their families with different languages as a result of the Tower of Babel judgement. It is appropriate to compare Scripture with Scripture in the context it is written. There are four verses listed above in chapter 10 (verses 5, 18, 20, and 32) which explain the statement (in verse 25) that "in his days the earth was divided," as the division of family groupings according to the languages God gave them into different lands across the face of the earth. Verse 25 was not referring to an actual physical division of the earth from one supercontinent into today's many continents.

Another Flood!

Let's stop and consider for a moment what would be the effect of the break-up of a supercontinent followed by the sprinting of the new continents into their present positions. In late 2004, there was an earthquake in the eastern Indian Ocean, resulting in movements of up to 15 or more feet along faults. The energy of the earthquake was transmitted through the water above, producing an enormous tsunami that devastated coastlines all around the Indian Ocean basin, killing more than 220,000 people. And even a few feet of movement on the San Andreas Fault in Southern California causes the ground to shake for many miles, often resulting in the collapse of freeways and other structures.

If the continents did indeed split apart in the days of Peleg, moving thousands of miles into their current positions in a catastrophic manner, the resulting devastation would have utterly destroyed the face of the earth and everything living on it. The ocean waters would have flooded over the continents in huge tsunamis, creating a second worldwide flood event!

In Genesis chapters 10 and 11, we see no written description of such an event. To the contrary, at the end of the Flood in Noah's day God made specific statements that He would never allow another worldwide Flood to ravage the earth's surface and its inhabitants (Genesis 8:21–22; Genesis 9:11). God specifically stated that He had set the boundaries around the land beyond which the waters would never again flood the earth (Psalm 104:8–9).

Of course, in order to shore up their belief that Genesis 10:25 is a reference to continental break-up during the days of Peleg, some may respond that God somehow miraculously held back the ocean waters to keep another flood from happening while this land division occurred. However, there is absolutely no indication in Scripture, not even a hint, that this was the case. Quite clearly, it is far better to err on the side of caution with regard to these Scriptures. This is particularly necessary when the context of Genesis chapter 10 has four other verses that confirm the meaning of verse 25 as referring to the division of people according to their languages into lands of their own across the face of the earth. Furthermore, this is in keeping with God's command to Noah and his family after the Flood to be fruitful and multiply, and to fill the earth (Genesis 9:1).

A Major Geographical Problem

There is also a major geographical flaw with the claim that the continents split apart in the days of Peleg. The description of the Flood of Noah's day in Genesis 8 says that on day 150 of that global, year-long event the ark ran aground in the mountains of Ararat. We read in verses 3-4:

> And the waters receded continually from the earth. At the end of the hundred and fifty days the waters decreased. Then the ark rested in the seventh month, the seventeenth day of the month, on the mountains of Ararat.

Why is this so significant? The mountains of Ararat should not be confused merely with the post-Flood volcano in Turkey called Mt. Ararat. As far as we can tell, the biblical reference to "the mountains of Ararat" speaks of mountains located in the region of eastern Turkey and eastward toward the Caspian Sea.

The buckling of the rock layers within these mountains indicate that they were formed by continental collisions. Thus, if a supercontinent such as Pangea broke apart in the days of Peleg to arrive at their present positions, then these mountains of Ararat would only have formed in the days of Peleg. Thus, they would not have existed on day 150 of the Flood for the ark to run aground on them!

The mountains of Ararat appear to have been caused by the collision of the Eurasian Plate with the Arabian and African Plates, perhaps influenced by the concurrent collision of the Indian Plate with the Eurasian Plate (figure 2). Thus, it would seem that most of the continental shifting between Europe, Asia, Africa, Arabia, and India most likely would have largely been completed by day 150 of the Genesis Flood.

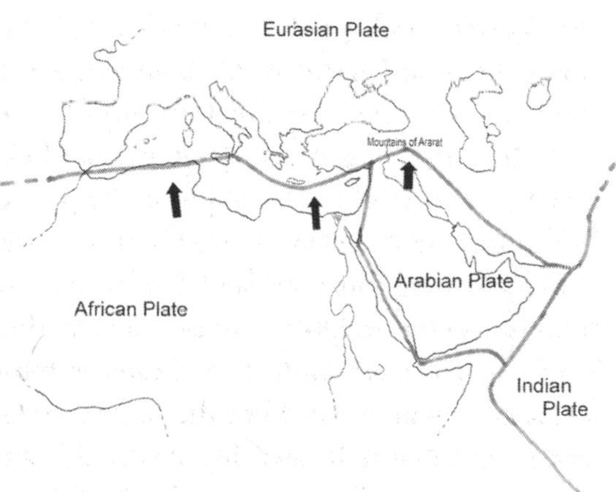

Figure 2: Plate movement resulted in the formation of the Mountains of Ararat.

Naturally, there still could have been comparatively minor adjustments after this point in the Flood, as the mountains of Ararat could still have been rising as further mountain building occurred after the ark ran aground. Again, there appear to be no hints in the biblical narrative of the Flood in Genesis 6–9 that there was any major continental shifting across the earth's surface after day 150, at least in the region of the mountains of Ararat. It's possible, however, that there still could have been some minor continental movement on the other side of the globe, with respect to North and South America, Australia, Antarctica, etc., and so this can't be ruled out entirely. However, according to Genesis 8:2, the fountains or springs of the great deep were stopped, and the windows of heaven were closed, on day 150, implying that the Flood waters possibly had reached their zenith at that point.

Furthermore, if the springs were associated with the rifting of the earth's crust and the seafloor spreading, and subduction and mantle convection that had moved the continental plates apart catastrophically, then the closure of these springs or fountains would seem to imply that the processes allowing for major movement of the continents would have stopped at this point, or at the very least, began to start decelerating, and eventually reach their present snail's pace.

All the primary geologic processes responsible for forcing the catastrophic continental movements during the Flood appear to have likewise begun to rapidly decelerate on and after day 150. Also, Genesis 8:3 indicates that the Flood waters began to steadily decrease and therefore recede from this time point onward, which would seem to indicate that the Flood waters were now subject to new land surfaces and topography rising and valleys sinking as a result of vertical earth movements. This is in stark contrast to the large horizontal movement and associated mountain-building that shifted the continents apart in the first portion of the Flood year.

Further Scientific Support for Continental Shift During the Flood

There are numerous evidences that support the contention that the pre-Flood supercontinent split and the resultant continents shifted apart catastrophically during the Flood. Several of these are highlighted below.

Folded Fossil-bearing Sediment

The fossil-bearing sedimentary layers produced by the Flood include the massive amount of plants buried and fossilized in coal beds. Many of these coal beds in the eastern United States can be traced right across Europe as far as Russia, a testimony to their global-scale formation during the Flood. There are also folded coal seams in the Appalachian Mountains and in the Ural Mountains of Russia. These deformed rock units formed by collisions of continents as a result of rapid continental movement. They were formed before other fossil-bearing sedimentary layers were deposited above the coal beds as a result of continued erosion elsewhere during the Flood. In order to fold and later bury these coal deposits, the continental division and shifting responsible for these mountain-building collisions had to have occurred during the Flood. This is also the same movement of continents that then subsequently separated what is now North and South America from Europe and Africa to form the Atlantic Ocean basins, all during the Flood.[1]

Basalts

Huge areas consisting of thick volcanic rock layers stacked on top of one

1. J.F. Dewey and J.M. Bird, "Mountain Belts and the New Global Tectonics," *Journal of Geophysical Research* 75 no. 14 (1970): 2625–2647; R.S. Dietz, "Geosynclines, Mountains and Continent-building," *Scientific American* 226 no. 3, as reproduced in *Continents Adrift and Continents Aground* (San Francisco, CA: W.H. Freeman and Company, 1976), p. 103–111.

another are found in a number of places on today's continents. Even secular geologists recognize these as catastrophic outpourings of huge volumes of lavas, so they call them flood basalts.[2] The two largest examples are the Siberian Traps and the Deccan Traps of India. A smaller example is the Columbia River Basalt of the U.S. Pacific Northwest. Flood basalts are found on every continent, usually with fossil-bearing sedimentary layers beneath them, and further fossil-bearing sedimentary layers above them, indicating they are also the result of catastrophic volcanic eruptions during the Genesis Flood.

The only way huge volumes of basalt lavas could be supplied for such catastrophic eruptions on such a grand scale was via huge mantle upwellings, called plumes. These plumes likely formed as a result of mantle-wide convection during catastrophic continental break-up and shifting. Since these flood basalts had to be produced during the Genesis Flood, then the rapid continental *sprint* and associated mantle processes also had to have occurred during the Flood.

Apes Buried First

In the post-Flood sediments of Africa (including some volcanic layers), we find fossilized remains of apes, and, by and large, in sediment layers *on top* of them are found fossilized human remains and other evidences of human occupation. This fossil sequence on the African continent is thus trumpeted by evolutionists as evidence of apes and then humans having progressively "evolved" from a common ancestor.

However, in the biblical model the apes started migrating from the Ararat area to Africa as soon as they left the ark, arriving early in the post-Flood period.[2] Noah's descendants stayed together at Babel and didn't migrate into Africa until after the confusion of languages. Thus, humans would have arrived in Africa long after the apes had arrived, and expectedly, we find apes buried and fossilized in the localized post-Flood sediment layers before humans. This logical fossil explanation requires that Africa was in its present position before Babel and the days of Peleg as a result of continental division and shifting having occurred during the Flood when the apes were still initially on board the ark.[3]

Conclusion

Though continental division and shifting in the days of Peleg appears feasible from a superficial reading of Genesis 10:25 in isolation, this concept has

2. S.A. Austin et al., "Catastrophic Plate Tectonics: A Global Flood Model of Earth History," in *Proceedings of the Third International Conference on Creationism*, R.E. Walsh, ed. (Pittsburgh, PA: Creation Science Fellowship, 1994), p. 609–621.
3. K.P. Wise, "Lucy Was Buried First: Babel Helps Explain the Sequence of Ape and Human Fossils," *Answers*, April–June, 2008, p. 66–68.

some major problems associated with it for the following reasons:

- When Genesis 10:25 is read within the context of the whole chapter, the four other verses (5, 18, 20, and 32) speaking of the division clearly emphasize that this was a linguistic and family division of all post-Flood people into different lands (geographical locations).
- Had the division of continents occurred during the days of Peleg, then the associated catastrophism would have resulted in another worldwide Flood, in violation of God's specific promise to Noah.
- Had the division of continents occurred during the days of Peleg, then the ark (with Peleg's ancestors) would have had no place to land, as the mountains of Ararat produced by continental collisions would not have yet existed.
- There is tremendous fossil and geologic evidence for continental division having occurred only during the Flood.

We, therefore, gently and lovingly encourage our brothers and sisters in Christ to refrain from claiming the division of continents occurred during the days of Peleg. The phrase "for in his days the earth was divided" in Genesis 10:25 needs to be kept and read within its context of Genesis 10 to give it its correct meaning. On the other hand, we also want to encourage people to realize that the Flood is the only major catastrophic event and the only logical mechanism for splitting apart the continents.

Answering a Few Objections[4]*

1. Objection: "To start with, the Hebrew word for 'earth' in Genesis 10:25, 10:32, and 11:1 is Hebrew #776 (*erets*) in the Strong's Concordance, which says this word means earth, field, ground, land and world. . . . In fact, the clear meaning of this Hebrew word for 'earth' . . . is a very strong indication that the Peleg reference has to do with actual breakup of the land mass."

Answer: There are other uses of this word, as Hebrew lexicons readily point out, meaning particular nations or inhabitants. For those not fluent in Hebrew, one needs to consult reputable Hebrew lexicons such as *The Brown-Driver-Briggs Hebrew and English Lexicon* (BDB) or *The Hebrew and Aramaic Lexicon of the Old Testament* by Koehler and Baumgartner (KB) to see how each Hebrew word, in its context, should be used. Naturally, these do not hit every

4. These are actual comments made to Answers in Genesis regarding the issue of an alleged continental split during the days of Peleg.

instance but representative instances (keep in mind *erets* is used well over 2,000 times in the Old Testament). BDB uses as one of its representative examples that Genesis 11:1 is in reference to inhabitants of earth.[5] However, the two brought up in Genesis 10 are not mentioned.

Though KB does not use any of the three pointed out, it does use 2 Chronicles 12:8, where *erets* is used for nations/kingdoms as well as several others to indicate countries and regions of people.[6]

So to exclude this definition may not be wise. And considering that BDB used *erets* specifically in Genesis 11:1 to refer to people confirms the point. According to leading Hebrew lexicons that utilize the context, these would be referring to the people being divided by language. Also, keep in mind that if one wants to argue for *erets* to mean "continent(s)," this is not even listed as a definition among the lexicons.

2. Objection: "You are incorrect that the Peleg reference comes in the middle of an account of the division of languages. It comes in the middle of a genealogy. The story of the division of languages comes afterwards, separately."

Answer: Genesis 10 is a breakdown of the language divisions that are discussed in more detail, with the chronological account in Genesis 11. Even Genesis 10 points out after each genealogy of Japheth, Ham, and Shem that it was a *linguistic division* in accordance with their family group to their nations. Consider the phrases in Genesis 10 that summarize and signify the context of language in these verses:

> Genesis 10:5 — From these the coastland peoples of the Gentiles were separated into their lands, everyone according to his *language*, according to their families, into their nations (emphasis added).
>
> Genesis 10:20 — These were the sons of Ham, according to their families, according to their *languages*, in their lands and in their nations (emphasis added).
>
> Genesis 10:31 — These were the sons of Shem, according to their families, according to their *languages*, in their lands, according to their nations (emphasis added).

The context of Genesis 10 is indeed referring to linguistic divisions from which the nations were being divided. Even a prominent Jewish historian understood this to mean a division of nations. Consider Josephus's comments here:

5. *Brown-Driver-Briggs Hebrew and English Lexicon* (Peabody, MA: Hendrickson Publishers, 2005), p. 76.
6. L. Koehler and W. Baumgartner, *Hebrew and Aramaic Lexicon of the Old Testament*, Volume 1 (Boston, MA: Brill Publishers, 2001), p. 90–91.

> Heber begat Joctan and Phaleg: he was called Phaleg, because he was born at the dispersion of the nations to their several countries; for Phaleg, among the Hebrews, signifies *division.*[7]

3. Objection: "Have you carefully looked at the word for 'divided' in each reference? They are two different Hebrew words: vs. 25 *palag* vs. 32 *parad.* The former can mean to split or cleave and the latter to scatter. . . . What is being divided appears different since the Hebrew verb is different in both verses."

Answer: The name of Peleg [Strong's Concordance #06389] in verse 25 is a variant of [#06388] *peleg,* which in turn is a derivation of [#06385] *palag.* This same root word for Peleg's name is also used in Genesis 10:25. It makes sense why this was used in direct reference to Peleg's name. But this is still different from verse 32 where [#06504] *parad* is used. However, they each appear in the same context.

Parad

Working backward, the *Theological Wordbook of the Old Testament* points out that *parad* is in reference to the scattering of peoples under comment 1806 (discussing *parad*). They in turn reference A. Wieder, "Ugaritic-Hebrew Lexicographical Notes," JBL 84:160–64, esp. p. 163–64.

In fact, *parad* is also the Hebrew word used in Genesis 10:5 where it states: "From these the coastland *peoples* of the Gentiles were separated [*parad*] into their lands, everyone according to his language, according to their families, into their nations." Later Mosaic writings in Deuteronomy 32:8 also use *parad* in reference to the split of nations.

Palag

This Hebrew word *palag* is used only three times in Scripture outside of Genesis 10. In 1 Chronicles 1:19 it repeats Genesis 10:25. In one case it refers to a splitting of a water channel when it overflows in poetic Job 38:25. The other usage is in Psalm 55:9 where it refers to splitting of languages. David was speaking of his enemies and was asking the Lord to judge them with the splitting of their tongues. Obviously, David was conjuring thoughts of the Tower of Babel and tongue-shifting there.

Peleg's name was a direct derivation of *palag,* and considering the context of Genesis 10, it makes sense this Hebrew name was indeed referring to the linguistic division. So there would be no reason to distance from this plain interpretation.

7. *The Works of Josephus, Complete and Unabridged,* trans. by William Whiston (Peabody, MA: Hendrickson Publishers, 1988), p. 37.

24

Vestigial Organs — Evidence for Evolution?

DR. DAVID N. MENTON

Vestigial organs have long been one of the classic arguments used as evidence for evolution. The argument goes like this: living organisms, including man, contain organs that were once functional in our evolutionary past, but that are now useless or have reduced function. This is considered by many to be compelling evidence for evolution. More importantly, vestigial organs are considered by some evolutionists to be evidence against creation because they reason a perfect Creator would not make useless organs.

The word *vestige* is derived from the Latin word *vestigium*, which literally means a "footprint." The Merriam-Webster's Dictionary defines a biological vestige as a "a bodily part or organ that is small and degenerate or imperfectly developed in comparison to one more fully developed in an earlier stage of the individual, in a past generation, or in closely related forms."

Darwin on "Rudimentary Organs"

Charles Darwin was perhaps the first to claim vestigial organs as evidence for evolution. In chapter 13 of his *Origin of Species*, Darwin discussed what he called "rudimentary, atrophied and aborted organs." He described these organs as "bearing the plain stamp of inutility [uselessness]" and said that they are "extremely common or even general throughout nature." Darwin speculated that these rudimentary organs once served a function necessary for survival, but over time that function became either diminished or nonexistent.

In Darwin's book *The Descent of Man*, he claimed about a dozen of man's anatomical features to be useless including the muscles of the ear, wisdom teeth, the appendix, the coccyx (tailbone), body hair, and the semilunar fold in the corner of the eye. To Darwin, this was strong evidence that man had evolved from primitive ancestors.

The List of "Vestigial Organs" Grows

In 1893 the German anatomist Robert Wiedersheim expanded Darwin's list of "useless organs" to 86. Listed among Wiedersheim's "vestigial" organs were such organs as the parathyroid, pineal and pituitary glands, as well as the thymus, tonsils, adenoids, appendix, third molars, and valves in veins.[1] All of these organs have been subsequently shown to have useful functions and indeed some have functions essential for life.

Wiedersheim's vestigial organs were presented as one of the so-called "proofs" of evolution in the famous Scopes "Monkey Trial" of 1925. Horatio Hackett Newman, a zoologist from the University of Chicago, stated on the witness stand that "there are, according to Robert Wiedersheim, no less than 180 [*sic*] vestigial structures in the human body, sufficient to make a man a veritable walking museum of antiquities."[2]

Vestigial Organs Still Used as Evidence for Evolution

For over 100 years, evolutionists have continued to use vestigial organs as evidence for evolution. In 1971 the *Encyclopedia Britannica* claimed there were more than 100 vestigial organs in man, and even as recently as 1981, some biology textbook authors were claiming as many as 100 vestigial organs in the human body.[3] One of the most popular current biology textbooks declares that "many species of animals have vestigial organs." Examples cited in humans include the appendix, "tailbone," and muscles that move the ear.[4]

In addition to textbooks, countless popular science magazines, evolution blogs, and websites continue to promote vestigial organs as evidence for evolution.

1. R. Wiedersheim, *The Structure of Man: An Index to His Past History* (London: Macmillan and Co., 1895).
2. *The World's Most Famous Court Trial* (Dayton, TN: Bryan College, 1990). This book is a word-for-word transcript of the famous court test of the Tennessee Anti-Evolution Act, at Dayton, July 10 to 21, 1925, including speeches and arguments of attorneys, testimony of noted scientists, and Bryan's last speech.
3. S.R. Scadding, "Do Vestigial Organs Provide Evidence for Evolution?" *Evolutionary Theory* 5 (1981): 173–176.
4. K.R. Miller and J. Levine, *Biology: Teachers Edition* (Upper Saddle River, NJ: Pearson Prentice Hall, 2006), p. 384.

A website sponsored by the Discovery Channel, for example, assures us that "the human body has something akin to its own junk drawer," and that this junk drawer "is full of vestigial organs, or souvenirs of our evolutionary past."[5]

Problems with Vestigial Organs as Evidence for Evolution

Why Do Useless Organs Persist?

Darwin himself pointed out a flaw in the vestigial organ argument. He wondered how once an organ is rendered useless, it can continue to be further reduced in size until the merest vestige is left. In chapter 14 of *Origin of Species* he declared, "It is scarcely possible that disuse can go on producing any further effect after the organ has once been rendered functionless. Some additional explanation is here requisite which I cannot give." Why, indeed, would useless organs continue to exist for millions of years after they ceased to have any selective advantage?

The Loss of Useful Organs Doesn't Explain Their Origin

A problem for using vestigial organs as evidence for "amoeba to man" evolution is that the chief burden of the macro evolutionary explanation is to account for the spontaneous origin of new functional organs — not the loss of functional organs. While evolution might require the loss of functional organs, it is the acquisition of fundamentally new organs that remains unexplained by random mutations and natural selection.

How Can We Be Certain an Organ Is Useless?

The problem with declaring any organ to be without function is discriminating between truly functionless organs and those that have functions that are simply unknown. Indeed, over the years nearly all of the organs once thought to be useless have been found to be functional. When we have no evidence for the function of an organ, it is well to bear in mind that absence of evidence is not evidence of absence.

Declaring Useful Organs to Be Useless Can Be Dangerous

Once an organ is considered to be useless, it may be ignored by most scientists, or even worse, surgically removed by physicians as a useless evolutionary leftover. The oft repeated claim that the human appendix is useless is a case in point. The evolutionist Alfred Romer in his book *The Vertebrate Body* said of the human appendix: "Its major importance would appear to be financial support of the surgical profession."[6] We can only wonder how many normal appendices

5. www.health.howstuffworks.com/vestigial-organ.htm/printable.
6. A. S. Romer and T. S. Parsons, *The Vertebrate Body* (Philadelphia: Saunders College Publishers, 1986), p. 389.

have been removed by surgeons since Darwin first claimed them to be a useless vestige. Even more frightening would be the surgical removal of a "useless" parathyroid or pituitary gland.

The Definition of Vestigial Organs Has Been Changed

As the list of "functionless" organs has grown smaller and smaller with advancing knowledge, the definition of vestigial organs has been modified to include those whose functions are claimed to have "changed" to serve different functions. But such a definition removes the burden of proof that vestigial organs are a vestige of evolution. Thus, the evolutionist might concede that the human coccyx ("tail bone") does indeed serve an important function in anchoring the pelvic diaphragm — but still insist, without evidence, that it was once used by our ancestors as a tail.

Circular Reasoning

The most conspicuous logical flaw in the use of vestigial organs as evidence for evolution is circular reasoning. Evolutionists first declare vestigial organs to be a result of evolution, and then they turn around and argue that their existence is evidence for evolution. This kind of argument would hardly stand up in a court of law.

There Are Other Explanations for Vestigial Organs

Vestiges of Embryology

Evolutionists insist on explaining vestigial organs only in terms of evolution, but other explanations are more plausible and even provable. For example, the human body does have many organs and structures that are clearly vestiges of our embryological development. While it is quite easy to prove that an organ or structure is a vestige of embryology, there can be no empirical evidence to support the speculation that an organ is a vestige of evolution.

There are several structures that function during the development of the embryo and fetus that appear to be no longer used after birth. Remnants of these once-functional structures persist throughout life. Such structures perfectly fit the definition of a vestige, but they are not vestiges of evolution. The following are a few examples of embryological vestiges.

Ligamentum arteriosum — obliterated remnant of the ductus arteriosus, an artery that shunted blood from the pulmonary trunk to the descending aorta, thus bypassing the lung during fetal development. In certain cases of congenital heart defects, the ductus arteriosus actually continues to function for some time after birth to keep the baby alive.

Ligamentum teres hepatis — obliterated remnant of the umbilical vein that shunted much of the oxygenated blood away from the liver to the inferior vena cava during fetal development.

Median umbilical ligament — an obliterated vestige of the allantois, a pouch extending off of the embryonic cloaca. The allantois disappears very early in gestation after functioning as a scaffolding to help construct the umbilical cord; this remnant is seen as a ligament extending from the bladder to the umbilicus (bellybutton).

Sexual Dimorphism

In most primates there are striking anatomical differences between males and females of the same species. These differences between the sexes are refered to as *sexual dimorphism.* The skulls of a male and female gorilla, for example, might not be recognized as from the same species if one had never seen them in the flesh. The difference between the sexes is not as dramatic in the case of humans, though they are dimorphic. The bodies of human males and females differ mostly in the organs related to reproduction.

Up until the end of the sixth week of embryological development, the reproductive organs of males and females are indistinguishable. After this time, the genital organs of both sexes develop from the same common starting tissues under the control of sex chromosomes (XX in the female and XY in the male) and various hormones. As a result of their embryological development from the same primordia, each sex contains vestigial components of the other sex.

Almost every organ of the female reproductive system can be found in a different or vestigial form in the male reproductive system (and vice versa). For example, in the male, the prostatic utricle (an out pouching of the prostatic urethra having no known function) is a remnant of the paramesonephric duct that develops into the uterus and oviducts of the female. Clearly, the vestigial organs of reproduction are not a result of evolution but rather embryological development.

Homology

Many vestigial organs are examples of homology but not necessarily of evolution. Homology is an underlying similarity between different kinds of animals recognized by both evolutionists and creationists. All terrestrial vertebrates, for example, share a widespread similarity (homology) of body parts. Evolutionists insist that this similarity is the result of evolution from a common ancestor. Creationists, on the other hand, argue that this similarity reflects the theme of a common Creator and the need to meet similar biological requirements.[7]

7. G.E. Parker, *Creation: Facts of Life* (Green Forest, AR: Master Books, 2006), p. 43–53.

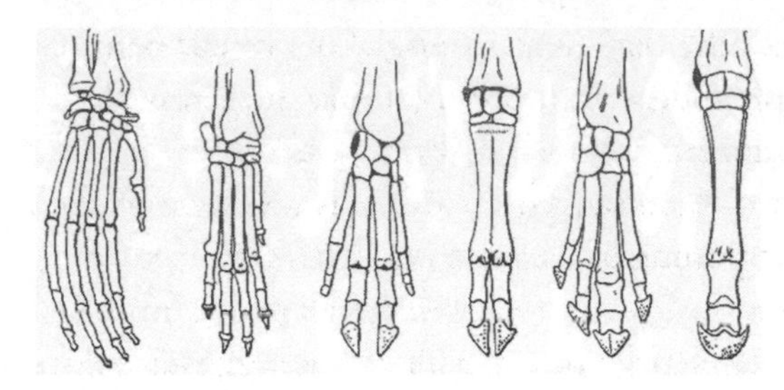

Homology in vertebrate limbs does not prove they came from a common ancestor.

For example, all vertebrates with true limbs (amphibians, reptiles, birds, and mammals) have the same basic limb structure at least during their embryological development. This standard vertebrate limb consists of an upper limb comprising one bone, a lower limb comprising two bones, and a hand or foot bearing five digits (fingers and toes). Thus, the limbs of all limbed vertebrates share fundamental similarities, with each being specialized to meet the needs of each species.

Horses have five digits while developing as an embryo, but generally all but one (the third digit) is absorbed before birth. Vestiges of the second and third metacarpal (and metatarsal) bones are visible in the modern horse as the splint bones. Some fossil horses, however, had three toes, but both three-toed and one-toed horses have been found together in the fossil record. In *National Geographic* magazine, for example, there is a picture of the feet of both a three-toed horse (Pliohippus) and a one-toed horse (Equus) that were found at the same volcanic site in Nebraska.[8]

Human hair is an example of a homologous structure declared to be vestigial by evolutionists. All mammals have hair. Hair may vary from the compacted hairs of a rhinoceros horn to the quills of a porcupine. To declare the unique hairs of one mammal to be vestigial to those of another is biological nonsense.

Evaluating Currently Claimed "Vestigial" Organs

It may prove useful for the reader to use the forgoing discussion of vestigial organs to evaluate some current claims for such structures. The website LiveScience lists what it regards as the top ten "vestigial" organs.[9] Five of these are found in humans, and are discussed below in order of their perceived importance by LiveScience.

The Appendix

Ever since Darwin, the appendix has been the prime example of a "useless"

8. M.R. Voorhies, "Ancient Ashfall Creates a Pompeii of Prehistoric Animals," *National Geographic*, January 1981, p. 74.
9. www.livescience.com/animals/top10_vestigial_organs.html.

organ. LiveScience says of the appendix that "it is a vestigial organ left behind from a plant-eating ancestor." In the middle of the 20th century, surgeons often removed the appendix electively during abdominal surgery, assuming it had no function. According to most evolutionists, the appendix is a vestige of the caecum (an expanded area at the beginning of the large intestine) left over from our plant-eating ancestors. But since humans have a well-developed caecum as well as an appendix, the appendix can hardly be considered a vestigial caecum. In his book *The Vertebrate Body*, evolutionist Alfred Romer said that the appendix is "frequently cited as a vestigial organ supposedly proving something about evolution. This is not the case. . . ."[10]

The important point is that the presence or absence of an appendix (or a caecum) reveals no evolutionary pattern whatever. An appendix is not found in any invertebrate, amphibian, reptile, or bird. Only a few diverse mammals have an appendix. The appendix is found, for example, in rabbits and some marsupials such as the wombat, but is not found in dogs, cats, horses, or ruminants. Both Old World and New World monkeys lack an appendix, while anthropoid apes and man have an appendix.[11]

The appendix is a complex, highly specialized organ with a rich blood supply — not what one would expect from a vestigial organ. The appendix is part of the gut associated lymphoid tissue (GALT), and has long been suspected of playing an immunological role much like that of the tonsils and adenoids (also once considered to be vestigial).

Recent evidence suggests that the appendix is well suited to serve as a "safe house" for commensal (mutually beneficial) bacteria in the large intestine. Specifically, the appendix is believed to provide support for beneficial bacterial growth by facilitating re-inoculation of the colon with essential bacteria in the event that the contents of the intestinal tract are purged following exposure to a pathogen.[12]

Male Breast Tissue and Nipples

It is surprising that evolutionists still continue to bring up the matter of the male breast (mammary gland) as a vestigial organ. Are they proposing that the males once nursed the young early in their evolution but no longer do so? Of course not. So how then does the evolutionist explain the male's vestigial mammary gland if it is not a consequence of evolution?

Vestigial mammary glands in males can only be understood in terms of

10. Romer and Parsons, *The Vertebrate Body*, p. 358.
11. J.W. Glover, "The Human Vermiform Appendix: A General Surgeon's Reflections," *Technical Journal* 3 no. 1 (1988): 31–38.
12. R.R. Bollinger et al., "Biofilms in the Large Bowel Suggest an Apparent Function of the Human Vermiform Appendix," *Journal of Theoretical Biology* 249 no. 4 (2007): 826–831.

embryology — not evolution. Mammary glands begin to develop in both males and females in the sixth week of gestation. At the time of birth, the rudimentary mammary glands of males and females are identical. In fact, both male and female mammary glands may be slightly enlarged at birth and secrete a fluid that is commonly known as "witches milk." This results from hormones that induce milk production in the mother being passed through the placenta to the fetal circulation.[13]

The male mammary gland is clearly a rudimentary or vestigial structure, but even the mammary gland of the nonlactating female might be considered vestigial. Female mammary glands are never fully developed and functional except during times of breast feeding the young. Should the evolutionist then consider the nonlactating female mammary gland to also be a vestige of evolution? The old evolutionist axiom that "nothing in biology makes sense except in the light of evolution" might better say that nothing in biology makes sense in the light of evolution.

Wisdom Teeth

Darwin was the first to popularize the notion that wisdom teeth are vestigial leftovers from our ape-like ancestors. The inherent racism of Darwinism is apparent when in his *Descent of Man*, Darwin declared that wisdom teeth are often lacking in "the more civilized races of man" in contrast to the "melanin (black) races where the wisdom teeth are furnished with three separate fangs, and are generally sound."[14]

Wisdom teeth, properly known as third molars, generally appear between the ages of 15 and 27 in both the upper and lower jaws of man. Many evolutionists consider them to be vestigial because unlike apes, third molars often fail to develop properly in man due to lack of space in the jaw. They argue that apes with their sloping face have longer jaws than man, and that when ape-like creatures evolved into humans with a vertical face and shorter jaws, there was no longer room for third molars.

Third molars are hardly useless vestiges. When there is adequate room for their development, they are fully functional molars and are used in chewing much as the first and second molars. Thinking them to be vestigial, many dentists in the past routinely removed third molars whether or not they were causing problems. It has been estimated that in America, only 20 percent of all young people with otherwise healthy teeth develop impacted

13. K.L. Moore, *The Developing Human* (Philadelphia, PA: W.B. Saunders Company, 1988), p. 427.
14. C. Darwin, *The Descent of Man and Selection in Relation to Sex* (New York, NY: D. Appleton and Company, 1896), p. 20.

third molars that require medical attention, while in the past, nearly nine out of ten American teenagers with dental insurance had their third molars extracted.[15]

The "Tailbone" (Coccyx)

The so-called "tailbone" is perhaps the most commonly touted example in man of a "useless" evolutionary vestige. According to evolutionary dogma, the tailbone, properly called the coccyx (because of its similarity to the shape of a cuckoo's beak), is a vestigial tail left over from our tailed monkey-like ancestors. Once again, many in the medical profession have been taken in by evolutionary speculation but mercifully, they have refrained from surgically removing the normal coccyx.

Even human abnormalities that have nothing to do with the coccyx have been declared to be "human tails." In a report in *The New England Journal of Medicine*, titled "Evolution and the Human Tail," Ledley described a two-inch long fleshy growth on the back of a baby, which he claimed to be a "human tail," though he conceded that it showed none of the distinctive biological characteristics of a tail! In fact, the "tail" was merely a fatty outgrowth of skin that wasn't even located in the right place on the back to be a tail! Still, Ledley declared that "even those of us who are familiar with the literature that defined our place in nature (Darwinism) — are rarely confronted with the relation between human beings and their primitive ancestors on a daily basis. The caudal appendage brings this reality to the fore and makes it tangible and inescapable."[16]

The human coccyx is a group of four or five small vertebrae fused into one bone at the lower end of our vertebral column. The coccyx is commonly called the "tailbone" because of its superficial similarity to a tail. The coccyx does occupy the same relative position at the end of our vertebral column as does the tail in tailed primates, but then, where else would it be? The vertebral column is a linear row of bones that supports the head at one end and the other must end somewhere. Wherever it ends, evolutionists will be sure to call it a vestigial tail.

Many modern biology textbooks give the erroneous impression that the human coccyx has no real function other than to remind us of our evolutionary ancestry. In fact, the coccyx has some very important functions. Six muscles converge from the ring-like bones of the pelvic brim to anchor on the coccyx,

15. A.J. MacGregor, *The Impacted Lower Wisdom Tooth* (New York, NY: Oxford University Press, 1985); a good review of wisdom teeth and the consequences of considering them to be evolutionary vestiges may be found at www.answersingenesis.org/tjv12/i3/wisdomteeth.asp
16. F.D. Ledley, "Evolution and the Human Tail: A Case Report." *N Engl J Med* 306 no. 20 (1982): 1212–1215.

forming a bowl-shaped muscular floor of the pelvis called the pelvic diaphragm. The incurved coccyx with its attached pelvic diaphragm supports the organs in our abdominal and pelvic cavities such as the urinary bladder, uterus, prostate, rectum, and anus. Without this critical muscular support, these organs could be easily herniated. The urethra, vagina, and anal canal pass through the muscular pelvic diaphragm, and thus the diaphragm serves as a sphincter for these structures.

Erector Pili and Body Hair

Evolutionists have long insisted that human body hair, and the small muscles (erector pili) attached to these hairs, are useless vestiges from our hairy ancestors. But human hair is as fully functional as that of any other mammal.

The body of man, like that of most mammals, is covered with hairs except for the palms and soles. But man, unlike other mammals, has mostly tiny colorless hairs called vellus hairs covering the seemingly "unhaired" parts of his body. This gives humans the appearance of being "hairless" with the exception of such areas as the scalp, axilla, chest, and genital regions. But in fact, if we count the tiny vellus hairs, humans have about as many hairs per square inch on their nose and forehead as they do on the top of their head. Indeed, hair density per square inch is approximately the same on the human body as it is for most primates.

Hair grows from tube-like structures in the skin called *hair follicles*. Most hair follicles are capable of making more than one type of hair depending in part on age, location, and hormonal stimulation. The first hairs to grow from the follicles of the developing baby are long silky hairs called *lanugo hairs*. These hairs, which cover most of the body, are usually shed before birth and are replaced with tiny vellus hairs. Thus, the newborn baby may appear to be mostly hairless, but in fact is covered with vellus hairs.

The long pigmented hairs on our scalp and elsewhere on our body are called *terminal hairs*. Terminal hairs grow from follicles that once produced lanugo and vellus hairs and with age may be replaced once again with vellus hairs. For example, after a boy reaches sexual maturity he may begin to lose terminal scalp hairs, which are replaced with vellus hairs, giving the appearance of baldness. Conversely, some vellus hairs on the face may be replaced with terminal hairs, producing a beard.

Evolutionists argue that human body hairs are vestigial (useless) because there are so few long terminal hairs compared to tiny vellus hairs. Hair serves as thermal insulation in most mammals, which is important because most animals are incapable of regulating their body temperature by sweating. Man, on the other hand, is a profuse sweater and can maintain body temperature over a much wider range of ambient temperature than nearly all other mammals. Long body hair of the type seen on most mammals would interfere with the evaporative water loss necessary for human thermoregulation by sweating.

In most mammals, hair serves as an important barrier to ultraviolet radiation from the sun. While human scalp hair serves a similar function on the typically exposed top of our head, our primary defense against UV damage is tanning and wearing clothes.

An important function of hair is its sensory function. All hair follicles, regardless of size, are supplied with sensory nerves so that they may be considered to be mechanoreceptors. Our hairs are like small levers that, when moved by any physical stimulus including air, send sensory signals to our brain. This is true of both the tiny vellus hairs and the long terminal hairs. This sensory function of hair can hardly be considered vestigial.

Another important function of hair follicles is the restoring of the epidermal skin surface following cuts and deep abrasions. Human hair follicles, regardless of size, serve as an important source of epidermal cells for recovering the skin's surface (reepithelialization) when broad areas of the epidermis are lost. If it were not for man's abundant hair follicles and sweat ducts, even routine skin abrasions might require a skin transplant.

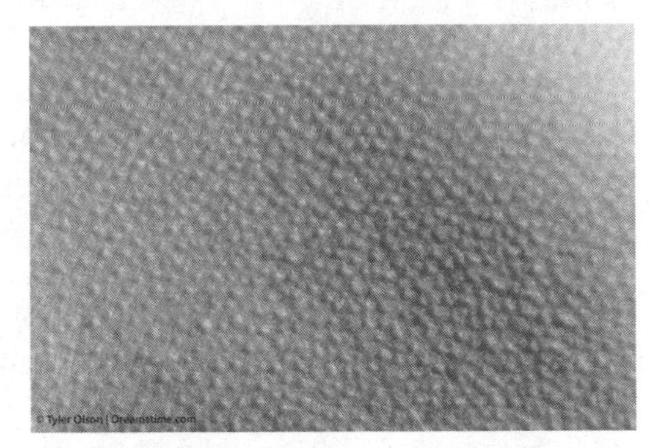

Goose bumps are not remnants of an evolutionary past, but serve several functions for humans.

All hairs are associated with muscles, and most have a muscle called the erector pili, which serves to move the hair from its normal inclined position to a more erect position. In the case of the vellus hairs of man this produces what is commonly called "goose bumps." This muscle is in a position to help squeeze oil from the sebaceous glands, which are also attached to the hair follicle. Erector pili muscles are supplied with nerves of the sympathetic nervous system, which is often associated with our response to "flight and fright" stimuli. Thus, when we are frightened we may get goose bumps. We also get goose bumps when we are chilled. Contraction of the erector pili muscles produces heat, and if this response is inadequate to warm the body, shivering may follow, which involves repeated contractions of the large body muscles.

Is the Argument for Vestigial Organs Vestigial?

Over the years, advancement in our understanding of biological science has raised serious doubts about vestigial organs as evidence for evolution. Creationists have subjected the evolutionary interpretation of vestigial organs to strong criticism.[17] Even some evolutionists are now urging that vestigial organs be downplayed or even abandoned as evidence for evolution. The evolutionist S.R. Scadding, for example, has critically examined vestigial organs as evidence for evolution. He concluded: "Since it is not possible to unambiguously identify useless structures, and since the structure of the argument used is not scientifically valid, I conclude that 'vestigial organs' provide no special evidence for the theory of evolution."[18] But like the long discredited recapitulation myth (that embryos pass through stages of their evolutionary history), vestigial organs continue to be used as evidence for evolution.

LET THERE BE TRUTH

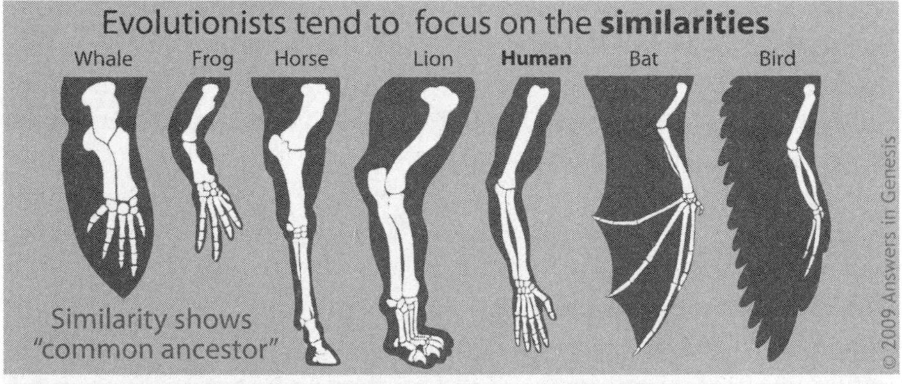

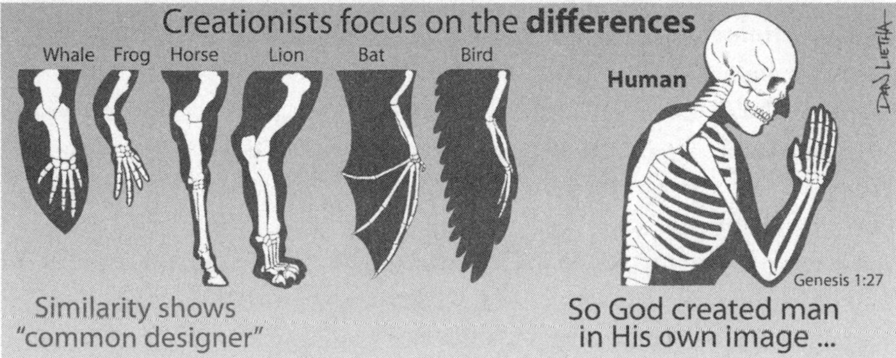

17. J. Bergman and G. Howe, *Vestigial Organs are Fully Functional* (Terre Haute, IN: Creation Research Society Books, 1990).
18. S.R. Scadding, "Do Vestigial Organs Provide Evidence for Evolution?" *Evolutionary Theory* 5 (1981): 173.

25

Is *Tiktaalik* Evolution's Greatest Missing Link?

DR. DAVID N. MENTON

In both the print and broadcast media in 2006 and 2007, reports of the discovery of the fossil fish known as *Tiktaalik* were hyped as convincing proof that, through a random chance process of evolution, fish sprouted legs and walked out onto the land, where they turned into amphibians, reptiles, mammals, and, ultimately people. But the media's excitement seems to stem not so much from being able to report a real scientific discovery as in being able to discredit the biblical account of creation.

A front page article in the *New York Times*,[1] for example, hailed *Tiktaalik* "as a powerful rebuttal to religious creationists, who hold a literal biblical view on the origins and development of life."

The whole idea of walking fish has come to be symbolic of the evolutionary worldview and its opposition to biblical Christianity. Many evolutionists display the familiar "Darwin fish" symbol on their automobiles, T-shirts, and office doors as a public declaration of their allegiance to evolution. The "Darwin fish" is a desecration of the fish symbol used by early Christians as a means of mutual identification during a time of persecution. Christians chose the

The walking fish has become symbolic of evolutionism.

1. John Noble Wilford, "Fossil Called Missing Link From Sea to Land Animals," *New York Times*, Late Edition — Final, Section A, Page 1, Column 5, April 6, 2006.

fish symbol because the individual letters of the Greek word *ichthys* (for "fish") served as an anagram for "Jesus Christ Son of God, Savior." Evolutionists have substituted the word "Darwin" for "*ichthys*" and have placed walking legs with feet on the fish. Thus, the Darwin fish reflects the fact that many evolutionists have indeed replaced Christianity with Darwinism. As for the legs on the Darwin fish, we will see that there are no known fish with true "legs" (and certainly no feet), and none capable of actually "walking" — except in the most trivial sense of the word.

We Must Be Cautious of Evolutionary Claims

In the next months and years, there will doubtless be further claims in the popular media of "irrefutable proofs" for evolution and, more importantly, "proofs" against the biblical account of creation. The popular media — as with tax-supported zoos, science museums, and public schools — are often zealous supporters of the quasi-scientific religion of materialism.

However, few reporters, teachers, or laymen have ever read the original scientific reports upon which grandiose evolutionary claims are based. Moreover, these reports are often convoluted, conflicting, and couched in unprovable assumptions that make evolutionary claims difficult to evaluate even for those who do examine the original scientific papers.

To evaluate the claims that there are fossil fish with legs that walked out of water to take up permanent residence on the land, one needs to understand something about fish, tetrapods (limbed vertebrates including humans), legs, and what is required anatomically to walk and swim. So let us begin by looking at the wide world of fish, and see which ones are supposed to be the "walkers."

There Are Lots of Fish!

The first thing to consider is that there are a *lot* of fish — both living and fossilized. Approximately 25,000 species of currently living fish have been identified, with 200–300 new species discovered — not evolved — every year. Indeed, fish comprise fully half of all known vertebrates!

It is not clear how many different fish species have been found as fossils, but some experts claim that there were once nearly a million species of fish! It appears that over time we have lost a lot of species of fish — and retained relatively fewer. But losing thousands of species of fish is hardly evolution — it's extinction. The question is, have we really gained any fundamentally *new* fish (to say nothing of fish that evolved true legs and walked out onto the land as permanent residents)?

Classification of Fish

Fish come in a bewildering variety of forms that defy consistent classification. As a result, there are competing classification schemes based on the particular bias of the classifier.

Basically, all species of fish have been divided into two main types — the jawless fish (hagfish and lampreys) and the jawed fish (all the rest). The jawed fish are, in turn, divided into two groups: the cartilaginous fish (such as the sharks and rays that have a skeleton made of flexible cartilage) and the much more numerous bony fish, which have hard bony skeletons.

Many of the so-called transitional forms have been greatly disputed, discovered (e.g., coelacanth), or dismissed, and *Tiktaalik* has recently been propped up as the "savior" of the evolutionary paradigm. How soon will it be before *Tiktaalik* is abandoned also?

Evolutionists believe that it took about 100 million years for invertebrates (animals with no bones) to evolve into vertebrates (animals with backbones). However, no compelling fossil evidence documents this purported major and unambiguous transition. While evolutionists believe that fish were the first true vertebrates, they're not sure which evolved first — cartilaginous or bony fish.

During the embryological development of vertebrates, most bones develop first as cartilage models that are later replaced by bone (called endochondral bone). Following the dictates of the embryonic recapitulation myth, it would be attractive for evolutionists to propose that cartilaginous fish evolved into bony fish, but most evolutionists consider the cartilaginous fish to be far too specialized to have been the ancestors of the bony fish.

Tiktaalik

The Bony Fish (*Osteicthyii*)

Bony fish are by far the most numerous of all fish, comprising about 24,000 living species, and they come in an amazing variety of forms and sizes (ranging from a half-inch-long sea horse weighing a fraction of an ounce to a 1,000-pound blue marlin). The purported evolutionary relationship of all these fish is at best highly speculative.

All bony fish have gills for breathing and fins for swimming. Starting from front to back, the most important fins for swimming are the paired pectoral fins (which are typically attached to the posterior margin of the skull), the generally smaller paired pelvic fins (that occupy a position near the anus), and the caudal fin (tail fin).

Bony fish are divided into two groups, the lobe-finned fish, known mostly from fossils, and the vastly more numerous ray-finned fish. Both have fins made up of bony rays, but the lobe-fins have fin rays mounted on a short, fleshy stalk supported by successive segments of bone. It is the superficial resemblance of these bony fins to tetrapod legs that has led evolutionists to speculate that the lobe-fin fish are the ancestors of tetrapods in the late Devonian (approximately 380 million years ago). So let's focus our investigation on the lobe-fins.

The Lobe-fin Fish (*Sarcopterygii*)

The lobe-finned fish have been divided into two rather dissimilar groups, the *Dipnoi* (lungfish) and the *Crossopterygii* (coelacanths and fossil relatives).

Lungfish (*Dipnoi*)

There are only three surviving types of lungfish. They are all eel-like in appearance, and have long and slender fleshy pectoral and pelvic fins, which are highly mobile. This group derives its name from the fact that these fish have air sacks ("lungs") that function at least partially in breathing (though all, at least in their immature state, have functional gills as well). The fact that these fish can breathe air, survive out of water for long periods of time, and have the ability to pull themselves along on their bellies (i.e., "walk") across mud flats with the aid of their fins, has caught the imagination of some evolutionists who consider them to be ancestral to tetrapods.

Many Living Fish Are Air-breathers and "Walkers"

But air-breathing fish are not uncommon among living fish species. For example, many popular aquarium fish (such as the paradise fish, betta, and gourami) are surface air-breathers that can actually drown if kept under water! Evolutionists are not even in agreement on whether lungs evolved before gills (as proposed by the famous vertebrate evolutionist Alfred Romer), or gills evolved before lungs.

Even the sort of "walking" that lungfish engage in is not uncommon among living fish species. Many fish are known to pull themselves along on their bellies, with the help of their pectoral fins, across large expanses of mud flats and even dry land. For example, the northern snakehead (*Channa argus*) and the walking catfish (*Clarias batrachus*) are air-breathing fish that can travel overland for considerable distances. The mudskippers are fish that breathe oxygen through their skin and "skip" along on land with the aid of their fleshy fins — indeed some of the larger species are said to skip faster than the average person can run! The climbing perch (*Anabas testudineus*) not only breathes air and "walks" on land but is even said to be capable of climbing trees! Yet *none* of these curious fish are considered by evolutionists to be ancestors of tetrapods — they are simply interesting and specialized fish. In fact there are even "flying fish" (with specialized fins that permit them to fly or glide in the air for hundreds of yards over water), but evolutionists have never considered them to be ancestors of birds.

Crossopterygians

Most evolutionists now look to fossil *Crossopterygians* for the ancestors of tetrapods — even though none of them are known to be capable of either walking or breathing out of water.

The distinguishing features of these fish are the division of the skull into anterior and posterior units (considered similar to embryonic tetrapod skulls); and fleshy pectoral fins containing bony elements (considered similar to tetrapod legs). These similarities have prompted evolutionists to confidently declare that *Crossopterygians* evolved into tetrapods.

Snakehead fish

According to evolutionists, the *Crossopterygians* flourished during the middle to late Devonian (extending from 385 million years ago to 365 million years ago) and all were once believed to have become extinct about 80 million years ago (even before the extinction of the dinosaurs).[2]

The Coelacanth — One of Many "Living Fossils"

However, in 1938 a fishing trawler netted a strange large blue fish in the Indian Ocean off the coast of Madagascar. This distinctive fish was soon identified as a *Crossopterygian* fish previously known only from the fossil record as the coelacanth.

Coelacanths are distinctly different from all other living fishes. They have an extra lobe on their tails (compared to other lobe-finned fish) and are the only living animal to have a fully functional joint in their cranium, which allows the front part of the head to be lifted when the fish is feeding.

The discovery of a coelacanth came as a surprise to evolutionists. (It was comparable to finding a living dinosaur, because these fish were believed to have become extinct 80 million years ago when they disappeared from the fossil record.) However, since 1938, dozens of living coelacanths have been found and studied, some as far as 7,000 miles away from the location of the first sightings![3]

Understandably, evolutionists are puzzled by how coelacanths could disappear for over "80 million years" and then turn up alive and well in the 20th century. They speculate that the fossilized coelacanths lived in environments favoring fossilization, whereas modern coelacanths live at great depths (over 600 feet) in caves and overhangs of steep marine reefs that don't favor fossil formation. This, however, is special pleading, since essentially no modern marine environment favors the formation of fossils and, indeed, none are being formed, as this would require rapid burial, which is not observed under normal conditions.

More importantly the coelacanth (and many other "living fossils") show that evolutionists can never assume that a plant or animal did not live during any particular period of assumed geologic time simply because it does not appear in the fossil record of this period. If 200-pound coelacanths can "hide" for "80 million years," it would seem anything can hide.

Another reason finding a living coelacanth caused so much surprise at the time of its discovery was that coelacanths were widely believed to be the

2. "New Fossils Fill the Evolutionary Gap Between Fish and Land Animals," www.nsf.gov/news/news_summ.jsp?cntn_id=106807, 2006.
3. Another was recently caught near Indonesia. See www.news.bbc.co.uk/2/hi/science/nature/6925784.stm.

ancestors of the tetrapods. Indeed, many evolutionists assumed that the very reason the coelacanths disappeared from the fossil record was because they evolved into land-dwelling tetrapods; yet here they were very much alive — and swimming!

Contrary to early suggestions of walking behavior, coelacanths have only been observed using their fins to swim.

Coelacanths Don't Walk

At the very least, evolutionists expected to observe some hint of walking behavior in the coelacanth, but the fish have done nothing to accommodate them. Although living coelacanths have often been observed swimming in their natural habitat, they have never been observed walking. Indeed, coelacanths have been observed swimming backward, upside-down, and even standing on their head! Alas — they absolutely refuse to walk on land or in the sea.

Evolutionists Look to Other Lobe-fins

Since living lobe-fin fish have not met expectations, evolutionists have turned to other fossilized lobe-fins for the ancestors of tetrapods. (After all, one can speculate endlessly about fossils without fear of contradiction — until they turn up alive.)

Currently, the three most popular Crossopterygian candidates for ancestors of tetrapods are *Eusthenopteron*, *Panderichthys*, and the recently discovered *Tiktaalik*.

Eusthenopteron

For several years, the evolutionist's "gold standard" of fish with "legs" has been the fossil fish *Eusthenopteron* (which, like the coelacanth, has fleshy pectoral fins with bones). If you have seen an artist's illustration in a textbook showing a fish walking out of the water, most likely it was *Eusthenopteron*.

Like most other jawed fish, *Eusthenopteron* has its pectoral fin girdle (bones that anchor the pectoral fins) attached to the back of its skull by means of a dermal bone called the *cleithrum*. Dermal bones develop directly from connective tissue cells under the skin, rather than from cartilage models as is the case for endochondral bones. (Fish scales, by the way, are dermal bones as well, and reside just under the superficial layer of the skin.)

Panderichthys

Panderichthys is yet another fossil *Crossopterygian* fish that has been declared to be an ancestor of tetrapods. *Panderichthys* lacks dorsal and ventral fins and has a relatively small tail fin (thus looking less obviously fish-like than *Eusthenopteron*).

Like the other *Crossopterygian* fish, *Panderichthys* has thick bony pectoral fins. Evolutionists argue that the shape of these fins and their pectoral girdle look more like that of tetrapods than *Eusthenopteron*. But Daeschler, Shubin, and Jenkins — the discoverers of *Tiktaalik* — claim that "*Panderichthys* possesses relatively few tetrapod synapomorphies, and provides only partial insight into the origin of major features of the skull, limbs, and axial skeleton of early tetrapods." As a result, they insist that "our understanding of major transformations at the fish-tetrapod transition has remained limited."[4]

Tiktaalik to the Rescue?

In the April 2006 issue of *Nature*, Daeschler et al. reported the discovery of several fossilized specimens of a *Crossopterygian* fish named *Tiktaalik roseae*. These well-preserved specimens were found in sedimentary layers of siltstone — cross-bedded with sandstones — in Arctic Canada.[4]

Like the other lobe-fin fish, *Tiktaalik* was declared to be late Devonian (between 385–359 million years old) by means of a "dating" method known as *palynomorph biostratigraphy*. This method presumes to date sedimentary rock layers on the basis of the assumed evolutionary age of pollen and spores contained in the rock. Most importantly, the discoverers of *Tiktaalik* claim that it "represents an intermediate between fish with fins and tetrapods with limbs."

Tiktaalik Is a Fish

Whatever else we might say about *Tiktaalik*, it *is a fish*. In a review article on *Tiktaalik* (appearing in the same issue of the scientific journal *Nature* that reported the discovery of *Tiktaalik*), fish evolution experts Ahlberg and Clack concede that "in some respects *Tiktaalik* and *Panderichthys* are straightforward fishes: they have small pelvic fins, retain fin rays in their paired appendages and have well-developed gill arches, suggesting that both animals remained mostly aquatic."[5]

In other respects, however, Ahlberg and Clack argue that *Tiktaalik* is more tetrapod-like than *Panderichthys* because "the bony gill cover has disappeared, and the skull has a longer snout." The authors weakly suggest that

4. Edward B. Daeschler, Neil H. Shubin, and Farish A. Jenkins, "A Devonian Tetrapod-like Fish and the Evolution of the Tetrapod Body Plan," *Nature* 440 no. 6 (2006): 757–763.
5. P.E. Ahlberg and J.A. Clack, News and Views, *Nature* 440 no. 6 (2006): 747–749.

the significance of all this is that "a longer snout suggests a shift from sucking towards snapping up prey, whereas the loss of gill cover bones probably correlates with reduced water flow through the gill chamber. The ribs also seem larger in *Tiktaalik*, which may mean it was better able to support its body out of water."

Without the author's evolutionary bias, of course, there is no reason to assume that *Tiktaalik* was anything other than exclusively aquatic. And how do we know that *Tiktaalik* lost its gill cover as opposed to never having one? The longer snout and lack of bony gill covers (found in many other exclusively aquatic living fish) are interpreted as indicating a reduced flow of water through the gills, which, in turn, is declared to be suggestive of partial air-breathing — but this is quite a stretch. Finally, what does any of this have to do with fish evolving into land-dwelling tetrapods?

Are the Pectoral Fins of *Tiktaalik* Really Legs?

Before we get into *Tiktaalik*'s "legs," it might be instructive to consider an old trick question. If we call our arms "legs," then how many legs would we have? The answer, of course, is *two legs* — just because we call our arms "legs" doesn't make them legs. The same might be said of the bony fins of *Crossopterygian* fish — we may call them "legs" but that doesn't necessarily make them legs.

Shubin et al. make much of the claim that *Tiktaalik*'s bony fins show a reduction in dermal bone and an increase in endochondral bone.[6] This is important to them because the limb bones of tetrapods are entirely endochondral. They further claim that the *cleithrum* (a dermal bone to which the pectoral fin is attached in fish) is detached from the skull, resembling the position of the scapula (shoulder blade) of a tetrapod. They also claim that the endochondral bones of the fin are more similar to those of a tetrapod in terms of structure and range of motion. However, none of this, if true, proves that *Tiktaalik*'s fins supported its weight out of water, or that it was capable of a true walking motion. (It certainly doesn't prove that these fish evolved into tetrapods.)

The Limbs of Tetrapods

The limbs of tetrapods share similar characteristic features. These unique features meet the special demands of walking on land. In the case of the forelimbs there is one bone nearest the body (proximal) called the *humerus* that articulates (flexibly joins) with two bones, the *radius* and *ulna,* farther away

6. Neil H. Shubin, Edward B. Daeschler, and Farish A. Jenkins, "The Pectoral Fin of Tiktaalik roseae and the Origin of the Tetrapod Limb," *Nature* 440 no. 6 (2006): 764–771.

from the body (distal). These in turn articulate with multiple wrist bones, which finally articulate with typically five digits. The hind limbs similarly consist of one proximal bone, the *femur*, which articulates with two distal bones, the *tibia* and *fibula*, which in turn articulate with ankle bones; and finally with typically five digits. In order to support the weight of the body on land, and permit walking, the most proximal bones of the limbs must be securely attached to the rest of the body. The humerus of the forelimb articulates with the pectoral girdle, which includes the *scapula* (shoulder blade) and the *clavicle* (collar bone). The only bony attachment of the pectoral girdle to the body is the clavicle.

The femur of the hind limb articulates with the pelvic girdle, which consists of fused bones collectively called the *pelvis* (hip bone). It is this hind limb — with its robust pelvic girdle securely attached to the vertebral column — that differs radically from that of any fish. (The tetrapod arrangement is important for bearing the weight of the animal on land.)

All tetrapod limb bones and their attachment girdles are endochondral bones. In the case of all fish, including *Tiktaalik*, the cleithrum and fin rays are dermal bones.

It is significant that the "earliest" true tetrapods recognized by evolutionists (such as *Acanthostega* and *Ichthyostega*) have all of the distinguishing features of tetrapod limbs (and their attachment girdles) and were clearly capable of walking and breathing on land. The structural differences between the tetrapod leg and the fish fin is easily understood when we realize that the buoyant density of water is about a thousand times greater than that of air. A fish has no need to support much of its weight in water where it is essentially weightless.

The Fins of Fish (including *Tiktaalik*)

Essentially all fish (including *Tiktaalik*) have small pelvic fins relative to their pectoral fins. The legs of tetrapods are *just the opposite*: the hind limbs attached to the pelvic girdle are almost always more robust than the forelimbs attached to the pectoral girdle. (This is particularly obvious in animals such as kangaroos and theropod dinosaurs.) Not only are the pelvic fins of all fish small, but they're *not even attached to the axial skeleton* (vertebral column) and thus can't bear weight on land.

While the endochondral bones in the pectoral fins of *Crossopterygians* have some similarity to bones in the forelimbs of tetrapods, there are significant differences. For example, there is nothing even remotely comparable to the digits in any fish. The bony rays of fish fins are dermal bones that are not related in any way to digits in their structure, function, or mode of development.

Clearly, fin rays are relatively fragile and unsuitable for actual walking and weight bearing.

Even the smaller endochondral bones in the distal fin of *Tiktaalik* are not related to digits. Ahlberg and Clack point out that "although these small distal bones bear some resemblance to tetrapod digits in terms of their function and range of movement, they are still very much components of a fin. There remains a large morphological gap between them and digits as seen in, for example *Acanthostega*: if the digits evolved from these distal bones, the process must have involved considerable developmental rearranging."[7]

So Is *Tiktaalik* a Missing Link?

Finally, what about the popular claim that *Tiktaalik* is the "missing link" between fish and tetrapods?

In their review article on *Tiktaalik*, Ahlberg and Clack tell us that "the concept of 'missing links' has a powerful grasp on the imagination: the rare transitional fossils that apparently capture the origins of major groups of organisms are uniquely evocative." The authors concede that the whole concept of "missing links" has been loaded with "unfounded notions of evolutionary 'progress' and with a mistaken emphasis on the single intermediate fossil as the key to understanding evolutionary transition."

Sadly, "unfounded notions" of this kind continue to be uncritically taught and accepted in the popular media and in our schools. Even more sadly, these unfounded notions have been used to undermine the authority of Holy Scripture.

7. Ahlberg and Clack, News and Views.

26

Why Is Mount St. Helens Important to the Origins Controversy?

DR. STEVEN A. AUSTIN

On May 18, 1980, a catastrophic geologic event occurred that not only shocked the world because of its explosive power, but challenged the foundation of evolutionary theory. That event was the eruption of Mount St. Helens in the state of Washington. The eruption of Mount St. Helens is regarded by many as the most significant geologic event of the 20th century, excelling all others in its extraordinary documentation and scientific study. Undeniable facts confront us. Although not the most powerful explosion of the last century, Mount St. Helens provided a significant learning experience within a natural laboratory for the understanding of catastrophic geologic processes.

On May 18, and also during later eruptions, certain critical energy thresholds were exceeded by potent geologic processes. These were able to accomplish significant changes in short order to the landscape (figure 1), providing us a rare, user-friendly opportunity to observe and understand the effects of catastrophic geologic processes.

What would 20 megatons of steam-blast energy do to a landscape? How would mudflows and giant water waves modify the earth? Geologists, who were accustomed to thinking about slow evolutionary processes forming geologic features, were astounded to witness many of these same features form rapidly at Mount St. Helens. Ultimately, the events and processes at the

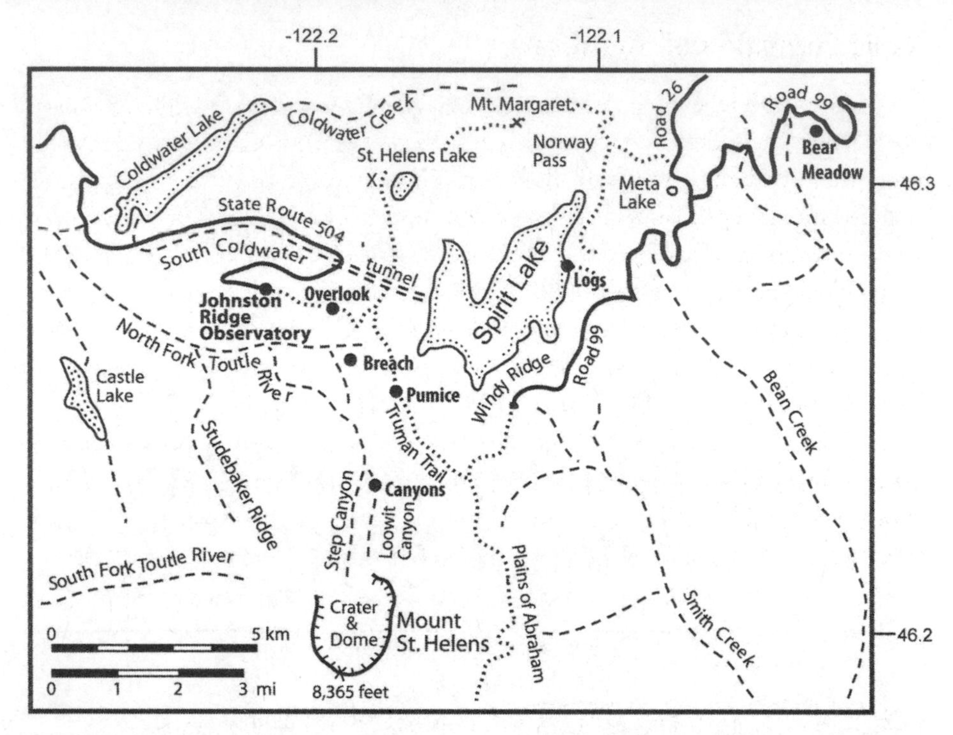

Figure 1. Map of the north flank of the volcano showing areas of special interest to understanding catastrophic geologic processes within Mount St. Helens National Volcanic Monument. "Overlook" is an observation post one mile east of Johnston Ridge Observatory on the ridge showing the eroded landscape on the North Fork of the Toutle River. "Breach" is the March 19, 1982, erosion feature with the "Little Grand Canyon" that is currently closed to off-trail activity without special use permit. "Pumice" is the Pumice Plain deposit consisting of various laminated pyroclastic flow deposits. "Canyons" displays the mudflow-eroded bedrock channels up to 600 feet deep on the north flank of the volcano. "Logs" is the shore observation locality on the Harmony Trail on the east side of Spirit Lake. "Bear Meadow" is the northeastern observation location outside the blast zone.

volcano challenge our way of thinking about how the earth works. Does the earth change piecemeal by slow and gradual processes, which accumulate small changes over immense periods of time? Or have rapid processes accomplished significant geologic changes in very short periods of time? What we have seen at Mount St. Helens has application to many geologic features. Can processes at Mount St. Helens explain the origin of finely laminated strata? Do canyons in hard rock bear evidence of catastrophic erosion? Have the Yellowstone "petrified forests" and coal deposits accumulated by catastrophic sedimentary processes? Was there a global flood on the earth?

Rapid Formation of Stratification

Up to 600 feet thickness of new strata have formed since 1980 at Mount St. Helens. These deposits accumulated from primary air blast, landslide, water wave on Spirit Lake, pyroclastic flows, mudflows, air fall, and stream water. Perhaps the most surprising accumulations are the pyroclastic flow deposits amassed from ground-hugging, fluidized slurries of fine volcanic debris that moved at high velocities off the north flank of the volcano. These deposits include fine pumice ash laminae beds from one millimeter thick to greater than one meter thick, each representing just a few seconds to several minutes of accumulation (see "Pumice" in figure 1).

Figure 2 shows 25 feet of the stratified deposit accumulated within three hours during the evening of June 12, 1980. It was deposited from pyroclastic flows generated by collapse of the eruption plume of debris over the volcano. The strata are very extensive and even contain thin laminae and crossbedding. Within the pyroclastic flow deposits are very thin laminae. It staggers the mind to think how the finest stratification has formed in an event of the

Figure 2. Deposits exposed by mudflow erosion on the North Fork of the Toutle River. The laminated and bedded pyroclastic flow deposit of June 12, 1980, is 25 feet thick in the middle of the cliff. That three-hour deposit is underlain by the pyroclastic flow deposit of May 18, 1980, and overlain by the mudflow deposit of March 19, 1982. (Photo by Steven A. Austin)

violence of a hurricane. Coarse and fine sediment were separated into distinct strata by the catastrophic flow process from a slurry moving at freeway speed. Conventionally, sedimentary laminae and beds are assumed to represent longer seasonal variations — or annual changes — as the layers accumulated very slowly. That is the typical uniformitarian interpretation. Furthermore, our natural way of thinking about catastrophic sedimentary process is that it homogenizes materials depositing coarse and fine together without obvious stratification. Mount St. Helens teaches us that stratification does form very rapidly by flow processes.

Rapid Erosion

If we reason from our everyday experience concerning the way rivers and creeks erode, we might assume that great time periods are needed to form deep canyons. At Mount St. Helens, however, very rapid erosion has occurred since the 1980 eruptions. These erosion features challenge our way of thinking about how landscapes form. What is exceptional at Mount St. Helens is the variety of new erosion features and their concentration within a limited and intensely studied area. There is no place in the blast zone at Mount St. Helens where the effects of recent erosion cannot be seen. That is what makes Mount St. Helens extraordinary! Scientists discovered that the kinds of processes causing erosion were as varied as the different features formed. The major agents of erosion unleashed at Mount St. Helens are listed in summary here.

1. Direct blast — the 20-megaton TNT equivalent, northward-directed steam blast of May 18 caused hot gas and rock fragments to abrade slopes around the mountain.
2. Pyroclastic flows — explosive blasts on and after May 18 created superheated, erosive "rivers" of ground-hugging volcanic ash and steam.
3. Debris avalanche — the movement of great masses of rock, ice, and debris over the earth's surface next to the volcano caused significant abrasion.
4. Mudflows — viscous streams of mud gouged out soft volcanic ash deposits and, to our astonishment, even the hardest rocks to form new canyons.
5. Water in channels — overland flow of floodwater caused extraordinary rill and gully patterns to appear, even in nearly level slopes.

6. Water waves — enormous water waves generated in Spirit Lake by the avalanche on May 18 inflicted severe erosion on slopes adjacent to the lake.
7. Jetting steam — eruptions of steam from buried glacier ice reamed holes through hot volcanic ash deposits, forming distinctive explosion pits.
8. Mass wasting — gravitational collapse induced significant changes to unstable slopes, especially those areas sculptured by other agents, leaving behind a varied landscape.

Two-thirds cubic mile of landslide and eruption debris from May 18, 1980, occupies 23 square miles of the North Fork of the Toutle River north and west of the crater (see figure 1). It was the largest debris avalanche observed in human history! This debris was deposited across the entire width of the valley along the uppermost 16 miles of the North Fork of the Toutle River. These deposits average 150 feet in thickness and form a hummocky surface that blocks the pre-1980 channel. Before the May 18 eruption, Spirit Lake had an outlet river draining westward into the Pacific Ocean.

From May 18, 1980, to March 19, 1982, the upper drainage area of the debris avalanche deposit was not connected to the Pacific Ocean, and water from Spirit Lake basin and the crater of the volcano did not connect to the Toutle River, due to debris blocking the valley. Because of this debris, there has been no natural outlet formed for Spirit Lake.

An explosive eruption of Mount St. Helens on March 19, 1982, melted a thick snowpack in the crater, creating a destructive, sheet-like flood of water, which became a mudflow. Breaching the deposits on the upper North Fork of the Toutle River (see "Breach" in figure 1). The most significant erosion occurred in the biggest steam explosion pit. The mudflow filled the big steam explosion pit with mud, which then overflowed the west rim of the pit as a deep ravine was cut into the 1980 deposits to the west.

The flow formed channels over much of the hummocky rockslide debris, allowing cataracts to erode headward, and established for the first time since 1980 a dendritic integration of channels on the Toutle's North Fork drainage. Erosion has occurred intermittently since then, but most of the streams were established in their present channel locations on March 19, 1982. Figure 2 is within the breach formed by the big mudflow that day. Bedrock was eroded up to 600 feet deep to form Step Canyon and Loowit Canyon on the north flank of the volcano (see "Canyons" in figure 1).

Individual canyons on the debris avalanche deposit have a depth of up to 140 feet and are cut through landslide debris and pumice from pyroclastic flows (see "Breach" in figure 1). That erosion left elevated plateaus north and south of a great breach, resembling the north and south rims of the Colorado River. Also, gully-headed side canyons and amphitheater-headed side canyons in the breach resemble side canyons in the Grand Canyon. The breach did not occur straight through the obstruction but has a meandering path, which reminds us of the meandering path of the Grand Canyon through the high plateaus of northern Arizona. The "Little Grand Canyon of the Toutle River" is a 1/40th-scale model of the real Grand Canyon of Arizona.

Small creeks that flow through the headwaters of the Toutle River today might seem, by present appearances, to have carved these canyons very slowly over a very long time period, except for the fact that the erosion was observed to have occurred rapidly! Geologists should learn that because the long time scale they have been trained to assign to landform development would lead to obvious error at Mount St. Helens, it also may be useless or misleading elsewhere.

Rapid Formation of Fossil Deposits

One million logs floated on Spirit Lake on the late afternoon of May 18, 1980, after they were uprooted and washed into the basin by the 860-foot-high water waves. Careful observation of the floating conifer logs in the lake indicates that such logs show a strong tendency to float upright, best seen from the eastern shore of the lake (see "Logs" in figure 1). Many upright deposited logs possess roots attached to the log, but many have no root ball, and those without roots also show strong tendency to float upright. It appears that the root end of these logs is denser wood and perhaps floods with water more easily, allowing the root ends to sink before the top of the log. All six of the common conifer species were observed to float in an upright position.

Hundreds of upright, fully submerged logs were located by sidescan sonar, and scuba divers verified that they were indeed trunks of trees that the sonar detected. It was estimated that 20,000 upright stumps existed on the floor of the lake in August 1985. It would appear that about ten percent of the deposited logs were in an upright position. If Spirit Lake were drained, the bottom would look like a forest of trees. These, however, did not grow where they are now, but have been replanted!

Scuba investigation of the upright-deposited logs shows that some are already solidly buried by sedimentation with more than three feet of sediment around their bases. Others, however, have none. This proves that the upright logs were deposited at different times, with their roots buried at different levels. If found buried in the rock strata, logs such as the ones in Spirit Lake might be interpreted as multiple forests that grew on different levels over periods of many thousands of years. The Spirit Lake upright-deposited logs, therefore, have considerable implications for interpreting "petrified forests" in the strata record. Direct application of the Spirit Lake logs may be made to the Yellowstone petrified forests. There at Yellowstone, at Specimen Ridge, geologists have commonly attributed the petrified upright logs to many thousands of years of forest growth, but the upright logs in Spirit Lake call that interpretation into question.

Rapid Formation of Peat Layer

The enormous log mat floating on Spirit Lake has lost its bark and branches by the abrasive action of wind and waves. Scuba investigations of the lake bottom showed that water-saturated sheets of conifer bark are especially abundant intermingled with volcanic sediment added from the lake shore, forming a layer of peat many inches thick. The peat shows coarse texture. The primary component is sheets of tree bark, which comprise about 25 percent, by volume, of the peat. Scuba divers recovered sheets of tree bark having lengths of greater than eight feet from the peat bed. Together with broken branch and root material, bark sheets impart the peat's noteworthy coarse texture and dominantly layered appearance.

The "Spirit Lake peat" contrasts strongly with peats that have accumulated in swamps. Typical swamp peats are very finely macerated by organic degradation processes. They are "coffee grounds to mashed potatoes" in general texture. Furthermore, swamp peats possess a homogeneous appearance because of the intense penetration of roots which dominate swamps. Root material is the dominant coarse component of modern swamp peats while bark sheets are extremely rare.

The Spirit Lake peat resembles, both compositionally and texturally, certain coal beds of the eastern United States, which also are dominated by tree bark and appear to have accumulated beneath floating log mats. Conventionally, coal is supposed to have accumulated from organic material built up in swamps by growth in place of plants. Because the accumulation of peat in swamps is a slow process, geologists have supposed that coal beds required about one thousand years to form each inch of coal. The peat layer in Spirit Lake reveals that "floating mat peat" can accumulate very rapidly and possesses textures resembling coal. Swamp peats, however, possess very rare bark-sheet material, because the intrusive action of tree roots disintegrates and homogenizes the peat. The Spirit Lake peat, in contrast, is texturally very similar to coal. Thus, at Spirit Lake, we may have seen the first stage in the formation of coal.

Conclusion

Mount St. Helens provides a rare opportunity to study transient geologic processes which, produced within a few months, changes what geologists might otherwise assume required many thousands of years. The volcano challenges our way of thinking about how the earth works, how it changes, and the time scale attached. These processes and their effects allow Mount St. Helens to serve as a miniature laboratory for catastrophism.

Catastrophism is documented as a viable theory of geologic change and may have far-reaching implications on other scientific disciplines and philosophical inquiries. Many scientists recognize that Darwin's theory (which assumed slow evolutionary change) may be in error. Darwin built his theory of the evolution of living things on the notion that earth has slowly evolved. With catastrophism, we have tools to interpret the stratigraphic record including the geologic evidence of the Genesis Flood. Mount St. Helens "speaks" directly to issues of our day.

Creationists have been intensely interested in the geologic formations at Mount St. Helens because they provide a very graphic and real explanation for features which are often supposed to support evolutionary theory and uniformitarian speculation. Mount St. Helens can also be used as a steppingstone to help us imagine what the Genesis Flood was like.

Bibliography

Arct, M.A., and A.V. Chadwick, "Dendrochronology in the Yellowstone Fossil Forest," *Geological Society of America, Abstracts with Programs* 15 (1983): 5.

Austin, S.A., "Depositional Environment of the Kentucky No. 12 Coal Bed (Middle Pennsylvanian) of Western Kentucky, with Special Reference to the Origin of Coal Lithotypes," Ph.D. dissertation, Pennsylvania State University, 1979, p. 411.

Austin, S.A., "Uniformitarianism — A Doctrine That Needs Rethinking," *Compass* 56 no. 2 (1979): 29–45.

Austin, S.A., "Rapid Erosion at Mount St. Helens," *Origins* 11 no. 2 (1984): 90–98.

Austin, S.A., *Catastrophes in Earth History: A Source Book of Geologic Evidence, Speculation, and Theory,* Technical Monograph No. 13 (El Cajon, CA: Institute for Creation Research, 1984).

Austin, S.A., "Floating Logs and Log Deposits of Spirit Lake, Mount St. Helens Volcano National Monument, Washington," *Geological Society of America, Abstracts with Programs* 23 (1991).

Austin, S.A., "The Dynamic Landscape on the North Flank of Mount St. Helens" in J.E. O'Connor, R.J. Dorsey, and I.P. Madlin, eds., "Volcanoes to Vineyards: Geologic Field Trips through the Dynamic Landscape of the Pacific Northwest," *Geological Society of America Field Guide* 15 (2009).

Chadwick, A.D., and T. Yamoto, "A Paleoecological Analysis of the Petrified Trees in the Specimen Creek Area of Yellowstone National Park, Montana, U.S.A.," *Paleogeography, Palaeoclimatology, Palaeoecology* 45 (1984): 39–48.

Coffin, H.G., "Mount St. Helens and Spirit Lake," *Origins* 10 (1983): 9–17.

Coffin, H.G., "Erect Floating Stumps in Spirit Lake, Washington," *Geology* 11 (1983): 298–299.

Coffin, H.G., "Sonar and Scuba Survey of a Submerged Allochthonous Forest in Spirit Lake, Washington," *Palaios* 2 (1987): 178–180.

Criswell, C.W., "Chronology and Pyroclastic Stratigraphy of the May 18, 1980, Eruption of Mount St. Helens, Washington," *Journal of Geophysical Research* 92 (1987): 10,237–10,266.

Foxworthy, B.L., and M. Hill, "Volcanic Eruptions of 1980 at Mount St. Helens — The First 100 Days," *United States Geological Survey Professional Paper 1249*: 1982.

Fritz, W.J., "Reinterpretation of the Depositional Environment of the Yellowstone Fossil Forests." *Geology* 8 (1980): 309–313.

Glicken, H., "Study of the Rockslide-Debris Avalanche of May 18, 1980, Mount St. Helens Volcano," Ph.D. dissertation., University of California, Santa Barbara, 1986.

Hickson, C.J., "The May 18, 1980, Eruption of Mount St. Helens, Washington State: A Synopsis of Events and Review of Phase 1 from an Eyewitness Perspective," *Geoscience Canada* 17 no. 3 (1990): 127–130.

Karowe, A.L., and T.M. Jefferson, "Burial of Trees by Eruptions of Mount St. Helens, Washington: Implications for the Interpretation of Fossil Forests," *Geological Magazine* 124 no. 3 (1987): 191–204.

Lipman, P.O., and D.R. Mullineaux, eds., "The 1980 Eruptions of Mount St. Helens, Washington," *U.S. Geological Survey Professional Paper* 1250, 1981.

Malone, S.D., "Mount St. Helens, the 1980 Re-awakening and Continuing Seismic Activity," *Geoscience Canada* 17 no. 3 (1990): 163–166.

Meyer, D.F., and H.A. Martinson, "Rates and Processes of Channel Development and Recovery Following the 1980 Eruption of Mount St. Helens, Washington," *Hydrological Sciences Journal* 34 (1989): 115–127.

Morris, J.D., and S.A. Austin, *Footprints in the Ash: The Explosive Story of Mount St. Helens* (Green Forest, AR: Master Books, 2003), p. 128.

Peterson, D.W., "Overview of the Effects and Influence of the Activity of Mount St. Helens in the 1980s," *Geoscience Canada* 17 (1990): 163–166.

Rosenfeld, C.L., and G.L. Beach, "Evolution of a Drainage Network: Remote Sensing Analysis of the North Fork Toutle River, Mount St. Helens, Washington," Corvallis, Oregon State University Water Resources Research Institute, WRRI-88, 1983.

Rowley, P.D., et al., "Proximal Bedded Deposits Related to Pyroclastic Flows of May 18, 1980, Mount St. Helens, Washington," *Geological Society of America Bulletin* 96 (1985): 1373–1383.

Scott, K.M., "Magnitude and Frequency of Lahars and Lahar-runout Flows in the Toutle-Cowlitz River System," *United States Geological Survey Professional Paper 1447-B*, 1989.

Waitt, R.B. Jr., et al., "Eruption-Triggered Avalanche, Flood, and Lahar at Mount St. Helens — Effects of Winter Snowpack," *Science* 221 (1983): 1394–1397.

Weaver, C.S., and S.D. Malone, "Overview of the Tectonic Setting and Recent Studies of Eruptions of Mount St. Helens, Washington," *Journal of Geophysical Research* 92 (1987): 10,149–10,154.

27

What Is the Best Argument for the Existence of God?

DR. JASON LISLE

There are a number of common arguments for the existence of God. But most of these arguments are not as effective as many Christians would like to think. Let's consider a hypothetical conversation between a Christian and an atheist.

> *Christian:* "Everything with a beginning requires a cause. The universe has a beginning and therefore requires a cause. That cause is God."
>
> *Atheist:* "Even if it were true that everything with a beginning requires a cause, how do you know that the cause of the universe is God? Why not a big bang? Maybe this universe sprang from another universe, as some physicists now believe."
>
> *Christian:* "The living creatures of this world clearly exhibit design. Therefore, they must have a designer. And that designer is God."
>
> *Atheist:* "The living creatures only *appear* to be designed. Natural selection can account for this apparent design. Poorly adapted organisms tend to die off, and do not pass on their genes."
>
> *Christian:* "But living creatures have irreducible complexity. All their essential parts must be in place at the same time, or the organism dies. So God must have created these parts all at the same time. A gradual evolutionary path simply will not work."

Atheist: "Just because you cannot imagine a gradual stepwise way of constructing an organism does not mean there isn't one."

Christian: "DNA has information in it — the instructions to form a living being. And information never comes about by chance; it always comes from a mind. So DNA proves that God created the first creatures."

Atheist: "There could be an undiscovered mechanism that generates information in the DNA. Give us time, and we will eventually discover it. And even if DNA did come from intelligence, why would you think that intelligence is God? Maybe aliens seeded life on earth."

Christian: "The Resurrection of Jesus proves the existence of God. Only God can raise the dead."

Atheist: "You don't really have any proof that Jesus rose from the dead. This section of the Bible is simply an embellished story. And even if it were true, it proves nothing. Perhaps under certain rare chemical conditions, a dead organism can come back to life. It certainly doesn't mean that there is a God."

Christian: "The Bible claims that God exists, and that it is His Word to us. Furthermore, what the Bible says must be true, since God cannot lie."

Atheist: "That is a circular argument. Only if we knew in advance that God existed would it be reasonable to even consider the possibility that the Bible is His Word. If God does not exist — as I contend — then there is no reason to trust the Bible."

Christian: "Predictive prophecy shows that the Bible really must be inspired by God. All of the Old Testament prophecies concerning Christ, for example, were fulfilled. The odds of that happening by chance are very low."

Atheist: "A low probability isn't the same as zero. People do win the lottery. Besides, maybe the Gospels have embellished what Jesus did, so that it would agree with the Old Testament prophecies. Perhaps some so-called prophetic books were actually written after the events they 'predict.' Maybe certain gifted individuals have abilities not yet understood by science and can occasionally predict the future. It certainly doesn't prove the Bible is inspired by God."

Christian: "I have personally experienced God, and so have many other Christians. He has saved us and transformed our lives. We know that He exists from experience."

Atheist: "Unfortunately, your personal experiences are not open to investigation; I have only your word for it. And second, how do you know that such subjective feelings are really the result of God? The right drug might produce similar feelings."

Not Conclusive

It should be noted that all the facts used by the Christian in the above hypothetical conversation are *true*. Yes, God is the first cause, the designer of life, the resurrected Christ, the Author of Scripture, and the Savior of Christians. Yet the way these facts are used is not decisive. That is, none of the above arguments really prove that God exists.

Some of the above arguments are very weak: appeals to personal experience, vicious circular reasoning, and appeals to a first cause. While the facts are true, the arguments do not come close to proving the existence of the biblical God. Some of the arguments seem stronger; I happen to think that irreducible complexity and information in DNA are strong confirmations of biblical creation. And predictive prophecy does confirm the inspiration of Scripture. Nonetheless, for each one of these arguments, the atheist was able to invent a "rescuing device." He was able to propose an explanation for this evidence that is compatible with his belief that God does not exist.

Moreover, most of the atheist's explanations are actually pretty reasonable, given his view of the world. He's not being illogical. He is being consistent with his position. Christians and atheists have different worldviews — different philosophies of life. And we must learn to argue on the level of worldviews if we are to argue in a cogent and effective fashion.

The Christian in the above hypothetical conversation did not have a correct approach to apologetics. He was arguing on the basis of specific evidences with someone who had a totally different professed worldview than his own. This approach is never conclusive, because the critic can always invoke a rescuing device to protect his worldview.[1] Thus, if we are to be effective, we must use an argument that deals with worldviews, and not simply isolated facts. The best argument for the existence of God will be a "big-picture" kind of argument.

God Doesn't Believe in Atheists

The Bible teaches that atheists are not *really* atheists. That is, those who profess to be atheists do ultimately believe in God in their heart-of-hearts. The

1. Of course, sometimes people are persuaded by such arguments. But that doesn't mean the argument is cogent. After all, people can be persuaded by very bad arguments.

Bible teaches that everyone knows God, because God has revealed Himself to all (Romans 1:19). In fact, the Bible tells us that God's existence is so obvious that anyone who suppresses this truth is "without excuse" (Romans 1:20). The atheist denies with his lips what he knows in his heart. But if they know God, then why do atheists claim that they do not believe in God?

The answer may be found in Romans 1:18. God is angry at unbelievers for their wickedness. And an all-powerful, all-knowing God who is angry at you is a terrifying prospect. So even though many atheists might claim that they are neutral, objective observers, and that their disbelief in God is purely rational, in reality, they are strongly motivated to reject the biblical God who is rightly angry with them. So they suppress that truth in unrighteousness. They convince themselves that they do not believe in God.[2] The atheist is intellectually schizophrenic — believing in God, but believing that he does not believe in God.[3]

Therefore, we do not really need to give the atheist any more specific evidences for God's existence. He already knows in his heart-of-hearts that God exists, but he doesn't want to believe it. Our goal is to expose the atheist's suppressed knowledge of God.[4] With gentleness and respect, we can show the atheist that he already knows about God, but is suppressing what he knows to be true.

Exposing the Inconsistency

Because an atheist does believe in God, but does not believe that he believes in God, he is simply a walking bundle of inconsistencies. One type to watch for is a *behavioral inconsistency*; this is where a person's behavior does not comport with what he claims to believe. For example, consider the atheist university professor who teaches that human beings are simply chemical accidents — the end result of a long and purposeless chain of biological evolution. But then he goes home and kisses his wife and hugs his children, as if they were *not* simply chemical accidents, but valuable, irreplaceable persons deserving of respect and worthy of love.

Consider the atheist who is outraged at seeing a violent murder on the ten o'clock news. He is very upset and hopes that the murderer will be punished for

2. This is called an "iterated belief" — a belief about a belief.
3. Self-deception is quite common. People frequently attempt to convince themselves of what they want to believe. The Bible tells us that those who hear God's Word but do not act on it are self-deceived (James 1:22).
4. In some cases, we can use scientific evidence to expose such inconsistency. Consider the evolutionist who admits that the probability of a cell forming by chance is infinitesimal. He is going against the odds. Yet, he decides to carry an umbrella with him when there is a 90 percent chance of rain.

his wicked actions. But in his view of the world, why should he be angry? In an atheistic, evolutionary universe where people are just animals, murder is no different than a lion killing an antelope. But we don't punish the lion! If people are just chemical accidents, then why punish one for killing another? We wouldn't get upset at baking soda for reacting with vinegar; that's just what chemicals do. The concepts that human beings are valuable, are not simply animals, are not simply chemicals, have genuine freedom to make choices, are responsible for their actions, and are bound by a universal objective moral code all stem from a Christian worldview. Such things simply do not make sense in an atheistic view of life.

Many atheists behave morally and expect others to behave morally as well. But absolute morality simply does not comport with atheism. Why should there be an absolute, objective standard of behavior that all people should obey if the universe and the people within it are simply accidents of nature? Of course, people can assert that there is a moral code. But who is to say what that moral code should be? Some people think it is okay to be racist; others think it is okay to kill babies, and others think we should kill people of other religions or ethnicities, etc. Who is to say which position should be followed? Any standard of our own creation would necessarily be subjective and arbitrary.

Now, some atheists might respond, "That's right! Morality is subjective. We each have the right to create our own moral code. And therefore, you cannot impose your personal morality on other people!" But of course, this statement is self-refuting, because when they say, "you cannot impose your personal morality on other people" they are imposing their personal moral code on other people. When push comes to shove, no one really believes that morality is merely a subjective, personal choice.

Logical Inconsistency

Another inconsistency occurs when atheists attempt to be rational. Rationality involves the use of laws of logic. Laws of logic prescribe the correct chain of reasoning between truth claims. For example, consider the argument: "If it is snowing outside, then it must be cold out. It is snowing. Therefore, it is cold out." This argument is correct because it uses a law of logic called *modus ponens*. Laws of logic, like *modus ponens*, are immaterial, universal, invariant, abstract entities. They are immaterial because you can't touch them or stub your toe on one. They are universal and invariant because they apply in all places and at all times (*modus ponens* works just as well in Africa as it does in the United States, and just as well on Friday as it does on Monday). And they are abstract because they deal with concepts.

Laws of logic stem from God's sovereign nature; they are a reflection of the way He thinks. They are immaterial, universal, invariant, abstract entities, because God is an immaterial (Spirit), omnipresent, unchanging God who has all knowledge (Colossians 2:3). Thus, all true statements will be governed by God's thinking — they will be logical. The law of non-contradiction, for example, stems from the fact that God does not deny Himself (2 Timothy 2:13). The Christian can account for laws of logic; they are the correct standard for reasoning because God is sovereign over all truth. We can know some of God's thoughts because God has revealed Himself to us through the words of Scripture and the person of Jesus Christ.

However, the atheist cannot account for laws of logic. He cannot make sense of them within his own worldview. How could there be immaterial, universal, invariant, abstract laws in a chance universe formed by a big bang? Why should there be an absolute standard of reasoning if everything is simply "molecules in motion"? Most atheists have a materialistic outlook — meaning they believe that everything that exists is material, or explained by material processes. But laws of logic are not material! You cannot pull a law of logic out of the refrigerator! If atheistic materialism is true, then there could be no laws of logic, since they are immaterial. Thus, logical reasoning would be impossible!

No one is denying that atheists are able to reason and use laws of logic. The point is that if atheism were true, the atheist would not be able to reason or use laws of logic because such things would not be meaningful. The fact that the atheist is able to reason demonstrates that he is wrong. By using that which makes no sense given his worldview, the atheist is being horribly inconsistent. He is using God's laws of logic, while denying the biblical God that makes such laws possible.

How could there be laws at all without a lawgiver? The atheist cannot account for (1) the existence of laws of logic, (2) why they are immaterial, (3) why they are universal, (4) why they do not change with time, and (5) how human beings can possibly know about them or their properties. But of course, all these things make perfect sense on the Christian system.

Laws of logic owe their existence to the biblical God. Yet they are required to reason rationally, to prove things. So the biblical God must exist in order for reasoning to be possible. Therefore, *the best proof of God's existence is that without Him we couldn't prove anything at all!* The existence of the biblical God is the prerequisite for knowledge and rationality. This is called the "transcendental argument for God" or TAG for short. It is a devastating and conclusive argument, one that only a few people have even attempted to refute (and none of them successfully).[5]

Proof Versus Persuasion

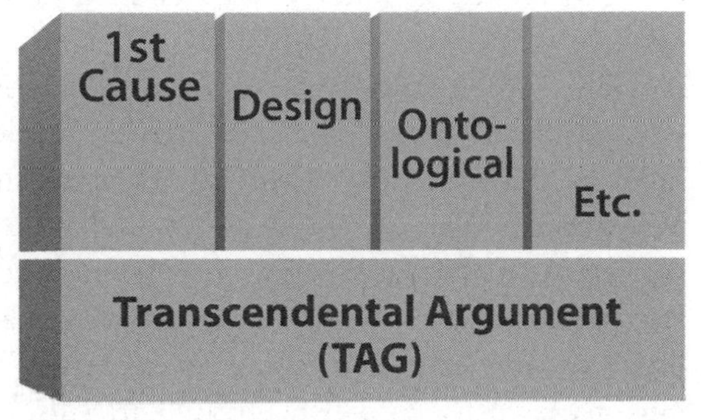

Other arguments for the existence of God (First Cause, Design, etc.) actually assume the transcendental argument before they can even make their argument.

Though the transcendental argument for God is deductively sound, not all atheists will be convinced upon hearing it. It may take time for them to even understand the argument in the first place. As I write this chapter, I am in the midst of an electronic exchange with an atheist who has not yet fully grasped the argument. Real-life discussions on this issue take time. But even if the atheist fully understands the argument, he may not be convinced. We must remember that there is a difference between proof and persuasion. Proof is objective, but persuasion is subjective. The transcendental argument does indeed objectively prove that God exists. However, that does not mean that the atheists will necessarily cry "uncle." Atheists are strongly motivated to not believe in the biblical God — a God who is rightly angry at them for their treason against Him.

But the atheist's denial of God is an emotional reaction, not a logical one. We might imagine a disobedient child who is about to be punished by his father. He might cover his eyes with his hands and say of his father, "You don't exist!" but that would hardly be rational. Atheists deny (with their lips) the biblical God, not for logical reasons, but for psychological reasons. We must also keep in mind that the unbeliever's problem is not simply an emotional

5. Perhaps most significantly, philosopher Michael Martin has attempted to rebut TAG indirectly by making a transcendental-style argument for the non-existence of God (TANG). Martin's argument has been refuted by John Frame, and independently by Michael Butler.

issue, but a deep spiritual problem (1 Corinthians 2:14). It is the Holy Spirit that must give him the ability to repent (1 Corinthians 12:3; 2 Timothy 2:25).

So we must keep in mind that it is not our job to convert people — nor can we. Our job is to give a defense of the faith in a way that is faithful to the Scriptures (1 Peter 3:15). It is the Holy Spirit that brings conversion. But God can use our arguments as part of the process by which He draws people to Himself.

28

Do Evolutionists Believe Darwin's Ideas about Evolution?

ROGER PATTERSON AND DR. TERRY MORTENSON

Charles Darwin first published his ideas on evolution over 150 years ago. In those 150 years we have come to understand the complexity of life, and many new scientific fields have shed light on the question of the validity of Darwin's evolutionary hypothesis. Few people have actually read the works of Darwin, and if they did they might be shocked to read some of Darwin's ideas. In this chapter we will take a look at what Darwin and other early evolutionists believed and how those ideas have changed over time.

Darwin was wrong on many points, and there would be few who would disagree with this claim. But if Darwin was wrong on some points, does that mean that the entire hypothesis of evolution is proven wrong?

What Is Evolution?

Like many words, *evolution* has many different uses depending on its context. The general concept of the word is "change over time." In that sense, one might say that a butterfly evolves from an egg to a caterpillar to a winged butterfly and a child evolves into an adult. There is no disputing that individual organisms change over time. However, using the word in this way is quite misleading for the origins debate. Darwin's hypothesis involves a very different concept.

As *evolution* is used in this chapter and in all science textbooks, natural history museums, and science programs on television, it refers to the biological idea that all life on earth has descended from a single common ancestor. There are many different variations on this theme as well as several explanations of how the first organism came into existence from non-living matter. Examining some of the historical evolutionary positions and comparing them to the ideas that are popular in scientific circles today shows how much those concepts have changed. In general, evolution will be used to refer to the concept of molecules turning into men over time. This concept of evolution is in direct opposition to the biblical account of creation presented in the Book of Genesis.[1]

Evolution – an Ancient Idea

The concept of molecules-to-man evolution is certainly not a new idea. Several Greek philosophers before the time of Christ wrote on the topic. For example, Lucretius and Empedocles promoted a form of natural selection that did not rely on any type of purpose. In *De Rerum Natura (On the Nature of Things)* Lucretius writes:

> And many species of animals must have perished at that time, unable by procreation to forge out the chain of posterity: for whatever you see feeding on the breath of life, either cunning or courage or at least quickness must have guarded and kept that kind from its earliest existence. . . . But those to which nature gave no such qualities, so that they could neither live by themselves at their own will, nor give us some usefulness for which we might suffer to feed them under our protection and be safe, these certainly lay at the mercy of others for prey and profit, being all hampered by their own fateful chains, until nature brought that race to destruction.[2]

This stands in opposition to the thinking of Aristotle, who promoted the idea of purpose in nature. Aristotle also imagined forms of life advancing through history, but he believed nature had the aim of producing beauty.[3] This idea of purpose in nature, or teleology, is later seen in the works of Thomas Aquinas and other Christian philosophers.

1. For an explanation of some of the contradictions between the biblical creation account and the widely held evolution story, see the article "Evolution vs. Creation: The Order of Events Matters!" at www.answersingenesis.org/docs2006/0404order.asp.
2. Sharon Kaye, "Was There No Evolutionary Thought in the Middle Ages? The Case of William of Ockham," *British Journal for the History of Philosophy* 14 no. 2 (2006): 225–244.
3. Henry Fairfield Osborn, *From the Greeks to Darwin* (London: Macmillan, 1913), p. 43–56.

The concept of evolution was not lost from Western thinking until Darwin rediscovered it — it was always present in various forms. Because much of the thinking was dominated by Aristotelian ideas, the idea of a purposeless evolutionary process was not popular. Most saw a purpose in nature and the interactions between living things. The dominance of the Roman Catholic Church in Europe (where modern science was born) and its adherence to Aristotelian philosophies also played a role in limiting the promotion of evolution and other contrary ideas as these would have been seen as heresy. As the Enlightenment took hold in Europe in the 17th and 18th centuries, explanations that looked beyond a directed cause became more popular.

Erasmus Darwin

Coming to the mid-to-late 18th century, Kant, Liebnitz, Buffon, and others began to talk openly of a natural force that has driven the change of organisms from simple to complex over time. The idea of evolution was well established in the literature, but there seemed to be no legitimate mechanism to adequately explain this idea in scientific terms. Following the spirit of the Greek poets Lucretius and Empedocles, Erasmus Darwin, the atheist grandfather of Charles, wrote some of his ideas in poetic verse. Brushing up against the idea of survival of the fittest, Erasmus spoke of the struggle for existence between different animals and even plants. This struggle is a part of the evolutionary process he outlines in his *Temple of Nature* (1803) in the section titled "Production of Life":

> Hence without parent by spontaneous birth
> Rise the first specks of animated earth;
> From Nature's womb the plant or insect swims,
> And buds or breathes, with microscopic limbs.[4]

And he continues:

> Organic Life beneath the shoreless waves
> Was born and nursed in Ocean's pearly caves;
> First forms minute, unseen by spheric glass,
> Move on the mud, or pierce the watery mass;
> These, as successive generations bloom,
> New powers acquire, and larger limbs assume;
> Whence countless groups of vegetation spring,
> And breathing realms of fin, and feet, and wing.[5]

4. Erasmus Darwin, *The Temple of Nature* (London: Jones & Company, 1825), p. 13.
5. Ibid., p. 14–15.

Starting with spontaneous generation from inanimate matter, Erasmus imagined life evolving into more complex forms over time. He did not identify any mechanisms that may have caused the change, other than general references to nature and a vague driving force.

In the introduction to this work, Erasmus Darwin states that it is not intended to instruct but rather to amuse, and he then includes many notes describing his ideas. Despite his claimed-to-be-innocent intentions, this poem lays out the gradual, simple-to-complex progression of matter to living creature — a view very consciously different from the biblical account of creation which the vast majority of his contemporaries knew and believed. He traces the development of life in the seas to life on land with the four-footed creatures eventually culminating in humans and the creation of society. There is no doubt that when Charles began his studies, the idea of evolution apart from the supernatural was present in Western thought (even in his own extended family). The arguments in support of special creation were certainly prominent, but evolutionary ideas were being pressed into mainstream thinking in the era of modernism.[6]

To underscore the early acceptance of evolution, the following passage from *Zoonomia* (3 vol., 1794–1796) illustrates Erasmus Darwin's belief that all life had come from a common "filament" of life.

> From thus meditating on the great similarity of the structure of the warm-blooded animals . . . would it be too bold to imagine that, in the great length of time since the earth began to exist, perhaps millions of ages before the commencement of the history of mankind would it be too bold to imagine that all warm-blooded animals have arisen from one living filament?[7]

Lamarckian Evolution or Use and Disuse

In France, and at the same time as Erasmus, Jean Baptiste Lamarck developed his theories of the origin and evolution of life. Initially, he had

6. Modernism was the dominant philosophy in Western culture from the late 18th to the late 20th centuries. This philosophy placed science as the supreme authority for determining truth. Science was viewed as the "savior" of mankind — eventually finding cures for all diseases, ending war, famine, etc. Though it has been largely replaced by post-modernism, this modernist thinking is still very prominent among scientists and many others in our culture. Post-modernism, on the other hand, is a radical skepticism about anyone's ability to know truth. Post-modernists argue that truth and morality are relative — there are no absolutes. It also reflects disenchantment with the promises made by modernist philosophers and scientists. Both philosophies reject Scripture as authoritative truth and are based on evolutionary thinking.
7. Erasmus Darwin, *Zoonomia*, volume 1 (Philadelphia, PA: Edward Earle, 1818), p. 397.

argued for the immutability of species, but in his later works he laid out a clear alternative to the special creation of plants and animals. Lamarck believed that the geology of the earth was the result of gradual processes acting over vast periods of time — a view later to be known as uniformitarianism. Lamarck developed four laws of evolution and put them forward in his *Philosophie Zoologique* published in 1809. Lamarck proposed that an internal force and the need for new organs caused creatures to develop new characteristics. Once developed, the use or disuse of the organs would determine how they would be passed on to a creature's offspring. This idea of the transmission or inheritance of acquired characteristics is the hallmark of this model of evolution.

Lamarck's mechanism of use and disuse of characters was widely rejected in his lifetime, especially by the prominent French naturalist Georges Cuvier, and was never supported by observations. Lamarck did attempt to explain how the characteristics were inherited, but there was still no clear biological mechanism of inheritance that would support his claims. Lamarck also proposed a tree of life with various branching structures that showed how life evolved from simple to complex forms. Much of what Lamarck proposed seems unreasonable to us today with a modern understanding of genetics. A husband and wife who are both bodybuilders will not have an extraordinarily muscular child — that acquired trait does not have any affect on the genetic information in the germ cells of the parents' bodies. However, recent research has revealed instances of bacterial inheritance that appear to be very Lamarckian in nature. Future research in this area may reveal that Lamarck was correct to some degree. But

In Lamarckian evolution, animals change due to environmental factors and the use or disuse of a feature. For example, a giraffe's neck will get longer over time as it continually stretches it to reach higher leaves on trees.

Darwin originally proposed that natural selection would be the primary mechanism acting to change organisms over millions of years. He was not aware of the role of mutations in heredity.

there are many good reasons to expect that this would provide no support for the idea of molecules-to-man evolution.[8]

Darwinian Evolution

Charles Darwin was at least familiar with all of these different views, and their influence can be found throughout his writings. Darwin often referred to the effects of natural selection along with the use or disuse of the parts. The legs and wings of the ostrich, the absence of feet and wings in beetles, and the absence of eyes in moles and cave-dwelling animals are all mentioned by Darwin as a result of use or disuse alongside natural selection.[9] Exactly how this process happened was a mystery to Darwin. He proposed the idea of "pangenesis" as the mechanism of passing traits from parent to offspring. This idea is not significantly different from Lamarck's, for it relies on the use and disuse of organs and structures that are passed on to offspring through pangenes over vast ages.

In his work *The Variation of Animals and Plants under Domestication*, Darwin suggested that gemmules are shed by body cells, and that the combination of these gemmules would determine the appearance and constitution of

8. Even if Lamarckian mechanisms are uncovered, the fossil record would not support the evolution story. See Duane Gish, *Evolution: The Fossils Still Say No*, (Santee, CA: Institute for Creation Research, 1996); Carl Werner, *Evolution: The Grand Experiment,* vol. 1 (Green Forest, AR: New Leaf Press, 2007); and *Living Fossils*, vol. 2 (Green Forest, AR: New Leaf Press, 2008). Natural selection can only "select" from existing genetic information (it cannot create new information), and mutations cause a loss or reshuffling of existing genetic information. See Terry Mortenson's DVD *Origin of the Species: Was Darwin Right?* (Answers in Genesis, 2007) and John Sanford, *Genetic Entropy and the Mystery of the Genome* (Lima NY: Elim Publishing, 2005). Also, what bacteria can do should not be directly applied to other forms of life because bacteria are categorically and significantly different. This is explained in Georgia Purdom's DVD *All Creatures Great and Small: Microbes and Creation* (Petersburg, KY: Answers in Genesis, 2009).
9. Charles Darwin, *The Origin of Species* (New York, NY: The Modern Library, 1993), p. 175–181.

the offspring. If the parent had a long neck, then more gemmules for a long neck would be passed to the offspring. In Darwin's defense, he was not aware of the work of his contemporary, Gregor Mendel. In his garden in the Czech lands, Mendel was studying the heredity of pea plants. Neither man knew of the existence of genes, or the DNA genes are composed of, but both of them understood there was a factor involved in transmitting characteristics from one generation to the next. Despite evidence from experiments conducted by his cousin Francis Galton, Darwin clung to his pangenesis hypothesis and defended it in his later work *Descent of Man*.

Darwin believed that all organisms had evolved by natural processes over vast expanses of time. In the introduction to *Origin of Species* he wrote:

> As many more individuals of each species are born than can possibly survive; and as, consequently, there is a frequently recurring struggle for existence, it follows that any being, if it vary however slightly in any manner profitable to itself, under the complex and sometimes varying conditions of life, will have a better chance of surviving, and thus be *naturally selected*. From the strong principle of inheritance, any selected variety will tend to propagate its new and modified form.[10]

Darwin's belief that slight modifications were selected to produce big changes in organisms over the course of millions of years was the foundation of his model for the evolution of life on earth. We know today that Darwin's notion of gemmules and pangenes leading to new features or the development of enhanced characteristics is a false notion. However, that does not mean, by itself, that Darwin's conclusion is wrong — just that his reasoning was faulty.

Neo-Darwinian Evolution and the Modern Synthesis

The discovery of DNA and the rediscovery of Mendel's work on heredity in pea plants have shown that Darwin's hereditary mechanism does not work. But his conclusion of molecules-to-man transformation over millions of years is still held as true by proponents of evolution. In the early 20th century, Mendelian genetics was rediscovered and it came to be understood that DNA was responsible for the transmission and storage of hereditary information. The scientific majority was still fixed on a naturalistic explanation for the evolution of organisms. That evolution happened was never a question — finding the mechanism was the goal of these naturalistic scientists.

10. Ibid., p. 21.

Mutation of genetic information came to be viewed as the likely mechanism for providing the raw material for natural selection to act on. Combining genetic studies of creatures in the lab and in the wild, models of speciation and change over time were developed and used to explain what was seen in the present. These small changes that resulted from mutations were believed to provide the genetic diversity that would lead to new forms over eons of time. This small change was referred to as "microevolution" since it involved small changes over a short amount of time. The evolutionists claim that the small changes add up to big changes over millions of years, leading to new kinds of life. Thus, microevolution leads to "macroevolution" in the evolutionary view. However, the acceptance of these terms just leads to confusion, and they should be avoided.

This is not fundamentally different from what Charles Darwin taught; it simply uses a different mechanism to explain the process. The problem is that the change in speciation and adaptation is heading in the opposite direction needed for macroevolution. The small changes seen in species as they adapt to their environments and form new species through mutation are the result of losses of information. Darwinian evolution requires the addition of traits (such as forelimbs changing into wings, and scales turning into feathers in dinosaur-to-bird evolution), which requires the addition of new information. Selecting from information that is already present in the genome and that was damaged through copying mistakes in the genes cannot be the process that adds new information to the genome.

Today, evolution has been combined with the study of embryology, genetics, the fossil record, molecular structures, plate tectonics, radiometric dating, anthropology, forensics, population studies, psychology, brain chemistry, etc. This leads to the intertwining of so many different ideas that the modern view of evolution can explain anything. It has become so plastic that it can be molded to explain any evidence, no matter how inconsistent the explanations may become. Even Darwin was willing to admit that there may be evidence that would invalidate his hypothesis. That is no longer the view held by the vast majority of evolutionists today — evolution has become a fact, even a scientific law (on par with the law of gravity), in the minds of many.

To help us see this more clearly, let us take a look at the idea of different races. Darwin published his views on the different races in *Descent of Man.* Though Darwin spoke against slavery, he clearly believed that the different people groups around the world were the result of various levels of evolutionary development. Darwin wrote:

> At some future period, not very distant as measured by centuries, the civilized races of man will almost certainly exterminate and

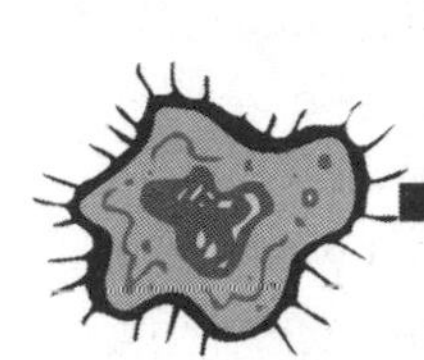

Natural Selection
+ Mutations
+
Millions of Years

After the discovery of DNA and its role in inheritance, evolutionists pointed to mutations in the DNA as the source for new traits. These accidental mutations provide differences in the offspring that can be selected for. This selection is believed to lead to new kinds of life.

> replace the savage races throughout the world. At the same time the anthropomorphous apes . . . will no doubt be exterminated. The break between man and his nearest allies will then be wider, for it will intervene between man in a more civilized state, as we may hope, even than the Caucasian, and some ape as low as a baboon, instead of as now between the negro or Australian [Aborigine] and the gorilla.[11]

This is the conclusion Darwin came to — that different rates of evolution would lead to different classes of humans. He often refers to the distinction between the civilized Europeans and the savages of various areas of the world. He concludes that some of these savages are so closely related to apes that there is no clear dividing line in human history "where the term 'man' ought to be used."[12] Consistent with his naturalistic view of the world, Darwin saw various groups of humans, whether they are distinct species or not, as less advanced than others. This naturally leads to racist attitudes and, as Dr. Stephen J. Gould noted, biological arguments for racism "increased by orders of magnitude following the acceptance of evolutionary theory,"[13] though this was likely only an excuse to act on underlying social prejudices.

Dr. James Watson (co-discoverer of the double-helix structure of the DNA molecule and a leading atheistic evolutionist) was caught in a storm of evolutionary racism in 2007. The *Times* of London reported in an interview:

> He says that he is "inherently gloomy about the prospect of Africa" because "all our social policies are based on the fact that their intelligence is the same as ours — whereas all the testing says

11. Charles Darwin, *The Origin of Species and The Descent of Man* (New York, NY: The Modern Library, 1936), p. 521.
12. Ibid., p. 541.
13. Stephen Jay Gould, *Ontogeny and Phylogeny* (Cambridge, MA: Belknap Press of Harvard University Press, 1977), p. 127.

> not really," and I know that this "hot potato" is going to be difficult to address. His hope is that everyone is equal, but he counters that "people who have to deal with black employees find this not true." He says that you should not discriminate on the basis of colour, because "there are many people of colour who are very talented, but don't promote them when they haven't succeeded at the lower level." He writes, "there is no firm reason to anticipate that the intellectual capacities of peoples geographically separated in their evolution should prove to have evolved identically. Our wanting to reserve equal powers of reason as some universal heritage of humanity will not be enough to make it so."[14]

Though he later stated that he did not intend to imply that black Africans are genetically inferior, he is being consistent with his evolutionary beliefs. His remarks were considered offensive, even by those who endorse evolution. This exposes an inconsistency in the thinking of many evolutionists today — if we evolved by random chance, we are nothing special. If humans evolved, it is only reasonable to conclude that different groups have evolved at different rates and with different abilities, and mental ability could be higher in one group than another. If the data supported this claim, in the evolutionary framework, then it should be embraced. Those who would suggest that evolution can explain why all humans have value must battle against those evolutionists who would disagree.

This exposes the inconsistent and plastic nature of evolution as an overarching framework — who gets to decide what evolution should mean? Darwin and Watson are applying the concepts in a consistent way and setting emotion and political correctness aside, when it is deemed necessary. Darwin noted that "it is only our natural prejudice and . . . arrogance" that lead us to believe we are special in the animal world.[15]

Without an objective standard, such as that provided by the Bible, the value and dignity of human beings are left up to the opinions of people and their biased interpretations of the world around us. God tells us through His Word that each human has dignity and is a special part of the creation because each one is made in the image of God. We are all of "one blood" in a line descended from Adam, the first man, who was made distinct from all animals and was *not* made by modifying any previously existing animal (Genesis 2:7).

14. Charlotte Hunt-Grubbe, "The Elementary DNA of Dr Watson," Times Online [London], October14, 2007, www.entertainment.timesonline.co.uk/tol/arts_and_entertainment/books/article2630748.ece.
15. Darwin, *The Origin of Species and The Descent of Man*, p. 411–412.

Saltation and Punctuated Equilibrium

Contrasted with Darwin's view of a gradual process of change acting over vast ages of time, others have seen the history of life on earth as one of giant leaps of rapid evolutionary change sprinkled through the millions of years. Darwin noted that the fossil record seemed to be missing the transitions from one kind of organism to the next that would confirm his gradualistic notion of evolution. Shortly after Darwin, there were proponents of evolutionary saltation — the notion that evolution happens in great leaps. The almost complete absence of transitional forms in the fossil record seemed to support this saltation concept and this was later coupled with genetics to provide a mechanism where "hopeful monsters" would appear and almost instantaneously produce a new kind of creature (e.g., changing a reptile into a bird). These "monsters" would be the foundation for new kinds of animals.

Saltation fell out of favor, but the inconsistency between the fossil record and the gradualism promoted by Darwin and others was still a problem. The work of Ernst Mayr, Stephen J. Gould, and Niles Eldredge was the foundation for the model of "punctuated equilibrium." This model explained great periods of stasis in the fossil record punctuated with occasional periods of rapid change in small populations of a certain kind of creature. This rapid change is relative to the geologic time scale — acting over tens of thousands of years rather than millions. This idea is not inconsistent with Darwin's grand evolutionary scheme. However, it seems that Darwin did not anticipate such a mechanism, though he commented that different organisms would have evolved at different rates. Whether evolution has occurred by gradual steps or rapid leaps (or some combination) is still a topic of debate among those who hold to the neo-Darwinian synthesis of mutations and natural selection as the driving forces of evolutionary change.

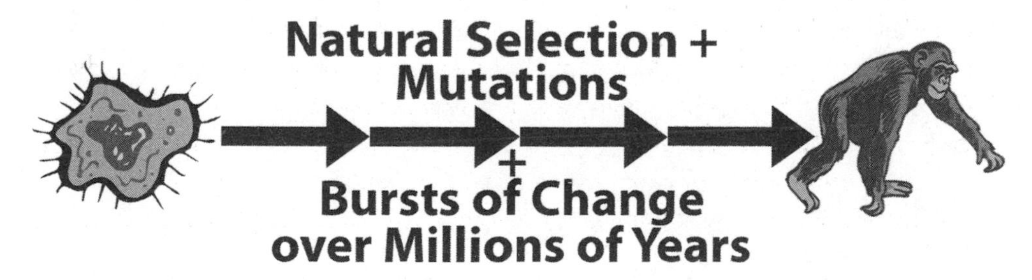

Contrary to Neo-Darwinism, punctuated equilibrium tries to account for the lack of fossil intermediates by appealing to rapid bursts of change interspersed in the millions of years. They still rely on mutations and natural selection, but at a much faster rate.

Conclusion

Sir Isaac Newton provided us with a general theory of gravity (and described laws in support of that theory) based on observational science. Even in light of modern understandings, those laws still apply today. Einstein did expand the concepts, but the functionality of Newtonian physics still applies today as much as ever.

The same cannot be said for Darwin's ideas. Darwin's hypothesized mechanism of natural selection (even with the added understanding of mutations) has failed to provide an explanation for the origin and diversity of life we see on earth today. His confident expectation that the fossil record would confirm his hypothesis has utterly failed, and the mind-boggling irreducible complexity seen in biological systems today defies the explanations of Darwin or his disciples. To say that evolutionary thinking today is Darwinian in nature can only mean that evolutionists believe that life has evolved from simpler to complex over time. Beyond that, what is called Darwinism today bears little resemblance to what Darwin actually wrote.

All of these ideas of the evolution of organisms from simple to complex are contrary to the clear teaching of Scripture that God made separate kinds of plants and animals and one kind of man, each to reproduce after its own kind. As such, these evolutionary ideas are bound to fail when attempting to describe the history of life and to predict the future changes to kinds of life in this universe where we live. When we start our thinking with the Bible, we can know we are starting on solid ground. Both the fossil record and the study of how plants, animals, and people change in the present fit perfectly with what the Bible says about creation, the Flood, and the Tower of Babel in Genesis 1–11. The Bible makes sense of the world around us.

29

What Are Some of the Best Flood Evidences?

DR. ANDREW A. SNELLING

Have you ever been "tongue-tied" when asked to provide geologic evidence that the Genesis Flood really did occur, just as the Bible describes? What follows is an overview of six geologic evidences for the Genesis Flood. Together, they will provide you with "ammunition" and a teaching tool for you and others.

Why is it that many people, including many Christians, can't see the geologic evidence for the Genesis Flood? It is usually because they have bought into the evolutionary idea that "the present is the key to the past." They are convinced that, because today's geological processes are so slow, the earth's rock layers took millions of years to form.

However, if the Genesis Flood really occurred, what evidence would we look for? We read in Genesis 7 and 8 that "the fountains of the great deep" were broken up and poured out water from inside the earth for 150 days (5 months). Plus, it rained torrentially and globally for 40 days and nights. ("The floodgates [or windows] of heaven were opened.") No wonder all the high hills and the mountains were covered, meaning the earth was covered by a global ocean. (". . . the world that then was, being overflowed with water, perished" 2 Peter 3:6; KJV.) All air-breathing life on the land was swept away and perished.

Wouldn't we expect to find billions of dead plants and animals buried and fossilized in sand, mud, and lime that were deposited rapidly by water in rock layers all over the earth? Of course! That's exactly what we find. Indeed, based on the biblical description of the Flood, there are six main geologic evidences that testify to its historicity.[1]

Evidence #1: Fossils of Sea Creatures High Above Sea Level

On every continent we find fossils of sea creatures in rock layers that today are high above sea level. For example, most of the rock layers in the walls of the Grand Canyon contain marine fossils. This includes the Kaibab Limestone at the top of the strata sequence and exposed at the rim of the canyon, which today is 7,000–8,000 feet above sea level.[2] This limestone was therefore deposited beneath lime sediment-charged ocean waters, which swept over northern Arizona (and beyond). Other rock layers of the Grand Canyon also contain large numbers of marine fossils. The best example is the Redwall Limestone, which commonly contains fossil brachiopods (a type of clam), corals, bryozoans (lace corals), crinoids (sea-lilies), bivalves (other types of clams), gastropods (marine snails), trilobites, cephalopods, and even fish teeth.[3] These marine fossils are found haphazardly preserved in this limestone bed. The crinoids, for example, are found with their columnals (disks), which in life are stacked on top of one another to make up their "stems," totally separated from one another in what can best be described as a "hash." Thus, these marine creatures were catastrophically destroyed and buried by the deposition of this lime sediment layer.

Fossil ammonites (coiled marine gastropods) are also found in limestone beds high in the Himalayas, reaching up to 30,000 feet above sea level.[4] All geologists agree that these marine fossils must have been buried in these limestone beds when the latter were deposited by ocean waters. So how did these marine limestone beds get to be high up in the Himalayas?

There is only one possible explanation — the ocean waters at some time in the past flooded over the continents. Could the continents have then sunk below today's sea level, so that the ocean waters flooded over them? No! Because the continents are made up of rocks that are less dense (lighter) than both the ocean floor

1. I want to acknowledge that these geologic evidences have also been elaborated on by my colleague Dr. Steve Austin at the Institute for Creation Research, in his book *Grand Canyon: Monument to Catastrophe* (Santee, CA: Institute for Creation Research, 1994), p. 51–52.
2. R.L. Hopkins and K.L. Thompson, "Kaibab Formation," in S.S. Beus and M. Morales, eds., *Grand Canyon Geology*, 2nd edition (New York, NY: Oxford University Press, 2003), p. 196–211.
3. S.S. Beus, "Redwall Limestone and Surprise Canyon Formation," in S.S. Beus and M. Morales, eds., *Grand Canyon Geology*, 2nd edition (New York, NY: Oxford University Press, New York, 2003), p. 115–135.
4. J.P. Davidson, W.E. Reed, and P.M. Davis, "The Rise and Fall of Mountain Ranges," in *Exploring Earth: An Introduction to Physical Geology* (Upper Saddle River, NJ: Prentice Hall, 1997), p. 242–247.

rocks and the mantle rocks beneath the continents. The continents, in fact, have an automatic tendency to rise, and thus "float" on the mantle rocks beneath, well above the level of the ocean floor rocks.[5] This is why the continents today have such high elevations compared to the deep ocean floor, and why the ocean basins can accommodate so much water. Rather, the sea level had to rise, so that the ocean waters then flooded up onto, and over, the continents. What would have caused that to happen? There had to be, in fact, two mechanisms to cause this.

First, if the volume of water in the ocean was increased, then sea level would rise. In Genesis 7:11 we read that at the initiation of the Flood all the fountains of the great deep were broken up. In other words, the earth's crust was cleaved open all around the globe and water burst forth from inside the earth. We then read in Genesis 7:24–8:2 that these fountains were open for 150 days. No wonder the ocean waters flooded up onto and over the continents.

Second, if the ocean floor itself rose, it would then have effectively "pushed" up the sea level. The catastrophic breakup of the earth's crust, referred to in Genesis 7:11, would not only have released huge volumes of water from inside the earth, but much molten rock.[6] The ocean floors would have been effectively replaced by hot lavas. Being less dense than the original ocean floors, these hot lavas would have had an expanded thickness, so the new ocean floors would have effectively risen, raising the sea level by up to more than 3,500 feet. When the ocean floors cooled and sank, the sea level would have fallen and the waters would have drained off the continents into new, deeper ocean basins.

Evidence #2: Rapid Burial of Plants and Animals

Countless billions of plant and animal fossils are found in extensive "graveyards" where they had to be buried rapidly on a massive scale. Often the fine details of the creatures are exquisitely preserved.

For example, billions of straight-shelled, chambered nautiloids (figure 1) are found fossilized with other marine creatures in a 7 feet (2 m) thick layer within the Redwall Limestone of Grand Canyon.[7] This fossil graveyard stretches for 180 miles (290 km) across northern Arizona and into southern Nevada,

5. J.P. Davidson, W.E. Reed, and P.M. Davis, "Isostasy," in *Exploring Earth: An Introduction to Physical Geology* (Upper Saddle River, NJ: Prentice Hall, 1997), p. 124–129.
6. A.A. Snelling, "A Catastrophic Breakup: A Scientific Look at Catastrophic Plate Tectonics," Answers April–June 2007, p. 44–48; A.A. Snelling, "Can Catastrophic Plate Tectonics Explain Flood Geology?" in Ken Ham, ed., *The New Answers Book 1* (Green Forest, AR: Master Books, 2006), p. 186–197.
7. S.A. Austin, "Nautiloid Mass Kill and Burial Event, Redwall Limestone (Lower Mississippian), Grand Canyon Region, Arizona and Nevada," in *Proceedings of the Fifth International Conference on Creationism*, R.L. Ivey, ed., (Pittsburgh, PA: Creation Science Fellowship, 2003), p. 55–99.

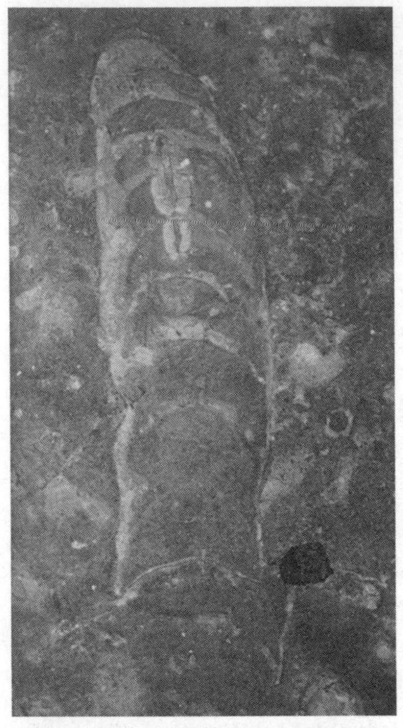

Figure1. Fossil nautiloids, found in the Redwall Limestone were buried rapidly.

covering an area of at least 10,500 square miles (30,000 km^2). These squid-like fossils are all different sizes, from small, young nautiloids to their bigger, older relatives. To form such a vast fossil graveyard required 24 cubic miles (100 km^3) of lime sand and silt, flowing in a thick-soup-like slurry at more than 16 feet (5 m) per second (more than 11 miles or 18 km per hour) to catastrophically overwhelm and bury this huge, living population of nautiloids.

Hundreds of thousands of marine creatures were buried with amphibians, spiders, scorpions, millipedes, insects, and reptiles in a fossil graveyard at Montceau-les-Mines, France.[8] At Florissant, Colorado, a wide variety of insects, freshwater mollusks, fish, birds, and several hundred plant species (including nuts and blossoms) are buried together.[9] Bees and birds have to be buried rapidly in order to be so well preserved.

Alligator, fish (including sunfish, deep sea bass, chubs, pickerel, herring, and gar-pike 3–7 feet [1–2 m] long), birds, turtles, mammals, mollusks, crustaceans, many varieties of insects, and palm leaves (7–9 feet [2–2.5 m] long) were buried together in the vast Green River Formation of Wyoming.[10] Notice in these examples how marine and land-dwelling creatures are found buried together. How could this have happened unless the ocean waters rose and swept over the continents in a global, catastrophic Flood?

Many trillions of microscopic marine creatures had to have catastrophically buried large ammonites and other marine creatures in the chalk beds of Britain.[11] These same beds also stretch right across Europe to the Middle East, as well as into the Midwest of the United States, forming a global-scale fossil

8. B. Heyler and C.M. Poplin, "The Fossils of Montceau-les-Mines," *Scientific American*, September 1988, p. 70–76.
9. T.D.A. Cockerell, "The Fossil Flora and Fauna of the Florissant Shales," *University of Colorado Studies* 3 (1906): 157–176.
10. L. Grande, "Paleontology of the Green River Formation with a Review of the Fish Fauna," *The Geological Survey of Wyoming Bulletin* 63 (1984).
11. J.M. Hancock, "The Petrology of the Chalk," *Proceedings of the Geologists' Association* 86 (1975): 499–536; B. Smith and D.J. Batten, "Fossils of the Chalk," *Field Guides to Fossils*, no. 2, 2nd edition (London: The Palaeontological Association, 2002).

graveyard. More than seven trillion tons of vegetation is buried in the world's coal beds found across every continent, including Antarctica.

Such was the speed at which many creatures were buried and fossilized — under catastrophic flood conditions — that they were exquisitely preserved. There was no destruction of many fish, which were buried so rapidly, virtually alive, that even fine details of fins and eye sockets have been preserved. Many trilobites have been so exquisitely preserved that even the compound lens systems in their eyes are still available for detailed study.

Mawsonites spriggi, when discovered, was identified as a fossilized jellyfish (figure 2). It was found in a sandstone bed that covers more than 400 square miles (1,040 km^2) of outback South Australia.[12] Millions of such soft-bodied marine creatures are exquisitely preserved in this sandstone bed. Consider what happens to soft-bodied creatures like jellyfish when washed up on a beach today. Because they consist only of soft "jelly," they melt in the sun and are also destroyed by waves crashing onto the beach. Based on this reality, the discoverer of these exquisitely preserved soft-bodied marine creatures concluded that all of them had to be buried in less than a day!

Some sea creatures were buried alive and fossilized so quickly that they were "caught in the act" of eating their last meal, or at the moment of giving birth to a baby! One minute a huge ichthyosaur had just given birth to her baby, then seconds later, without time to escape, mother and baby were buried and "snap frozen" in a catastrophic "avalanche" of lime mud.

Figure 2. Soft-bodied marine creatures, such as this fossilized jellyfish (*Mawsonites spriggi*), are finely preserved in a sandstone bed.

These are but a few examples of the many hundreds of fossil graveyards found all over the globe that are now well-documented in the geological literature.[13] The countless billions of fossils in these graveyards, in many cases exquisitely preserved, testify to the rapid burial of plants and animals on a global scale in a watery cataclysm and its immediate aftermath.

12. R.C. Sprigg, "Early Cambrian (?) Jellyfishes from the Flinders Ranges, South Australia," *Transactions of the Royal Society of South Australia* 71 no. 2 (1947): 212–224; M.F. Glaessner and M. Wade, "The Late Precambrian Fossils from Ediacara, South Australia," *Palaeontology* 9 (1966): 599–628.
13. For example: D.J. Bottjer et al., eds., *Exceptional Fossil Preservation: A Unique View on the Evolution of Marine Life* (New York, NY: Columbia University Press, 2002).

Evidence #3: Rapidly Deposited Sediment Layers Spread Across Vast Areas

On every continent are found layers of sedimentary rocks over vast areas. Many of these can be traced all the way across continents, and even between continents. Furthermore, geologists find evidence that the sediments were deposited rapidly.

Consider the sedimentary rock layers exposed in the walls of the Grand Canyon. This sequence of layers is not unique to that region of the United States. For more than 50 years geologists have recognized that these strata belong to six megasequences (very thick, distinctive sequences of sedimentary rock layers) that can be traced right across North America.[14]

The lowest of the Grand Canyon's sedimentary layers is the Tapeats Sandstone, belonging to the Sauk Megasequence. It and its equivalents cover much of the United States. We can hardly imagine what forces were necessary to deposit such a vast, continent-wide series of deposits. Yet at the base of this sequence are huge boulders and sand beds deposited by storms. Both are evidence that massive forces deposited these layers rapidly and violently right across the entire United States. Slow-and-gradual (present-day uniformitarian) processes cannot account for this evidence, but the Genesis Flood surely can!

The Grand Canyon's Redwall Limestone belongs to the Kaskaskia Megasequence. The *same* limestones appear in many places across North America, as far as Tennessee and Pennsylvania. These limestones also appear in the exact same position in the strata sequences, and they have the exact same fossils and other features in them. What is even more remarkable is that the same Carboniferous limestone beds also appear in England, again containing the same fossils and other features.

The Cretaceous chalk beds of southern England are well known because they appear as spectacular white cliffs along the coast. The same chalk beds can be traced westward across England and appear again in Northern Ireland. In the opposite direction, these same chalk beds can be traced across France, the Netherlands, Germany, Poland, southern Scandinavia, and other parts of Europe to Turkey, then to Israel and Egypt in the Middle East, and even as far as Kazakhstan.[15]

Remarkably, the same chalk beds with the same fossils in them, and with the same distinctive strata above and below them, are also found in the Midwest United States, from Nebraska in the north to Texas in the south, and in the Perth Basin of Western Australia.

---

14. L.L. Sloss, "Sequences in the Cratonic Interior of North America," *Geological Society of America Bulletin* 74 (1963): 93–114.
15. D.V. Ager, *The Nature of the Stratigraphical Record* (London: Macmillan, 1973), p. 1–2.

Consider another feature — coal beds. In the northern hemisphere, the Upper Carboniferous (Pennsylvanian) coal beds of the eastern and Midwest United States are the same coal beds, with the same plant fossils, in Britain and Europe, stretching halfway around the globe, from Texas to the Donetz Basin north of the Caspian Sea in the former USSR.[16] In the southern hemisphere, the same Permian coal beds are found in Australia, Antarctica, India, South Africa, and even South America! These beds share the same kind of plant fossils across the region (but they are different from those in the Pennsylvanian coal beds).

The buff-colored Coconino Sandstone is very distinctive in the walls of the Grand Canyon. It has an average thickness of 315 feet and covers an area of at least 200,000 square miles eastward across adjoining states.[17] So the volume of sand in the Coconino Sandstone layer is at least 10,000 cubic miles!

This layer also contains physical features called cross beds. While the overall layer of sandstone is horizontal, these features are clearly visible as sloped beds. These cross beds are remnants of the sand waves produced by the water currents that deposited the sand (like sand dunes, but underwater). So it can be demonstrated that water, flowing at 3–5 miles per hour, deposited the Coconino Sandstone as massive sheets of sand, with sand waves up to 60 feet high.[18] At this rate, the whole Coconino Sandstone layer (all 10,000 cubic miles of sand) would have been deposited in just a few days!

Sediment layers that spread across vast continents are evidence that water covered the continents in the past. Even more dramatic are the fossil-bearing sediment layers that were deposited rapidly right across many or most of the continents at the same time. To catastrophically deposit such extensive sediment layers implies global flooding of the continents. And these are only a few examples.[19]

Evidence #4: Sediment Transported Long Distances

When the Flood waters swept over the continents and rapidly deposited sediment layers across vast areas, these sediments had to have been transported from distant sources.

16. Ibid., p. 6–7.
17. D.L. Baars, "Permian System of Colorado Plateau," *American Association of Petroleum Geologists Bulletin* 46 (1962): 200–201; J.M. Hills and F.E. Kottlowski, *Correlation of Stratigraphic Units of North America-Southwest/Southwest Mid-Continent Region* (Tulsa, OK: American Association of Petroleum Geologists, 1983); R.C. Blakey and R. Knepp, "Pennsylvanian and Permian Geology of Arizona," in J.P. Jenney and S.J. Reynolds, eds., "Geologic Evolution of Arizona," *Arizona Geological Society Digest* 17 (1989): 313–347.
18. A.A. Snelling and S.A. Austin, "Startling Evidence of Noah's Flood," *Creation Ex Nihilo* 15 no. 1 (1992): 46–50; S.A. Austin, ed., *Grand Canyon: Monument to Catastrophe* (Santee, CA: Institute for Creation Research, 1994), p. 28–36.
19. Ager, *The Nature of the Stratigraphical Record*, p. 1–13.

For example, as was mentioned above, the Coconino Sandstone, seen spectacularly in the walls of the Grand Canyon, has an average thickness of 315 feet, covers an area of at least 200,000 square miles, and thus contains at least 10,000 cubic miles of sand.[20] Where did this sand come from and how do we know?

The sand grains are pure quartz (a natural glass mineral), which is why the Coconino Sandstone is such a distinctive buff color. Directly underneath it is the strikingly different red-brown Hermit Formation, consisting of siltstone and shale. Sand for the Coconino Sandstone could not have come from the underlying Hermit Formation.

The sloping remnants of sand "waves" in the Coconino Sandstone point to the south, indicating the water that deposited the sand flowed from the north.[21] Another clue is that the Coconino Sandstone thins to zero to the north in Utah, but the Hermit Formation spreads further into Utah and beyond. So the Coconino's pure quartz sand had to come from a source even further north, above the red-brown Hermit.

The Grand Canyon has another layer with sands that must have come from far away — the sandstone beds within the Supai Group strata between the Hermit Formation and the Redwall Limestone. In this case, the sand "wave" remnants point to the southeast, so the sand grains had to be deposited by water flowing from a source in the north and *west*. However, to the north and west of the Grand Canyon we find only Redwall Limestone underneath the Supai Group, so there is no nearby source of quartz sand for these sandstone beds.[22] Thus, an incredibly long distance must be postulated for the source of Supai Group sand grains, probably from a source as far away as northern Utah or even Wyoming.[23]

Higher in the strata sequence is the Navajo Sandstone of southern Utah, best seen in the spectacular mesas and cliffs in and around Zion National Park. The Navajo Sandstone is well above the Kaibab Limestone, which forms the rim rock of Grand Canyon. Like Grand Canyon sandstone, this sandstone also consists of very pure quartz sand, giving it a distinctive brilliant white color, and it also contains remnants of sand "waves."

20. D.L. Baars, "Permian System of Colorado Plateau," *American Association of Petroleum Geologists Bulletin* 46 (1962): 200–201; J.M. Hills and F.E. Kottlowski, *Correlation of Stratigraphic Units of North America-Southwest/Southwest Mid-Continent Region* (Tulsa, OK: American Association of Petroleum Geologists, 1983); R.C. Blakey and R. Knepp, "Pennsylvanian and Permian Geology of Arizona," in J.P. Jenney and S.J. Reynolds, eds., "Geologic Evolution of Arizona," *Arizona Geological Society Digest* 17 (1989): 313–347.
21. Austin, *Grand Canyon: Monument to Catastrophe*, p. 36.
22. J.S. Shelton, *Geology Illustrated* (San Francisco, CA: WH Freeman, 1966), p. 280.
23. R.C. Blakey, "Stratigraphy of the Supai Group (Pennsylvanian-Permian), Mogollon Rim, Arizona," in S.S. Beus and R.R. Rawson, eds., *Carboniferous Stratigraphy in the Grand Canyon Country, Northern Arizona and Southern Nevada* (Falls Church, VA: American Geological Institute, 1979), p. 102.

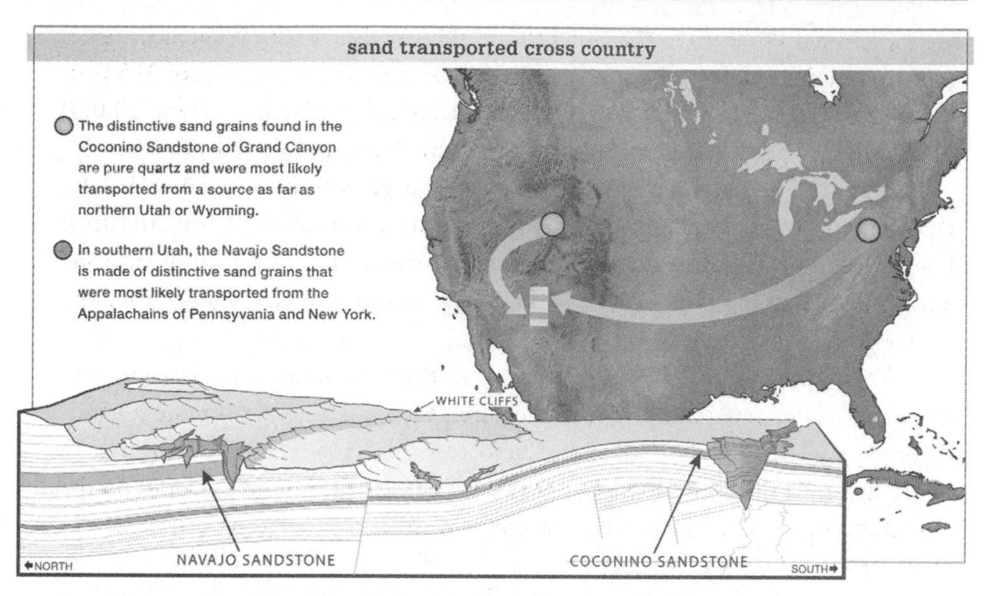

Figure 3: The deposition of these layers defies any uniformitarian explanation.

However, we have to look even farther for the original rocks that eroded to form the sand in this sandstone layer. Fortunately, within this sandstone we find grains of the mineral zircon, which is relatively easy to trace to its source because zircon usually contains radioactive uranium. By "dating" these zircon grains, using the uranium-lead (U-Pb) radioactive method, it has been postulated that the sand grains in the Navajo Sandstone came from the Appalachians of Pennsylvania and New York, and from former mountains farther north in Canada. If this is true, the sand grains were transported about 1,250 miles right across North America[24] (figure 3).

This "discovery" poses somewhat of a dilemma for conventional uniformitarian (slow-and-gradual) geologists, because no known sediment transport system, even today, is capable of carrying sand right across the entire North American continent during the required millions of years. It must have been water over an area even bigger than the continent. All they can do is postulate that some unknown transcontinental river system must have done the job. But even in their scientific belief system of earth history, it is impossible for such a river to have persisted for millions of years.

Yet the evidence is overwhelming that the water was flowing in one direction. More than half a million measurements have been collected from 15,615 localities recording water current direction indicators throughout the geologic

24. J.M. Rahl et al., "Combined Single-grain (U-Th)/He and U/Pb Dating of Detrital Zircons from the Navajo Sandstone, Utah," *Geology* 31 no. 9 (2003): 761–764.

record of North America. Based on these measurements, water moved sediments right across the continent, from the east and northeast to the west and southwest throughout the so-called Paleozoic.[25] This pattern continued on up into the Mesozoic, when the Navajo Sandstone was deposited, although some water currents shifted more southward. How could water be flowing right across the North American continent consistently for hundreds of millions of years? Absolutely impossible!

The only logical and viable explanation is the global cataclysmic Genesis Flood. Only the water currents of a global ocean, lasting a few months, could have transported such huge volumes of sediments right across North America to deposit the thick strata sequences which blanket the continent.[26]

Evidence #5: Rapid or No Erosion Between Strata

If the fossil-bearing layers took hundreds of millions of years to accumulate, then we would expect to find many examples of weathering and erosion after successive layers were deposited. The boundaries between many sedimentary strata should be broken by lots of topographic relief with weathered surfaces. After all, shouldn't periods of weathering and erosion for millions of years follow each deposition?

On the other hand, in the cataclysmic global Flood most of the fossil-bearing layers would have accumulated in just over one year. Under such catastrophic conditions, even if land surfaces were briefly exposed to erosion, such erosion (called sheet erosion) would have been rapid and widespread, leaving behind flat and smooth surfaces. The erosion would not create the localized topographic relief (hills and valleys) we see forming at today's snail's pace. So if the Genesis Flood caused the fossil-bearing geologic record, then we would only expect evidence of rapid or no erosion at the boundaries between sedimentary strata.

At the boundaries between some sedimentary layers we find evidence of only rapid erosion. In most other cases, the boundaries are flat, featureless, and knife-edge, with absolutely no evidence of any erosion, as would be expected during the Genesis Flood.

The Grand Canyon offers numerous examples of strata boundaries that are consistent with deposition during the Genesis Flood.[27] However, we will focus

25. S.R. Dickinson and G.E. Gehrels, "U-Pb Ages of Detrital Zircons from Permian and Jurassic Eolian Sandstones of the Colorado Plateau, USA: Paleogeographic Implications," *Sedimentary Geology* 163 (2003): 29–66.
26. A.V. Chadwick, "Megatrends in North American Paleocurrents," www.origins.swau.edu/papers/global/paleocurrents/default.html.
27. Austin, *Grand Canyon: Monument to Catastrophe*, p. 42–52.

here on just four, which are typical of all the others, appearing at the bases of the Tapeats Sandstone, Redwall Limestone, Hermit Formation, and Coconino Sandstone.

The strata below the Tapeats Sandstone has been rapidly eroded and then extensively scraped flat (planed off). We know that this erosion occurred on a large scale because we see its effects from one end of the Grand Canyon to the other. This massive erosion affected many different underlying rock layers —granites and metamorphic rocks — and tilted sedimentary strata.

There are two evidences that this large-scale erosion was also rapid. First, we don't see any evidence of weathering below the boundary — we don't see the expected soils.[28] Second, we find boulders and features known as "storm beds" in the Tapeats Sandstone above the boundary.[29] Storm beds are sheets of sand with unique internal features only produced by storms, such as hurricanes. Boulders and storm beds aren't deposited slowly.

Below the base of the Redwall Limestone the underlying Muav Limestone has been rapidly eroded in a few localized places to form channels. These channels were later filled with lime sand to form the Temple Butte Limestone. Apart from these rare exceptions, the boundary between the Muav and Redwall Limestones, as well as between the Temple Butte and Redwall Limestones, are flat and featureless, hallmarks of continuous deposition.

Indeed, in some locations the boundary between the Muav and Redwall Limestones is impossible to find because the Muav Limestone continued to be deposited after the Redwall Limestone began.[30] These two formations appear to intertongue (thin beds of each formation are interleaved with one another), so the boundary is gradational. This feature presents profound problems for uniformitarian geology. The Muav Limestone was supposedly deposited 500–520 million years ago,[31] the Temple Butte Limestone was deposited about 100 million years later (380–400 million years ago),[32] and then the Redwall Limestone was deposited several million years later (330–340 million years ago).[33] It is

28. N.E.A. Hinds, "Ep-Archean and Ep-Algonkian Intervals in Western North America," *Carnegie Institution of Washington Publication* 463, vol. 1, 1935.
29. A.V. Chadwick, "Megabreccias: Evidence for catastrophism," *Origins* 5 (1978): 39–46.
30. A.A. Snelling, "The Case of the 'Missing' Geologic Time," *Creation Ex Nihilo* 14, no. 3 (1992): 30–35.
31. L.T. Middleton and D.K. Elliott, "Tonto Group," in S.S. Beus and M. Morales, eds., *Grand Canyon Geology*, 2nd edition (New York, NY: Oxford University Press, 2003), p. 90–106.
32. S.S. Beus, "Temple Butte Formation," in S.S. Beus and M. Morales, eds., *Grand Canyon Geology*, 2nd edition (New York, NY: Oxford University Press, 2003), p. 107–114.
33. S.S. Beus, "Redwall Limestone and Surprise Canyon Formation," in S.S. Beus and M. Morales, eds., *Grand Canyon Geology*, 2nd edition (New York, NY: Oxford University Press, 2003), p. 115–135.

Figure 4. The flat, featureless boundary between these two layers indicates that the top layer (Coconino Sandstone) was laid down right after the bottom layer (Hermit Formation), before any erosion could occur.

much more logical to believe that these limestones were deposited continuously, without any intervening millions of years.

The boundary between the Hermit Formation and the Esplanade Sandstone is often cited as evidence of erosion that occurred over millions of years after sediments had stopped building up.[34] However, the evidence indicates that water was still depositing material, even as erosion occurred. In places, the Hermit Formation's silty shales are intermingled (intertongued) with the Esplanade Sandstone, indicating that a continuous flow of water carried both silty mud and quartz sand into place. Thus, there were no millions of years between these layers.[35]

Finally, the boundary between the Coconino Sandstone and the Hermit Formation is flat, featureless, and knife-edge from one end of the Grand Canyon to the other (figure 4). There is absolutely no evidence of any erosion on the Hermit Formation before the Coconino Sandstone was deposited. That alone is amazing.

The fossil-bearing portion of the geologic record consists of tens of thousands of feet of sedimentary layers, of which about 4,500 feet are exposed in the walls of the Grand Canyon. If this enormous thickness of sediments were deposited over 500 or more million years, then some boundaries between layers

34. L.F. Noble, "A Section of Paleozoic Formations of the Grand Canyon at the Bass Trail," *U.S. Geological Survey Professional Paper* 131-B, 1923, p. 63–64.
35. E.D. McKee, "The Supai Group of Grand Canyon," *U.S. Geological Survey Professional Paper* 1173, 1982, p. 169–202; R.C. Blakey, "Stratigraphy and Geologic History of Pennsylvanian and Permian rocks, Mogollon Rim Region, Central Arizona and Vicinity," *Geological Society of America Bulletin* 102 (1990): 1189–1217; R.C. Blakey, "Supai Group and Hermit Formation," in S.S. Beus and M. Morales, eds., *Grand Canyon Geology*, 2nd edition (New York, NY: Oxford University Press, 2003), p. 136–162.

should show evidence of millions of years of slow erosion, just as erosion is occurring on some land surfaces today. On the other hand, if this enormous thickness of sediments were all deposited in just over a year during the global cataclysmic Genesis Flood, then the boundaries between the layers should show evidence of continuous rapid deposition, with only occasional evidence of rapid erosion, or of no erosion at all. And that's exactly what we find, as illustrated by strata boundaries in the Grand Canyon.

Evidence #6: Many Strata Laid Down in Rapid Succession

The sedimentary units in the Grand Canyon are thought, by uniformitarian geologists, to have been deposited and deformed over the past 500 million years. If it really did take millions of years for these sedimentary sequences to be deposited, then individual sediment layers would not have been deposited rapidly, nor would the sequences have been laid down continuously. In contrast, if the Genesis Flood deposited all these strata in a little more than a year, then the individual layers would have been deposited in rapid succession.

Do we see evidence in the walls of the Grand Canyon that the sedimentary layers were all laid down in quick succession? Yes, absolutely! The entire sequence of sedimentary strata was still soft during subsequent folding and experienced only limited fracturing. These rock layers would have broken and shattered unless all the strata were immediately folded while the sediment was still relatively soft and pliable (figure 5).

When solid, hard rock is bent (or folded) it invariably fractures and breaks because it is brittle.[36] Rock will bend only if it is still soft and pliable — "plastic" like modeling clay or children's play-dough. If such modeling clay is allowed to dry and/or is baked in an oven, it is no longer pliable but hard and brittle, so any attempt to bend it will cause it to break and shatter.

When sediments are deposited by water in a layer, some water is trapped between the sediment grains. Clay particles may also be among the sediment grains. The pressure of other sediment layers on top of each layer squeezes the particles closer together and forces out much of the water. The internal heat of the earth may also cause additional dehydration of the sediments. Removal of the water dries the sediment layer and converts the chemicals that were in the water and between the clay particles into a natural cement. This cement transforms the originally soft and wet sediment layer into a hard, brittle rock layer.

36. E.S. Hills, "Physics of Deformation," *Elements of Structural Geology* (London: Methuen & Co., 1970), p. 77–103; G.H. Davis and S.J. Reynolds, "Kinematic Analysis," *Structural Geology of Rocks and Regions*, 2nd edition (New York, NY: John Wiley & Sons, 1996), p. 38–97.

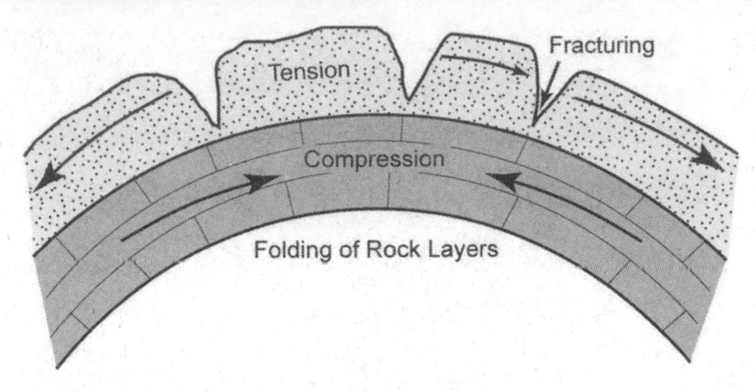

Figure 5. When solid, hard rock is bent (or folded) it invariably fractures and breaks because it is brittle. Rock will bend only if it is still soft and pliable, like modeling clay. If clay is allowed to dry out, it is no longer pliable but hard and brittle, so any attempt to bend it will cause it to break and shatter.

This process, known technically as diagenesis, can be exceedingly rapid.[37] It is known to occur within hours but generally takes days or months, depending on the prevailing conditions. It doesn't take millions of years, even under today's slow-and-gradual geologic conditions.

The 4,500-foot sequence of sedimentary layers in the walls of the Grand Canyon stands well above today's sea level. Earth movements in the past pushed up this sedimentary sequence to form the Kaibab Plateau. However, the eastern portion of the sequence (in the eastern Grand Canyon and Marble Canyon) was not pushed up as much and is about 2,500 feet lower than the height of the Kaibab Plateau. The boundary between the Kaibab Plateau and the less uplifted eastern canyons is marked by a large, step-like fold, producing what is called the East Kaibab Monocline.

It's possible to see these folded sedimentary layers in several side canyons. For example, the folded Tapeats Sandstone can be seen in Carbon Canyon (figure 6). Notice that these sandstone layers were bent 90° (a right angle), yet the rock was not fractured or broken in the fold axis or hinge line (apex) of the fold. Similarly, the folded Muav and Redwall Limestone layers can be seen along nearby Kwagunt Creek. The folding of these limestones did not cause them to fracture and break either, as would be expected for ancient, brittle rocks. The obvious conclusion is that these sandstone and limestone layers were all folded and bent while the sediments were still soft and pliable, and very soon after they were deposited.

Herein lies an insurmountable dilemma for uniformitarian (long-age) geologists. They maintain that the Tapeats Sandstone and Muav Limestone were

37. Z.L. Sujkowski, "Diagenesis," *Bulletin of the American Association of Petroleum Geologists* 42 (1958): 2694–2697; H. Blatt, *Sedimentary Petrology*, 2nd edition (New York, NY: W.H. Freeman and Company, 1992).

Figure 6. It is possible to see these folded sedimentary layers in several side canyons. All these layers had to be soft and pliable at the same time in order for these layers to be folded without fracturing. Here the folded Tapeats Sandstone can be seen in Carbon Canyon.

deposited 500–520 million years ago;[38] the Redwall Limestone, 330–340 million years ago;[39] then the Kaibab Limestone at the top of the sequence, supposedly 260 million years ago.[40] However, the Tapeats Sandstone was supposedly deposited some 440 million years before the Kaibab Plateau was uplifted, which caused the folding (supposedly only about 60 million years ago).[41] How could the Tapeats Sandstone and Muav Limestone still be soft and pliable, as though they had just been deposited, and not subjected yet to diagenesis, without fracturing and shattering when they were folded 440 million years after their deposition?

The conventional explanation is that under the pressure and heat of burial, the hardened sandstone and limestone layers were bent so slowly they behaved as though they were plastic and thus did not break.[42] However, pressure and

38. L.T. Middleton and D.K. Elliott, "Tonto Group," in S.S. Beus and M. Morales, eds., *Grand Canyon Geology*, 2nd edition (New York, NY: Oxford University Press, 2003), p. 90–106.
39. S.S. Beus, "Redwall Limestone and Surprise Canyon Formation," in S.S. Beus and M. Morales, eds., *Grand Canyon Geology*, 2nd edition (New York, NY: Oxford University Press, 2003), p. 115–135.
40. R.L. Hopkins and K.L. Thompson, "Kaibab Formation," in S.S. Beus and M. Morales, eds., *Grand Canyon Geology*, 2nd edition (New York, NY: Oxford University Press, 2003), p. 196–211.
41. P.W. Huntoon, "Post-Precambrian Tectonism in the Grand Canyon Region," in S.S. Beus and M. Morales, eds., *Grand Canyon Geology*, 2nd edition (New York, NY: Oxford University Press, 2003), p. 222–259.
42. E.S. Hills, "Environment, Time and Material," *Elements of Structural Geology* (London: Methuen & Co., 1970), p. 104–139; G.H. Davis and S.J. Reynolds, "Dynamic Analysis," *Structural Geology of Rocks and Regions*, 2nd edition (New York, NY: John Wiley & Sons, 1996), p. 98–149.

heat would have caused detectable changes in the minerals of these rocks, telltale signs of metamorphism.[43] But such metamorphic minerals or re-crystallization due to such plastic behavior[44] is not observed in these rocks. The sandstone and limestone in the folds are identical to sedimentary layers elsewhere.

The only logical conclusion is that the 440-million year delay between deposition and folding never happened! Instead, the Tapeats-Kaibab strata sequence was laid down in rapid succession early during the year of the Genesis Flood, followed by uplift of the Kaibab Plateau within the last months of the Flood. This alone explains the folding of the whole strata sequence without appreciable fracturing.

Conclusion

In this chapter we have documented that, when we accept God's eyewitness account of the Flood in Genesis 7–8 as an actual event in earth history, then we find that the geologic evidence is absolutely in harmony with the Word of God. As the ocean waters flooded over the continents, they must have buried plants and animals in rapid succession. These rapidly deposited sediment layers were spread across vast areas, preserving fossils of sea creatures in layers that are high above the current (receded) sea level. The sand and other sediments in these layers were transported long distances from their original sources. We know that many of these sedimentary strata were laid down in rapid succession because we don't find evidence of slow erosion between the strata.

Jesus Christ our Creator (John 1:1–3; Colossians 1:16–17), who is the Truth and would never tell us a lie, said that during the "days of Noah" (Matthew 24:37; Luke 17:26–27) "Noah entered the ark" and "the Flood came and took them all away" (Matthew 24:38–39). He spoke of these events as real, literal history, describing a global Flood that destroyed all land life not on the ark. Therefore, we must believe what He told us, rather than believe the ideas of fallible scientists who weren't there to see what happened in the earth's past. Thus, we shouldn't be surprised when the geologic evidence in God's world (rightly understood by asking the right questions) agrees exactly with God's Word, affirmed by Jesus Christ.

43. R.H. Vernon, *Metamorphic Processes: Reactions and Microstructure Development* (London: George Allen & Unwin, 1976); K. Bucher and M. Frey, *Petrogenesis of Metamorphic Rocks*, 7th edition (Berlin: Springer-Verlag, 2002).
44. Vernon, *Metamorphic Processes: Reactions and Microstructure Development*; G.H. Davis and S.J. Reynolds, "Deformation Mechanisms and Microstructures," *Structural Geology of Rocks and Regions*, 2nd edition (New York, NY: John Wiley & Sons, 1996), p. 150–202.

30

What Are Some Good Questions to Ask an Evolutionist?

MIKE RIDDLE AND DR. JASON LISLE

A football coach recruited the best defensive players he could find. His strategy was to have the best defense in the conference. All through the season the opposing teams were unable to score many points. When the season was over his team posted a record of zero wins, ten losses, and two ties. How could this happen? The answer is they had no offense.

A Christian Game Plan

This is where many Christians are in their efforts to witness to unbelievers. The Bible instructs believers to have answers when challenged by any and all who oppose the Word of God (defense — 1 Peter 3:15). The Bible also instructs believers to bring down all strongholds and anything that exalts itself against the knowledge of God (offense — 2 Corinthians 10:4–5). Sadly, while many Christians lack the knowledge to challenge unbelievers (offense), they also lack a defense.

What is meant by defense and offense in Christian witnessing? Defense means that the Christian can answer questions such as: How do you fit dinosaurs into the Bible? Where did Cain get his wife? How could Adam name all the animals in one day? What about carbon-14 dating? Does God really exist? Couldn't God have used evolution?

Offense means the Christian can ask the unbeliever questions that challenge his or her worldview. The strategy of asking good questions can be used to demonstrate to unbelievers that their belief in evolution is a sort of "blind" faith and is not something derived from empirical science. They can also illustrate to the compromised Christian (a person who professes to believe in both the Bible and ideas such as evolution or millions of years) that God's Word is a completely accurate record and is not to be modified by secular opinions of what is possible.

There are several different types of questions that are useful in apologetics; we will cover four general categories of questions in this chapter. Questions can be used to help us assess and clarify the worldview of the critic. What does he really believe, and how is he using the terms? We will call these "clarification questions." We can ask "foundation questions" about the most basic laws of science, and the beginning of first things. There are "textbook questions" — questions that can expose inconsistency in common textbook claims. These are particularly useful in public school settings. And finally, there are worldview questions — questions that can be used to show that the evolutionary worldview is utterly, intellectually defective.

Clarification Questions

These questions are used to help explain the meaning of words or terms. A definition in science needs to be clear and precise. It should include all the attributes that distinguish it from all other entities. If any of these attributes are missing, then the definition becomes ambiguous.

- What do you mean by *evolution*?
- What do you mean by *theory*?
- What is meant by a *fact* in science?

Let's examine some examples of the importance of establishing definitions.

"Evolution is change over time." This is not a legitimate definition because it includes everything in the universe.

"Evolution is genetic change in a species over time." While this may be one definition of "evolution," it is not the claim at issue in the origins debate. Such a definition includes all forms of change, including changes that both creationists and evolutionists believe in (e.g., information-decreasing mutations). Therefore, this does not adequately define the type of evolution relevant to origins; that is, Neo-Darwinian evolution that suggests that an amoeba can change into a man over millions of years.

"Evolution means both micro and macro changes." This is a common use of evolution in textbooks. Dog varieties or different beak sizes of finches thus become examples of evolution. This definition includes both variety within the kinds and Neo-Darwinian evolution (molecules to man). The definition tacitly implies that small observed changes, sometimes referred to as microevolution, will lead to large unobserved changes (macroevolution), which begs the question at issue.

From these examples we see that it is important to establish definitions of terms prior to any discussion.

Foundation Questions

These questions aim at the core, or foundation, of the unbeliever's evidence.

- What is the ultimate cause of the universe?
- How did life originate?
- Where did the dinosaurs come from?
- Where are all the millions of transitional fossils in the Precambrian and Cambrian layers?
- Since information is nonmaterial and in all observed cases always requires an intelligent sender, how did all the information contained in DNA originate?
- How do we know that is true?
- Has that ever been observed?
- Are there any assumptions in what you are describing?

In this chapter we will analyze the cause of the universe question. Analysis of the other questions can be found in the *New Answers Books 1 & 2*.

Question: What caused the universe to come into existence and where did the original energy or matter come from?

This is an important question because it aims at the very foundation or beginning of the entire evolution worldview. Without a cause (and a mass/energy source) there can be no big bang, evolution of stars, or life. Some evolutionists may scoff at such a question by stating it is not a legitimate question. Others might state that science does not deal with such questions or we can't know such things. In either case this is a "brush-off" to avoid the question. There are only three possible responses to this question:

1. The universe created itself.
2. The universe has always existed.
3. The universe had to be created.

Response 1: The universe created itself.

For something to create itself it would have to both exist (in order to have the power to act) and not exist (in order to be created) at the same time. This is a contradiction — an illogical position to take. Based on all known scientific understanding and logic we know that *from nothing, nothing comes*. Therefore, this is not a legitimate response. A person arguing this way has violated the law of non-contradiction and is ignoring good science. This now leaves two possible choices.

Response 2: The universe has always existed (no beginning).

In order to analyze this response we need to understand some basics about the second law of thermodynamics. The second law is concerned with heat — the flow of thermal energy. Everything in the universe is losing its available energy to do work. To illustrate this concept we will use the example called "No Refills."

You have just been given a new car for FREE! All expenses for the lifetime of the car are paid. Sounds like a good deal. However, there is one catch. You are only allowed to have one tank of gas and never allowed to refill the tank. Once you have driven the car and used up all the gas, the car can no longer be used for transportation. In other words, the gas (energy source) has been used up and cannot be reused to propel the car. This is what the second law of thermodynamics deals with. Usable energy is constantly becoming less usable for doing work. Unless the car obtains new fuel from an outside source, it will cease to function after it exhausts its first tank of gas.

Likewise, the universe is constantly converting useful energy into less usable forms. As one example, stars are fueled by hydrogen gas that is used up as it is converted into heavier elements. But the problem is this: for any given region of space, there is only a finite amount of available energy. There is just only so much hydrogen available per cubic meter. This means that unless the universe obtains new useable energy from an outside source, it will cease to function in a finite amount of time. Stars will no longer be possible, once the hydrogen is gone.[1]

However, there is no "outside source" available. The universe is everything, according to the secular worldview. Like the car, the universe would cease to function after its first "tank of gas" is exhausted. But if the universe were infinitely old, it should have used up that energy a long time ago. Putting it another

1. Some stars are thought to be powered by fusion of heavier elements, eventually resulting in iron. But eventually, these heavier elements would be used up as well. Nuclear reactions of elements heavier than iron are endothermic, and cannot power a star.

way, if stars have eternally been processing hydrogen into heavier elements, then there would be no hydrogen left! But there is. The fact that the universe *still* contains useable energy indicates that it is not infinitely old — it had a beginning.

Response 3: The universe had to be created.

Since the universe could not create itself and it had to have a beginning, the only logical solution is that the universe had to be created! This leaves us with the original question to the evolutionist, "Where did the matter come from to create the universe?" Any reply not recognizing that the universe was created ignores the laws of science and good logic.

When asking this question, be prepared to answer the challenge, "Where did God come from?" This question indicates a misunderstanding of the nature of God. It suggests that God is within (or "bound by") the universe and that God is part of the chain of effects within time — all of which require a cause. We should be prepared to correct the misunderstanding, and point out that God does not require a cause since He has always existed, is beyond time, and is not part of the physical universe. God is a spirit, not a sequence of energetic reactions, and so the laws of thermodynamics (which place a finite limit on the age of the universe) do not apply to Him.

> Remember the former things of old, For I am God, and there is no other; I am God, and there is none like Me (Isaiah 46:9).

Textbook Questions for the Classroom

These questions are used to help students in the classroom critically think through information in a textbook or further explore statements made by a teacher.

- While some molecules do combine to form larger structures such as amino acids, it has been shown that this always results in a mixture of left- and right-handed amino acids that is not used in life. Since this is true, is there some other explanation for how the molecules useful for life might have formed? (Be prepared for an answer involving "given enough time it could happen.")[2]
- Since oxygen is known to destroy molecular bonds, and since the lack of oxygen in the atmosphere (meaning no ozone) would cause all potential life to be destroyed by ultraviolet rays, how could life have formed? (Be prepared to follow up with a question about hydrolysis — water decomposing molecules.)

2. For responses involving "given enough time it could happen," see chapter 16, "Does Evolution Have a . . . Chance?"

- Since water breaks down the bonds between amino acids (a process called hydrolysis), how could life have started in the oceans?
- The National Academy of Sciences defines a theory as "a comprehensive explanation of some aspect of nature that is supported by a vast body of evidence" and science as "the use of evidence to construct testable explanations and predictions of natural phenomena."[3] Does this mean scientists can reproduce how life originated or test any step of the process for how life evolved? If not, then how can evolution qualify as a theory?
- Microsoft uses intelligent programmers and complex codes to create the Windows operating system. However, information in DNA is millions of times more dense and complex. How could the process of evolution, using natural processes and chance, solve the problem of complex information sequencing without intelligence? (Be prepared for an answer involving "given enough time it could happen.")
- Bill Gates (founder and former CEO of Microsoft) recognized that the processing capabilities of DNA are "like a computer program but far, far more advanced than any software ever created."[4] Using all their intelligence and all the modern advances in science, have scientists ever created DNA or RNA in a laboratory through unguided naturalistic processes? If not, then isn't the origin of life still an unverified assumption?
- DNA, RNA, and proteins all need each other as an integrated unit. Even if only one of them existed, the many parts needed for life could not sit idle and wait for the other parts to evolve because they would dissolve or deteriorate. Is there any compelling (observable) evidence for how all these components evolved at the same time or separately over time?
- Isn't it true that whenever we see interdependent complex structures or codes we automatically assume an intelligent person had to put them together? So why do we assume that DNA, or RNA, or a cell, which is more complex than any computer ever designed, happened by chance? Doesn't that seem to go against good science and logical thought?

3. National Academy of Sciences: Institute of Medicine, *Science, Evolution, and Creationism* (Washington, DC: The National Academies Press, 2008), p. 10–11.
4. Bill Gates, *The Road Ahead* (London: Penguin Books, 1996), p. 228.

- Is there any observed case where random chance events created complex molecules with enormous amounts of information like that found in DNA or RNA? If not, then why should we assume it happened in the past?
- A living cell is composed of millions of parts all working together and is considered more complex than any man-made machine. Then, since the process of evolution has no blueprints (cannot plan for the future) for building something, since over time things tend to deteriorate unless there is a mechanism in place to sustain them, since virtually all known mutations decrease genetic information (or are neutral), since natural selection would not be operating until the first cell formed, how could the process of evolution ever assemble something as complex as a living cell with all its information content?
- Since we started with finches and the finches stayed finches, isn't this just an example of variety within a kind?
- Since we started with bacteria, and the bacteria that became resistant to the antibiotic remained bacteria, isn't this just another example of variety within a kind?
- What naturalistic evidence could actually disprove that evolution is the explanation for life on earth (or the formation of the universe)?

It is important to remember that whenever asking questions of a teacher or instructor, asking the questions at an appropriate time and in a respectful manner is extremely important. More questions related to specific topics can also be found in the books *Evolution Exposed: Biology*[5] and *Earth Science*[6] by Roger Patterson.

Worldview Questions

These are the questions that can stop people in their tracks. A series of well-stated worldview questions can expose the inconsistency of non-biblical worldviews. It is the Christian worldview alone that makes science, knowledge, and ethics possible. We can help unbelievers see this by asking the right questions.

5. Roger Patterson, *Evolution Exposed: Biology* (Petersburg, KY: Answers in Genesis, 2009).
6. Roger Patterson, *Evolution Exposed: Earth Science* (Petersburg, KY: Answers in Genesis, 2008).

- How do you account for the existence and nature of laws? In particular, how do you account for (1) laws of morality, (2) laws of nature, and (3) laws of logic? (Laws of morality make sense in the Christian worldview where God created human beings in His own image [according to a natural reading of Genesis] and therefore has the right to set the rules for our behavior.)
- If we are simply chemical accidents, as evolutionists contend, why should we feel compelled to behave in a particular fashion?
- If laws of morality are just what bring the most happiness to the most people, then why would it be wrong to kill just one innocent person if it happened to make everyone else a lot happier?
- If laws of morality are just the adopted social custom, then why was what Hitler did wrong? (Laws of nature make sense in the Christian worldview; God upholds the entire universe by His power. God is beyond time, and has promised to uphold the future as He has the past [Genesis 8:22].)
- In your worldview, why do the different objects in the universe obey the same laws of nature?
- Do you have confidence that laws of nature will apply in the future as they have in the past? If not, then why did you bother to answer my question? You assumed your vocal cords and my ears would work in the future as they have in the past, otherwise I could not understand your answer.
- Since you have not experienced the future, how do you know that the laws of nature will behave in the future as they have in the past? The answer "it's always been that way before" is not legitimate because it assumes that the future will be like the past, which is the very question I'm asking.
- In the Christian worldview, it makes sense to have universal, immaterial, unchanging laws of logic. These are God's standard for correct reasoning. How do you account for the existence and properties of laws of logic?
- Do you believe laws of logic are universal (applying everywhere)? If so, why (since you do not have universal knowledge)?

- Why do we all believe laws of logic will be the same tomorrow as they are today, since we are not beyond time and have not experienced the future?
- How can you have immaterial laws if the universe is material only?
- Why does the material universe feel compelled to obey immaterial laws?
- How does the material brain have access to these immaterial laws?

If you ask these questions properly, and are prepared for the common unsound responses, you can dismantle the evolutionary worldview. There is simply no good rebuttal to the Christian position, though many will make attempts. See *The Ultimate Proof of Creation*[7] by Dr. Jason Lisle for more information on worldview apologetics, and for examples of using these kinds of questions in actual dialogues.

Conclusion

The importance of asking questions is an essential part of Christian apologetics. Jesus often used the technique of asking questions. In Mark 11:29–33 Jesus refutes the chief priests, scribes, and elders by asking them a question.

> But Jesus answered and said to them, "I also will ask you one question; then answer Me, and I will tell you by what authority I do these things: The baptism of John — was it from heaven or from men? Answer Me."
>
> And they reasoned among themselves, saying, "If we say, 'From heaven,' He will say, 'Why then did you not believe him?' But if we say, 'From men' " — they feared the people, for all counted John to have been a prophet indeed. So they answered and said to Jesus, "We do not know."
>
> And Jesus answered and said to them, "Neither will I tell you by what authority I do these things."

Jesus used good questions to show the foolishness of those who attempt to argue with God. We can do the same, by learning to think biblically, and knowing just a few of the many inconsistencies of the evolutionary worldview.

7. Jason Lisle, *The Ultimate Proof of Creation* (Green Forest, AR: Master Books, 2009).

31

What about Bacteria?

DR. JOE FRANCIS

When my children were toddlers, it seemed to my wife and me that they were always sniffling or coughing, or fighting off a cold or the flu. Many a night was spent rocking a feverish child to sleep. The two of us viewed with fear such ordinary places as the church nursery, seeing it as a breeding ground for infections.

My wife and I count our blessings, however, that our long nights were the only hardship we faced. Before the development of antibiotics and vaccines, infections were a leading cause of death among children. Most families lost at least one child to scarlet fever, diphtheria, pneumonia, measles, or smallpox.

Doctors now know that these maladies are caused by bacteria or viruses (collectively known as microbes).[1] As scientists continue to learn more about microbes, they are discovering that microbes employ intricate mechanisms to attack the human body. This raises a question: If God finished creation in six days and declared it "very good," where did these disease-causing designs come from?

Finding the answer has great potential to help mankind. A better understanding of God's original purpose for microbes could help scientists see how they have changed and to find revolutionary new ways to treat infectious diseases.

Based on the creation account in Genesis, it appears that God originally made microbes to perform only beneficial functions. If so, one would expect

1. Viruses are considered to be a separate category, but for the sake of this discussion we will include them as microbes.

many present-day bacteria to continue to perform their "very good" functions. Creation biologists predicted this and have documented examples.[2]

The Matrix

Imagine a futuristic city where vehicles are run by highly efficient acid-powered motors that produce little or no pollution. On the way home, your vehicle attaches itself to an airborne mega-transport ship, studded with hundreds of other vehicles. With the combined power of the multiple motors — complete with propellers — the mega-transport travels smoothly through rough weather and treacherous conditions to your home.

After detaching from the ship, you park in your driveway, which senses your car's dimensions and molds a raised platform to fit the car's shape, locking it securely 20 feet off the ground.

Imagine that as you're sleeping an airborne probe flies over your neighborhood and attaches to your home and car, inserting new instructions to update the operating software.

Whenever any cars in the city get the least bit outdated, tiny vehicles prowling the city track them down, attack them, and dismantle the parts. Then, using the old parts, each tiny vehicle can transform itself into a shiny new car, ready and waiting for you in the morning.

Your Gut Is a Thriving City

Futuristic city? Not really. These are just some of the things that bacteria do every day in our digestive systems. In fact, the human digestive system is the most densely populated ecosystem on earth, with hundreds of species of bacteria, yeast, and viruses interacting daily in this environment.[3]

Each species of bacteria is present in such high numbers that the total population is in the trillions. In fact, if we consider all the bacteria in the human body, there are ten for every human cell. This means that, by sheer numbers alone, you are more bacteria than human!

---

2. Only about 8 percent of the identified bacteria cause disease. For past predictions by creation biologists, see A. Gillen, *The Genesis of Germs* (Green Forest, AR: Master Books, 2007); J. Francis, "The Role of Virulence Factors in the Establishment of Beneficial Ecological Relationships of Vibrio cholera and Vibrio fischeri," *Occasional Papers of the BSG* 8 (2006); Francis and Wood, "The CT Toxin of Vibrio cholera, Its Structure, Function, and Origin," *Occasional Papers of the BSG* 11 (2008); and J. Francis and T. Wood, *Stadium Integrale* 16 (2009): 88, "Cholera Toxin and the Origin of Cholera Disease."
3 Steve Gill et al., "Metagenomic Analysis of the Human Distal Gut Microbiome," *Science* 312 (2006): 1355–1359.

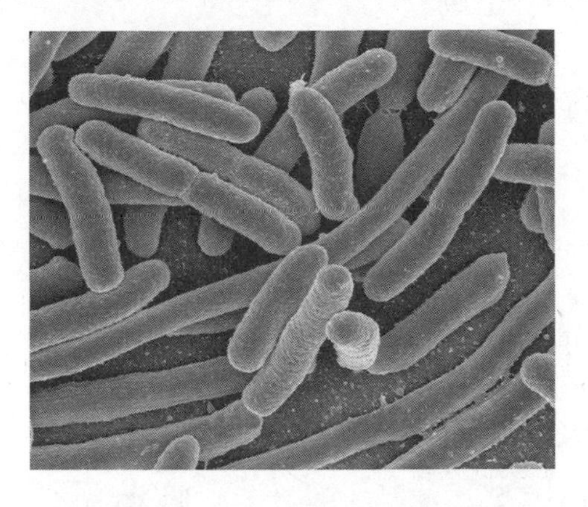

Escherichia coli (E. coli) is a bacterium commonly found in the lower intestine. Most E. coli strains are harmless and can produce vitamin K2 or prevent harmful bacteria from successfully invading the intestine. Picture copyright of Rocky Mountain Laboratories.

In the intestines, good bacteria provide nutrients, break down waste, and act as an immune system that prevents harmful bacteria from infecting our body. In fact, the human digestive system may need bacteria to be present before it can develop properly after birth.[4] Similar to the vehicles in the futuristic city above, many bacteria have elaborately designed mechanisms to move around in this dynamic, ever-changing environment. It is as though they were created to live there.

Microbes, Microbes, Everywhere

Microbes are found not only in the human body but also in every environment on earth, from high in the atmosphere to deep below the earth's surface, where they survive by eating things like oil and rocks. Microbes thrive in boiling hot springs, ice and snow, the dry heat of deserts, acids, high salt concentrations, rubber stoppers in bottles, and even hand soap.

Microbes Are Our Friends

While some microbes do cause disease, most do not. About 5,000 species of bacteria have been identified, but only about eight percent cause disease. While most species of disease-causing bacteria

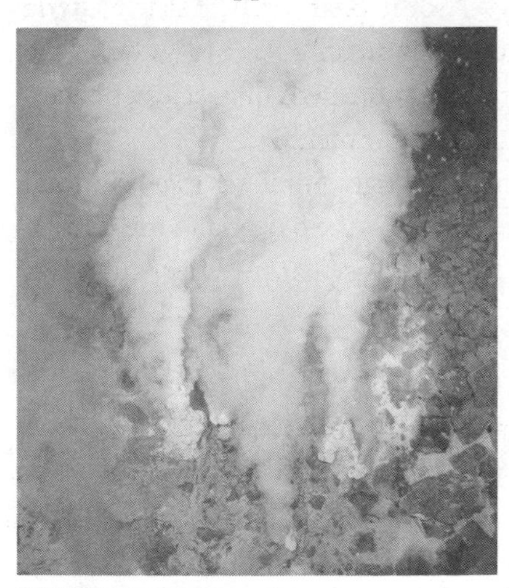

Seafloor vents — On the seafloor are vents where superheated water spews toxic chemicals into the ocean. Numerous microbes, uniquely designed to withstand the extreme heat, feed on these minerals. They are the main food source for whole communities of organisms.

4. Recent research has also shown that the heart is decreased in size in animals that develop without intestinal bacteria. Peter Turnbaugh et al., "The Human Microbiome Project," *Nature* 449 (2007): 804–810.

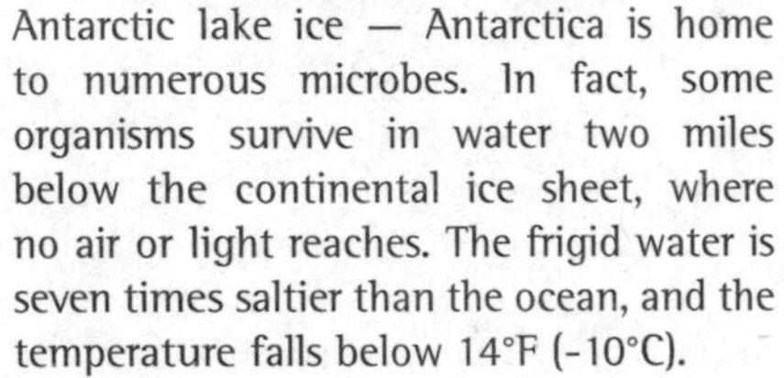

Antarctic lake ice — Antarctica is home to numerous microbes. In fact, some organisms survive in water two miles below the continental ice sheet, where no air or light reaches. The frigid water is seven times saltier than the ocean, and the temperature falls below 14°F (-10°C).

Acidic hot springs — Hot springs, such as those in Yellowstone National Park, are home to a spectrum of microbes. They can survive temperatures well above 100°F (35°C) and acids potent enough to dissolve iron.

have been carefully identified (for obvious reasons), microbiologists estimate that 10 million other species of unidentified bacteria fill the earth. So the disease-causing species may account for only a tiny fraction of all bacterial species.

If most bacteria and other microbes don't cause disease, just what are they doing? Since the Bible states that God made everything "very good" at creation, creationists would expect to see the microbes' very good function all around us, on a grand scale.

Quite remarkably we find that microbes play a vital role in distributing and recycling nutrients all over the planet.[5] For example, every living thing needs carbon, oxygen, hydrogen, and nitrogen. Many bacteria specialize in recycling these nutrients through the air, water, and land. This crucial process, called biogeochemical cycling, takes place on an unimaginably huge scale (see "The Necessary Matrix of Bacteria").

Many, many microbes must work in concert to perform this cycling. Once thought to be a sterile wasteland, the deep earth appears to be a major chemical factory, filled with a mass of bacteria that could be greater than the combined mass of all plants and animals living on the surface.

Without the millions of different microbes, the earth's vast resources would be useless to us. We need their help to get the necessary chemicals out of the earth and into our bodies. We couldn't even eat steak or salad without bacteria

5. See J.W. Francis, "The Organosubstrate of Life: A Creationist Perspective of Microbes and Viruses," *Proceedings of the Fifth International Conference on Creationism*, 2003.

THE NECESSARY MATRIX OF BACTERIA

Bacteria are almost everywhere, busily sustaining life in ways we rarely see or appreciate. God designed bacteria, in many cases, to make inaccessible atoms available to us. A matrix of bacteria works around the clock to provide many vital ingredients of life.

OXYGEN-PRODUCING ↑

Cyanobacteria in the oceans break apart the bonds of carbon dioxide, making oxygen available to living things. Perhaps the most abundant creature on earth, these microbes may release more oxygen than all green plants combined.

NITROGEN-FIXING ↑

Our atmosphere is rich in nitrogen, but the majority is unusable because the atomic bond is too strong to break. The bacteria in the genus *Rhizobium*, which live in and around plants, fix the nitrogen, making it usable to the plants. Most animals get their nitrogen indirectly from these nitrogen-fixing bacteria.

← CARBON-RECYCLING

Many different bacteria recycle carbon, an essential building block of life. One specific duty is to break down dead plant matter and sea creatures. Without these bacteria, our forests would be choked with branches and leaves, and our oceans littered with exoskeletons.

ROCK-EATING →

Many essential nutrients in the soil come from weathered rocks. A group of bacteria, known as lithotrophs, actually speed up this process by feeding on the minerals within the rocks. As these rocks break down, they enrich the soil, thus benefitting the plants that we eat.

RAIN-MAKING ↑

Some bacteria even help to make it rain! This recent discovery supports the biomatrix concept that microbes assist life cycles throughout our world.

in our stomach to help break food down. So every day, throughout the day, God displays His infinite love and wisdom, caring for every living thing even at the lowest, molecular level.

Microbes play a vital role in distributing and recycling nutrients for living things all over the planet.

Consider just one example — nitrogen recycling. Unlike the oxygen in the atmosphere, the nitrogen that we breathe is basically useless to humans and animals. The chemical bonds are just too strong. But a few bacteria and other microbes have the incredible ability to break the bonds of nitrogen and make it useful to living things.

In fact, many plants have specialized organs attached to their roots that house these nitrogen-loving bacteria. This relationship between plants and bacteria is a common phenomenon called mutualism, a form of symbiosis. It is a relationship whereby each partner benefits by living with the other partner.

Nothing Lives Alone

All creatures on earth live in symbiotic partnerships, including lowly single-celled pond-dwelling organisms. It appears that the Creator wants us to "clearly see" in these pervasive symbiotic relationships how much we depend on others — and ultimately Him — for life. From the very beginning of time, all the different creatures on earth had to be alive and working together, and we continue to depend on them (and God) for a healthy life.

So what are all these symbiotic microbes doing? Creationists have noted several major things, such as providing nutrition and influencing reproduction of insects. Let's consider just a couple of other interesting examples from the animal kingdom.

Defending plants and animals

Microbes are also involved in defending plants and animals against attack by other organisms. For example, consider that in the early 1900s a fungus almost wiped out the majestic American chestnut tree. A few trees survived the blight, however, and they were found to possess a virus that modified the blight, causing the fungus to be less potent. Now scientists are breeding resistant chestnut trees that could once again grace American forests.

It seems likely that God originally designed certain viruses as part of the immune system of plants.

Bioluminescence

Another interesting partnership is the bioluminescent (light-producing) bacteria that grow inside special light organs in creatures such as the Hawaiian bobtail squid.[6] The bioluminescence may help protect the squid against predators that swim under them at night. Perhaps the glowing squid appears as moonlight to predators lurking below, or perhaps the squid uses the light to see its way through murky water or at night. Whatever the bacteria's function, recent studies show that bioluminescent bacteria play an important role in the great depths of the ocean.

These are just a couple of the interesting symbiotic partnerships of bacteria and other microbes. Their amazing abundance and their life-supporting functions suggest that the Creator — our "living God" (Psalm 84:2) — made microbes to form a massive, life-sustaining, life-promoting biomatrix on earth.

When you look closely at the microbial world, two major themes are inescapable. One is that our living God intended to "fill the earth" with life, evidenced by the pervasive, life-sustaining biomatrix of microbes, animals, and humans. Second is the Creator's emphasis on relationships. A vast multitude of living things interact with each other as God designed it to be and as He sustains it.

> For in Him we live and move and have our being (Acts 17:28).

Good Designs Gone Bad

So what mechanism caused some of these "very good" microbes to go bad? Did God directly modify them, or did they change over time? At least three possible changes may have occurred, or a combination of all three:

1. Displacement. Microbes were originally designed to perform beneficial functions in restricted places, but after the Fall they spread to other places and began to cause disruption and disease.
2. Modification. Microbes were physically modified to become pathogenic (disease-causing). [7]
3. Uncontrolled growth. Their numbers were designed to remain within safe ranges, but now they fluctuate, causing either under- or over-population that results in disease and disruption of a once-balanced system.

---

6. E.G. Ruby, "Lessons from a Cooperative Bacterial-Animal Association: The Vibrio Fischeri-Euprymna Scolopes Light Organ Symbiosis," *Annual Review of Microbiology* 50 (1996): 591–624.
7. It is not yet known whether these modifications occurred directly by God or indirectly by the changed environment of the cursed post-Fall world.

Scripture hints at examples of helpful creations that have gone bad, such as thorns and thistles. Yeast is an example of a good thing that becomes invasive and harmful when it spreads too rapidly (see 1 Corinthians 5:6–8). In fact, yeast can cause severe infection, such as thrush and candidiasis in humans. Let's consider examples of other common disease-causing microbes.

Displaced Cholera

It seems that many microbes once had a good purpose but have changed as a result of the Fall and now cause disease.

Cholera is a severe intestinal illness that humans get from contaminated water or food. It leads to severe diarrhea, shock, and even death. In its most virulent form, it can kill within three hours of infection. Cholera is caused by the bacterium *Vibrio cholera*, which produces a variety of toxins. Interestingly, most species related to *Vibrio cholera* grow harmlessly on the surface of practically all shelled ocean creatures and some fish. There they perform a valuable task: breaking down chitin, the main component of the hard outside shell, or exoskeleton, of crabs, shrimp, lobsters, and many other sea creatures. Without their help, oceans and beaches would be littered with billions of shells. The breakdown of chitin also returns precious nutrients like carbon and nitrogen back to the ocean.

Even more fascinating, some of the cholera components that are toxic to the human intestines are used to break down chitin. So creationists hypothesize that *Vibrio cholera* originally broke down chitin in the ocean, but after Adam's Fall, God allowed them to spread beyond their proper place.

Disease-causing versions of *Vibrio cholera* may also have been genetically modified after the Fall. We have discovered that they have some extra DNA, apparently inserted by viruses, which allows the bacteria to produce toxin. Other types of cholera lack this DNA and are typically nontoxic.

Modified *E. Coli*

Another bacterium that appears to be modified is *Escherichia coli*. Normally, each person carries millions of harmless *E. coli* in his or her intestines, where it helps keep the digestive track running smoothly. *E. coli* is so intimately associated with the human body that health departments check for it when they want to confirm human activity in or near a waterway. Unfortunately, viruses appear to have infected some *E. coli* and introduced their own DNA into the *E. coli*'s DNA. For instance, one strain of *E. coli*[8] has an extra piece of DNA that

8. A bacterial strain is like a subspecies. *E. coli* is one species, but it has many subspecies or strains, which differ just slightly from one another. The harmless strain of *E. coli* that is

produces lethal toxins. If you remove the offending DNA, you remove much of this bacterium's disease-causing potential.

But why would *E. coli* carry a toxin in the first place? What was this toxin created to do? No one can say for sure, but we do know that this strain of *E. coli* lives harmlessly in the gut of farm animals, where it has been shown to help protect against cancer-causing viruses.[9] So creationists hypothesize that the disease-causing abilities of this strain may have been acquired by the displacement or modification of a harmless *E. coli*.

In recent years medical researchers have also discovered that beneficial *E. coli* may protect our intestines from disease-causing bacteria. In fact, some physicians are administering a strain of *E. coli* to "at-risk" newborns to shield the babies from diarrhea-causing bacteria.[10]

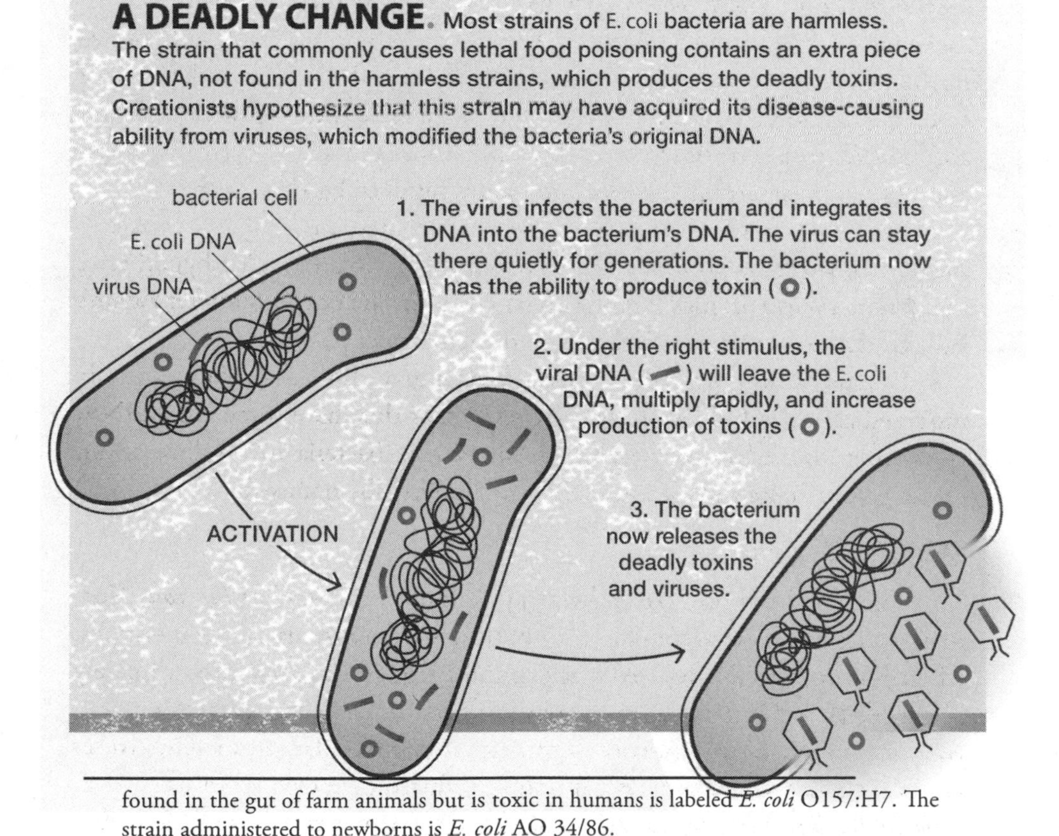

found in the gut of farm animals but is toxic in humans is labeled *E. coli* O157:H7. The strain administered to newborns is *E. coli* AO 34/86.

9. C. Zimmer, *Microcosm: E. coli and the New Science of Life* (New York, NY: Pantheon, 2008).
10. See reference 8.

New Treatment Ideas

This concept, that intestinal health depends on the presence of beneficial bacteria, forms the basis of an entirely new area of medicine called probiotics. Several over-the-counter products are now available that may help boost beneficial bacteria populations in the gut.

Also, a new theory in medicine called the hygiene hypothesis is based on this idea. The proposal is that humans should be exposed to microbes early in life; and if they are not, a variety of disease conditions may result, including asthma, multiple sclerosis, and colitis.

Scripture clearly shows that plants, which now have thorns and thistles as a result of the Fall, once had only good functions. Considering this example, Christians can begin to imagine how all of God's creatures once had beneficial roles; and perhaps, in some cases, this knowledge can be used to fight disease.

At least one creation researcher is already investigating such ideas and is proposing ways in which certain bacteria can be used to fight cancer.[11] This kind of medical treatment represents a very promising and exciting new area of research. Best of all, it flows from our understanding of God's beneficent creation, which He graciously allows to persist in a fallen world.

11. Luke Kim, "Bacterial Attenuation and Its Link to Innate Oncolytic Potention," *Answers Research Journal* 1 (2008): 117–122.

32

Unicorns in the Bible?

DR. ELIZABETH MITCHELL

Some people claim the Bible is a book of fairy tales because it mentions unicorns. However, the biblical unicorn was a real animal, not an imaginary creature. The Bible refers to the unicorn in the context of familiar animals, such as peacocks, lambs, lions, bullocks, goats, donkeys, horses, dogs, eagles, and calves (Job 39:9–12).[1] In Job 38–41, God reminded Job of the characteristics of a variety of impressive animals He had created, showing Job that God was far above man in power and strength.[2]

Job had to be familiar with the animals on God's list for the illustration to be effective. God points out in Job 39:9–12 that the unicorn, "whose strength is great," is useless for agricultural work, refusing to serve man or "harrow (plow) the valley." This visual aid gave Job a glimpse of God's greatness. An imaginary fantasy animal would have defeated the purpose of God's illustration.

Modern readers have trouble with the Bible's unicorns because we forget that a single-horned feature is not uncommon on God's menu for animal design. (Consider the rhinoceros and narwhal.) The Bible describes unicorns skipping like calves (Psalm 29:6), traveling like bullocks, and bleeding when they die (Isaiah

1. In addition to Job 39:9–10, the unicorn is mentioned in Numbers 23:22, 24:8; Deuteronomy 33:17; Psalm 22:21, 29:6, 92:10; Isaiah 34:7.
2. In Job, God's list of impressive real animals goes on to discuss peacocks, ostriches, horses, hawks, and eagles. God builds up to a crescendo, commanding Job to look at the behemoth, which He had created on the same day He created man (Job 40:15). The behemoth's description matches that of a sauropod dinosaur. Following the behemoth, the list concludes with the leviathan, a powerful, fiery sea creature. See "Could Behemoth Have Been a Dinosaur?" www.answersingenesis.org/behemoth.

(Courtesy: Domenichino, Virgin and Unicorn, [working under Annibale Carracci], Fresco, 1604 – 1605, Farnese Palace, Rome)

34:7). The presence of a very strong horn on this powerful, independent-minded creature is intended to make readers think of strength.

The absence of a unicorn in the modern world should not cause us to doubt its past existence. (Think of the dodo bird. It does not exist today, but we do not doubt that it existed in the past.) Eighteenth century reports from southern Africa described rock drawings and eyewitness accounts of fierce, single-horned, equine-like animals. One such report describes "a single horn, directly in front, about as long as one's arm, and at the base about as thick. . . . [It] had a sharp point; it was not attached to the bone of the forehead, but fixed only in the skin."[3]

The *elasmotherium*, an extinct giant rhinoceros, provides another possibility for the unicorn's identity. The *elasmotherium*'s 33-inch-long skull has a huge bony protuberance on the frontal bone consistent with the support structure for a massive horn.[4] In fact, archaeologist Austen Henry Layard, in his 1849 book *Nineveh and Its Remains*, sketched a single-horned creature from an obelisk in company with two-horned bovine animals; he identified the single-horned animal as an Indian rhinoceros.[5] The biblical unicorn could have been the *elasmotherium*.[6]

Assyrian archaeology provides one other possible solution to the unicorn identity crisis. The biblical unicorn could have been an aurochs (a kind of wild ox known to the Assyrians as rimu).[7] The aurochs's horns were symmetrical and

3. Edward Robinson, ed., *Calmet's Dictionary of the Holy Bible* revised edition (Boston, MA: Crocker and Brewster, 1832), p. 907–908.
4. The report in *Nature* described a 33-inch-long skull with a bony frontal protuberance more than three feet in circumference. This bony protuberance with its associated structures is thought to have supported a horn over a yard long. Norman Lockyer, "The Elasmotherium," *Nature: International Weekly Journal of Science*, August 8, 1878, p. 388.
5. Austen Henry Layard, *Nineveh and Its Remains* (London: John Murray, 1849), p. 435.
6. A margin note on Isaiah 34:7 placed in the King James Version in 1769 mentions this possible identity, and the Latin Vulgate translates the same Hebrew word as "unicorn" in some contexts and "rhinoceros" in others.
7. *Aurochs* is both singular and plural, like *sheep*.

often appeared as one in profile, as can be seen on Ashurnasirpal II's palace relief and Esarhaddon's stone prism.[8] Fighting rimu was a popular sport for Assyrian kings. On a broken obelisk, for instance, Tiglath-Pileser I boasted of slaying them in the Lebanese mountains.[9]

Extinct since about 1627, aurochs, *Bos primigenius*, were huge bovine creatures.[10] Julius Caesar described them in his *Gallic Wars* as:

> . . . a little below the elephant in size, and of the appearance, color, and shape of a bull. Their strength and speed are extraordinary; they spare neither man nor wild beast which they have espied. . . . Not even when taken very young can they be rendered familiar to men and tamed. The size, shape, and appearance of their horns differ much from the horns of our oxen. These they anxiously seek after, and bind at the tips with silver, and use as cups at their most sumptuous entertainments.[11]

The aurochs's highly prized horns would have been a symbol of great strength to the ancient Bible reader.

One scholarly urge to identify the biblical unicorn with the Assyrian aurochs springs from a similarity between the Assyrian word *rimu* and the Hebrew word *re'em*. We must be very careful when dealing with anglicized transliterated words from languages that do not share the English alphabet and phonetic structure.[12] However, similar words in Ugaritic and Akkadian (other languages of the ancient Middle East) as well as Aramaic mean "wild bull" or "buffalo," and an Arabic cognate means "white antelope."

However, the linguistics of the text cannot conclusively prove how many horns the biblical unicorn had. While modern translations typically translate *re'em* as "wild ox," the King James Version (1611), Luther's German Bible (1534), the Septuagint, and the Latin Vulgate translated this Hebrew word with words meaning "one-horned animal."[13]

---

8. Viewable at www.britishmuseum.org.
9. Algernon Heber-Percy, *A Visit to Bashan and Argob* (London: The Religious Tract Society, 1895), p. 150.
10. Brittanica Concise Encyclopedia, 2007, s.v. "Aurochs."
11. Julius Caesar, *Gallic Wars*, Book 6, chapter 28, www.classics.mit.edu/Caesar/gallic.6.6.html.
12 Elizabeth Mitchell, "Doesn't Egyptian Chronology Prove That the Bible Is Unreliable?" in *The New Answer Book 2*, Ken Ham, ed. (Green Forest, AR: Master Books, 2008), p. 245–264.
13 Some writers who hold to the two-horned identity think that the KJV translators substituted the plural *unicorns* for the singular *an unicorn* in Deuteronomy 33:17 because they were uncomfortable with the idea of a two-horned unicorn. However, the KJV translators themselves noted the literal translation an unicorn in their own margin note.

The importance of the biblical unicorn is not so much its specific identity — much as we would like to know — but its reality. The Bible is clearly describing a real animal. The unicorn mentioned in the Bible was a powerful animal possessing one or two strong horns — not the fantasy animal that has been popularized in movies and books. Whatever it was, it is now likely extinct like many other animals. To think of the biblical unicorn as a fantasy animal is to demean God's Word, which is true in every detail.

They likely chose the plural rendering to fit the context of the verse. Deuteronomy 33:17 states, "His [Joseph's] glory is like the firstling of his bullock, and his horns are like the horns of unicorns: with them he shall push the people together to the ends of the earth: and they are the ten thousands of Ephraim, and they are the thousands of Manasseh" (KJV). The verse compares the tribal descendants of Joseph's "horns," meaning descendants of his two sons Ephraim and Manasseh, with the strong horns of unicorns. "Horns" is plural because there are two sons in view, and "unicorn" is referenced because the unicorn's horn is so incredibly strong.

33

Doesn't the Bible Support Slavery?

PAUL TAYLOR AND BODIE HODGE

The issue of slavery usually conjures up thoughts of the harsh "race-based" slavery that was common by Europeans toward those of African descent in the latter few centuries. However, slavery has a much longer history and needs to be addressed biblically.[1]

Some "white"[2] Christians have used the Bible to convince themselves that owning slaves is okay and that slaves should obey their "earthly masters." Regrettably and shamefully, "white" Christians have frequently taken verses of Scripture out of context to justify the most despicable acts. In some cases, it could be argued that these people were not really Christians; they were not really born again but were adhering to a form of Christianity for traditional or national reasons. Nevertheless, we have to concede that there are genuine "white" Christians who have believed the vilest calumnies about the nature of "black" people and have sought support for their disgraceful views from the pages of the Bible.

But what does the Bible really teach?

1. It should be noted that Answers in Genesis strongly opposes both racism and slavery.
2. We are using the term "white" to refer to peoples of European origin and "black" to refer to peoples primarily of African origin. We are actually not too thrilled about these terms either since all people are really the same color just different shades, but for the sake of understanding, we will use them in this chapter.

Greek and Hebrew Words for "Slave"

The Hebrew and Greek words used for "slave" are also the same words used for "servant" and "bondservant," as shown by the following table.

	Hebrew, (Old Testament)	Greek, (New Testament)	Meaning
1	עבד ebed		Slave, servant, bondservant
2	עבד abad		Serve, work, labor
3	שִׁפחה shiphchah		Maid, maidservant, slave-girl
4	אמה amah		Maid servant, female slave
5		δουλος doulos	Servant, slave, bondservant
6		συνδουλος sundoulos	Fellow servant, slave
7		παιδισκη paidiske	Bondwoman, maid, female slave

In essence, there are two kinds of slavery described in the Bible: a servant or bondservant who was paid a wage, and the enslavement of an individual without pay. Which types of "slavery" did the Bible condemn?

A Brief History of Slavery

It is important to note that neither slavery in New Testament times nor slavery under the Mosaic covenant have anything to do with the sort of slavery where "black" people were bought and sold as property by "white" people in the well-known slave trade of the last few centuries. No "white" Christian should think that he or she could use any slightly positive comment about slavery in this chapter to justify the historic slave trade, which is still a major stain on the histories of both the United States and the UK.

The United States and the UK were not the only countries in history to delve into harsh slavery and so be stained.

1. The Code of Hammurabi discussed slavery soon after 2242 B.C. (the date assigned by Archbishop Ussher to the Tower of Babel incident).
2. Ham's son Mizraim founded Egypt (still called Mizraim in Hebrew). Egypt was the first well-documented nation in the Bible to have harsh slavery, which was imposed on Joseph, the son of Israel, in 1728 B.C. (according to Archbishop Ussher). Later, the Egyptians were slave masters to the rest of the Israelites until Moses, by the hand of God, freed them.
3. The Israelites were again enslaved by Assyrian and Babylonian captors about 1,000 years later.
4. "Black" Moors enslaved "whites" during their conquering of Spain and Portugal on the Iberian Peninsula in the eighth century A.D. for over 400 years. The Moors even took slaves as far north as Scandinavia. The Moorish and Middle Eastern slave market was quite extensive.
5. Norse raiders of Scandinavia enslaved other European peoples and took them back as property beginning in the eighth century A.D.
6. Even in modern times, slavery is still alive, such as in the Sudan and Darfur.

We find many other examples of harsh slavery from cultures throughout the world. At any rate, these few examples indicate that harsh slavery was/is a reality, and, in all cases, is an unacceptable act by biblical standards (as we will see).

The extreme kindness to be shown to slaves/servants commanded in the Bible among the Israelites was often prefaced by a reminder that they too were slaves at the hand of the Egyptians. In other words, they were to treat slaves/servants in a way that they wanted to be treated.

Slavery in the Bible

But was slavery in the Bible the same as harsh slavery? For example, slaves and masters are addressed in Paul's epistles. The term "slave" in Ephesians 6:5 is better translated "bondservant." The Bible in no way gives full support to the practice of bondservants, who were certainly not paid the first century equivalent of the minimum wage. Nevertheless, they were paid something (Colossians 4:1) and were therefore in a state more akin to a lifetime employment contract rather than "racial" slavery. Moreover, Paul gives clear instructions that Christian "masters" are to treat such people with respect and as equals. Their employment position did not affect their standing in the Church.

Other passages in Leviticus show us the importance of treating "aliens" and foreigners well, and how, if they believe, they become part of the people of God (for example, Rahab and Ruth, to name but two). Also, the existence of slavery in Leviticus 25 underlines the importance of redemption, and enables the New Testament writers to point out that we are slaves to sin, but are redeemed by the blood of Jesus. Such slavery is a living allegory, and does not justify the race-based form of slavery practiced from about the 16th to 19th centuries.

As we already know, harsh slavery was common in the Middle East as far back as ancient Egypt. If God had simply ignored it, then there would have been no rules for the treatment of slaves/bondservants, and people could have treated them harshly with no rights. But the God-given rights and rules for their protection showed that God cared for them as well.

This is often misconstrued as an endorsement of harsh slavery, which it is not. God listed slave traders among the worst of sinners in 1 Timothy 1:10 ("kidnappers/men stealers/slave traders"). This is no new teaching, as Moses was not fond of forced slavery either:

> He who kidnaps a man and sells him, or if he is found in his hand, shall surely be put to death (Exodus 21:16).

In fact, take note of the punishment of Egypt, when the Lord freed the Israelites (Exodus chapters 3–15). God predicted this punishment well in advance:

> Then He said to Abram: "Know certainly that your descendants will be strangers in a land that is not theirs, and will serve them, and they will afflict them four hundred years. And also the nation whom they serve I will judge; afterward they shall come out with great possessions" (Genesis 15:13–14).

Had God not protected slaves/bondservants by such commands, then many people surrounding them who did have harsh slavery would have loved to move in where there were no governing principles as to the treatment of slaves. It would have given a "green light" to slave owners from neighboring areas to come and settle there. But with the rules in place, it discouraged such slavery in their realm.

In fact, the laws and regulations over slavery are a sure sign that slavery isn't good in the same way the Law came to expose and limit sin (Romans 5:13). One reverend explained it this way:

> In giving laws to regulate slavery, God is not saying it is a good thing. In fact, by giving laws about it at all, He is plainly stating it is a bad thing. We don't make laws to limit or regulate good things. After all, you won't find laws that tell us it is wrong to be too healthy or that if water is too clean we have to add pollution to it. Therefore, the fact slavery is included in the regulations of the Old Testament at all assumes that it is a bad thing which needs regulation to prevent the damage from being too great.[3]

Does the Bible Support Harsh Slavery?

There are several passages that are commonly used to suggest that the Bible condones harsh slavery. However, when we read these passages in context, we find that they clearly oppose harsh slavery.

> If you buy a Hebrew servant, he shall serve six years; and in the seventh he shall go out free and pay nothing. If he comes in by himself, he shall go out by himself; if he comes in married, then his wife shall go out with him. If his master has given him a wife, and she has borne him sons or daughters, the wife and her children shall be her master's, and he shall go out by himself. But if the servant plainly says, "I love my master, my wife, and my children; I will not go out free," then his master shall bring him to the judges. He shall also bring him to the door, or to the doorpost, and his master shall pierce his ear with an awl; and he shall serve him forever (Exodus 21:2–6).

This is the first type of bankruptcy law we've encountered. With this, a government doesn't step in, but a person who has lost himself or herself to debt can sell the only thing they have left: their ability to perform labor. This is a loan. In six years the loan is paid off, and they are set free. Bondservants who did this made a wage, had their debt covered, had a home to stay in, on-the-job training, and did it for only six years. This almost sounds better than college, which doesn't cover debt and you have to pay for it!

Regarding Exodus 21:4, if he (the bondservant) is willing to walk away from his wife and kids, then it is his own fault. And he would be the one in

3. Personal correspondence with Reverend Mathew Anderson, Ottumwa, Iowa, 2/3/2007.

defiance of the law of marriage. He has every right to stay with his family. On the other hand, his wife, since she is a servant as well, must repay her debt until she can go free. Otherwise, a woman could be deceitful by racking up debt and then selling herself into slavery to have her debts covered, only to marry someone with a short time left on his term, and then go free with him. That would be cruel to the master who was trying to help her out. So this provision is to protect those who are trying to help people out of their debt.

This is not a forced agreement either. The bondservants enter into service on their own accord. In the same respect, a foreigner can also sell himself or herself into servitude. Although the rules are slightly different, it would still be by their own accord in light of Exodus 21:16 above.

> If men contend with each other, and one strikes the other with a stone or with his fist, and he does not die but is confined to his bed, if he rises again and walks about outside with his staff, then he who struck him shall be acquitted. He shall only pay for the loss of his time, and shall provide for him to be thoroughly healed. And if a man beats his male or female servant with a rod, so that he dies under his hand, he shall surely be punished. Notwithstanding, if he remains alive a day or two, he shall not be punished; for he is his property (Exodus 21:18–21).

This passage follows closely after Moses' decree against slave traders in Exodus 21:16. We include verses 18 and 19 to show the parallel to servants among the Israelites. The rules still apply for their protection if they already have servants or if someone sells himself or herself into service.

Regarding Exodus 21:20–21, consider that many of those who sold themselves into servitude were those who had lost everything, indicating that they were often times the "lazy" ones. In order to get them up to par on a working level, they may require discipline. And the Bible does say to give discipline — even fathers were to give their children "the rod;" to withhold it is considered unloving (Proverbs 13:24, 23:13). So beating with a rod (or more appropriately "a branch") is not harsh, but required for discipline. Even the Apostle Paul reveals he was beaten with a rod three times (2 Corinthians 11:25), and he didn't die from it. In fact, the equivalent in today's culture (spanking) was commonplace in public schools until just a few years ago. Only recently has this been deemed "inappropriate."

According to verses 20–21, if an owner severely beat his servant, and the servant died, then he would be punished — that was the law. However, if the servant survived for a couple of days, it is probable that the master was punishing him and not intending to kill him, or that he may have died from another cause. In this case there is no penalty other than that the owner loses the servant who is his temporary property — he suffers the loss.[4]

Some have also complained that God is sexist in his treatment of servants (though sexism is outside the realm of this chapter, we will still address this claim).

> If a man sells his daughter as a servant, she is not to go free as menservants do. If she does not please the master who has selected her for himself, he must let her be redeemed. He has no right to sell her to foreigners, because he has broken faith with her (Exodus 21:7–8; NIV).

There is a stark delineation between male servants and the female servants in Exodus 21:7. A Hebrew male could sell himself into servitude for his labor (to cover his debts, etc.) and be released after six years. A Hebrew female could be sold into servitude, with permission of her father, not for labor purposes but for marriage. Verse 8 discusses breaking faith with her, which means that they have entered into a marriage covenant (see Malachi 2:14). If God approved of the female leaving in six years, then marriage is no longer a life-long covenant. So God is honoring the sanctity of marriage here.

Imagine what would happen if this rule wasn't in place. It would mean that men would have the free reign to marry a woman for six years and then "trade" her in for another woman. This is not approved of in the Bible. Of course, when a man buys a male servant, they are not married, and so the male servants were to be set free.

> I am the Lord your God, who brought you out of the land of Egypt, to give you the land of Canaan and to be your God. And if one of your brethren who dwells by you becomes poor, and sells himself to you, you shall not compel him to serve as a slave. As a hired servant and a sojourner he shall be with you, and shall serve you until the Year of Jubilee. And then he shall depart from you — he and his children with him — and shall return to his own family. He shall return to the possession of his fathers. For they are My servants, whom I brought out of the land of Egypt; they shall not be sold as slaves. You shall not rule over him with rigor, but you shall fear your

4. There seems to be some debate as to the proper translation of verse 21. Several versions (NIV, HCSB, NLT) translate it as ". . . if the servant recovers after a day or two," rather than "remains alive a day or two." If this is the proper translation, it obviously makes this a moot point.

> God. And as for your male and female slaves whom you may have — from the nations that are around you, from them you may buy male and female slaves. Moreover you may buy the children of the strangers who dwell among you, and their families who are with you, which they beget in your land; and they shall become your property. And you may take them as an inheritance for your children after you, to inherit them as a possession; they shall be your permanent slaves. But regarding your brethren, the children of Israel, you shall not rule over one another with rigor (Leviticus 25:38–46).

God prefaces this passage specifically with a reminder that the Lord saved them from their bondage of slavery in Egypt. Again, if one becomes poor, he can sell himself into slavery/servitude and be released as was already discussed.

Verse 44 discusses slaves that they may *already* have from nations around them. They can be bought and sold. It doesn't say to seek them out or have forced slavery. Hence, it is not giving an endorsement of seeking new slaves or encouraging the slave trade. At this point, the Israelites had just come out of slavery and were about to enter the Holy Land. They shouldn't have had many servants. Also, this doesn't restrict other people in cultures around them from selling themselves as bondservants. But as discussed already, there are passages for the proper and godly treatment of servants/slaves.

Sadly, some Israelite kings later tried to institute forced slavery, for example Solomon (1 Kings 9:15) and Rehoboam with Adoniram (1 Kings 12:18). Both fell from favor in God's sight and were found to follow after evil (1 Kings 11:6; 2 Chronicles 12:14).

> Blessed is that servant whom his master will find so doing when he comes. Truly, I say to you that he will make him ruler over all that he has. But if that servant says in his heart, "My master is delaying his coming," and begins to beat the male and female servants, and to eat and drink and be drunk, the master of that servant will come on a day when he is not looking for him, and at an hour when he is not aware, and will cut him in two and appoint him his portion with the unbelievers. And that servant who knew his master's will, and did not prepare himself or do according to his will, shall be beaten with many stripes. But he who did not know, yet committed things deserving of stripes, shall be beaten with few. For everyone to whom much is given, from him much will be required; and to whom much has been committed, of him they will ask the more (Luke 12:43–48).

As for Jesus's supposed support for beating slaves, this is in the context of a parable. Parables are stories Jesus told to help us understand spiritual truths. For example, in one parable Jesus likens God to a judge (Luke 18:1–5). The judge is unjust, but eventually gives justice to the widow when she persists. The point of that story was not to tell us that God is like an unjust judge — on the contrary, He is completely just. The point of the parable is to tell us to be persistent in prayer. Similarly, Luke 12:47–48 does not justify beating slaves. It is not a parable telling us how masters are to behave. It is a parable telling us that we must be ready for when Jesus Himself returns. One will be rewarded with eternal life through Christ, or with eternal punishment (Matthew 25:46).

> Bondservants, be obedient to those who are your masters according to the flesh, with fear and trembling, in sincerity of heart, as to Christ; not with eyeservice, as men–pleasers, but as bondservants of Christ, doing the will of God from the heart, with goodwill doing service, as to the Lord, and not to men, knowing that whatever good anyone does, he will receive the same from the Lord, whether he is a slave or free. And you, masters, do the same things to them, giving up threatening, knowing that your own Master also is in heaven, and there is no partiality with Him (Ephesians 6:5–9).

Again, Paul in Ephesians is not giving an endorsement to slavery/bondservants and masters, but gives them both the same commands, showing that God views them as equals in Christ. Again, bondservants were to be paid fair wages:

> Masters, give your bondservants what is just and fair, knowing that you also have a Master in heaven (Colossians 4:1).

Christians Led the Fight to Abolish Slavery

The slavery of "black" people by "white" people in the 16th to 19th centuries (and probably longer) was harshly unjust, like many cultures before. This harsh slavery is not discussed in Moses' writings because such slavery was forbidden in Hebrew culture. This is not surprising. Paul tells us in Romans 1:30 that people are capable of inventing new ways of doing evil. Peter even reveals that some slave owners were already being disobedient and treating slaves/bondservants harshly (1 Peter 2:18). Of course, the Bible gives no endorsement of such treatment. "White" on "black" slavery was opposed by Christians such as William Wilberforce, but not by examining passages on slavery because the slaveries were of different types.[5] "Racial" slavery was opposed because it was seen to be contrary to the value that God places on every human being, and the fact that God "has made from one blood every nation of men to dwell on all the face of the earth" (Acts 17:26). The last letter that the revival evangelist John Wesley ever wrote was to William Wilberforce, encouraging Wilberforce in his endeavors to see slavery abolished. In the letter, Wesley describes slavery as "execrable villainy."

> Reading this morning a tract wrote by a poor African, I was particularly struck by that circumstance that a man who has a black skin, being wronged or outraged by a white man, can have no redress; it being a "law" in our colonies that the oath of a black against a white goes for nothing. What villainy is this?[6]

Wesley concentrated on the value of a man, irrespective of the color of his skin. It is this principle of the value God places on human beings — a biblical principle — which was Wesley's motivation in opposing slavery.

The famous hymnwriter John Newton at one time actually captained slave ships. He did so even after his conversion to Christianity, because he was influenced by the prevailing attitudes of his society; it took time for him to realize his errors. But realize them he did — and he spent the latter part of his life campaigning against slavery. He wrote movingly and disturbingly of the suffering of slaves in the ships' galleys in his pamphlet "Thoughts upon the African Slave Trade."

> If the slaves and their rooms can be constantly aired, and they are not detained too long on board, perhaps there are not many who die; but the contrary is often their lot. They are kept down, by the weather, to breathe a hot and corrupted air, sometimes for a week: this added to the galling of their irons, and the despondency which seizes their spirits when thus confined, soon becomes fatal. . . . I believe, upon an average between the more healthy, and the more sickly voyages, and including all contingencies, one fourth of the whole purchase may be allotted to the article of mortality: that is, if the English ships purchase *sixty thousand* slaves annually, upon the whole extent of the coast, the annual loss of lives cannot be much less than *fifteen thousand.* [7]

5. Paul Taylor, "William Wilberforce: A Leader for Biblical Equality," *Answers* magazine, December 2006, online at www.answersingenesis.org/articles/am/v2/n1/william-wilberforce.
6. John Wesley's letter to William Wilberforce, February 24, 1791. Wesley died six days later.
7. J. Newton, *Thoughts upon the African Slave Trade*, 1787.

Like Wesley, it was the biblical value of human life which was the deciding factor in Newton's opposition to slavery in his latter years.

The use of the term "one blood" in Acts 17:26 is very significant. If "races" were really of different "bloods," then we could not all be saved by the shedding of the blood of one Savior. It is because the entire human race can be seen to be descended from one man — Adam — that we know we can trust in one Savior, Jesus Christ (the "Last Adam").

Many other Christians could be named in the fight to abolish slavery, which seemed to culminate with Abraham Lincoln in the mid 1800s (slavery was one of the reasons for the Civil War in the United States).

Is the Bible Racist?

Some "white" Christians have assumed that the so-called "curse of Ham" (Genesis 9:25) was to cause Ham's descendents to be black and to be cursed. While it is likely that African peoples are descended from Ham (Cush, Phut, and Mizraim), it is not likely that they are descended from Canaan (the curse was actually declared on Canaan, not Ham).

However, there is no evidence from Genesis that the curse had anything to do with skin color. Others have suggested that the "mark of Cain" in Genesis 4 was that he was turned dark-skinned. Again, there is no evidence of this in Scripture, and in any case, Cain's descendants were more or less wiped out in the Flood.

Incidentally, the use of such passages to attempt to justify some sort of evil associated with dark skin is based on an assumption that the other characters in the accounts were light-skinned, like "white" Anglo-Saxons today. That assumption can also not be found in Scripture, and is very unlikely to be true. Very light skin and very dark skin are actually the *extremes* of skin color, caused by the minimum and maximum of melanin production, and are more likely, therefore, to be the genetically selected results of populations moving away from each other after the Tower of Babel incident recorded in Genesis 11.

The issue of racism is just one of many reasons why Answers in Genesis opposes evolution. Darwinian evolution can easily be used to suggest that some "races" are more evolved than others, that is, the common belief is that "blacks" are less evolved. Biblical Christianity cannot be used that way — unless it is twisted by people who have deliberately misunderstood what the Bible actually teaches. On top of this, rejecting the Bible, a book that is not racist, because one may think evolution is superior is a sad alternative. Recall Darwin's prediction of non-white "races":

> At some future period, not very distant as measured by centuries, the civilized races of man will almost certainly exterminate and replace the savage races throughout the world. At the same time the anthropomorphous apes . . . will no doubt be exterminated. The break between man and his nearest allies will then be wider, for it will intervene between man in a more civilized state, as we may hope, even than the Caucasian, and some ape as low as a baboon, instead of as now between the negro or Australian [aborigine] and the gorilla.[8]

Conclusion

Though this short chapter couldn't delve into every verse regarding slavery, the basic principles are the same. In light of what we've learned, here are a few pointers to remember:

1. Slaves under the Mosaic Law were different from the harshly treated slaves of other societies; they were more like servants or bondservants.
2. The Bible doesn't give an endorsement of slave traders but just the opposite (1 Timothy 1:10). A slave/bondservant was acquired when a person voluntarily entered into it when he needed to pay off his debts.
3. The Bible recognizes that slavery is a reality in this sin-cursed world and doesn't ignore it, but instead gives regulations for good treatment by both masters and servants and reveals they are equal under Christ.
4. Israelites could sell themselves as slaves/bondservants to have their debts covered, make a wage, have housing, and be set free after six years. Foreigners could sell themselves as slaves/bondservants as well.
5. Biblical Christians led the fight to abolish harsh slavery in modern times.

8. Charles Darwin, *The Descent of Man*, 2nd ed. (New York, NY: A.L. Burt, 1874), p. 178.

34

Why Did God Make Viruses?

DR. JEAN K. LIGHTNER

There are some fundamental differences in how creationists and evolutionists view life. Biblical creationists believe that God created various forms of life according to their kinds with the ability to reproduce and fill the earth (Genesis 1:21, 22, 24–28). This view includes the concepts that God had purpose in what He created and that it originally was very good (Isaiah 45:18; Genesis 1:31).

In contrast, evolutionists view life as all descending from a single common ancestor by chance processes. Evolutionary arguments tend to imply that life isn't really very complex or well designed. For example, 100 years ago a cell was promoted as being nothing more than a blob of protoplasm, implying that it wouldn't be difficult for it to arise by chance. This proved to be wrong; cells are incredibly complex structures.[1] At one time evolutionists argued that organs or structures with no known function actually had no function; at the time this included hundreds of organs and structures in the human body. Instead these were believed to be vestiges of evolution. This argument has become rather vestigial itself, as these organs have been found to have function.[2]

1. C. Wieland, "Chemical Soup Is Not Your Ancestor!" *Creation* 16 no. 2 (1994):46–47; see Harvard video, *Inner life of a Cell* at www.multimedia.mcb.harvard.edu/media.html.
2. D. DeWitt, "Setting the Record Straight on Vestigial Organs," www.answersingenesis.org/articles/aid/v3/n1/setting-record-straight-vestigial; see chapter 24, "Vestigial Organs — Evidence for Evolution?" in this volume.

Yet this argument reappeared in genetics. Most of the DNA in our bodies does not code for proteins, so it was labeled "junk DNA" by evolutionists who assumed it has no function. As research continues, it is becoming clear that this DNA has numerous essential functions.[3] The evolutionary worldview has a dismal track record for anticipating the astounding complexity in life uncovered by scientific research.

If God created everything good and with a purpose, why are there disease-causing bacteria and viruses in the world? It is true that we first learned about bacteria and viruses because of the problems they cause. Bacteria have been studied in considerable detail and are now recognized to be mainly helpful and absolutely essential for life on earth; bacteria that cause disease (which developed as a result of the Fall) are the exceptions, not the rule.[4] But what about viruses: what purpose could they possibly have?

What Is a Virus?

Viruses are a bit of an enigma. They contain DNA or RNA that are found in all living things. This is packaged in a protein coat. Despite this, viruses are not usually considered living because they are not made up of cells and cannot reproduce by themselves. Instead, the virus will inject the DNA or RNA into a living cell, and the cell will make copies of the virus and assemble them so they can spread.[5]

Viruses vary considerably in their ability to cause disease. Many known viruses are not associated with disease at all. Others cause mild symptoms that may often go undetected. Some, like the HIV virus that causes AIDS in people, appear to have come from another species where they do not cause disease. Given our current knowledge of viruses, it is quite reasonable to believe that disease-causing viruses are descended from viruses that were once not harmful.[6] It has been suggested that they have played an important role in maintaining life on earth — somewhat similar to the way bacteria do.[7] In fact, they may play a role in solving an intriguing puzzle that faces creationists.

3. G. Purdom, "'Junk' DNA — Past, Present, and Future, Part 1," www.answersingenesis.org/articles/aid/v2/n1/junk-dna-part-1; J. Lightner, "The Smell of Change in Our Understanding of Pseudogenes," www.answersingenesis.org/articles/aid/v3/n1/smell-of-change-pseudogenes.
4. See chapter 31, "What About Bacteria?" in this volume.
5. J. Bergman, "Did God Make Pathogenic Viruses?" *Technical Journal* 13 no. 1 (1999): 115–125.
6. J.R. Lucas and T.C. Wood, "The Origin of Viral Disease: A Foray into Creationist Virology," in *Exploring the History of Life: Proceedings of the Fifth BSG Conference* and *Occasional Papers of the BSG* 8 (2006): 13.
7. Bergman, "Did God Make Pathogenic Viruses?"; see chapter 31, "What About Bacteria?" in this volume.

A Creationist Puzzle

The biblical record tells of a global Flood when all created kinds of unclean[8] land animals were reduced to a population of two, the pair that was preserved with Noah on the ark (Genesis 7). After the Flood, these animals reproduced and filled the earth again (Genesis 8:15–19). Today many of these kinds are represented by whole families. For example, the dog family (Canidae) is believed to represent a created kind.[9] However, this is a very diverse group of animals. There are foxes that are adapted to living in the arctic, and others that live in the desert. There is incredible variety seen in modern domestic dog breeds. Where did all this variety come from? And how could it arise so quickly given that the Flood occurred around 4,300 years ago?[10]

The answer to this puzzle is probably quite complex. Some of the variety would have been carried by the pair of animals on the ark. When parents pass traits on to their offspring, these traits can appear in new combinations in the offspring (Mendelian genetics). Natural selection can weed some existing traits out of a population. However, a close examination reveals that genetic changes have also arisen in this time.[11] Many of these changes do not appear accidental and do not directly cause disease. For this reason, some creationists have proposed that God "designed animals to be able to undergo genetic mutations which would enable them to adapt to a wide range of environmental challenges while minimizing risk."[12]

Isn't That Evolution?

It is important to recognize that biologists use several distinct definitions for *evolution* that are often blurred together as if they are synonymous.[13] *Evolution* is sometimes defined as "change in the genetic makeup (or gene frequency) of a population over time." This has been observed; both creationists and evolutionists recognize this as important in building models to help us

8. Unclean animals probably included all non-ruminants. See Leviticus 11; Deuteronomy 14:1–8.
9. T.C. Wood, "The Current Status of Baraminology," *Creation Research Society Quarterly* 43 no. 3 (2006): 149–158.
10. J. Ussher, *The Annals of the World*, L. and M. Pierce, trans. and ed. (Green Forest, AR: Master Books, 2003).
11. This is clear because the two animals on the ark could carry up to four alleles for any one gene. Today there are some genes where considerably more than four alleles exist in animals from the same created kind.
12. J.K. Lightner, "Karyotypic and Allelic Diversity in the Canid Baramin (Canidae)," *Journal of Creation* 23 no. 1 (2009): 94–98.
13. See "An Introduction to Evolution" on the Understanding Evolution website, www.evolution.berkeley.edu/evolibrary/search/topicbrowse2.php?topic_id=41.

understand what likely happened in the past. A second definition of *evolution* involves the idea that all life descended from a common ancestor over millions of years through naturalistic processes. This has *not* been observed. In fact, it is in direct opposition to the testimony God (the eyewitness to creation) gives us in the Bible. The idea that all life has a common ancestor requires the *assumption* that the Bible's history is false, and the *assumption* that changes which do occur could produce the variety of life we see today from a single-celled ancestor.[14]

With regard to the first definition of evolution, creationists and evolutionists differ in the pattern of genetic changes they should expect to see. The creation model predicts that degenerative changes can occur because mankind sinned and brought death into the world (Genesis 3). It also predicts that adaptive changes could occur because God cares for His creation and intends for the earth to be inhabited (Psalm 147:8–9; Matthew 6:25–34; Isaiah 45:18). Both types of changes have been observed. The fact that some foxes are adapted to live in the arctic while others are adapted to live in the desert fits perfectly with this biblical teaching. While evolutionists accept that these types of changes occur, their model requires that most genetic changes add information to the genome. This pattern has *not* been observed. Without this pattern, they cannot account for the many organs and complex biochemical pathways that exist in animals today.[15] Scientific observations show that there is an overall pattern of decay seen in the genome, which is the opposite of what the evolutionary model would predict.[16]

Another difference is the source of the genetic change. Evolutionists assume that random mutations and natural selection can account for the genetic changes that are seen. Since the underlying mechanism is naturalistic, changes were expected to be very slow. Contrary to their expectations, rapid adaptation has been observed,[17] and evolutionists have had to adjust their thinking to accept this. Furthermore, detailed studies of the pattern in genetic differences within related animals don't make sense if mutations are assumed to always be essentially random events.[18] Something else is clearly going on here. It appears

14. See "Misconceptions about Evolution and the Mechanisms of Evolution: Evolution and Religion Are Incompatible" on the Understanding Evolution website, www.evolution.berkeley.edu/evolibrary/misconceptions_faq#d1. Note how religious beliefs are said to have nothing to do with the real (material) world; this is in stark contrast with the biblical teaching that God, as the Creator of all, is relevant to every aspect of life.
15. See L. Spetner, *Not By Chance!* (New York, NY: Judaica Press, 1998).
16. See J. Sanford, *Genetic Entropy and the Mystery of the Genome* (Lima, NY: Elim Publishing, 2005).
17. See www.answersingenesis.org/articles/aid/v3/n1/life-designed-to-adapt.
18. J.K. Lightner, "Karyotype Variability within the Cattle Monobaramin," *Answers Research Journal* 1 (2008): 77–88; J.K. Lightner, "Genetics of Coat Color I," *Answers Research Journal* 1 (2008): 109–166.

that God has placed some incredible programming into the genomes of the animals He created, and viruses may play some role in this.

Evidence of Horizontal Gene Transfer

Interestingly, there are some portions of DNA in animals that look like they came from a virus.[19] While some of these were likely originally present in the genome since they have essential functions, others may have been introduced by viruses.[20] A number of years ago, one creationist proposed that horizontal gene flow (genes picked up from somewhere in the environment rather than inherited from parents) may help to explain rapid adaptation and the interesting pattern of DNA in animals. In fact, the author lists 13 different biological phenomena that might be explained by horizontal gene flow.[21] Since viruses carry genetic material (DNA or RNA), they are the most logical agents to suspect in transferring genes. While horizontal gene transfer would not change the identity of an animal (i.e., it would still belong to the same kind), it could rapidly provide a source of genetic variability that allows for rapid adaptation. If this is the case, then viruses were created "good" (as in Genesis 1), with a support role much like bacteria are known to have.

While the evidence is largely circumstantial, further scientific investigation does seem to support these ideas.[22] In fact, a recent *PNAS* article has brought some new information to light. Previous studies had suggested horizontal transfer between closely related species. This study identified a large section of DNA (~2.9 kb) that was approximately 96 percent identical in a marsupial (opossum), several placentals (mouse, rat, bushbaby, tenrec, and little brown bat), a reptile (anole lizard), and an amphibian (African clawed frog). It was absent from the 27 other animals surveyed (which included human and Jamaican fruit bat).

19. Traditionally, this DNA has been assumed to be the result of viral infection. Recently, several creationists have presented evidence that some (RNA) viruses may actually be escapees. In other words, the genes were originally in the DNA of the animals and were able to move around within the cell (by copying on to RNA). At some point the viruses became independent and can now travel between animals. For more on this intriguing idea see Y. Liu. "The Natural History of Retroviruses: Exogenization vs Endogenization" *Answers Research Journal* 2 (2009): 97–106.
20. Y. Liu, "Were Retroviruses Created Good?" *Answers*, October–December 2006, online bonus content, www.answersingenesis.org/articles/am/v1/n2/were-retroviruses-created-good.
21. T. Wood, "The Aging Process: Rapid Post-Flood Intrabaraminic Diversification Caused by Altruistic Genetic Elements (AGES)," *Origins* 54 (2002).
22. T. Wood, "Perspectives on Aging: A Young Earth Creation Diversification Model," in *Proceedings of the Fifth International Conference on Creationism*, Robert L. Ivey, Jr., ed. (Pittsburgh, PA: Creation Science Fellowship, 2003), p. 479–489.

This sequence appears to have been incorporated into an existing functional gene in rats and mice, although its specific function is not yet known.[23] Because of the pattern observed, it appears that horizontal gene transfer was concentrated at some time in the past and perhaps occurred via a DNA virus.[24] Interestingly, several species (anole and opossum) are from Central/South America, several are restricted to Africa (bushbaby, tenrec), and the others have a wider geographical distribution.[25] This suggests that the transfer may have occurred early post-Flood or been intercontinental in scope.[26]

Since most scientists are heavily influenced by the evolutionary worldview, they often miss indicators of purpose. For example, the section of DNA discussed above is a transposon (a type of mobile genetic element or transposable element). After the putative transfer, it was copied and integrated into several different parts of the genome in the various species. This requires that the proper tools (e.g., enzymes) be in place so that the section of DNA can be incorporated into the genome initially, then modified and copied appropriately. Given that decay has occurred over time, it is not surprising to creationists that there are examples of transposons where this process doesn't work properly and disease occurs.

Diseases draw attention and research dollars, so the problems associated with transposons have been recognized before the benefits are understood (much like was true of bacteria). Many people still view these mobile genetic elements as "parasitic" or "selfish." However, they are quite widespread in the genome of plants, animals, and man. If their insertion was always purely "random," it seems they should more consistently cause problems in a complex system such

23. J.K. Pace II et al., "Repeated Horizontal Transfer of a DNA Transposon in Mammals and Other Tetrapods," *PNAS* 105 no. 44 (2008): 17,023–17,028.
24. The authors are evolutionists who carry in the assumption of common ancestry. Although creationists could argue that some kinds were created with these sequences and others were not, it appears more likely that they result from horizontal gene transfer. Also, the authors used evolutionary assumptions to estimate the time the horizontal transfer occurred (which was essentially the same for all species). When this type of estimate was done with mitochondrial DNA, the estimated mutation rate was significantly off compared to actual measured mutation rates. A. Gibbons, "Calibrating the Mitochondrial Clock," *Science* 279 no. 5347 (1998): 28–29.
25. See comment by Cedric, one of the authors of the *PNAS* article, on "Space Invader DNA Jumped Across Mammalian Genomes," www.scienceblogs.com/notrocketscience/2008/11/space_invader_dna_jumped_across_mammalian_genomes.php.
26. The creation model predicts a high concentration of horizontal gene transfer post-Flood as animals were migrating out and filling various ecological niches. There is also a chance that animals on the ark may have already carried these sequences. Further intrabaraminic comparisons may help to clarify the timing of horizontal gene flow for this particular case.

as the genome.[27] Therefore, it seems more logical to believe that transposons have purpose and were designed in a way to benefit their possessor.

The Bible Explains the Paradox

The biblical view explains an important paradox we see in the world around us. It anticipates the complexity that is constantly being uncovered by scientific research; God is an all-wise Creator and would be expected to use awesome design patterns and programming. It also explains the decay observed because mankind sinned and brought death into the world; the world is now in bondage to decay (Romans 8:20–21). This is an exciting time to be a creationist researcher, as the tremendous volume of scientific research is helping to provide answers to questions that have been asked for decades.

27. Some accidental insertions may not cause obvious problems because the genome contains a high amount of redundancy. Redundancy is a hallmark of excellent design that militates against system failure. It is also inconsistent with the notion that life arose by chance. Such accidental insertions do, however, contribute to the deterioration of the genome.

35

Wasn't the Bible Written by Mere Men?

BODIE HODGE

> All Scripture is given by inspiration of God, and is profitable for doctrine, for reproof, for correction, for instruction in righteousness, that the man of God may be complete, thoroughly equipped for every good work (2 Timothy 3:16–17).

A Bigger Problem than You Might Think

It truly is a secular age. I had the opportunity to speak to a student-led club at a government school a couple of years ago. At the end of the lecture, I began answering questions the students had. Even though there was a very negative tone coming from many of the questioners, I remained courteous in each response.

Most of the questions were common ones and fairly easy to answer. The questions began with issues related to the creation-evolution debate, such as dinosaurs and radiometric dating. After those were answered, the questions became more impassioned and were directed toward God and the Bible, such as "Who created God?" and "Isn't the Bible full of contradictions?" At the end, one statement came up that I didn't get to respond to. The bell rang and out they ran. I really wish they had brought this up sooner so I could have responded to the claim that the Bible was written by mere men. We were getting closer to the heart of the issue.

I didn't realize how important this was until I saw a statistic of young people who had walked away from the church. Out of 1,000 young adults surveyed who have left church, 44 percent of them said that they did not believe the accounts in the Bible were true and accurate. When asked what made them answer this way, the most common response (24 percent) was that *the Bible was written by men*. The rest of the results, from that 44 percent, are shown below.[1]

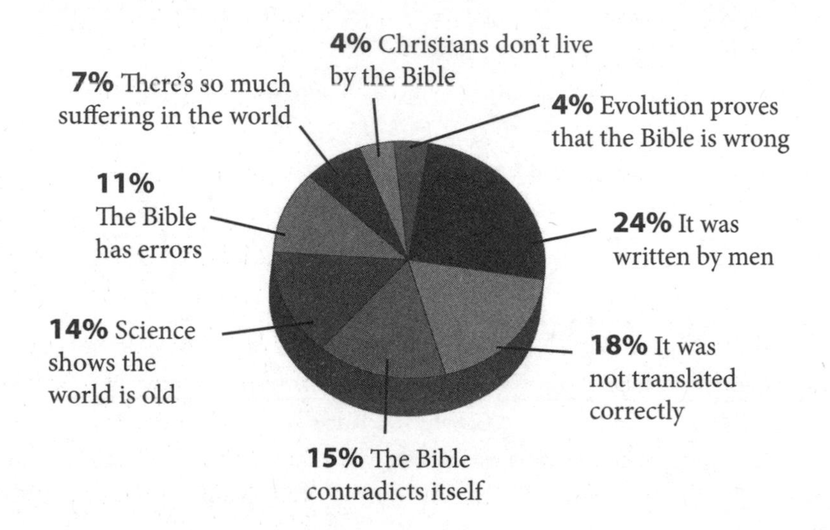

Even though 24 percent directly claimed this, take note that there are related answers such as 11 percent believing the Bible to have errors, which means God could not have been involved since God does not make errors (Psalm 12:6; Deuteronomy 32:4). Also, claiming that the Bible contradicts itself would imply that God was not involved since God cannot deny Himself (2 Timothy 2:13), and thus contradict Himself. So at least 50 percent would, in one way or another, dispute that a perfect God was responsible for the Bible!

So What Is the Answer?

When it comes to the authorship of the Bible, of course men were involved — Christians would be the first to point this out. Paul wrote letters to early churches and these became Scripture. David wrote many of the Psalms, Moses wrote the Pentateuch (the first five books of the Bible), and so on. In fact, it is estimated that over 40 different human authors were involved.[2] So this is not the real issue.

The real issue is whether God had any involvement in the authorship of the Bible. Let's think about this for a moment. When someone claims that the Bible was written by men *and not God*, this is an absolute statement that reveals something extraordinary. It reveals that the person saying this is claiming to be transcendent! For a person to validate the claim that God did not inspire the

1. Ken Ham and Britt Beemer, *Already Gone* (Green Forest, AR: Master Books, 2009), p. 107.
2. Josh McDowell, *A Ready Defense* (Nashville, TN: Thomas Nelson Publishers, 1993), p. 27.

human authors of the Bible means he must be omniscient, omnipresent, and omnipotent!

1. *Omniscient:* This person is claiming to be an all-knowing authority on the subject of God's inspiration in order to refute God's claim that Scripture was inspired by Him (2 Timothy 3:16).
2. *Omnipresent:* This person is claiming that he was present, both spiritually and physically, to observe that God had no part in aiding any of the biblical authors as they penned Scripture.
3. *Omnipotent:* This person is claiming that, had God tried to inspire the biblical authors, they had the power to stop such an action.

So the person making the claim that the Bible was merely written by men alone is claiming to be God, since these three attributes belong to God alone. This is a religious issue of humanism versus Christianity. People who make such claims (perhaps unwittingly) are claiming that *they* are the ultimate authority over God and are trying to convince others that God is *subservient* to them. As we respond to claims such as these, this needs to be revealed.

What Is a Good Response?

I like to respond to this claim with a question that reveals this real issue — and there are several ways to do this. For example, referring to omnipresence, you can ask, "Do you really believe that you are omnipresent? The only way for you to make your point that God had no involvement would be if you were omnipresent." Then point out that this person is claiming to be God when he or she makes the statement that God had no involvement in the Bible.

Or, in regard to omnipotence, perhaps ask, "How is it that you are powerful enough to stop God from inspiring the authors?" Or you could direct the question to the rest of the listeners by simply asking, "Since the only way to refute the fact that God inspired the Bible is to use attributes of God such as omnipresence, omnipotence, and omniscience, do the rest of you think this person is God?" You may have to explain it further from this point so the listeners will better understand.

If you are not sure you can remember these types of questions, then remember that you can always lead the person down the path by first asking an easier question such as, "How do you know that God was not involved?" But then you will have to listen carefully to the response to know how to respond after that.

Other responses include undercutting the entire position by pointing out that any type of reasoning apart from the Bible is merely arbitrary. So the person trying to make a logical argument against the claims of the Bible (i.e., that God inspired the authors) is doing so only because he or she is assuming (though unintentionally) the Bible is true and that logic and truth exist! It is good to point out these types of presuppositions and inconsistencies.[3]

Someone may respond and say, "What if I claim that Shakespeare was inspired by God — then you would have to be omniscient, omnipresent, and omnipotent to refute it."

Actually, it is irrelevant *for me* to be omniscient, omnipresent, and omnipotent to refute such a claim. God, who is omniscient, omnipresent, and omnipotent, refutes this claim from what He has already stated in the Bible. Nowhere has God authenticated Shakespeare's writings as Scripture, unlike Christ the Creator-God's (John 1; Colossians 1; Hebrews 1) approval of the Old Testament prophetic works and the New Testament apostolic works — the cap of the canon is already sealed.[4]

Conclusion

Sadly, in today's society, children, whether churched or not, are being heavily exposed to the religion of humanism. This religion reigns in state schools. So it is logical that the younger generations are thinking in terms of humanism and applying that to their view of the Bible.

The student mentioned earlier was applying the religion of humanism (i.e., man, not God, is the authority) to the Bible when he claimed that it was written by men. He viewed himself, and not God, as the authority; and he further reasoned that there is no God at all and therefore the Bible could not have had God's involvement.

Therefore, his statement that the Bible was written by men is merely a religious claim made by a man claiming the attributes of God. It is good to point this out as many people follow this same thought process, failing to realize the implications most of the time.

> You shall have no other gods before Me (Exodus 20:3).

If one can expose the false religion of humanism, then unbelievers may be more open to realizing that they are being deceived. After all, unbelievers are not the enemy; rather, the false principalities and dark powers that are at work to deceive are the enemy (Ephesians 6:12).

3. Jason Lisle, "Feedback: Put the Bible Down," Answers in Genesis, www.answersingenesis.org/articles/2008/12/05/feedback-put-the-bible-down.
4. Bodie Hodge, "A Look at the Canon: How Do We Know that the 66 Books of the Bible Are from God?" Answers in Genesis, www.answersingenesis.org/articles/aid/v3/n1/look-at-the-canon.

36

Isn't the God of the Old Testament Harsh, Brutal, and Downright Evil?

BODIE HODGE

Have you ever heard questions such as:

How could God kill all the innocent people, even children, in the Flood?

Why would God send Joshua and the Israelites into Canaan to exterminate the innocent Canaanites living in the land?

Do you really believe a loving God would send people to an eternal hell?

This view of God is commonly referred to in the secular media, atheistic books, and so on. There is a common claim that the God of the Old Testament (even in the New Testament) seems very harsh, brutal, and even evil.[1]

An initial response to this claim can simply be, "How can the atheist or non-Christian say God is harsh, brutal, and evil when they deny the Bible, the very book that defines harsh, brutal, and evil?" Even further, in atheistic, materialistic,

1. For example, atheist Richard Dawkins wrote that the God of the Old Testament is, "arguably the most unpleasant character in all fiction: jealous and proud of it; a petty, unjust, unforgiving control-freak; a vindictive, bloodthirsty ethnic cleanser; a misogynistic, homophobic, racist, infanticidal, genocidal, filicidal, pestilential, megalomaniacal, sadomasochistic, capriciously malevolent bully." Richard Dawkins, *The God Delusion* (Boston, MA: Houghton Mifflin Co., 2006), p. 31.

and evolutionary worldviews, such things are neither right nor wrong because there is no God in their view to establish what is right or wrong. The same people who profess to believe in a naturalistic view where animals rape, murder, and eat their own kind are those who attack the loving God of the Bible and try to call Him evil (Isaiah 5:20).

But a closer look at such claims against the God of the Bible shows that these claims have no merit. Claiming that God is evil or harsh is an attack on God's character, and every Christian should be prepared to have an answer for such attacks (1 Peter 3:15).

The intent of many of those who make such claims is to make a good God look evil in order to justify their rejection of Him, His Word, or even His existence. But if God really doesn't exist and the Bible isn't His Word, then those who attack God and His Word by calling Him harsh and evil shouldn't even care to attack Him. By attacking Him, they show that they know He exists and are simply suppressing that knowledge (see Romans 1:20–25). They are trying to justify their rebellion against God. Few that I have spoken with realize that when they attack God's character in an effort to make a case against His existence they are refuting their own position.

Some of the events in the Bible that people commonly use to justify that claim that God is harsh, include events in Genesis such as the Fall of man, the Flood, and the destruction of Sodom and Gomorrah. And then they proceed to the Canaanites, Egyptians, Benjamites, or even non-Christians in general.[2] So Genesis seems to be a good place to begin.

The Fall: Adam and Eve

Often people ask how God could sentence all of mankind to die because of Adam and Eve's sin. Adam and the Eve knew the punishment for sin (Genesis 2:17), but they sinned anyway, going against the plain commandment of God. Adam knowingly sinned (1 Timothy 2:14), so his punishment was brought upon himself. Most people fail to realize, however, that all mankind sinned in Adam as we were in the body of our ancestor when he sinned (Hebrews 7:10). Due to Adam's sin, we also receive a sin nature, and we sin ourselves (Romans 5:12). So we also die because of sin — we are no different from Adam and Eve. However, we should stop to consider the blessing that is found amidst the curse. When Adam and the woman sinned, God offered the first prophecy of Jesus Christ in Genesis 3:15. The curse of sin would be erased by the seed of a woman (the result of a

2. Of course, there are other instances that can be found in Scripture where people may try to claim God is harsh, brutal, or evil, but these examples should suffice to answer this particular issue.

virgin birth) sent to save mankind. A means of salvation was already being offered.

On top of this, the first man and woman should have died right then, but God is patient and gave them a "grace period," covering their sin by sacrificing animals (when He made coats of skins in Genesis 3:21) in their place; sin is punishable by death, so something had to die (Hebrews 9:22). Abel followed this pattern (Genesis 4:4), as did Noah (Genesis 8:20), Abraham (Genesis 22:13), and the Israelites. These animal sacrifices were not sufficient to take away sins (Hebrews 10:4) — only a perfect, sinless sacrifice, fulfilled in the death of Jesus Christ, could (Hebrews 4:15; 9:13–14). It was Christ's sacrifice alone that was sufficient to cover the sins of the whole world (1 John 2:2). The infinite Son died to pay the penalty for the infinite punishment from an infinitely Holy God.

Sacrifices made by the Lord for Adam and Eve to provide them coats of skin (Genesis 3:21)

So there are two blessings so far: a final means of salvation in Christ and a grace period of the penalty for sin being covered instead of bringing about *instant* death. But there is another blessing that few may notice without reading the rest of the Bible. By being sentenced to die, man wouldn't be forced to live in a sin-cursed world for all eternity — this is why the path to the Tree of Life was guarded (Genesis 3:22–24)! By dying in this sin-cursed world with Christ as Savior, one inherits the new heaven and new earth, which are restored to perfection, where there is no Curse, death, or suffering for eternity (Revelation 21:4, 22:3). Death will have no sting (1 Corinthians 15:53–56) for those in Christ.

So in this instance,

Noah offered sacrifices of clean animals after the Flood (Genesis 8:20–21).

man sinned and God acted justly by punishing that sin, and even went much further by offering three blessings: a grace period, a means of salvation, and a perfect place to live an eternal life without sin, death, or the Curse. Imagine if a thief went before a judge and the judge said, "You have broken the law so you deserve 50 years in jail with no parole, but I will give you 1 year in jail, and you don't have to begin serving that for six months so you may set your affairs in order. After 1 year, I'll give you a guaranteed release, and on top of that, I'll buy you a million-dollar home and prepare it for you." It seems strange that people would say that the judge would be harsh and evil for sentencing the thief to a year in jail. What would be stranger still is if the thief refused the generous offer.

The Flood

God is often attacked for killing "all the innocent people, and even children," in the Flood. In fact, some have specifically said, "But the children . . . how could God kill the little children?" The response: "If the earth was filled with violence and evil, it makes one wonder how many children were still alive anyway. After all, in today's culture, where evil has a foothold, it is children that seem to bear the brunt of much violence (e.g., hundreds of millions of abortions). Even if there were some children left, God provided the ark. Why did the parents of those children refuse to let them board? Why did they insist on putting their children in harm's way? If anyone is to blame, it is the parents and guardians who stopped them from coming to the ark."

Why blame God for something when He provided a means of salvation, which the parents refused? Imagine if a boater came to rescue a woman and her child who were on top of a roof with floodwaters rising. The boater says, "Please get in and I can save you." The woman says, "No, we will stay because I don't believe you." Then the boater patiently waits and even tries to explain what will happen, yet she continues to refuse over and over again. The boater even asks for her to send her child and she still refuses and swats the boater away . . . and then finally they drown. Is it appropriate to blame the boater for the death of the child?

People had the opportunity to come in the ark but they refused.

But consider this, judging Scripture by Scripture, it says that no one is truly innocent (Romans 3:23), and all will eventually die anyway — a repercussion of our own actions (1 Corinthians 15:22; Romans 6:23). Second, what brought such a judgment on the people before the Flood?

> Then the LORD saw that the wickedness of man was great in the earth, and that every intent of the thoughts of his heart was only evil continually (Genesis 6:5).

What a strong statement! *Every* intention and thought was evil *all* the time. Imagine the murders, rapes, thefts, child sacrifices, cannibalism, and so on. This was happening continually. Yet this was about 120 years (maximum) before the Flood (Genesis 6:3). So God was still patient, allowing time for repentance and change (1 Peter 3:20). God even called Noah to be a preacher of righteousness (2 Peter 2:5), yet people still refused to listen and continued in their evil ways.

God even went so far as to offer a way of salvation! He provided an ark through Noah and his family, and yet others didn't come. Only Noah's family was saved (2 Peter 2:5). The means of salvation, preaching of righteousness, and God's patience were there, yet everyone else refused and received their judgment.

As an aside, the claim of children dying in the Flood has always been of interest, especially when skeptics and atheists bring it up. The hypocrisy is astounding since these skeptics and atheists often support the murder of babies as we have seen in the abortion debate. If people really were evil and their thoughts evil all the time, then abortion, child murder, and child sacrifice were likely commonplace. Disobedience to God would likely mean disobeying God's command to be fruitful and multiply (Genesis 1:28). Resisting this command would result in drastically fewer children, so one could wonder if many children were even around at the time of the Flood. Noah himself had no children until he was 500 years old (lending to the view that children may have been few and far between in those days). Even so, children are sinners and can also have evil intentions and thoughts (Romans 3:23). Today, for example, we see children killing children in school, child thieves, rape among children, and so on. But if children and infants didn't make it to the ark (the means of salvation at the time), whose fault is it but their own and/or parents/guardians who refused to let them?! So why blame God when He offered them a means to be saved?

Sodom and Gomorrah

In Genesis 18:20–33, the Lord revealed to Abraham that Sodom and Gomorrah had sinned exceedingly. Their wickedness was not revealed in its entirety, but we are aware of their acts of sodomy (later in the chapter) that had overtaken them in their actions, enough to rape.

Abraham asked if God would sweep away the righteous with the wicked. He asked the Lord if there were 50 righteous, would the Lord spare it; He said yes. He asked the Lord if there were 40 righteous, would the Lord spare it; He said yes. He asked the Lord if there were 30 righteous, would the Lord spare it; He said yes. He asked the Lord if there were 20 righteous, would the Lord spare it; He said yes. He asked the Lord if there were 10 righteous, would the Lord spare it; He said yes.

This reveals how wicked and sinful the people were. They were without excuse and judgment was finally coming. This also reveals something interesting about the Flood. If God would spare Sodom and Gomorrah for only 10 righteous people, then would God have spared the earth if 10 people were righteous before the Flood? It appears that He did. Methuselah and Lamech, Noah's father and grandfather, *may* have been among those that made 10 (along with Noah, his wife, and his three sons and their wives). Of course, there may have been others who were righteous too, up until the Flood. But at the time of the Flood, we can surmise there were only eight (Methuselah and Lamech had died just before the Flood).

Lot and his family numbered less than 10 in Sodom and Gomorrah (Lot, his wife, his two daughters, his two sons-in-law, only made six). Yet, God provided a means of salvation for them — the angels helped them get to safety.

Were there children in Sodom and Gomorrah? The Bible doesn't reveal any, and homosexual behavior was rampant, so there may not have been many, if any, children. Since God made it clear that not even 10 people were righteous in the city, then even the children (if any) were being extremely sinful. But like all these situations, if the children and/or the parents/guardians refused to let them have salvation and righteous teachings, whose fault is it? It is not the fault of God, who did provide a way, but the fault of those who suppressed the truth.

God was just and gave the people of Sodom and Gomorrah, and the five cities of the plain, what they asked for (their due punishment). They wanted a life without God and His goodness . . . and God gave that to them.

The Egyptians

In this instance, God used Moses and Aaron (Exodus 5–15) to judge the Egyptians for the wickedness they were inflicting on the Israelites through harsh slavery (Exodus 1:8–14), murdering their children (Exodus 1:22), and so on. God struck the land with many plagues and disasters because Pharaoh continued to sin and the nation of Egypt followed after him in sin. It culminated with the death of the firstborn in Egypt, even though this judgment could easily have been averted had Pharaoh listened and released the Israelites from their oppression — the blood is on Pharaoh's head. Even Pharaoh and his army's final demise was on his own head, not God's. In fact, each plague could easily have been averted had Pharaoh responded to what God said through Moses and Aaron. So a means of salvation from the plagues was given, but Pharaoh and the Egyptians rejected it.

The Canaanites

As for God using people to do His bidding, this is nothing new, as we saw with Moses and Aaron and the Egyptians. God used people to build an ark, His temple, and so on. God used judges and kings to ward off attacks and to provide justice, among other functions. So the concept is nothing new. With the Canaanites, God used the Israelites to enact His judgment under Joshua's leadership.

The Canaanites were far from innocent! God was patient with them as they continued in their sin. Among the Canaanite tribes when Joshua invaded were the Amorites whose sin was prophesied to Abraham. Abraham received the prophecy that the sin of the Amorites had not reached its full measure (Genesis 15:16). During this time, Abraham met Melchizedek, a noble, kingly priest in the land of Canaan. But Melchizedek's ministry surely had an influence on the Canaanites as it took several hundred years before their sin overtook them. Had they continued to listen to what he taught, they probably wouldn't have been in this situation.

When Joshua entered the land of Canaan, the Amorites' sin *had* reached its full measure and it was time for judgment. Leviticus 18:2–30 points out the horrendous crimes that were going on in the land of Canaan. They were having sex with their mothers, sisters, and so on. Men were having sex with other men. They were giving their children to be sacrificed to Molech (vs. 21). They were having sex with animals (vs. 23). So it is impossible to make the claim that those tribes were innocent and undeserving of punishment.

But one can't neglect that children sin, too. As previously pointed out, today there are kids killing kids, kids thieving, kids raping, etc. So the innocence of children is a farce. In fact, if they were sacrificing their children, then how many children were alive when Joshua entered the Promised Land anyway?

At Jericho, both young and old were to be destroyed (Joshua 5:13–6:21), so at least Jericho had young. Yet Jericho is also the place that Christ Himself appeared as a theophany to lead Joshua into battle. Jericho must have been very bad to warrant a physical appearance of Christ to have judgment poured out on them. Perhaps all the sins listed in Leviticus 18 were going on there as well! Yet even in Jericho, there was a means of salvation as Rahab and her family were saved. She can even be found in the lineage of Christ (Matthew 1:5).

The Benjamites

The Benjamites asked for it as well (Judges 19:22–25, 20:13) and sided with the wicked. So no one can claim the Benjamites were innocent either. Sadly, the Benjamites knew the consequences of their actions prior to sinning. They were Israelites who had no excuse for not knowing what Moses wrote. They should have known better, but chose to sin deliberately (Leviticus 18, especially verses 26–30). They also brought it on themselves.

Had the Benjamites repented, the Lord would have forgiven them. The Israelites had extensive means of sacrifice to cover sin and to expel the wicked from among them. However, the Benjamites refused this means of salvation and sinned against God.

Non-Christians

When discussing eternal salvation in Christ with non-Christians, they often ask, "Do you really believe a loving God would send people to an eternal hell?" The response is: only if they sin! And the fact is, all have sinned, all fall short of the glory of God (Romans 3:23). The fascinating thing is that some will *not* spend eternity in hell. Everyone deserves that punishment, including me, but God has provided a means of salvation just as He did in the Old Testament situations described above. If one refuses to receive this salvation, can God be blamed?

Jesus Christ was born to save mankind.

There is only one God; He is God of both the Old Testament and New Testament, even though some try to suggest there are different presentations. In both the Old and New Testaments, people had the opportunity to get back to a right relationship with Him by repenting, asking forgiveness of their sin, and receiving Christ as their Lord and Savior.[3] In both Testaments, God judges sin. Mercy and patience were to be found through God's vessels: Noah, with his preaching for years, and Abraham, with his pleading for Sodom and

3. Although those alive before the time of Christ did not know His name, they still knew of the coming Messiah, as prophesied in Genesis 3:15 and many other places. Their salvation from sin was secured by their faith in the work that He would do on the Cross.

Gomorrah (even Lot urged the people not to be so wicked) — just as mercy and patience are still available today (John 7:37–38).

And He has provided a means of salvation in Jesus Christ (1 Peter 3:18), just as the ark was with the Flood and the angels were in urging Lot and his family to flee Sodom and Gomorrah. No one can blame God for not providing a merciful alternative or call Him "evil" for providing justice against sin.

Conclusion

Naturally, there are plenty of other examples in Scripture where these same principles apply. Consider the analogy of a person who steals and gets caught. When he stands before the judge, the judge finds him guilty and imposes a fine. But then the judge offers to pay the fine. Instead of accepting, the thief refuses and blames the whole mess on the judge who acted justly and even offered a way out!

This is really what is happening in today's culture. Mankind sins and gets caught. People are found guilty by a Holy God. God steps in and offers a means of salvation from the punishment of the crime (which is eternal death), even so far as to die in their place so that they can have eternal life. Yet in all this, the sinners still say no to God and then proceed to blame Him for the situation they are in! It simply doesn't make sense.

In summary:

Event/people	Were they sinning?	Did God provide justice?	Did God provide a means of salvation?
The Fall: Adam and Eve	Yes	Yes	Yes
The Flood	Yes	Yes	Yes
Sodom and Gomorrah	Yes	Yes	Yes
The Egyptians	Yes	Yes	Yes
The Canaanites	Yes	Yes	Yes
The Benjamites	Yes	Yes	Yes
Non-Christians	Yes	Yes	Yes

In light of this, God should not be blamed, but those who were punished for their sin retain the blame. God did provide a means of salvation in each of these cases even though He was not obligated to do so. God should not be blamed. Interestingly enough, individuals who say God is cruel want justice when they are wronged, for example, if someone steals from them, attacks them, or offends them in any way. They really have a double standard.

We are all sinners already under the death penalty (Romans 3:23). But again, God has provided a means of salvation in Christ. It would be nice if people realized that they should hate sin (Romans 12:9) and love God (Deuteronomy 6:5) who acts justly against sin (2 Thessalonians 1:5–10). Yet He offers abundant mercy to those who love Him (Exodus 20:6; Deuteronomy 7:9; Ephesians 2:4). Please consider this, if you haven't already.

37

Who Sinned First — Adam or Satan?

BODIE HODGE

When Christians or others speak of Adam as the first sinner, this comes from the Apostle Paul where he states:

> Therefore, just as through one man sin entered into the world, and death through sin, and thus death spread to all men, because all sinned (Romans 5:12).

It means that sin *entered the world* through Adam — that he is the one credited with sin's entrance and hence the subsequent entrance of death and suffering and the need for a Savior — a last Adam (1 Corinthians 15:45). When we look back at Genesis, it is true that Satan rebelled, and also Eve sinned, prior to Adam's disobedience.

The Sin of Eve

There were several things that Eve did wrong prior to eating the fruit. When the serpent (who was speaking the words of Satan) asked in Genesis 3:1: "Has God indeed said, 'You shall not eat of every tree of the garden'?" her response was less than perfect:

> And the woman [Eve] said to the serpent, "We may eat the fruit of the trees of the garden; but of the fruit of the tree which is in the

midst of the garden, God has said, 'You shall not eat it, *nor shall you touch it*, lest you die' " (Genesis 3:2–3; emphasis added).

Compare this to what God had commanded in Genesis 2:16–17:

> And the LORD God commanded the man, saying, "Of every tree of the garden you may freely eat; but of the tree of the knowledge of good and evil you shall not eat, for in the day that you eat of it you shall surely die."

A possible depiction of the serpent as shown in the Creation Museum

Eve made three mistakes in her response:

1. She added the command not to *touch* the fruit: "nor shall you touch it." This seems to be in direct contradiction with the command of Adam to tend the Garden (Genesis 2:15), which would probably constitute touching the tree and the fruit from time to time. It also makes the command from God to be exceptionally harsh.
2. She omitted that God allowed them to *freely* eat from *every* tree. This makes God out to be less than gracious.
3. She amended the meaning of die. Let me explain. The Hebrew in Genesis 2:17 is "die die" (*muwth – muwth*), which is often translated as "surely die" or literally as "dying you shall die," which indicates the beginning of dying — an ingressive sense. In other words, if they had eaten the fruit, then Adam and Eve would have *begun to die* and would return to dust (which is what happened when they ate in Genesis 3:19). If they were meant to die right then, Genesis 2:17 should have used *muwth* only once as is used in the Hebrew meaning dead, died, or die in an absolute sense, and not *beginning to* die or *surely* die as die-die is commonly used. What Eve said was "die" (*muwth*) once instead of the way God said it in Genesis 2:17 as "die-die" (*muwth – muwth*). So she changed God's word to appear harsher again by saying they would die almost immediately.

Often we are led to believe that Satan merely deceived Eve with the statement that "You will not surely die?" in Genesis 3:4. But we neglect the cleverness and cunning that God indicates that the serpent had in Genesis 3:1. Note also that the exchange seems to suggest that Eve may have been willingly led. That is, she had already changed what God had said.

If you take a closer look, the serpent argued against Eve with an extremely clever ploy. He went back and argued against her incorrect words using the phraseology that God used in Genesis 2:17 ("die-die," muwth-muwth). This, in a deceptive way, used the proper sense of die that God stated in Genesis 2:17 against Eve's mistaken view. Imagine the conversation in simplified terms like this:

> God says: Don't eat or you will *begin* to die.
> Eve says: We can't eat or we will die *immediately*.
> Serpent says: You will not *begin* to die?

This was very clever of Satan — using God's Words against her to deceive her. This is not an isolated incident. When Satan tempted Jesus (Matthew 4:1–11), Jesus said, "It is written" and quoted Scripture (Matthew 4:4). The second time, Satan tried quoting Scripture (i.e., God) deceptively, just as he had done to Eve (Matthew 4:5–6). Of course, Jesus was not deceived, and corrected Satan's twisted use of Scripture with a proper use of Scripture (Matthew 4:7). Because of Eve's mistaken response of God's command, it was easier for her to be deceived by Satan's misuse of what God had said.

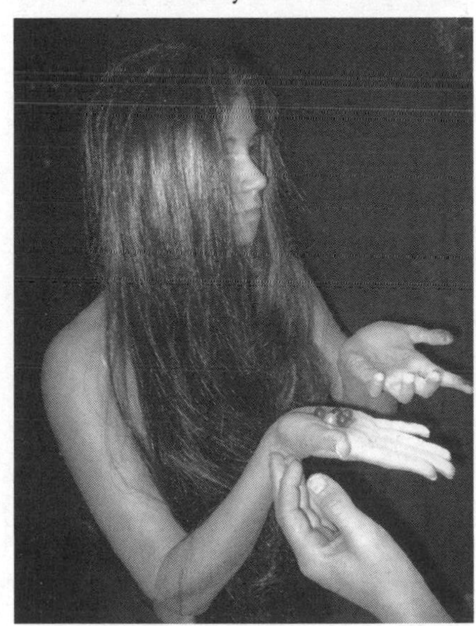

Eve offering Adam the fruit, as presented in the Creation Museum

Another point that can be brought out about Eve was her adoption of Satan's reduction of "Lord God" to simply "God" in Genesis 3:3. This mimicked the way Satan addressed God when he questioned Eve in Genesis 3:1. Satan had degraded God by not using the term God had used in Genesis 2:16–17 and Eve followed suit.

From her response, though, she started down the slope into sin by being enticed by her own thoughts about the fruit (James 1:14–15). This culminated with her eating the forbidden fruit and giving some to her husband, who also ate. Eve sinned against God by eating the fruit from the Tree of the Knowledge of Good and Evil prior to Adam eating it. However, upon a closer look at the text, their eyes were not opened until after Adam ate — likely only moments later (Genesis 3:7). Since Adam was created first (Eve coming from him, but both being created in God's image), and he had been given the command directly, and since he was the responsible party for his wife, it required his sin to bring about the Fall of mankind. When Adam ate and sinned, they knew something was wrong and felt ashamed (Genesis 3:7). Sin and death had entered into the creation.

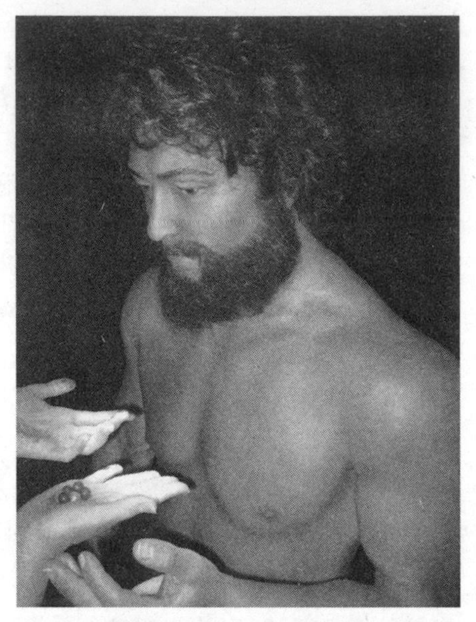

Adam taking the fruit from Eve, as depicted in the Creation Museum

The Sin of Satan

Like Eve, Satan had sinned prior to Adam's disobedience. His sin was pride in his beauty (Ezekiel 28:15–17) and in trying to ascend to be like God while in heaven (Isaiah 14:12–14). He was cast out when imperfection was found in him (Isaiah 14:12; Ezekiel 28:15) and then we find his influence in the Garden of Eden (Ezekiel 28:13; Genesis 3).

Unlike Adam, Satan was never given dominion over the world (Genesis 1:28). So his sin did not affect the creation, but merely his own person. This is likely why Satan went after those who were given dominion. Continuing in his path as an enemy of God, he apparently wanted to do the most damage, so it was likely that his deception of Eve happened soon after his own fall.

The Responsibility of Adam

Adam failed at his responsibilities in two ways. He should have stopped his wife from eating, since he was there to observe exactly what she was about to eat (Genesis 3:6). Instead of correcting the words of his wife (Genesis 3:17), he listened to her and ate while not being deceived (1 Timothy 2:14).

We could also argue that Adam failed to keep and guard the Garden as he was commanded in Genesis 2:15. God, knowing Satan would fall, gave this command to Adam, but Adam did not complete the task. God knew that Adam would fall short and had a plan specially prepared.

Many people have asked, "Why do we have to die for something Adam did?" The answer is simple — we are without excuse since we sin, too (Romans 3:23, 5:12). This has caused some to ask: "Why did we have to inherit a sin nature from Adam, causing us to sin?" We read in Hebrews 7:9–10:

> Even Levi, who receives tithes, paid tithes through Abraham, so to speak, for he was still in the loins of his father when Melchizedek met him.

If we follow this argument, then all of us were ultimately *in Adam* when he sinned. So, although we often blame Adam, the life we have was in Adam when he sinned, and the sin nature we received was because we were in Adam when he sinned. We share in the blame and the sin, as well as the punishment.

But look back further. Everyone's life (including Eve's) came through Adam and ultimately came from God (Genesis 2:17). God owns us and gives us our very being (Hebrews 1:3), and it is He whom we should follow instead of our own sinful inclinations. Since the sin of Adam, all men have had the need for a Savior, Jesus Christ, the Son of God who would step into history to become a man and take the punishment for humanity's sin. Such a loving act shows that God truly loves mankind and wants to see us return to Him. God — as the Author of life, the Sustainer of life, and Redeemer of life — is truly the One to whom we owe all things.

38

How Can Someone Start a New Life in Christ?

CECIL EGGERT

The Creator God tells us in the Book of Genesis about the origin of all things in six days — matter, light, earth, sun, moon, animals, and mankind. His desire was that all of His creation would live in a perfect world where God and man could enjoy everything He had made . . . forever. Can you imagine living in a perfect world?

There was a perfect relationship between the Creator God and man; there was no death, disease, or suffering. Fear between man and animals was non-existent, and every emotional, physical, mental, and spiritual need that Adam and Eve had was met by their Creator. The role of man was clearly defined: Adam and Eve were in charge of an orderly earth that was "very good" (Genesis 1:31)!

Just imagine! God created man in His image, to have a relationship with Him, and gave him a perfect world to care for where mankind was the pinnacle of His creation! When God created Adam and Eve, He didn't make them to be just obedient puppets; they had the freedom to choose and to make their own decisions.

The Fall

One day Adam chose to disobey God's command and go his own way.

> And the LORD God commanded the man, saying, "Of every tree of the garden you may freely eat; but of the tree of the knowledge of good and evil you shall not eat, for in the day that you eat of it you shall surely die" (Genesis 2:16–17).

> Then to Adam He said, "Because you have heeded the voice of your wife, and have eaten from the tree of which I commanded you, saying, 'You shall not eat of it': Cursed is the ground for your sake; in toil you shall eat of it all the days of your life. Both thorns and thistles it shall bring forth for you, and you shall eat the herb of the field. In the sweat of your face you shall eat bread till you return to the ground, for out of it you were taken; for dust you are, and to dust you shall return" (Genesis 3:17–19).

God called Adam's disobedience *sin*. With Adam's sin the process of death had begun. As Adam sinned and died, so do all of us. Romans 5:12 in the New Testament tells us "Therefore, just as through one man sin entered the world, and death through sin, and thus death spread to all men, because all sinned." Sin changed everything: it severed our relationship with God and introduced pain, suffering, and death into the world. This sin affected all of humanity, including you and me. The world was no longer the perfect place that God had originally created it to be.

Sin now corrupted everything (Genesis 3; Romans 8:20–22). When Adam and Eve sinned, it truly was the saddest day in the universe. But God had an eternal plan. While God, being just and holy, had to punish man's sin (or disobedience), He still desired to have a loving relationship with mankind. God made a promise to Adam and Eve. God told Satan, who had deceived Eve: "And I will put enmity between you and the woman, and between your seed and her Seed; He shall bruise your head, and you shall bruise His heel" (Genesis 3:15). This promise was that in the future, He would send a perfect sacrifice from the offspring ("seed") of Eve that would conquer Satan and restore the relationship that had been broken because of sin.

Until the perfect sacrifice was provided, animals were to be used as sacrifices for sin. The first example of this blood sacrifice was demonstrated as animals were slain and the skin was used to cover the nakedness of Adam and Eve: "Also for Adam and his wife the LORD God made tunics of skin, and clothed them" (Genesis 3:21). While this animal skin only represented a "covering" of Adam and Eve's sin, it was a picture of a coming blood sacrifice that God would provide to "cleanse" man from his sin once and for all.

Adam and Eve now had hope for a future restored relationship between them and their Creator God. From Adam to Noah to Abraham, people continued to sacrifice animals. Through Moses, God revealed His law, and the people's need for an unblemished sacrifice to be offered for sin. So, in obedience to God, the Israelites shed the blood of perfect lambs year after year for the forgiveness of sins. These temporary sacrifices only symbolized what was to come in the promised Messiah; the One who would provide the ultimate and perfect sacrifice for the sins of the world.

The Messiah

Throughout Old Testament times, the prophets declared the message of God's love, mercy, and justice, preparing the way for the coming of Messiah. Just as the prophets foretold, the Messiah came to earth, born of a virgin.

> Now in the sixth month the angel Gabriel was sent by God to a city of Galilee named Nazareth, to a virgin betrothed to a man whose name was Joseph, of the house of David. The virgin's name was Mary. . . . Then the angel said to her, "Do not be afraid, Mary, for you have found favor with God. And behold, you will conceive in your womb and bring forth a Son, and shall call His name JESUS (Luke 1:26–31).

Two thousand years ago, our loving Creator God kept His promise of Genesis 3:15 as He stepped into history in the person of Jesus Christ: "In the beginning was the Word, and the Word was with God, and the Word was God. . . . And the Word became flesh and dwelt among us, and we beheld His glory, the glory as of the only begotten of the Father, full of grace and truth" (John 1:1, 14).

He wrapped himself in the flesh of His creation to become the sinless sacrifice to die for the sins of the world.

> For God so loved the world that He gave His only begotten Son, that whoever believes in Him should not perish but have everlasting life (John 3:16).

Jesus's life was everything the prophets foretold. The sinless Son of God was born of the virgin Mary, grew in knowledge and stature, and began His public ministry when He was in His thirties.

During His ministry, Jesus healed the sick, restored the blind, raised the dead, and told them how they could receive eternal life. He did these miraculous acts to show that He truly was the Son of God.

> And truly Jesus did many other signs in the presence of His disciples, which are not written in this book; but these are written that you may believe that Jesus is the Christ, the Son of God, and that believing you may have life in His name (John 20:30–31).

The time came for Jesus to become the perfect sacrifice — to die for the sins of the world and to restore that broken relationship between God and man, once and for all. He would willingly pay the penalty that you and I would have had to pay for our sin (Romans 6:23).

While nailed to the Cross, just before He died, Jesus cried out the word *tetelestai*. This Greek word means, "the debt is paid" or "paid in full." The Cross showed God's love for us. "But God demonstrates His own love toward us, in that while we were still sinners, Christ died for us" (Romans 5:8). Christ had finished what He came to do, to become the perfect sacrifice for sin and to restore man's relationship with the Creator. This was God's eternal plan.

But it doesn't end with Jesus' death on the Cross. Jesus didn't remain in the tomb; He rose from the dead, conquering death. "He is not here; for He is risen" (Matthew 28:6). No longer was the temporary sacrifice of the unblemished animals necessary. The "Lamb of God," Jesus Christ, became the perfect and final sacrifice. You see, in Adam we all die, but in Jesus we have true life and will live forever with Him in a new heaven and new earth that God is preparing, where there will be no more sin, suffering, or death. The first man Adam brought sin and death into the world; the last Adam — Jesus Christ — brings life to the world.

> For since by man came death, by Man also came the resurrection of the dead. For as in Adam all die, even so in Christ all shall be made alive (1 Corinthians 15:21–22).

God offers us the opportunity to be forgiven, spotless, and loved. When we understand and accept what God has done through His son Jesus Christ, we have a restored relationship with our Creator. The Bible makes it clear: God's gift of salvation is offered to us, not just to hear or agree with intellectually, but to respond to in faith (John 14:6; Romans 6:23). This gift is something that we receive by faith (Eph. 2:8–9; Titus 3:5).

There Is a Decision

God calls upon men everywhere to repent of their sin and to place their faith in Christ. Those who repent and believe will have their sins forgiven, a restored relationship with their Creator, and life with Him for eternity. The Bible makes clear the eternal destiny of those who reject Him — they will be separated from Him forever in a place called hell (Revelation 20:15).

The Questions You Must Answer

Do you recognize that you are a sinner in need of salvation? Sin is disobedience to God's commands. God's commands are summarized in the Ten Commandments.

God says "do not lie." Have you ever told a lie?

God says "do not steal." Have you ever taken something that doesn't belong to you?

God says "do not covet." Have you ever been jealous of something that someone else has?

If you have disobeyed these or any other of God's commands, then you are a sinner. Your sin prevents you from having a relationship with your Creator.

Would you like to receive Jesus Christ's sacrifice on the Cross as payment for your sin, submit your life to Him, and receive the free gift of eternal life? Because this is such an important matter, let's clarify what this decision involves. You need to:

Repent. Understand that you have disobeyed the Creator's commands. Tell God you are sorry for your sins. Be willing to turn from anything that is not pleasing to Him. He will show you His plan for you as you grow in your relationship with Him and read His Word.

Receive Christ as your Savior and Lord. Believe that Jesus lived, died, and rose again in payment for your sin (John 3:16, Romans 10:9). Jesus says, "I am the door. If anyone enters by Me, he will be saved" (John 10:9).

Rely on God's strength. God does not promise that life as a Christian will be easy or that you will be healthy and wealthy. In fact, you can expect trials in life that will test your faith (James 1:2–3; 1 Peter 1:6–9). However, God promises that He will give you the strength to bear those burdens (1 Corinthians 10:13).

Jesus told His followers in Luke 14:25–33 that they should count the cost before following Him. If this is what you really want, and your desire is to make Him the center of your life, you can receive the Creator's gift (eternal life through faith in Jesus Christ) right now. The Bible tells us:

> For with the heart one believes unto righteousness, and with the mouth confession is made unto salvation. . . . For "whoever calls on the name of the LORD shall be saved" (Romans 10:10–13).

You can go to God in prayer right now, right where you are, and ask Him for this gift. Here's a suggested prayer to help you:

> Lord Jesus, I know that I am a sinner and do not deserve eternal life, but I believe You died for me and rose from the grave to pay the price for my sin. Please forgive me of my sins and save me. I repent of my sins and now place my trust in You for eternal life. I receive the free gift of eternal life. Amen.

Look at what Jesus promises to those who believe in Him: "Most assuredly, I say to you, he who believes in Me has everlasting life" (John 6:47). And, "But as many as received Him, to them He gave the right to become children of God, to those who believe in His name" (John 1:12). We want to share in your joy if you have just made this life-changing decision. Our desire is to help you grow in your understanding of Jesus Christ and God's Word. Would you please give us a call, write, or email us and tell us your story? We would love to hear from you!

We would like to know if you have made this life-changing decision or have questions on how you can receive eternal life. We also encourage you to contact a Bible-believing church in your area where the pastor accepts the accuracy and authority of the Bible from its very first verse in Genesis (including the Genesis accounts of a recent creation and a global Noah's Flood).

A Challenge as You Take This Message to Others

The C.A.R.E Factor

It has been said; "People don't care how much you know until they know how much you care." First Peter 3:15 says, "But sanctify the Lord God in your hearts, and always be ready to give a defense to everyone who asks you a reason for the hope that is in you, with meekness and fear." Colossians 4:5–6 says, "Walk in wisdom toward those who are outside, redeeming the time. Let your speech always be with grace, seasoned with salt, that you may know how you ought to answer each one."

With all the equipping and knowledge we gain through the resources available to us today, it is possible for us to have an arsenal of answers without having a heart of compassion for those who need the gospel. The following acrostic will help each of us as we share this message with heart and purpose.

The Heart

C — Compassion
Compassion is cultivated as we view each person as a soul who will spend eternity with or without God.

A — Acceptance
Accept the person as an individual who has been created in the image of God.

R — Respect
Respect each person and treat him or her with dignity. The cultivation of good listening skills is critical to the proper communication of the gospel message.

E — Encouragement
Encourage the person along the way as you help answer his or her questions.

The Purpose

C — Connecting
Connect to others in common areas of life by being yourself and being transparent. Let your heart connect to their heart.

A — Assessing
Assess the worldview of your prospect before responding so you can understand his or her questions and know how to properly answer them.

R — Responding
Responding graciously is just as important as having accurate information.

E — Evangelizing
Evangelization can only be accomplished when we share the person and work of Jesus Christ. Remember, sharing the gospel message is His mandate.

As we answer a person's questions, it may take many encounters before we are able to share the saving knowledge of Christ. A balance of grace and truth will always be in order during this process. A word of caution — grace without truth is compromise, and truth without grace is heartless. The practice of fear and meekness and grace and truth can speak as loudly as the answers we provide through His Word. As we prepare ourselves with answers to the questions of this age, let us not forget to equip ourselves with the C.A.R.E. Factor as we pray, love, and go to the lost.

Contributors

Steve A. Austin

Dr. Steven Austin earned a Ph.D. in geology from Pennsylvania State University. As a full-time scientist with the Institute for Creation Research, he participated in professional, peer-reviewed studies at Mount St. Helens and the Grand Canyon. His research has been published in the prestigious International Geology Review. Dr. Austin is now conducting additional studies in the Grand Canyon, and researching the earthquake destruction of archaeological sites in Jordan.

David A. DeWitt

Dr. David DeWitt earned a Ph.D. in neuroscience from Case Western Reserve University in Cleveland, Ohio. He is a professor of biology and director of the Center for Creation Studies at Liberty University (Lynchburg, Virginia). Dr. DeWitt's research has focused on Alzheimer's disease, and he has written a number of articles for peer-reviewed journals such as *Brain Research* and *Experimental Neurology*.

Don B. DeYoung

Dr. Don DeYoung is chairman of the department of physical science at Grace College, Indiana. He also serves on the faculty of the Institute for Creation Research, Dallas. His writings have appeared in *The Journal of Chemical Physics, The Creation Research Society Quarterly*, and elsewhere. Dr. DeYoung has also written numerous books on Bible-science topics, including object lessons for children.

Cecil Eggert

Cecil Eggert serves as advancement officer at Answers in Genesis. He has a B.S. degree from Hyles-Anderson College and is currently completing his M.S. in biblical counseling from Trinity College of the Bible and Seminary. Cecil served as an associate pastor for 29 years, culminating as pastor of outreach at Calvary Baptist Church in Covington, Kentucky, before joining the staff of Answers in Genesis.

Danny Faulkner

Dr. Danny Faulkner has a B.S. (math), M.S. (physics), M.A. and Ph.D. (astronomy, Indiana University). He is a full professor at the University of South Carolina–Lancaster, where he teaches physics and astronomy. Danny has written numerous articles in astronomical journals and is the author of *Universe by Design*.

Joe Francis

Dr. Joe Francis, professor of biological sciences at Master's College, earned his Ph.D. from Wayne State University and was a post-doctoral fellow at the University of Michigan Medical School. He serves as a board member of the Creation Biology Study Group.

Ken Ham

CEO/president of Answers in Genesis, Ken Ham is one of the most in-demand Christian speakers in North America. A native Australian now residing near Cincinnati, Ham has the unique ability to communicate deep biblical truths and historical facts through apologetics. He is the author of numerous books on evangelism, dinosaurs, and the negative fruits of evolutionary thinking, including *The Lie: Evolution* and *Already Gone.*

Bodie Hodge

Bodie attended Southern Illinois University at Carbondale and received a B.S. and M.S. in mechanical engineering. His specialty was a subset of mechanical engineering based in advanced materials processing, particularly starting powders. Currently, Bodie is a speaker, writer, and researcher for Answers in Genesis–USA.

Jean K. Lightner

Dr. Jean Lightner earned her undergraduate degree in animal science. After earning a M.S. and D.V.M., she worked for three years as a veterinary medical officer for the U.S. Department of Agriculture. From here, she resigned to stay at home to raise and teach her four children. She has contributed both technical articles and laymen articles to several creationists' magazines, journals, and websites.

Jason Lisle

Dr. Lisle received his Ph.D. in astrophysics from the University of Colorado at Boulder. He specializes in solar astrophysics and has interests in the physics of relativity and biblical models of cosmology. Dr. Lisle has published a number of books, including *Taking Back Astronomy* and *The Ultimate Proof of Creation*, plus articles in both secular and creationist literature. He is a speaker, researcher, and writer for Answers in Genesis–USA.

Tim Lovett

Tim Lovett earned his degree in mechanical engineering from Sydney University (Australia) and was an instructor for 12 years in technical college engineering courses. Tim has studied the Flood and the ark for 15 years and is widely recognized for his cutting-edge research on the design and structure of Noah's ark. He is author of the book *Noah's Ark: Thinking Outside the Box*.

David N. Menton

Now retired, Dr. David Menton served as a biomedical research technician at Mayo Clinic and then as an associate professor of anatomy at Washington University School of Medicine (St. Louis) for more than 30 years. He was a consulting editor in histology for five editions of *Stedman's Medical Dictionary*, and has received numerous awards for his teaching. Dr. Menton has a Ph.D. in cell biology from Brown University and is currently a speaker, researcher, and writer for Answers in Genesis–USA.

Elizabeth Mitchell

Dr. Mitchell earned her M.D. from Vanderbilt University School of Medicine and practiced medicine for seven years until she retired to be a stay-at-home mom. Her interests in ancient history strengthened when she began to homeschool her daughters. She desires to make history come alive and to correlate it with biblical history.

Tommy Mitchell

Dr. Tommy Mitchell is a graduate of Vanderbilt University School of Medicine. He received his M.D. in 1984 and completed his residency in internal medicine in 1987. For 20 years Tommy practiced medicine in his hometown of Gallatin, Tennessee. In 1991, he was elected a Fellow of the American College of Physicians. Dr. Mitchell has been active in creation ministry for many years. He felt the Lord's call to full time service, and in 2007 he withdrew from the active practice of medicine to join Answers in Genesis–USA as a full-time speaker and writer.

John D. Morris

Dr. John Morris is president of the Institute for Creation Research in Dallas, Texas. The author of numerous books on creation, including *The Young Earth*, Dr. Morris has led several expeditions to Mt. Ararat in search of Noah's ark. A frequent conference speaker, Dr. Morris also hosts the daily radio program *Back to Genesis*.

Terry Mortenson

Dr. Terry Mortenson earned a Ph.D. in the history of geology from Coventry University in England. His thesis focused on the "scriptural geologists," a group of men in the early 19th century who fought the rise of old-earth geological theories. A former missionary (mostly in Eastern Europe), Dr. Mortenson has researched and spoken on creation and evolution for many years. He is now a speaker, writer, and researcher with Answers in Genesis–USA.

Michael Oard

Now retired after 36 years in the U.S. National Weather Service and in research meteorology, Mike Oard holds a masters degree in atmospheric science and has published research articles in journals of the American Meteorological Association and elsewhere. An active creationist, Oard has also published articles in various creationist periodicals and in the *Proceedings of the International Conference on Creationism*. He serves on the board of the Creation Research Society.

Roger Patterson

Roger Patterson earned his B.S. Ed. degree in biology from Montana State University. Before coming to work at *Answers in Genesis*, he taught for eight years in Wyoming's public school system and assisted the Wyoming Department of Education in developing assessments and standards for children in public schools. Roger now serves on the Educational Resources team at Answers in Genesis–USA.

Georgia Purdom

Dr. Purdom received her Ph.D. in molecular genetics from Ohio State University. Her professional accomplishments include winning a variety of honors, serving as professor of biology at Mt. Vernon Nazarene University (Ohio), and the publication of papers in the *Journal of Neuroscience*, the *Journal of Bone and Mineral Research*, and the *Journal of Leukocyte Biology*. Dr. Purdom is also a member of the Creation Research Society, American Society for Microbiology, and American Society for Cell Biology.

Mike Riddle

Mike holds a degree in mathematics and a graduate degree in education. He has been involved in creation ministry for more than 25 years. Prior to getting involved in creation ministry, Mike was a captain in the U.S. Marines and a national champion in track and field. Mike also spent over 20 years in the computer field where he managed U.S. Sprint's worldwide technical training and Microsoft's worldwide engineer training. Currently, Mike is a speaker, writer, and researcher for Answers in Genesis–USA.

Andrew A. Snelling

Dr. Andrew A. Snelling received his Ph.D. (geology) from the University of Sydney (Australia). After research experience in the mineral exploration industry, he was founding editor of the *Creation Ex Nihilo Technical Journal* (Australia). He also served as a professor of geology at the Institute for Creation Research. In 2007 he joined Answers in Genesis–USA as director of research. A member of several professional geological societies, Dr. Snelling has written numerous technical papers in geological journals, and creationist publications.

Paul F. Taylor

Paul F. Taylor is the senior speaker for Answers in Genesis (UK/Europe). He holds a B.S. in chemistry from Nottingham University and a masters in science education from Cardiff University. He is the author of several books, including *Cain and Abel*, *In the Beginning*, and *The Six Days of Genesis*. Paul and his wife, Geri, have five children between them.

Tom Vail

Tom Vail has been a professional guide in the Grand Canyon since 1980. He and his wife, Paula, started Canyon Ministries in 1997 to offer Christ-centered rafting tours through the Grand Canyon. Tom is author and compiler of *Grand Canyon: A Different View*. He is also co-author of the True North Series providing biblically based guide books on our national parks, including *Your Guide to the Grand Canyon* and *Your Guide to Zion and Bryce Canyon National Parks*.

John Woodmorappe

John Woodmorappe has been a researcher in the areas of biology, geology, and paleontology for over 20 years. He has a B.A. in biology, a B.A. in geology, and an M.A. in geology. John has also been a public school science teacher. He is the author of many peer-reviewed technical articles in creationist literature.

Index